∫

Musical Influence on American Poetry

MUSICAL INFLUENCE on AMERICAN POETRY

BY CHARMENZ S. LENHART

THE UNIVERSITY OF GEORGIA PRESS • ATHENS

FOR MY PARENTS

EVERETT
Poet
and
EDMEE
Musician

Contents

Preface

OF LATE MUCH INTEREST HAS BEEN AROUSED AMONG SCHOLARS IN the influence which music has had upon letters. This influence, long tacitly recognized by literary men, has come but slowly to the attention of the scholar despite the number of essays on music and letters written during the nineteenth century—a century which felt most strongly the effects of *synaesthesia*.

There are several understandable reasons why this influence has not been sufficiently explored. First, any careful study of the interrelationship of these two arts must be based, at least partially, upon an historical grasp and appreciation of both fields, in addition to an exact understanding of the working, the mechanics, and the science of music.

The science of music, or musicology, is a comparatively new field of study. It was not until 1863 that F. Chrysander called for a scientific approach to the study of music in his *Jahrbücher für Musikalische Wissenschaft*. Guido Adler wrote the first important article on musicology in "Umfang, Methode und Ziel der Musikwissenschaft" for the *Vierteljahrsschrift für Musikwissenschaft* in 1885. Music histories made a similarly belated appearance, and many of the first were pioneering efforts like that of Charles Burney near the close of the eighteenth century.

The first history of American music did not appear until 1883, when Frederic Louis Ritter, a carefully trained German musicologist and historian, wrote his *Music in America,* a text still in use. No course in musicology was even offered in an American university until 1917 when the University of California made such a course available to students.

The types and kinds of writings which have dealt with music and poetry, even in the recent past, have not always been purely scholarly. Many were simply intuitive recognitions of the parallels of the two arts. The approaches to this subject vary greatly from the essays of Sidney Lanier to the comparisons of James Huneker; from the volumes of Wilhelm Ambros to the writings of Romain Rolland, James Joyce, Marcel Proust, and, more recently, Jacques Barzun. Of these, Sidney Lanier covered a greater area in his close discussion of the arts than any writer before or since, for he touched upon the science of music, the rhythmical similarities in poetry and music, the question of sound in verse, the historical relationships, the appearance of music in poetry and drama, and the background of music in historical time. Later studies which treat any of these subjects with greater understanding are indebted to his pioneering work.

The significance of this twentieth century movement in the field of letters is shown, in part, by the number of scholarly books which lately have been written about music and letters. During the twenties and thirties a series of individual studies of music in the Shakespearean period, of music in Shakespeare's work, such as those of E. W. Naylor and John Murray Gibbon, appeared. More recently studies of music in the works of Milton, Shelley, and Browning, and in the writings of the Romantic period, in general, have been made. Recent biographers have taken more carefully into account the musical interests of the men they treat. Fagin's study of Poe, and Holloway and Schyberg's studies of Whitman are good examples of this trend, as is Gay Wilson Allen's *Solitary Singer*.

The most important writer on the two arts of poetry and letters since Sidney Lanier is Calvin S. Brown of the University of Georgia, who published his *Music and Literature* in 1948, and *Tones into Words* in 1953. Robert Faner's doctoral dissertation, published as *Walt Whitman & Opera* (1951), is the first thorough study of its kind of an American poet and the influence music had upon him.

The purpose of this particular study is to continue the research already begun in this direction in the hope that further light will be shed upon the creative act in American poetry. Since the historical development of American poetry has paralleled in many ways the development of music, the kinds of poetry written in a century often have depended upon the kinds of music heard in that century. It is true that all poets cannot be said to have been influenced by music, nor can the bulk of poetry be accounted for in that light, but the bulk of lyric poetry—and it is with lyric poetry and poets that this study is chiefly concerned—has had some hitherto unexplored relationship with the music of a given period. The growth of musical interest from the seventeenth to the nineteenth century is phenomenal, and within the nineteenth century the growth from the song conception to the symphonic can be traced almost exactly in the lyric poetry of that period.

The limits of this study must be initially recognized. It is not an attempt to deal either with the ballads or the folk materials which constitute so important a portion of American poetry. It is not an attempt to deal with the sentimental ballads and the popular lyrics of the day. These would constitute a study in themselves. It is directly concerned with those lyrical poets in America who were recognized literary figures, and with their poems or that segment of their verse which reveals the influence of music.

The approach here has been three-fold: historical, personal, and textual. For this reason the study is arranged chronologically to indicate not only the historical parallels that occurred in the two arts in America, but also to illustrate the reaction of a poet born in a certain musical period and climate and his use of the musical theories, terminology, and forms commonly known in his day. How much any given poet may have known of music has been gathered from his own writings on the subject and from what is known of his musical interests. How much he has borrowed from music in the way of imagery, form, and sound depends not only upon the individual poet but also upon the time in which he lived. The nineteenth century was a period of tremendous growth in musical interest among the poets.

The poetic text itself is the basis for examination and serves as proof for the thesis. The influence of music upon this poetic text may be observed in a variety of ways: there may be direct reference to music; there may be an attempt to imitate some musical form such as the symphony or the sonata, or to cast verses into forms of known musical origin such as the hymn, the sonnet, the ode, the villanelle, the ballad; there may be an attempt to create the impression of music by the flow of the lines after the fashion of musical phrases, by the combinations of sounds, by rapid and slower pacing; there may be a deliberate effort to write lyrics to be sung.

Since it is obviously impossible to deal with the poetic text of any great number of poets in any detail, and since any discussion of the influence of music upon a poet's style must deal with the texts, this discussion is limited to three of the more important nineteenth century poets, making it possible to see at close hand how music affects verse. The effect of music upon verse often lies in the poet's borrowing of form or of imagery; often there is also an attempt on the poet's part to simulate sounds of music or to call up certain memories or "impressions." The reader, then, should be aware of the fact that poets conscious of music make some attempt at one or a combination of these qualities in their verse, and that often all kinds of musical borrowings may be apparent in a single poem. For that reason the rhythmic theories of the poets also come in for scrutiny.

This is a study, first of all, of the conscious efforts of poets to duplicate a musical idea, and of the kinds of poetry that often resulted. It also considers poetry which is written with only vague musical knowledge, or with the hope of achieving musical sound in verse. It is, in short, an attempt to bring together for the first time those evidences of the American poet's awareness of music. In order properly to prepare the reader for this approach, the first chapter has been devoted to a brief history of music in America during the past three centuries.

It is a very real pleasure to be able to acknowledge here the material aid, the encouragement, and the interest of Professor John T. Flanagan of the University of Illinois, who had more to do with the preparation of this manuscript than anyone other than myself. I should also like to acknowledge the encouragement and interest of the late President Morgan L. Combs of Mary Washington College of the University of Virginia, who read much of this book in manuscript. I wish to express appreciation for the letters and criticisms of Conrad Aiken. Acknowledgement is also due to Miss Frieda Thies, Librarian of the Sidney Lanier Room at the Johns Hopkins University; to David Mearns, Librarian of the Manuscript Division of the Library of Congress; to the staff of the Rare Book Room at the Library of Congress; to the staff of the Trent Manuscript Collection at Duke University; to Bayard Q. Morgan for his correspondence and his manuscript on "Question Melodies in English"; and to the following poets for personal letters to the writer: Babette Deutsch, Ezra Pound, Louis Untermeyer, William Carlos Williams, the late John Gould Fletcher, and William Rose

Benét. Acknowledgement is also due to Dr. Carrol Quenzel, Librarian of Mary Washington College; to Miss Eva Fay Benton, Librarian of the University of Illinois; and especially to the late professors Sidney Glenn and Arthur Christy, and Mrs. Hobart Peer of the University of Illinois for their encouragement and their faith. And finally, my greatest debt is due the late Julia Gehren Steffen, my grandmother, who was a life-long inspiration to me.

CHARMENZ S. LENHART

America's
Musical
Background

THE ENGLISH COLONISTS WHO
came in successive migratory waves to America in the early seventeenth century brought with them in their hymnals, their songs, their virginals and other key-board instruments, and their chests of viols a rich European musical heritage.

Choral music had reached unparalleled heights in England at the start of the century, and the great English choral schools surpassed even those of the Italians and the Flemish.[1] Renaissance England was a land of song where popular ballads were sung on the streets, and metrical psalmody swept the courts of England as it did those of continental Europe. Some of the finest composers of the late sixteenth century resided in England—men like Dowland, Morley, Thomas Campion, and Byrd, to name a few. These men composed such sweet "ayres" that many of the poems of the day were written especially for their musical settings.[2] These, along with the sonnets which were written to be sung and the numerous lyrics, constituted a large portion of the secular music of the day. Excelling in the composition of the madrigal, Morley alone left a wealth of music that made English musical history bright.

Sacred choral music had had, by the seventeenth century, a long and chequered career. Gregorian chant was the melodic basis for most of the sacred songs, and its peculiar modal texture had already escaped into the melodies of balladry. Balladry, in turn, with its easy "rocking horse" metres, became the favorite metrical pattern for the rhymed setting of psalms that was popular in the

1

late sixteenth century and was known as metrical psalmody. Actually an offshoot of the Reformation, metrical psalmody achieved popularity even in the Catholic courts of Europe.[3] Martin Luther, whose hymn collection had appeared in 1524, was one of the hymnists to take advantage of ballad metre for the rhythms of his songs. His hymns, collected from a variety of sources—secular as well as sacred[4]—had tremendous popularity and have appeared in various forms in hymn books of widely disparate origin ever since. Calvin, on the other hand, owed to the Catholic court the melodies for the hymnals which the Puritans adopted at Geneva, for Calvin drew upon the melodies of two French court composers, Clement Marot and Theodore Beza, who introduced the French forms of the ballades into his psalter.[5]

The keyboard instruments—the organs and the family of instruments called clavecins—had a development largely Italian, Spanish, and German, rather than English. Germany became, in the seventeenth century, the great organ-building center, and soon branched off into the building of other kinds of instruments, chiefly the lute and key-board instruments. Italy's leading instrumental contribution came in the development of the stringed instruments, one example of which was the omnipresent "chest of viols" that could be found in every country house in England at the time the Puritans and Pilgrims began their migrations. Instruments in the century had relative degrees of popularity which depended a great deal upon where the instrument was used; the violin or "fiddle," because of its harshness and brilliance, was scorned by aristocratic musicians, who preferred the viol since it was never played in the taverns.

Musically this pre-Bach period is most famed for the development of keyboard music and for the development of the homophonic opera and oratorio which originated in Italy about 1600. The greatest composers of the period were Italian—men like Corelli (1653-1713), Monteverdi (1567-1643), Scarlatti (1659-1725), and Vitali (1644-1692). Aside from Monteverdi, these men were largely writers of chamber music, the forms of which developed from the clustering together of the various dance tunes of the day.

It is a mistake to think of the English Puritans, and thus of the American Puritans, as in any way cut off from the mainstream of music which coursed powerfully through the century. Percy Scholes's book, *The Puritans and Music,* has done much to explode the myth that either Puritan group was in any way unmusical.

Scholes's interest had been stirred by the research of Oscar G. Sonneck, longtime chief of the Music Division at the Library of Congress, whose pioneering study of musical conditions in America in the eighteenth century led him to believe that America had had a considerable musical history long before the year 1700. Knowing of the strong love for music of such noted English Puritans as Oliver Cromwell and John Milton, Sonneck wrote that it would be strange indeed if "Providence [had been prompted] to send to our shores, out of all the millions who inhabited Europe, just those few thousand beings who had no music in their souls."[6] Providence had *not* sent us unmusical souls; for though the chief English composer of theatre music and the cantata ode, Henry Purcell, was not born until 1658, the Puritans, as well as the settlers of the Virginia colonies, were far from unmusical folk.

The spurious writings of a Reverend Samuel Peters, a disappointed Tory during the Revolution, have done much to mislead readers. When Peters returned to England, he wrote *A General History of Connecticut* in which he fabricated the notorious Connecticut "Blue Laws." These allegedly demonstrated the Puritan dislike for many social activities, including music, and they pointed out that the Puritans primarily disliked instrumental music. The Duyckinck brothers, in their *Cyclopedia of American Literature,* said of the Peters history: "A sober critic would go mad over an attempt to correct its mis-statement."[7] Peters claimed that the Puritans disliked music altogether and only sang songs in church because it was required of them. He said they had two beloved instruments, however, the trumpet and the drum, both used to call people to meetings, etc. He asserted that the Puritans did not enjoy dancing and thus had no need for orchestras of any sort such as were popular all over Europe in the seventeenth century.

While it has not been found that musical interest among the earliest Puritan settlers was as great as that of their British cousins, lack of material evidence does not in itself prove that there actually was less musical interest here.

The Pilgrims in 1620 brought with them Henry Ainsworth's *Book of Psalmes,* especially written for them and published at Amsterdam in 1612. They continued to use this text for the psalms until 1692, when the Massachusetts Bay Colony absorbed Plymouth and the *Bay Psalm Book* superseded Ainsworth. The music appeared with the words in the Ainsworth edition.

The leader of the "Mayflower" Pilgrims, Robert Browne, was a "keen music lover" and an excellent lutanist, whose children were taught music. One of his sons regularly took his viol to church to serve as bass for the psalms.[8] And Edward Winslowe wrote in his diary of the Pilgrim departure from Leyden:

They, I say, that stayed at Leyden feasted us that were to go, at our pastor's house . . . where we refreshed ourselves, after tears, with singing of psalms, making joyful melody in our hearts, as well as with the voice, there being many of our congregation very expert in music; and indeed it was the sweetest melody that ever mine ears heard. . . .[9]

Though the Pilgrim settlement has not yet attracted the musical scholar's attention as a center of culture as the Puritan settlements have, and though the greater portion of writings from this early colonial period are of Puritan origin, it may be presumed that the Pilgrims had no particular feeling against music, and, indeed, probably welcomed it as a means to glorify God.

The Puritans, because of the nature of their settlement, remained much closer to their English friends than the Pilgrims, both before and during the period of the Commonwealth. Cromwell was a friend of John Cotton; and another colonist, John Oxenbridge, was a friend of the great Puritan poets Milton and Marvell. Milton was a good friend of Roger Williams, and was also on friendly terms with John Winthrop, Jr., and the Reverend John Clarke of Rhode Island.[10] Several of the colonists belonged to the Royal Society of London, and many of the more important books written by colonists were sent to England for publication. Wigglesworth's *Day of Doom* was twice reprinted in England (1673, 1711), and the *Bay Psalm Book* achieved real popularity there, running through eighteen editions. Conversely, the Puritans eagerly kept in touch with the literary developments of the day, and read Milton's 1645 edition quite soon after its appearance.

Musically this meant, of course, that what went on in England among the Puritans went on in large part here. Milton wrote in his *Areopagitica:*

If we think to regulat Printing, thereby to rectifie manners, we must regulat all recreations and pastimes, all that is delightful to man. . . . No musick must be heard, *no song be set or sung,* but what is grave and *Doric.* There must be licensing dancers, that no gesture, motion, or deportment be taught our youth but what by their allowance shall be thought honest; for such *Plato* was provided of; it will ask more than the work of twenty licensers to examin all the lutes, the violins, and the ghitterns in every house; they must not be suffer'd to prattle as they doe, but must be licenc'd what they may say. And who shall silence all the airs and madrigalls, that whisper softnes in chambers? . . . The villages also must have their visitors to enquire what lectures the bagpipe, and the rebbeck reads ev'n to the ballatry, and the gammuth of every *municipal* fidler, for these are the Country-man's *Arcadias*. . . .[11]

It may be assumed that this revealing account of the omnipresence of music was quite as typical of the Puritan colonies—on a lesser scale, of course—as it was of the mother country.

The Puritans brought with them the Anglican psalm book of 1563, the "Old Version," or Sternhold and Hopkins' *Whole Book of Psalms,* which they replaced with the *Bay Psalm Book* in 1640. The one hundred and fifty psalms were sung to forty-six tunes, but the enterprising nature of the colonists was such that they demanded their own texts and set about composing metrical versions of the psalms with boundless ambition.

For many years instrumental music was assumed to be non-existent in Puritan colonies, largely because historians found so few references to it.

One of the reasons that credence was ever given to the idea that the Puritans were opposed to music of an instrumental nature was that few references to the playing of any instruments could be found in America. In a day when Hengrave House in England boasted a staggering collection of viols and other stringed instruments, and when every Sussex village had orchestras of flutes, clarinets, bassoons, trombones, serpents, violins, cellos, etc., while one church even boasted of having nine bassoons,[12] America seemed completely devoid of any instruments except the jew's-harp, the trumpet, and the drum.

Samuel Eliot Morison, however, records a letter from a nephew to an uncle in England in which the nephew, Harvard student Josiah Flynt, asked for a violin. The uncle answered:

Musick I had almost forgot. I suspect you seek it both to [sic] soon, and to [sic] much. This be assured of that if you be not excellent at it Its worth nothing at all. And if you be excellent it will take up so much of your mind and time that you will be worth little else. . . .[13]

A Reverend Edmund Brown of Sudbury "bequeathed a 'base vyol' and sundry books of music in his will," and Nathaniel Rogers of Ipswich left a treble viol. A collegemate of the aforesaid Josiah Flynt left a guitar and a viol in 1681, and Morison suggests that these instruments may have been part of an orchestra in which the students idled away their time—idleness being a Puritan sin. Seaborn Cotton, son of John Cotton, copied ballads into his commonplace book, and Elnathan Chauncey put several measures of music into his.[14]

Thus it can be surmised, despite the scarcity of evidence, that the Puritan felt as any other seventeenth century figure might have about the use of instruments. Samuel Sewall, for instance, was a great music lover, and in his diaries made frequent references to his enjoyment of dinner music.[15] He was something of a lutanist, for he speaks of "skrewing the strings of a lute." Strangely enough, he apparently shared the Biblical preference for the trumpet, for he wrote of its sound as that of which he was most fond. He also wrote of going to "Mr. Hiller's to enquire for my wife's virginal."[16] On a visit to Harvard College he deplored that he had not heard any music in the halls, and when he was in England in 1689 he frequently wrote of the concerts that he had attended there.

Massachusetts had her own lute and fiddle maker by 1691, but unfortunately he robbed a Dutchman and came to an untimely end. At almost the same time Thomas Symnes wrote of music at Harvard College in the seventeenth century:

Music was studied, known and approved in our College, for many years after its first founding. This is evident from the Musical Theses, which were formerly printed; and from some writings containing some tunes, with directions for *singing by note,* as they are now sung.[17]

The papers he referred to were burned in the College Library fire of 1764. The real objection that the Puritans had to music seems to have been directed at the use of musical instruments in churches. Aside from this ban, which several churches today maintain—some even ban the organ—the early colonial fathers were by no means opposed to music. John Cotton, a good Puritan, wrote in 1647 that he had no objection whatsoever to dancing, "yea though mixed," "nor do we forbid the private use of any instrument."[18] He did object to any kind of music in church except singing. From his own statements, so shortly after the Puritan migration, it can certainly be seen that the American Puritan enjoyed his dance music and his chamber music just as any other Englishman of the mid-century period would have.

Increase Mather wrote of music: "Indeed the sweetness and delightfulness of music has a natural power to lenifie melancholy passions."

The Virginia colonists have left still fewer references to music than have their Northern brothers. However, the early appearance of chamber music and opera in Williamsburg at the Governor's Palace toward the end of the century indicates an ardent support of music all through the seventeenth century.

Though the main musical direction in America in the seventeenth century was toward religious music, during the eighteenth century a decided interest in music of a secular nature developed, and an influx of foreign musicians to our shores began around the turn of the century. At the mid-century point, native American composers began to assume some importance in the musical world, and the successive migrations of the Moravians and other German sects began to be apparent in the German names that appeared on the early public concert programs. Music moved out of the church and into the chamber and concert hall after 1731.[19]

The traditions of the polyphonic and homophonic schools of music were conspicuous early in the century in America. Bach (1685-1750), whose works represent the instrumental culmination of the baroque polyphonic tradition, was relatively unknown in Europe outside the north German cities until the early part of the nineteenth century, but he was not unknown in America; for by 1773 his name began to appear on programs in Boston and New York, though his oratorios remained unknown. Handel (1685-1759), who left Germany quite early in his musical career to live in London, was known in America sooner and more widely than Bach because of the love for oratorio music which America had early acquired. Handel's music was played extensively in America by 1770, and William Tuckey brought to New York a performance of the "Messiah" in the same year. (Germany did not hear the "Messiah" until 1772.) Handel's operatic overtures were popular with the American orchestras of the day which were assembled from the amateur musicians of the various communities. Haydn (1732-1809) was, of course, born too late to have much influence upon eighteenth century American composers, but his music, primarily the symphonies, was played here as early as 1785 in Philadelphia. And when Haydn left the little German court and came to be lionized by London society, he wrote his great oratorios after the fashion of Handel—a fact which so excited the Bostonians that they formed the historic Handel and Haydn Society in 1815 for the performance of these oratorios. It was Mozart (1756-1791) who had an almost immediate transference to America, for his string quartets were played while they were still in manuscript by the Wissahickon German Pietists and the Moravians at Bethlehem.[20] It must be remembered, though, that Mozart was born late in the century, and that his influence could hardly have been widespread, so that Haydn's name was the more familiar as the century closed.

Perhaps because America grew prouder of her native arts as she moved into the pre-Revolutionary days, she began to give more attention to her native composers; or perhaps it was because there were so few composers of any importance in America, that the names of Francis Hopkinson, James Lyon, and William Billings loomed large. These men were the first American composers of any real stature, and they were productive in the second half of the century and not the early part. When the great German composers began to be heard here, the work of Americans became less popular.

Eighteenth century musical development in America varied with particular cities and centers of culture. Boston became one of those centers of culture, disseminating musical influence over a wide area. As early as 1685 a dancing master had made plans—though in vain—to set himself up in Boston, and by 1716 the *Boston News-Letter* carried this item:

This is to give notice that there is lately just come over from England a choice collection of Instruments, consisting of Flageolets, Flutes, Hautboys, Bass-Viols, Violins, Bows, Strings, Reeds for Hautboys, Books of Instruction for all these Instruments, Books of Ruled Paper. To be sold at The Dancing School of Mr. Sustone in Sudbury Street near The Orange Tree, Boston. Note: Any person may have all instruments of Musick mended, or Virginalls and Spinnets Strung and Tuned at a reasonable Rate, and likewise be taught to Play on any of these instruments above mentioned; dancing taught by a true and easier method than has been heretofore.[21]

The notice indicates that by 1716 there were in Boston not only performers on virginals and spinets but there were also students of composition and composers (would-be), as well as dancing masters. Though Boston long remained Puritan in its attitude toward drama, and passed an anti-theatre law in 1750 after several plays had been seen by Bostonians, it was most receptive to music, and public concerts began in Boston at the same time that they began in Germany, and not long after the introduction of the "Concerts Spirituel" in France.[22] A Boston concert announced in an advertisement in the *Boston News-Letter* of December, 1731, precedes by three and a half months the first concert at Charleston, South Carolina, which was quite a music center and saw ballad opera as early as 1735. The concert in Boston was an instrumental one: "There will be performed a *Concert of Music* on sundry instruments at Mr. Pelham's great Room, being the House of the late Dr. Noyes near the Sun Tavern."[23] There is no indication from the advertisement that this was even a "first" performance of any kind, and it may well be assumed that American papers, like German, did not for some time carry musical items.[24] A few years later (1744) Faneuil Hall was being used for concerts of music, and by 1754 there was a regular Concert Hall at Hanover and Court streets, where "select pieces by the Masters" were given. There is evidence that by the late fifties a series of regular yearly subscription concerts was being given, and by 1766 concert subscriptions were an established custom.[25] It is an additional tribute to Boston that the great German musician, Karl Theodore Pachelbel, came to live there in 1732-33. A harpsichordist, he gave in 1736 the first public concert New York had ever heard.

Pachelbel was, of course, familiar with the polyphonic and contrapuntal tradition which Bach was still sponsoring in the eighteenth century, and he must have done much to familiarize Americans with Bach's music—especially the harpsichord music, most of which remained unpublished during Bach's liftetime.

Boston still remained, in this century, the center of sacred musical practice, and the first organ was installed in the Brattle Street Church in 1711. Singing schools for the improvement of church music were founded, and hymns finally crept into the church service, though for many years metrical psalmody was the only approved song-portion of the service. Singing schools began trying to teach by note the melodies that had been lost through teaching "by ear" or "rote." The elder members of the churches made immediate outcry, for they had more difficulty learning to read music, and thus felt less a part of the singing service than they had when all of the tunes were familiar. The effort to replace "lining out" with "read" music began to show almost immediate results. Samuel Sewall wrote in his Diary in 1720: "At night Dr. Mather preaches in the School-House to the young musicians

from Revelations 14.3. . . . House was full and the singing extra-
ordinarily Excellent, such as has hardly been heard before in
Boston. Sung four times out of Tate and Brady. . . ."[26]

The "fuguing composer," William Billings (1746-1800), was
the first to use the pitch pipe to establish the pitches for melodies,
a practice which soon became the custom of song leaders generally.
Billings was a Boston tanner and a composer of polyphonic church
music. He was relatively unschooled, but his fugal music was hailed
with great delight in his own day; and he claimed that his fugues
were

more than twenty times as powerful as the old slow tunes. Each part
striving for mastery and victory, the audience entertained and delighted, their minds surprisingly agitated and extremely fluctuated,
sometimes declaring for one part and sometimes for another. Now the
solemn bass demands their attention; next the manly tenor; now the
lofty counter; now the volatile treble. Now here, now there, now here
again! O ecstatic! Rush on, you sons of harmony.[27]

Billings represented, strangely enough, the polyphonic tradition
in America at a time when its long European development was at
the point of dying out. Bostonians hailed these "new tunes" and
regarded his work as far more interesting since actually Billings'
fugues sounded much more like a series of lively rounds than had
their old chorales.

Billings was a child of nature who discredited "rules" in his
compositions, insisting that the sole guide must be "Nature" and
that "Every Composer should be his own carver."[28] He wrote his
New England Psalm Singer in the Handelian manner in 1770,
and enjoyed great vogue during the Revolution with his stirring
tunes to patriotic lyrics. He was one of the chief leaders in the
revival of interest in the singing school, and the singing society
he founded in 1774 at Stoughton, Massachusetts, became the
Stoughton Musical Society in 1786—the earliest one in America.
In 1790 the members sang a performance of Handel's *Messiah*
without music or accompaniment in a song contest to win over the
First Church in Dorchester, whose choir was supported by a bass
viol. Billings was at the height of his popularity in 1790, and traces
of his influence can still be found in the fugues of the Sacred Harp
singers in the rural South.[29]

The cantata ode which developed in the English courts through
the work of Matthew Locke (1632-1677) and John Blow (1648-

1708) found its finest composer in the short-lived Henry Purcell. There is a tendency to forget the debt America owes musically to Purcell (1658-1695), for the English composer did not write successfully in the forms that are familiar to us today. He wrote, it is true, for the church, the theatre, and for instrumental combinations, but his music is that of the purely English tradition and owes far more to the sixteenth century masque composers than it does to anything else. Handel's influence upon posterity is entirely different and is strongly based upon his Italian teachings. Purcell tended to write the lighter, more fanciful music of the earlier period; and the chief foreign influence upon his work was that of the French through Lulli, the operatic composer who inspired Purcell's "Dido and Aeneas."

Purcell was one of the greatest of the cantata ode writers in England. Since this ode was indigenous as a form to the English, it was natural that he should have been influenced here by an English composer. His teacher was John Blow, one of the fine writers of ode music, who can be said to have created the form which the cantata ode took in the seventeenth century. After Purcell's untimely death, the pure stream of English composition ended, for Italian opera and the great German composers literally snuffed the life out of native English music, and, aside from John Gay's *Beggar's Opera* (1728), England ceded the making of great music to other countries. The influence of Purcell and Blow, however, can be found in the "occasional" musical compositions heard in American cities such as Philadelphia and Boston, where in the eighteenth century a composer like Francis Hopkinson devoted a portion of his time to the writing of music and verse for such "occasions."

Ballad opera was another musical genre popular for some time in America, and Italian opera had something of a struggle to establish itself here for that very reason. One of the best imitators of ballad opera in America was James Ralph of Philadelphia, whose *Fashionable Lady* was successful in 1730. It was the War of 1812 which dealt the death stroke to ballad opera.

The Philadelphians, because of the Quakers who were violently opposed to music, secular and sacred, had quite an internal struggle to hear opera and theatre music at all. But the Pennsylvania Moravians and Episcopalians were ardent champions of secular music and rallied against the Quakers. Though no ballad opera company could play Philadelphia until 1754, the Moravians succeeded in triumphing so that opera presented by the Hallam Company, a theatrical group popular in the South and in New York, was finally well received. It was not until 1766 that Philadelphia had a successful operatic season. It must not be assumed, however, that Philadelphia was unmusical, for College Hall presented the *Masque of Alfred* with music by Dr. Arne in January, 1757, an ambitious undertaking. The Moravians had founded the first *Singstunde* in 1742, and the history of chamber music in Pennsylvania will be bright when it is written, for the Moravians were constant practitioners of the art, and in their archives have been found Haydn quartets and symphonies, and Mozart trios and three symphonies which date back to 1785.[30] It is believed that *The Creation* and *The Seasons* had their American premières in Philadelphia. In addition, the city supported a dancing master in 1710 who taught dancing in boarding schools in 1728, and though the first public notice of a concert does not appear until 1757, it hardly seems plausible that none was given earlier. A Collegium Musicum was founded in 1744, and by 1759 the College of Philadelphia had an Orpheus Club, devoted to music.

From 1750 to 1850 Philadelphia's musical life was brightest and the city was, until the Civil War, the chief American music center. Then New York, with Italian opera seasons, began to assume musical leadership. But throughout the eighteenth century, Philadelphia was the center of much musical activity, for which the Moravians were largely responsible.

There is reason to believe that the first organs in America were brought over by the Moravians (a fact which would seem natural since Germany was a great organ-building country) because the Swedes borrowed an organ from them as early as 1703 for the dedication of the Gloria Dei Church. Christopher Witt was building organs in Pennsylvania as early as 1704. Witt was also the translator of the hymns of Johannes Kelpius, the great Moravian hymnist.

The Moravians had established a Collegium Musicum in this country before 1750, almost as soon as similar organizations were being established in Germany. They were responsible for the introduction of the trombone into the country in 1754 and have since been famous for their trombone choirs. They believed strongly in lay singing as well as in sacred song, and Bethlehem's fame as the Bach center of America continued to spread. Franklin wrote of a visit he paid the Moravians in 1756: "I was at their church, where I was entertain'd with good musick, the organ being accompanied with violins, hautboys, flutes, clarinets, etc."[31]

Philadelphia was also famous for her musical societies, and one of the more famous, the Urania or Uranian Academy, was founded in 1787 to promote the singing of great choral works. One of the Academy's most effective presentations was the "Hallelujah Chorus." Two famous members of the Academy were Benjamin Rush and Francis Hopkinson. The Uranian Society lasted until 1800.

Francis Hopkinson (1737-1791) was America's, and Philadelphia's, first important native composer. He was considered something of a *bon vivant* in his own world. He carried on a lengthy correspondence with Thomas Jefferson on the quilling of the harpsichord, was a close friend of Benjamin West, and was so skillful in musical mechanics that he was able to supply a keyboard for Benjamin Franklin's musical glasses. Hopkinson was himself the inventor of the belharmonica, one of the briefly popular eighteenth century instruments.

Hopkinson was famous in his period as a psalmist, teacher, organist, harpsichordist, essayist, composer, poet, judge, and "Improver of the harpsichord." He has long been considered the best candidate for the honor of being the first composer in America. He published his "My Days Have Been So Wondrous Free" in 1759, two years before the earliest issue of James Lyon's *Urania*. He wrote Washington at the time that he dedicated his seven *Songs for the Harpsichord* to him in 1788: "I cannot, I believe be refused the Credit of being the first Native of the United States who has produced a Musical Composition."[32]

Lawyer Hopkinson was frequently heard in small concerts in Philadelphia; he was a graduate of the College of Philadelphia in 1757, taking his M.A. in 1760 and honorary LL.D. in 1790. The identity of his music teachers can only be conjectured from those who were then available in Philadelphia. He certainly studied late in life with James Bremner, a harpsichordist, and the center of a chamber music circle which included players of the German flute, French horn, and various stringed instruments. Hopkinson had in his library the works of Handel, Arne, Corelli, Pergolesi, Scarlatti, Vivaldi, Purcell, and Pepusch, as well as the "Water Music" of Handel in manuscript. Hopkinson was an ardent odist who played for commencements at the college, even composing odes for them. He was an organist also, and tried his hand at the composition of what can be called the first American opera—*The Temple of Minerva* (1781)—titled originally an oratorio, though it is very similar in form to the cantata ode. However, his songs are his most important musical work. He wrote a "Collection of Psalm Tunes with a Few Anthems . . ." for the use of the United Churches of Christ Church and St. Peter's Church in Philadelphia. Since Hopkinson came from a musical family, it was natural that he should know the English psalmists of the day, Arnold, Williams, and Tansúr, and the American psalmists, Tufts and Lyon. He became somewhat an authority on church music and wrote an anthem from Psalm 114, as well as a "Psalm of Thanksgiving" for Easter services (1766) at Christ's Church. He also wrote music for the 23rd Psalm and a long metre Doxology for the Dutch. He wrote two more songs: "A Toast to George Washington" and an "Ode to the Memory of James Bremner."

The cantata or "libretto" ode was a form dear to the hearts of Philadelphians, and Hopkinson seems to have done his share in composing music for special occasions in this city. These odes were formed upon a pattern similar to that of the oratorio and cantata, with solos, duets, and choruses. The odes were in great demand in Philadelphia for every dedication service or for celebrations by any society. Hopkinson wrote several of his cantata odes for the college commencements at Philadelphia. The form of the cantata ode was a comparatively simple one, since the poet needed only to vary the type of material to be used in arias, recitatives, and choruses, while the musician was not expected to be a great composer at all. The "libretto" was so brief that it almost argued against "greatness." It is difficult today to determine the reason for the success and popularity everywhere of the cantata ode. But it was an imitation of the English court fashion and came to an end only about the time of the rise of lyricism in American verse and the era of the great composers.

Today Hopkinson is remembered for his songs and church music, while his ode music is forgotten. The periodic revival of interest in the harpsichord brings to attention the body of harpsichord music which he left. He was typically an eighteenth century figure in his latitude of interests. Had he been born in Europe where he might have received the proper training in composition and where he could have known the great musical libraries, Hopkinson might have left something of a more ambitious nature. And yet it is doubtful, since all musical forms were in a state of flux in his day, and he was not the type of man to shape a new form such as Haydn had evolved. Hopkinson is important here only because he was America's first native composer.

Philadelphia and Boston both had fuller musical developments in the century than did New York, but the controversy over whether opera should be presented in English or Italian took place chiefly in New York, and as the century waned visiting artists began to find their best reception in New York.

Ballad opera probably appeared as early as 1732 in New York, and by 1750 Kean and Murray opened a theatre which presented seven ballad operas. Pachelbel gave concerts in New York in 1736, and the Hallam Company presented several seasons of plays with singing and dancing. Visiting artists' concerts became customary events thereafter, with men like Dienval, a violinist, flutist, and teacher of many wind instruments, presenting concerts. From 1760 to 1767 regular subscription concerts were the order of the day in New York. After that they were discontinued for six years. The first open air concerts were given at Ranelagh Gardens in 1765, and were soon followed by concerts in the King's Arms Garden on Broadway, and by vocal and instrumental music in the Vaux Hall Gardens. In 1774 an Harmonic Society was founded and in the same year French and Italian virtuosi appeared in concerts.

Before the Revolution there appeared in New York an American Opera Company with a repertoire of over two hundred operas, and by 1793 New York's own opera company was singing opera in English. All through the 1790's any number of operas were sung in English. Successful Italian opera in America was a nineteenth century development.

In addition to these growing musical centers, New Jersey, Maryland, Virginia, and the Carolinas had a considerable musical life. Colleges like William and Mary provided classes in music; and in Charleston, South Carolina, the St. Cecilia Society, the first musical society in America, was founded in 1762, nine years before a similar musical society of any importance was founded in Vienna. It remained in existence until 1912. By 1754 Charleston had opened a regular theatre for plays and operas, and it was Charleston that witnessed the first ballad opera production recorded in America: *Flora, or Hob in the Wall* in 1735. Although orchestras had played for many years in the various chamber combinations and for public affairs, in 1752 the Kean and Murray Company opened its new theatre in Upper Marlborough, Mary-

land, with the first orchestral accompaniment to opera in the
presentation of Gay's *Beggar's Opera*.[33]

The hymns of Watts and Wesley contributed to the development
of sacred music in eighteenth-century America. Singing schools
were opened everywhere to improve the quality of church music,
and John Tufts devoted much time to the teaching of note reading
and the general improvement of church singing in his travels
around the country to establish "singing schools."

Another of America's famous eighteenth century composers was
James Lyon of Newark, New Jersey. Lyon (1735-1794), interested
in spreading and "improving" the quality of psalmody through
the American colonies, brought out, by subscription, in 1762 his
psalm melodies entitled *Urania*. Lyon was handicapped by not
being able to drink at the "pure stream of English psalmody," but
he imitated as best he could the English composers of the day. He
was not a "fuguing" composer as Billings had been, but still his
anthems are too ornate for the taste of our day.[34] Unlike the
English psalmodists, he gave no space to organ accompaniment or
instrumental preludes. Sonneck wrote of Lyon:

James Lyon used English publications more freely than American. The
extent to which he copied the favorite English psalmodists of the day
shows how well he had studied their works. Unless his acquaintanceship with English psalmody was exceptional in the Colonies, it would
be of singular importance for proving the lively intercourses between
Great Britain and British America even in musical matters.[35]

Lyon was never very popular in the colonies, but his psalmody
was used "for concert purposes" for several years.[36] In 1784, An-
drew Adgate was the moving spirit behind an "institution for the
Encouragement of Church Music" called the Uranian Society and
later the Uranian Academy, where Lyon, Billings, and Handel all
shared musical honors on a program in May, 1786.

American concert programs of the eighteenth century were
strangely constructed, it seems to us, for a popular method of
presenting a work in the day was to present only a portion of it.
Thus only a popular portion of a symphony might be heard. Then,
too, the names of minor native composers appeared on programs
along with names such as Handel and Haydn. American concert
programs were usually scaled to meet the requirements of small
and restless audiences, and America, like all of Europe, was largely
chamber music conscious.

While public favor was still active in support of home-grown talent, many amateur musicians tried their hands at writing music, and since instruments in the century were in a period of growth and development, there was also a considerable faddism among the devotees of various types of instruments.

Jefferson, Washington, and Franklin were among the famous men of their day who took delight in music. Washington was frequently in Williamsburg concert audiences, as well as at opera when it was given there. His account books list records of expenditures "for concert" also in Philadelphia and in New York. He owned several violins, which, it is believed, he played. Jefferson, who was himself a flutist, violinist, and composer, longed to import impoverished European musicians for a private chamber orchestra at Monticello. Franklin attended concerts frequently, and liked working with musical instruments. He experimented with the harmonica (or "armonica"), an extremely resonant instrument which had a certain vogue because of the sustained eerie quality of its tone.

It is interesting at this point to make some further reference to one of America's great men, the friend of D'Alembert and Voltaire, of Francis Hopkinson, William Billings, and John Dickinson—Benjamin Franklin. Though it is widely known that Franklin was interested in the concert music of his day, not only in Pennsylvania but in Europe as well, and that he was the improver of a musical instrument he called the harmonica (which he hoped would supplant the harpsichord and which "was well enough regarded to attract virtuosi and outstanding composers, among them Mozart and Beethoven"), very few are aware that Franklin was a serious critic of the whole body of song and poetry—that is, that he was interested in the interrelationship of the two. He learned to play the harp, guitar, and violin, and a composition for a string quartet for three *violini con violoncello* bears his name, although the inscription is in Italian and indicates that someone else had a hand in it.[37] He was the first American music publisher, releasing the *Ephrata Hymns* in 1730, Watts's *Psalms* in 1729 and 1741, and *The Singing Master's Guide to His Scholars* in 1730. In addition, he published *Divine and Moral Songs for Children* in 1737 and 1747, and a *New Year's Ode* by Colley Cibber, Esq., Poet Laureate, set to music by Dr. Green. Franklin felt that the Scottish tunes (the ballads were very popular since large Scotch-Irish immigrations took place in 1714) were better suited to poetry than were contemporary opera scores. He said:

They were composed by the minstrels of those days to be played on the harp accompanied by the voice. The harp was strung with wire, which gives a sound of long continuance, and had no contrivances like that in the modern harpsichord, by which the sound of the preceding could be stopt, the moment a succeeding note began. To avoid *actual* discord, it was therefore necessary that the succeeding emphatic note should be a chord with the preceding, as their sounds must exist at the same time. . . . The connoisseurs in modern music will say I have no taste; but I cannot help adding that I believe our ancestors, in hearing a good song, distinctly articulated, sung to one of those tunes and accompanied by the harp, felt more real pleasure than is communicated by the generality of modern opera exclusive of that arising from the scenery and dancing. . . .[38]

In many ways Franklin's criticism of opera and oratorio may be compared to that of his English predecessor, Addison, who criticized Italian opera from the external or theatrical point of view. Franklin shows an understanding of the problem facing the composer who is trying to weld verse and voice:

. . . by what I can learn of *their* songs, the music was simple, conformed itself to the usual pronunciation of words, as to measure, cadence or emphasis, never disguised and confounded the language by making a long syllable short or a short one long when sung; their singing was only more pleasing, because of a more melodious manner of speaking; it was capable of all of the graces of prose oratory while it added the pleasure of harmony. A modern song, on the contrary, neglects all the properties and beauties of common speech, and in their place introduces its defects and absurdities as so many graces. . . . I must endeavor to support this charge by proof. Here is the first song I lay my hands on. It happens to be a composition of one of our greatest masters, the ever-famous Handel. It is not one of his juvenile performances, before his taste could be improved and formed . . . it is greatly admired by all his admirers and is really excellent in its kind. It is called "The Additional Favorite Song in Judas Maccabeus." Now I reckon among its defects and improprieties of common speech the following: 1. *Wrong placing the accent or emphasis,* by laying it on words of no importance, or on wrong syllables. 2. *Drawling;* or extending the sound of words and syllables beyond their natural length. 3. *Stuttering;* or making many syllables of one. 4. *Unintelligibleness;* the result of the three foregoing united. 5. *Tautology;* and 6. *Screaming;* without cause. . . . Give this whole song to any taught singer and let her sing it to any company that have ever heard it; you will find they will not understand three words in ten. I send you inclosed the song with its music at length. Read the words without repetitions.

Observe how few they are, and what a shower of notes attend them. You will then perhaps be inclined to think with me, that though the words might be the principal part of an ancient song, they are small of importance in a modern one; they are in short, only a *pretence for singing.*[29]

Thus it can be seen that an amateur musician like Franklin regarded critically the works of Handel, even writing a kind of critique upon the eighteenth century style of musical setting for songs. His interest in composition and in various new instruments is surely some indication of how extensive was the interest in music during the century. Franklin, of course, heard music abroad as well as at home, and thus heard much opera and was in every way better equipped to try his hand at music criticism than most Americans of his period. Actually music criticism was comparatively new in Europe too, though the Bach polyphonic style was being volubly "criticized" in the North German papers. This criticism was rarely objective and depended upon the particular musical clique in journalistic supremacy. In America, a New England psalmist, Oliver Holden, attempted vainly to establish a musical magazine for competent criticism in the *Massachusetts Musical Magazine* (1795).

After 1780, America was unable to support a sufficiently rich native musical growth against the influx of foreign musicians. It is certainly a mistake, however, to believe that America was slower to develop musically than any country in Europe. The eighteenth century saw the birth of modern music, and few of the important cities in Europe were more musically active than American cities. To recapitulate, Paris did not institute its public concerts until 1725, when it began a series known as the Concerts Spiritual. Germany remained a series of little states, each with its own ruler and courtly musicians who composed for the chapels and the chamber music groups centered there. It was England, actually, which offered the fullest freedom for the development of a composer's talent, and it was for this reason that Handel decided to remain in England during his most creative years. And Haydn achieved his first international fame when he came as an old man to England. It is obviously true that the great Germanic tradition that began in England with these men blighted England's native musical growth. After 1750, native English music declined, for Purcell had no worthy successors. The importance of this fact to America was that her musical currents flowed from England in the century. As it ended, America suffered the same inundation of her native talent that England had, and Italian and German musical forms and composers even brought to an end the popular ballad opera in English.

III

The most musically active century in modern times was the nineteenth. It was inevitable that the flowering of musical forms and the growth in instrumental techniques, as well as the growing audience for public concerts, should have an influence upon America. American audiences in great numbers sprang up virtually overnight; concert halls and opera houses were built in the cities, and even small towns had their concert series brought down from larger places. The ready transference of musical compositions across the waters frequently resulted in America's hearing music here almost immediately following its European debut.

The New York Philharmonic Society was founded in April of 1842. On November 24, the Vienna Philharmonic gave its first concert, *eleven* days before the New York Philharmonic's first season began. H. E. Krehbiel wrote:

In a sense, Vienna and New York entered simultaneously upon one phase of artistic culture. Is the phenomenon not startling? The court of Austria, already the Imperial Court of Germany, supported the most elaborate musical institution when the Dutch adventurers made their first settlement on Manhattan. . . . From that time down to the present the Austrian capital has led the world in the appreciation and encouragement of the art; yet in the most potent phase of instrumental culture it does not antedate New York. . . .[40]

Long before the turn of the nineteenth century, unnamed orchestras of various sorts had sprung up in America,[41] and as early as 1810 there was a Philharmonic Society in Boston.[42]

New York witnessed the steady transfer of musical prodigies from Europe here, and most of the famous musicians of the day sooner or later came to American shores. One of the most famous of these was the Norwegian, Ole Bull (1810-1880), whose violin playing in 1843 captured American audiences everywhere. New England was, strangely enough, particularly impressed by Ole Bull's playing, and he stayed in America in the hope of founding an American school of composition. He offered at one time (1855) a thousand dollar prize to the American composer of an opera on an American theme, an offer made too briefly. Ole Bull served for a short time as manager of the American Academy of Music in New York, and his concerts stimulated such wild public demonstrations that a series of violinists of the stature of Remenyi and Vieuxtemps began to concertize here. The Swedish singer Jenny Lind (1820-1887) came to America in 1850 under the auspices of P. T. Barnum and sang in New York with unprecedented success. She earned over $100,000 during her stay, and did much to stimulate interest in her native Scandinavian songs. Another famous figure of the mid-fifties was Mme. Henrietta Sontag, who toured America in 1853 and sang operatic selections at Niblo's Gardens and under Max Maretzek in New York. Adelina Patti, the child prodigy from a musically precocious operatic family, may be said to have made her debut as early as 1847, while still a child, in a tour with Ole Bull. However, her adult debut took place in 1859 with extravagant recognition on every hand. Mme. Malibran (1808-1836), the short-lived daughter of Manuel Garcia, who came to America with her father's operatic troupe, was one of the two great contraltos of the period and was highly praised by Poe. Finally she married de Beriot, the violinist, and did not return to this country after 1827. Mme. Marietta Alboni came to America in 1851 with the Havana Operatic Company, and it has repeatedly been said of her that, though she was no actress, it is doubtful whether a greater contralto has ever been heard in this country. She was greatest in performances of *Norma,* and Walt Whitman spoke highly in her praise. Mario, Marchese di Candia (1812-1883), and Guila Grisi (1812-1869) came to America in 1854 for the first time and sang in New York with great success. Heine celebrated their beautiful voices and their love affair in verse. Mario returned after Grisi's death in 1874. Pianists Henri Herz and Sigismund Thalberg toured America in 1845 and 1856-57. Until the time of Louis Gottschalk (1829-1869), New Orleans pianist, these were the greatest piano virtuosi. William Mason (1829-1908), son of Lowell Mason, who went abroad to study with Lizst, was one of the fine piano virtuosi and composers of the period.

The first successful season of Italian opera was presented in New York in 1825 by the Garcia Company, and the season opened with resounding success but little financial reward. Lorenzo Da Ponte, Mozart's librettist for *Don Giovanni,* was at that time living in New York, and it was due to his efforts that the first season included both *Don Giovanni* and *Barber of Seville*. In 1832 Da Ponte was largely responsible for the formation of the Italian opera company which bore the name of Montressor. The first American opera house for the production of Italian opera—German and French opera came to popularity later—was opened in New York in 1833. Audiences who heard opera before this time in New York had to go either to Niblo's Gardens or to the Park Street Theatre. The Astor Place Theatre was not built until 1847 when the Havana Company under the management of Torrens made its celebrated appearance, bringing such singers as Badiali and Miss Ostinelli (Signora Biscaccianti).

After 1840 the demand to hear foreign opera was so great in America that American opera companies were forced to present foreign operas as well as operas in English. With the advent of Max Maretzek in New York in 1848, opera seasons began in earnest. Maretzek brought the first German operatic performances to America in 1855-56, and in 1855 Richard Wagner, then engaged in writing the "Ring" music, was sorely tempted to come to America by an offer of $12,000. In 1859, Carl Bergmann, conductor of the Germania Orchestra, gave a performance of Wagner's *Tannhäuser* in an obscure New York theatre. From that time on the history of German opera in America is the history of Wagner's extensive American successes. Theodore Thomas and Leopold Damrosch for many years carried on a spectacular rivalry in their efforts to be the first to bring to New York the greatest music of contemporaries, particularly anything new of Wagner's.

New York, however, was not the first great operatic center for foreign opera, nor was it the best for many years. It was New Orleans that first boasted of an Italian opera company in 1810, and it was not long thereafter that the *Barber of Seville,* the opening presentation, was made a part of the regular season there.

The list of foreign operas familiar to and beloved by nineteenth century audiences differs in many ways from ours today. For one thing, Verdi, while prominent, was more famed for what we call his lesser operas, and was no greater as a composer in that day than Donizetti and Bellini. Operas like *Norma, La Sonnambula, La gazza Ladra, Robert le Diable, I Puritani,* were exceedingly popular, although they are rarely heard today.

Native American operas were composed by William Henry Fry of Philadelphia and George Bristow of New York. Fry (1815-1864) wrote *Leonora,* which had a kind of momentary success, in 1845;

it was the first publicly performed native grand opera in America. Fry, one of the chief advocates of American music, became music editor of the *Tribune* in 1852. Bristow (1825-1898) wrote the second American opera, *Rip Van Winkle*. Light operas like James Hewitt's *Robin Hood* were far more successful in English than were the grand operas.

New York was indeed fortunate in the men who developed the symphonic program there. Beginning with the Parisian, Louis A. Jullien (1812-1860), who was something of a chauvinist and delighted in startling his audiences by playing "Fireman's Quadrilles" with action suited to the music, New York fell largely under the sway of Theodore Thomas (1835-1905) and his rival, Leopold Damrosch from Bavaria.

Thomas had a greater hand in the musical development of nineteenth century America than any other figure, and he devoted his life to a "series of programs progressively planned" to cultivate the public's liking for the best in musical literature. Thomas organized his own orchestra in 1862 and toured America with it in 1869. He directed the New York Philharmonic in 1877 and built the Chicago Symphony in 1891. He pioneered in the effort to bring Wagner to American audiences and asked American composers Dudley Buck, George Chadwick, John Knowles Paine, and Arthur William Foote for commissioned works. Damrosch, on the other hand, conducted the New York *Männergesangverein Arion* and organized a New York Oratorio Society in 1874. He briefly conducted the New York Philharmonic and came to direct the Symphony Society of New York. He joined with Thomas and H. E. Krehbiel in the worship of Wagner. New York heard Berlioz as early as 1846, and America was one of the few countries where his works were given frequent hearings. Orchestral rivalry centered constantly about the presentation of new works.

Philadelphia, as early as 1809, had a club calling itself the Amateurs of Music founded expressly for the purpose of hearing and performing string quartets and other chamber music. The Mason string quartet, founded in New York by William Mason in 1855 with Theodore Thomas playing first violin, often appeared in Philadelphia; while the Hupfelds of Philadelphia gave many string quartet concerts from 1810 on. Philadelphia had a Musical Fund Society Hall in 1824 whose foundation was for the performance of string quartets, and in 1825 Philadelphia had an academy of music. The Musical Fund Orchestra of over a hundred members

played a different Beethoven symphony each year. The Society
had been founded in 1816 to stimulate interest in the chamber
music of Beethoven and Boccherini. Philadelphia, as early as 1815,
had a regular concert series during the winter season, managed by
Benjamin Carr. The manufacture of pianos took place chiefly in
Philadelphia during the century.

A great number of organizations for the performance of the
sacred music of the great German composers grew up in Philadelphia. The Philadelphia Haydn Society of 1809, the Handelian
Society of 1815, and the St. Cecilia Society of 1824 are typical
examples of the interest in music in this period. In addition, an
Anacreontic Society was formed in 1833 along with a Philharmonic
Society, and in 1835 the Männerchor Society of Philadelphia came
into being.

Philadelphia supported a number of writers of music criticism—
such men as William Fry, called the "American Berlioz" because
he was typically a romantic composer; John S. Dwight, editor of
Dwight's Journal of Music (1852); and Richard Storrs Willis,
editor of *Musical Tunes and the Musical World* (1854).

Boston remained, in the century, one of the chief musical centers
of America. Here most of the excitement over the full dawn of the
romantic movement with the advent of Beethoven's music took
place, and it was here, earlier still, that the famed Handel and
Haydn Society was founded in 1815 for the performance of the
oratorios of these two composers. This Society was one of the most
active and musically satisfying groups in America and its oratorio
concerts were undertaken with great care. The Society commissioned a work from Beethoven in 1823, but he was then busy with
his Ninth Symphony, and the commission was never fulfilled. It
has been said that the performances of these works by the Handel
and Haydn Society were so fine, as were those of Mendelssohn
somewhat later, that they have scarcely since been equalled in
America.

Boston boasted of a Philharmonic Society founded by Gottlieb
Graupner in 1809. In 1817 the small chamber orchestra began to
draw larger audiences. By 1815 a typical program included a
Haydn overture, a violin concerto, a Symphony Concertante
(Kreutzer), and three selected songs. Boylston Hall, the concert
hall for the important Handel and Haydn Society, also housed the
Philharmonic Concerts. James Monroe records hearing lengthy
concerts by both organizations in 1817. At the same time Salem

itself was musically active. Here bound volumes of parts were found containing Pleyel's edition of Haydn, Mozart, Kreutzer, and Poull's quartets. Dr. Henry K. Oliver referred to concerts by the Salem Glee Club which were "Occasionally varied by the introduction of instrumental quartet and quintet playing of music by Mozart and Haydn" with two violins, viola, and violoncello.[43]

Gottlieb Graupner (1767-1836), one of Boston's outstanding musicians, did much to further the growth of musical interest in the outlying communities around Boston. He taught music not only in the Boston academies but also in Salem and Concord where many oratorio concerts were held and operatic performances were heard. John Sullivan Dwight (1813-1893) was one of the most influential musicians in Boston during the mid-century period. He founded the Harvard Musical Association in 1837, the Harvard Choir, and his *Journal* in 1852. His articles had wide circulation and actually constituted the first serious music criticism in America.[44] Lowell Mason (1792-1872) was a tremendous musical influence in Boston because it was he who began the teaching of music in the schools of Boston in 1831 and founded the Boston Academy of Music in 1833. Mason also initiated the first music conventions and helped to bring out the Handel and Haydn Society's *Collection* in 1821 which borrowed the tunes of Handel, Haydn, Mozart, and Beethoven. John Parker tried to establish a music magazine in *The Euterpeiad,* or *Musical Intelligencer* in 1820, but it lasted only two years, though it was several times revived.

Between 1845 and 1860 America became a mecca for more than a million and a quarter Germans who emigrated to the Middle West. This Middle Western migration has been called the "Invasion of 1848." Musically it was responsible for the growth of interest in chamber music and the symphony in the Middle West, an interest which came astonishingly early by comparison. The first all-German orchestra, the Germania, appeared in America in 1848 with widespread acclaim for its performances of Beethoven, Mendelssohn, and Wagner; the orchestra gave performances of *Tannhäuser* here in 1852-53, during which period it played six of Beethoven's nine symphonies. In Milwaukee in 1850 there was a fine string quartet season, and in the same period Theodore Thomas took his orchestra on a tour of the Western states. The Mendelssohn Quintette Club toured in 1859 as far west as Topeka, Kansas, and gave concerts in towns like Saginaw, Michigan.

But even before the musical "Invasion of 1848" the Middle West had music of a superior quality. By 1819 Cincinnati had a Haydn Society; in 1838 St. Louis had a Musical Fund Society, and in 1849 Milwaukee formed a *Musikverein*. Chicago in the 1830's was hearing visiting artists; in 1840 the city heard several ballad singers, and in 1850 formed her own Philharmonic Society. In that year, too, she heard a performance of Italian opera for the first time. In 1860 Chicago supported a full season of chamber music recitals, following hard on the heels of the development of string quartets in the East. Travellers from the East were always surprised when they heard music from piano keys coming from a log cabin, but it should also be remembered that Philadelphia and Boston were the great centers of pianoforte manufacture in America, and the Chickering firm soon began exporting pianos even to Europe. The number of pianos in American homes after 1800 was astonishing. In 1829 more than 2,000 pianos were built and sold in America. The last city to turn from the use of the harpsichord and clavier was Williamsburg, Virginia.

How seriously the nineteenth century man regarded music may be gathered from Margaret Fuller's writings in the *Dial* in 1840-42. In her columns devoted to "Concerts of the Past Winter," she wrote much of Beethoven and his influence. She was most anxious to improve audience-appreciation of the German masters, and, like writers in the twentieth century, frequently deplored America's musical taste. Unconsciously, perhaps, her feeling for music reflects German philosophical thinking. Music was important in the scheme of things—of first importance—and Bostonians must set out to learn to appreciate this greatest of media.

Of all the great nineteenth century composers, it was Beethoven (1770-1827) who captured the public taste in America, as he had everywhere in Europe. It is now believed that Beethoven may have been heard in America as early as 1811 when the composer was forty-one. It is certain that his First Symphony was heard in Lexington, Kentucky, in 1817, and that a septette gave a performance of the "Eroica" Symphony in 1825. Considering the kind of orchestra and chorus necessary for a proper performance of the Ninth Symphony, it is not surprising that a full performance in America was not given until 1846 in New York. The Bostonians, however, were hearing selections from his *Mount of Olives in* 1818.

Descriptive music came to America in the writings of Mendelssohn and Schumann, Liszt, Berlioz, Chopin, and Grieg, along with nationalism and the tone poem or symphonic poem. Grieg, in particular, introduced America to the Northern school of music, and his own compositions were prepared for by the presence of Ole Bull in America. Brahms and Wagner had an almost immediate transference to America, and the Wagner cult grew strong here in the seventies and eighties—so strong that Dwight, no fancier of Wagner, refused to continue his *Journal* because he so deplored the musical taste of the day.

America saw a typically indigenous musical growth in the minstrel shows which toured from 1829-1860. These, along with the "singing families" like the Hutchinsons of New Hampshire and the Cheneys of Vermont, specialized in the sentimental ballads of the day, and constituted the chief sources of truly popular concert music. The two greatest minstrel writers were Dan Emmett and Stephen Foster. Foster (1826-1864), certainly one of America's greatest song writers, was completely untrained as a musician and wrote his own lyrics. Though his songs reflect Negro life, he was not a Southerner and knew the Negro only through spirituals and the minstrel show. Emmett (1815-1904), best remembered for his "Old Dan Tucker" and "Dixie," was the leader of the Virginia Minstrels, the popular show first appearing in 1843 in Boston. But Emmett never achieved the widespread popularity as a composer that Foster did. Foster's first songs were written for the E. P. Christy show: songs like "Old Folks at Home," "De Camptown Races," "Oh! Susanna," and "Old Dog Tray." He left about a hundred and seventy-five songs, many of which were immediately absorbed as folk melodies of the day.

A composer often associated with Stephen Foster as a song writer is Ethelbert Nevin (1862-1901), whose "Mighty Lak a Rose" and "The Rosary" are still among America's best loved songs. John Knowles Paine (1839-1906) is sometimes called the "dean" of American music, even though his work is infrequently performed today. He was a symphonist and wrote a better *Centennial Hymn,* it has been said, than Richard Wagner's. George Chadwick, Horatio Parker, Arthur William Foote, and Dudley Buck were the best of the mid-century song writers in America. Edward Mac-Dowell (1861-1908), the "American Grieg," has gained a kind of immortality with his Indian suites. He was a musical impressionist and a miniaturist, and represented America in the trend toward nationalism and impressionism—typical of late nineteenth century music everywhere in Europe.

The history of American music since the half-century mark is actually the history of European music, for works of great composers since then have been as frequently played here as they have been in other cities in the western hemisphere. The tremendous growth in America's musical interest from 1750 on nearly parallels the rise of romanticism in American poetry.

This very brief history of music in America appears here as the introductory chapter to this study in the hope that it will help readers to realize that America did not differ substantially from other countries in the kinds and quality of music that she heard in each period, and that the characteristically "new" music of each period was certainly heard as soon here as it was in England. Though England was the chief source for America's knowledge of seventeenth century music, it must be remembered that there were no internationally famed Protestant composers in the period and that little music was published. Because of her German settlements, America was nearer to the Germanic musical springs than to the English in the following century, and the crescendo of musical interest that culminated in America's great nineteenth century orchestras speaks for itself.

Seventeenth
Century
American Poetry

THE FIRST VOLUME OF VERSE
published in the New World was the *Bay Psalm Book* in 1640.[1]
Regardless of the lack of merit the volume possesses as poetry, it is
significant that only ten years after the arrival of the Puritans the
founding fathers engaged themselves in making psalm verses to be
sung. Psalm-singing, which was inherent in the Protestant movement in every country and in every branch of that movement, was
of especial interest to the Puritan who was only too glad to substitute matter from the Bible for Popish plain-chant music, made up
as it was of the compositions of St. Ambrose and Gregory I. Moreover, the fact that the congregation as a whole could take part in
psalm-singing made it popular. Both Luther and Calvin had
realized its efficaciousness and had drawn on the rollicking secular
tunes of the day for their psalms. All of Protestant England knew
and sang these psalms in the time of Elizabeth and welcomed a
form of harmony as distinguished from the single line of plain-
chant. In addition, the ballad or common metres of the new
metrical psalmody contrasted favorably in the people's ears with
the unmeasured music of plain-chant and the motet.

The rendering of the psalms into vernacular poetry was a
favorite pastime of poets of the day, and the *Bay Psalm Book* was
only part of the general movement in England which had resulted
in the Sternhold and Hopkins (1562-63) edition that the Puritans
brought with them, and in the work of Henry Ainsworth (1612).
Ainsworth had used his predecessors' tunes, but attempted his own
translations for the Pilgrims, then at Amsterdam, who found the

sense of Sternhold and Hopkins obscure, and many of the psalms impossible of proper execution to the melodies. It has been generally agreed that Ainsworth's attempts, published at Amsterdam and brought to America by the Pilgrims, have almost as many impossible passages in them as Sternhold's and Hopkins's. Obviously neither of the two English attempts was satisfactory.

In 1636, thirty "pious and learned ministers,"[2] largely under the direction of Richard Mather, Thomas Welde, and John Eliot, set about attempting a more accurate translation of the psalms which would not "add to, vary, or detract from" the psalms, and would present the very sense of them.

The preface to the *Bay Psalm Book,* apparently written by Richard Mather, reveals how the Puritan reasoned away the use of musical instruments—familiar to the harper David—in metrical psalmody:

Touching the first, certainly the singing of Davids psalmes was an acceptable worship of God, not only in his owne, but in succeeding times . . . some things in it [this worship] indeed were cerimoniall, as their musicall instruments &c but what cerimony was there in singing prayse with the words of David . . . was everything of David typicall? . . . If they were typicall because the cerimony of musicall instruments was joyned with them, then their prayers were also typicall, because they had that ceremony of incense admixt with them: but wee know that prayer then was a morall duty, notwithstanding the incense; and soe singing those psalms notwithstanding their musical instruments.[3]

The writer of the preface is very positive about the duty of *all* the members of the congregation to sing.

Therefore not some select members, but this whole Church is commended to teach one another in all the severall sorts of Davids psalms. . . .[4]

And he continues in that vein, indicating that it is a moral duty for the Puritan to sing.

Further, the writer of the preface holds that metrical psalmody accords with the wishes of God, since the psalms were written in the Hebrew tongue to be sung as poetry; so in translation into the tongue of each country, the style of the original must be preserved. But, he hastens to add, God was manifestly wise in holding from us the "framework" of Hebrew verse, as well as the Hebrew tunes to which it was sung, "lest we should think ourselves bound to imitate them." Only the "grave sort of tunes" and the "graver sort of verses" were acceptable.[5]

The translations of the psalms into English metre were strict, and paraphrase was shunned. Every attention was given the original, and only in a few instances was it necessary to contract or dilate the Hebrew word "for the sense and the verse sake." The poets realized that their translations were not elegant or "smooth," but considered this nothing to cavil at since "God's Altar needs not our pollishings, for wee have respected rather a plaine translation . . . and soe have attended Conscience rather than Elegance, fidelity rather than poetry, in translating the hebrew words into english language. . . ."[6]

The chief concern of this study is the effect of the music upon the poetic line, and the kinds of verses that resulted from the melodic patterns. No music appeared with the *Bay Psalm Book* until the ninth edition in 1698, presumably from a fear that written notes might give rise to instrumental performances of the psalms in addition to the singing of them. But then any musician so desiring could have played the tunes by ear.

Melodies for the psalms of the *Bay Psalm Book* appear to have been largely taken from Ravenscroft, according to a note at the end of the 1698 edition. Ravenscroft's collection of psalm melodies had been published in England in 1621 so that the Puritans leaving England were as familiar with those tunes, perhaps, as they were with those of the "new" Sternhold and Hopkins (1592). There is also little doubt that the writers of the *Bay Psalm Book* also knew Ainsworth's tunes published in 1612 at Amsterdam supposedly to improve the general quality of Pilgrim music, which had become an object of ridicule to visitors to the church, so poor had the Pilgrims' singing become. The writer of the preface to the 1640 edition mentions the Puritans' difficulties with Ainsworth's[7] tunes, which they replaced in part with some of the later ones.

Another psalter which probably yielded some melodies to the *Bay Psalm Book* was the *Scottish Psalter*, published in 1635. The *Scottish Psalter* is of interest because it contained a great many part-songs, which were the unique gift of Scotland, despite the disapproval of Calvin, who felt that harmony was sensual. Scottish song schools continued to flourish during the height of Calvin's influence, and Scottish psalms were much richer in harmony than Calvin approved of. But the modal character of the *Scottish Psalter* is of chief interest since it seems to have been a Protestant attempt "to bring the old melodies back into practicable singing form."[8]

The Ainsworth psalter tunes which the Pilgrims had substituted for tunes from Sternhold and Hopkins numbered thirty, of which better than half are derivative from French song forms, probably from the Anglo-Genevan Psalter which the Puritans knew from the time of Mary. Apparently the French forms "had not the strength to strike root permanently" though Macdougall suggests that it was probably the ten-syllable line that was difficult to sing.[9] At any rate it is apparent that the *Bay Psalm Book* of 1640 was not drawing heavily on Ainsworth's tunes but instead had returned to the ballad style or common metre of Sternhold and Hopkins and Ravenscroft.

Despite serious efforts on the part of musicologists to determine exactly the melodies of the *Bay Psalm Book,* opinion remains divided as to which tunes were used, and even how many of them were known to the Puritans. Several assertions have been made that the Puritans sang the original *Bay Psalm Book* verses to only about five of these best known tunes. But Macdougall questions this statement, asserting that, after all, in addition to the Sternhold and Hopkins tunes which the Puritans knew, and those of the *Scottish Psalter* with its one hundred tunes, the Puritans almost certainly knew Ainsworth as well as Este with his tunes in four parts "harmonized by ten of the best musicians of the period." Though it is reasonable to assume that the Puritans would know more than "five tunes," one cannot be certain from any contemporary accounts that they did.[10]

The *Bay Psalm Book* in its ninth edition had thirteen tunes arranged with melody and bass only. The tunes were Oxford, Lichfield, Low Dutch Tune, York, Windsor, Cambridge Short Tune, David's, Martyr's, Hackney, and tunes known only as Psalm 100, Psalm 115, and Psalm 148.[11] How many of these were known to the Puritans in 1640 must remain pure conjecture.

Originally in America all of the tunes were given out a line at a time by the deacon himself or by some singing member of the congregation who had a good sense of pitch with which to start the song. Since this method proceeded from line to line of unfamiliar tunes it was known as "lining out"; Samuel Sewall related in his diary his dismay at finding that he set the tune of "Windsor" and ended up with "High Dutch," an experience fairly common in that day.[12]

There were no approved methods for teaching the melodies of songs besides "lining out," which continued until the publication of volumes of psalms and hymns with music scored inside. When Playford's *Whole Book of Psalms* appeared in 1677, it was still difficult for the Puritans to accept the use of notes for their music, and lengthy debates ensued as to God's wish in the matter. Many in the congregation felt that the use of notes would lead to the worship of God by musical instruments; others that it was a plot by the young of the community to seize the reins from their elders who could not read music.[13] Those who felt concerned over printed notes leading to instrumental practice of the psalms must have had their worst fears confirmed when Playford wrote of the printed melodies in his 1677 edition:

And since many of our churches are lately furnished with organs, it will be useful for the organist and likewise for such students in the universities as shall practice song, to a Lute or a Violl.[14]

This was anathema to the average Puritan even in 1677, for many had objected even to the New Version of Tate and Brady with notes.

The verses in the *Bay Psalm Book* are, of course, wholly dependent upon the tunes to which they were to be set, though the majority of them are in common ballad metre: 8-6-8-6-8-6-8-6 or in double common metre twice the length. The few verses which do not follow this scheme are probably set to the more varied French metrics of a tune from the Ainsworth psalter. For instance, the easy flow of the eight-syllable line is frequently broken for a six- or five-syllable one, but there is on the whole little of this deviation.

As poetry the *Bay Psalm Book* reflects exactly the purpose of its authors. It was *not* written to be *read;* it made no pretence to any beauty as poetry, and it is like poetry only in being metrical. It cannot, of course, be compared to the prose rendering of the *King James Bible* since the musical line of the latter would be unmeasured music or plain-chant. A part of the rudeness of the verses can be attributed to the metre which today (since the eighteenth century, actually) we associate closely with satire and doggerel. The jog-trot rhythms of the metrical psalms seem to us to be particularly unsuited to the "graver tunes" the Bay Psalm fathers felt they were writing for. In all fairness, the *Bay Psalm Book* should not be judged from this remove. Ballad metre was the easiest to recall and the most natural for the singing of hymns and psalms.

It is important to remember, too, in judging the *Bay Psalm Book*, that none of the metrical psalm translations of the day, English or American, achieved anything like an harmonious arrangement of verse. Though tradition has it that Francis Quarles sent his own metrical translations of Psalms 16, 25, 51, 88, 113 and 137 with John Josselyn on his trip to Boston, there is no evidence that they were incorporated into the *Bay Psalm Book*. The Anglo-Puritan Quarles, a musician as well as a poet, might well have written verses of unusual excellence, but they were rejected as not suited to the desires of the "thirty pious divines." Recalling the beauties of the communal King James translations in 1611, the church fathers may have hoped that communal psalm translations, dedicated to the spirit of the original, might excel those done by individuals. Certainly even so eminent a poet as John Milton, trying his hand at metrical psalmody, produced nine-versed psalms as wooden as any his colleagues wrote.[15]

Since the "learned and pious" ministers themselves obviously knew the tunes to which they were forming their verses, and since several psalms must have been written for the same tune, a sameness is apparent in the poetry. Most of the verses are written for four measure phrases in either three-four or four-four time. Many of the psalms are wholly iambic, and this might be expected since it is common in music to begin with an anacrusis. Psalms like the twenty-third have almost certainly been written with the second syllable receiving the heavy accent. It might be well to note here too that verses written *for* music are more often subject to metrical variations of the milder sort—such as a change from trochaic feet in one line to iambic in another—because the final note in a semi-cadence varies often from one through four beats, which variation is bound to affect the metrics of the next verse line. To illustrate, let us look at the twenty-third Psalm:

> The Lord to mee a shepheard is,
>   want therefore shall not I.
> Hee in the folds of tender-graace,
>   doth cause mee down to lie;
> To waters calme me gently leads
>   Restore my soule doth hee;
> He doth in paths of righteousness:
>   for his names sake leade mee.

> Yea though in valley of deaths shade
>   I walk, none ill I'le feare:
> because thou are with mee, thy rod
>   and staffe my comfort are.
> For mee a table thou hast spread,
>   in presence of my foes:
> thou dost annoynt my head with oyle,
>   my cup it over-flowes.
> Goodnes & mercy surely shall
>   all my dayes follow mee:
> and in the Lords house I shall dwell
>   so long as dayes shall bee.

The wording of the verse indicates clearly where the rest will fall. On the whole the verse is regular, metrically. We would regard its metrical pattern as iambic tetrameter. However, there are deliberate departures from that pattern in "because thou art with mee, thy rod/and staffe my comfort are," and in the final quatrain. Throughout the rest of the verse, each line musically has begun with an "upbeat." The one possible exception occurs in the line beginning "Yea though" where it might be argued that each word is equally as long as the other. But lines eleven and twelve call for some pretty obvious syncopation—that is the crowding of three syllables into the time value of two—if the word "thou" is emphasized as it should be in the line. If not, aside from a certain awkwardness which arises from a too careful literal translation, even these lines can be read iambically. For that matter, so can "Goodnes & Mercy . . . ," though here again the sense of the line would indicate a temporary substitution of the dactylic foot.

The psalm is so familiar to readers in the King James version that the metrical version seems even cruder by contrast. Many of the lines are distorted by the necessity of literal translation and rhyme, a job obviously beyond this poet. The stiffness seems almost un-English, as if the language itself were in the process of breaking away from synthetic structure.

In order to see the actual influence of music on these *Bay Psalm* verses, another psalm revealing the same poetic crudity as Psalm 23, probably by the same "pious" minister, illustrates that it was evidently written with another melody in mind. Psalm 24, which reveals in prose translation no great metrical difference, appears here in prevailing trimeter metre, with a peculiar starkness of expression:

The earth Iehovahs is,
  and the fulnesse of it:
the habitable world; & they
  that there upon doe sit.
Because upon the seas,
  hee hath it firmly layd:
and it upon the water-floods
  most sollidly hath stayd.
The mountaine of the Lord,
  who shall thereto ascend?
and in his place of holynes,
  who is it that shall stand?
The clean in hands, & pure
  in heart; to vanity
who hath not lifted up his soule,
  nor sworne deceitfully.
From God he shall receive
  a benediction,
and righteousness from the strong-God
  of his salvation.
This is the progenie
  of them that seek thy face:
of them that doe inquire for him:
  of Iacob 'tis the race.   Selah . . .

Following the "Selah" or musical interlude, the mood of the
verse changes to one of complete exaltation of the Lord—the
"glorious-King." It seems strange to see the presence of the word
Selah, since to the Hebrew it suggested an instrumental interlude
during which the congregation meditated. At a signal, the interlude concluded, the verse, modified in mood, continued.

Psalm 24 is, if anything, even more compressed and unpoetic
than Psalm 23. However, it should always be borne in mind that
these verses were *sung* rather than read, and lines like three and
four in stanza one, in all probability are smoothed out through
the easy substitutions of note values in a melody. A word or words
like "& they," appearing in as awkward a spot as they do, *look* on
the printed page much worse than they might sound if glossed
over in the melody. Printing tends to make even *sung* words all
look of equal value. Certainly as poetry, Psalm 24 has reached
a nadir.

The many obvious metrical infelicities that occur in Psalm 24—
if one reads properly the punctuation—*must* have been cleared up

by the melodic pattern. Notes can be held or foreshortened. Such verses do not always indicate a bad ear on the part of the poet. They may be an indication that he is writing to some familiar tune, and fitting words to time value rather than to each note.

Another psalm which indicates that it was written to a different tune and incidentally *is* better verse is Psalm 4:

> God of my justice, when I call
>   answer me: when distrest
> thou hast inlarg'd me, show me grace,
>   and heare thou my request . . .

The second line of this stanza indicates some lengthening of "answer me" in the melody. If the sense of the second and third lines had been clearer, one might assume this psalm to have been versed by a different minister. The psalm styles have their differences, and within the limits set, one can discern a lesser or greater poet. Psalm 91, for instance, which suffers by comparison with the free flowing prose-poetic line of the King James version, is superior to Psalm 23:

> He that within the secret place
>   of the most high doth dwell,
> he under the Almightyes shade
>   shall lodge himself *full well.*
> My hope he is, & my fortresse,
>   I to the Lord will say:
> he is my God; & I in him
>   my confidence will stay . . .

There is more regard here for poetry as such, and a trifle more of the necessary padding in words and phrases to fill out the line than in the more literal translations. At any rate, the poem reads more easily.

One of the best of the metrical versions is Psalm 121 which is in true ballad metre, is regular, and possesses a certain smoothness that many of the verses lack. And Psalm 141 is rather beautifully versed:

> O God, my Lord, on thee I call,
>   doe thou make hast to mee:
> and harken thou unto my voice,
>   When I cry unto thee.

> And let my pray'r directed be
>   as incense in thy sight:
> and the up-lifting of my hands
>   as sacrifice at night . . .

Critics of the *Bay Psalm Book* who are unable to account for its long popularity both here and abroad will be interested in an occasion that Foote tells about. He attended the Harvard Tercentenary at which the 78th Psalm from the *Bay Psalm Book* was sung to the "York tune." He wrote:

The great congregation included men and women of a world-wide diversity of background to practically all of whom both work and music were utterly unknown. Hardly any of them sang the 1st stanza, but by the time the sixth stanza was reached a great volume of singing arose, for they had discovered not only that the crude old verse could be sung but that both it and the old tune had a simple dignity and austere beauty all their own.[16]

Perhaps the best proof that the *Bay Psalm Book* in its own day was well regarded and that it met the need for which it was written was its immediate and prolonged adoption by both English and Colonial churches. In 1651 a "revised and enlarged edition," *The Psalms, Hymns and Spiritual Songs of the Old and New Testament,* was printed at Cambridge. It was this volume that was adopted in 1667 at Salem and Ipswich, and finally at Plymouth by the Pilgrims in 1692. In England the last edition of the *Bay Psalm Book* appeared in 1754; and in Scotland, where it was quite popular, "half a dozen Scotch editions appeared between 1732 and 1759."[17] But this anticipates the history of sacred music in the eighteenth century.

In summary, it should be said that the first volume of verse published in the New World showed unmistakable signs of having been written to known melodies. These melodies influenced the stanza structure and often the wording of the lines. If it were possible for us now to hear the metrical psalms from this book sung to the original melodies for which they were written, critics would in all probability temper the harshness of their criticisms.

SECULAR VERSE

> I heard the merry grasshopper then sing,
> The black clad cricket bear a second part,
> They kept one tune, and plaid on the same string,
> Seeming to glory in their little Art.

> Shall creatures abject, thus their voices raise?
> And in their kind resound their maker's praise!
> Whilst I as mute, can warble forth no higher layes.
>
> *Contemplations.* ANNE BRADSTREET

The division between sacred and secular verse in the seventeenth century is an arbitrary one since most of the printed verse was written to glorify God. American poets were imitative of the late Elizabethans and the influence of John Milton grew stronger as the century ended.[18] The American poets, it should not be forgotten, were Englishmen, and their verse does not differ in kind from English verse of the period.

A surprising number of colonists were poets, but then a goodly number of the Puritans who settled New England were educated men. Jantz,[19] who has published much of the heretofore neglected verse of the period, feels that scholars have woefully overlooked not only the quantity of seventeenth century American verse, but the quality of it. He has divided the American poets into three overlapping groups: the founding fathers, the first native-born group, and the later established poets.

The poetic technique of one of the founding fathers, John Fiske (1601-1677), interested Jantz, who said it had a musical parallel:

It was quite sometime after I had transcribed the poems from his manuscript that it dawned on me that his poetic will and technique were something quite unknown to the present and therefore at first uncomprehensible. However, once the basic understanding of his poetic intent was achieved it suddenly became clear that here was a true master of a remarkable technique . . . this man composed his poems in somewhat the way that Buxtehude and Bach composed their music. His method of procedure, like John Wilson's, is to derive an appropriate Anagram from the name of the person to be celebrated, take this Anagram as the basic theme and develop his poem contrapuntally about it . . . he is the purist and the master of this forgotten technique . . . critics are fond of pointing to the Anagram as one of the surest indications of the low style of Puritan poetry . . . did not Bach do something similar to Fiske, when, using the letters of his name as his musical theme, he developed it into a glorious figure? One may safely infer John Fiske is following an old European poetic tradition. . . .[20]

If there was such a tradition, poetically speaking, surely only the minor poets were familiar with it, and even then indulged in it only as Bach did as a musical joke. Neither composer, incidentally, was born when Fiske wrote.

Most of the printed seventeenth century American verse appeared as broadside verse,[21] or else was squeezed into any available space in the ubiquitous almanacs of the day. In addition, everyone with any poetic pretentions wrote elegies,[22] a considerable body of which still survive. Recent studies by Jantz and Wright point up the need for separate editions of some of the works of seventeenth century poets. Jantz, who has published much seventeenth century verse for the first time, as well as republished some material, calls attention to the large body of verse in the *Magnalia Christi Americana* (written 1697; published 1702), Morton's *New England's Memorial*, in Roger Williams's *Key to the Language of America,* and in lesser works. However, most of this verse, aside from the broadside verses which were often composed to be sung to familiar tunes, gives little evidence of musical awareness. A poem of Richard Steere's, published by Jantz, did contain some musical imagery of a pastoral nature. This type of imagery was common in the eighteenth century too. Steere's verse, a portion of which appears here, makes reference to the music of nature:

> Sweet Musickes pleasant and *harmonious sounds;*
> The chirping notes of winged Choresters,
> and *Purling Murmurs* of the Gliding brooks,
> *Modulate Accents* of a well *Tun'd* voice,
> Joyn'd with the Sweet Allurements of the *Lute* . . .
> Pleasing discourses, Histories and Novals
> Amrous Converse, which Innocent and clean
> All give a Charming Sweetness to the Muse.[23]

This verse is very like the sort of thing being written in England at the same time, and proves that all the colonists did not give themselves up wholly to Indian fighting and the exigencies of environment. Thomas Dudley, Nathaniel Ward, Charles Chauncey, and John Wilson were names familiar as poets to the colonists.

Anne Bradstreet, the most famed of the colonial poets, was the daughter of the poet Governor Thomas Dudley, who died with a volume of verse in his pocket. Born in 1612 in England and brought up in the household of the Earl of Lincoln, Anne Bradstreet was but a part of old England transplanted to the New World. Between 1630 and 1642 she wrote some four hundred pages of verse. Her verses were first published in London in 1650 with the familiarly pretentious title of *The Tenth Muse Lately Sprung up in America.* Though Milton's poems appeared in 1645, there is no evidence that Anne Bradstreet knew them. Rather, the French Huguenot poet, Du Bartas, whose "Semaine" in 1578 had won Sidney's endorsement, seems to have exerted the same influence upon Mrs. Bradstreet that he exerted upon seventeenth century English poets. (Milton, for instance, was interested in Du Bartas, perhaps because the latter was the first to tell the story of the creation in verse.)

Du Bartas, in his own lifetime, rivalled Ronsard in popularity. The characteristic that undoubtedly accounted most for his popularity was the tremendous span of learning that appeared in his verse. Nathaniel Ward, in his dedication to Mrs. Bradstreet, called her a "right Du Bartas [*sic*] Girle" because of her interest in Du Bartas, whom she undoubtedly knew through Sylvester's translation.

The scope of Anne Bradstreet's verse is large. She too, like her master, Du Bartas, paraded an extensive knowledge of ancient and modern history, of medicines, and of the arts. Her verse reveals her as an ardent Puritan. Because of her position in the poetic world of her day, it is important to this study to ascertain whether music played any part in her verse.

By way of purely negative approach, it is of interest to note that in addressing the mother church in England, Mrs. Bradstreet lists a number of the items it is necessary to "root out" in order to please the Puritan:

> These are the dayes the Churches foes to crush,
> To root out Popelings head, tail, branch and rush;
> Let's bring *Baal's* vestments forth to make a fire,
> Their Mytires, Surplices, and all their Tire,
> Copes, Rotchets, Crossiers, and such empty trash,
> And let their Names consume, but let the flash
> Light Christendome . . .[24]

Here there is no mention made of the burning of organs or any other instrument—matters once believed a part of the Puritan process of purification. However, Anne Bradstreet does make slighting reference to another musical instrument besides the organ; she apparently shared her century's contempt for the violin:

> From pipe to pot, from pot to words and blows,
> For he that loveth wine, wanteth no woes.
> Whole nights with *Ruffians, Roarers Fidlers* spend,
> To all obscenity *mine ears* I lend . . .

> Cards, Dice and Oathes concomitant I love,
> To playes, to masques, to Taverns still I move,
> And in a word, if what I am you'd hear,
> Seek out a British brutish Cavaler.[25]

There can be no doubt that the violin was a low instrument when a Puritan associated it with a "Cavaler."

But these are minor matters. Of chief interest here is the question of whether Mrs. Bradstreet made use of music at all in her imagery, whether her references show any real knowledge of music, and whether any of her verse forms were affected by music.

In her larger works included in the *Tenth Muse,* she displays a knowledge of myths, events, and medicine. In the "Four Humours of Man," in the section titled "Blood," she has a description of the psalmist, David:

> No pattern, nor no pattron will I bring
> But *David, Judah's* most heroick King,
> Whose glorious deeds in Arms the world can tell,
> A rosie cheek Musitian thou know'st well;
> He knew well how to handle Sword and Harp,
> And how to strike full sweet, as well as sharp . . .[26]

Another passage that reveals a limited knowledge of music occurs in a tribute, actually an "Elegy upon that Honourable and renowned Knight Sir Philip Sidney":

> *Calliope* with *Terpsichore* did sing
> Of poesie, and of musicke, he was King:
> Which makes me now with Silvester confess,
> But *Sidney's* Muse can sing his worthiness . . .[27]

These references, of course, prove nothing except that the lady apparently made the standard overtures to figures associated with music. It may be important that she chooses only David for her "pattern and pattron" in making her verses, and the reference to his handling both sword and harp as both "sweet" and "sharp" reads like a pun. I doubt that it was so intended.

Another common classical allusion is made in her poem written "In Honour of Du Bartas." She honors Du Bartas's knowledge of "physick, musick, and state policy," saying that she feels in such awe of him that she is more "senseless than the stones to *Amphion's* lute."[28]

There is more evidence than this, however, that our first

American poet to achieve fame outside our boundaries had some liking for music. In one verse she wrote: "Sweet musick raps my brave harmonious soul, My high thoughts elevate beyond the pole. . . ."[29]

Unless "raps" is a variant spelling for "wraps," the sense of the first line is somewhat obscure. It could be assumed that the use of "harmonious" here is actually suggested by the reference to music, and not used in the sense of "agreeable." At any rate, the suggestion that music elevates thought, or aids in the process, is obvious.

At another point in her verse, referring to old age, she wrote: "My skin is wrinkled, and my cheeks are pale, *No more rejoyce at musicks pleasing noise,* But waking glad to hear the cocks shrill voice. . . ."[30] The passage indicates that music was for her, at one time, more than a passing pleasure. The term "noise" for "sound" was common in the century, and frequently found in the Bible.

There are not, on the whole, many references to music in the poetry of Anne Bradstreet. The few references she does make are in the pastoral tradition. Exact musical terms seldom appear except with reference to singing, and she reveals familiarity with the terminology of vocal, rather than with instrumental music. Occasionally her musical images are blurred somewhat through her handling of them, as for instance, when there occurs a mixing of vocal and instrumental terms within four lines of a verse from "Contemplation":

> I heard the merry grasshopper then *sing,*
> The black clad Cricket *bear a second part,*
> They kept *one tune,* and *plaid on the same string,*
> Seeming to glory in their little Art . . .[31]

Here, with a little mixed imagery, she reveals that she is familiar, as most Puritans must have been, with the "bearing of parts." This is not the same thing as singing a part now, for harmony rather than polyphony is the order of our day. But seventeenth century musicians "bore" parts in madrigals and motets wholly disparate from each other, and requiring considerably more musicianship from the singer than is required today. To "bear a second part" might well imply something in the nature of a fugue; on the other hand, it could mean something as simple as an entry in rondo form. Both the cricket and the grasshopper are playing "one tune"—that is, to sound their "maker's praise," as the verse goes on to say, but they are also playing this tune on the same string—a musical feat a little difficult to understand.

Another reference to a "sweet concert" of music occurs in "The Prologue to the Tenth Muse" where the poet compares her art to that of music from broken strings:

> From school boyes tongue no rhet'rick we expect
> Nor yet a *sweet Consort* from *broken strings*
> Nor perfect beauty, where's a main defect:
> My foolish, broken, blemish'd Muse so sings
> And this to mend, alas, no Art is able,
> 'Cause nature, made it so irreparable.[32]

But the majority of references to music in her verse are references to "sing," "singing praises," and to pastoral images revolving around song. A typical example of this sort of musical reference appears here:

> The dawning morn with songs thou dost prevent,
> Sets *hundred notes* unto thy feathered crew,
> So each one tunes his *pretty instrument,*
> And *warbling* out the old, begins anew,
> And thus they pass their youth in summer season,
> Then follow thee into a better Region
> Where winter's never felt by that sweet airy legion.[33]

Aside from these, Anne Bradstreet reveals musical influence in only one other respect, and that one is rather oblique.

The fashion of the day in church worship in America was for psalm-singing. Hymns were not rightly a *part* of the service until late in the century. However, it was a common practice to sing hymns in the home and at meetings, and they differed only in subject matter—in that they weren't *psalms*—not in metre. The writing of hymns was popular in the century, and many a poet turned his hand to this form, perhaps because the stanzas themselves were simple, and the technique easily mastered. At any rate, Anne Bradstreet left a number of hymns, based upon the most intimate happenings of her life and unpublished at the time of her death. They are found among her "Religious Experiences and Occasional Pieces," and are surely the very best of her poems for all their simplicity. A portion of one will give the reader some idea of their nature:

> What God is like to him I serve,
> What Saviour like to mine?
> O, never let me from thee swerve,
> For truly I am thine . . . [34]

These hymns are among her most beautiful poems, much more pleasing to modern tastes than the rather stiffly paraded knowledge of humours, ages, and monarchies. Actually the major portion of her verse is a kind of seventeenth century didacticism. She instructs the reader in many matters, but not in music. However, I think it must be pointed out, in summary, that Anne Bradstreet was by no means insensitive to the appeals of music, nor did she shun reference to song and music as an appealing art.

Michael Wigglesworth's *Day of Doom* (1662) is set to ballad metre and thunders in content if not in metre, after the fashion of the great music of the *Dies Irae*. Wigglesworth speaks of trumpet sounds and angel calls, and the poem alternates in mood between the two, though it is less partial to angel calls. The opening section of his poem anticipates the opening of Milton's *Paradise Lost* (1667), albeit Wigglesworth's explanation to man of God's workings is much more horrifying, if less poetically conceived.

There is one other poet who gives evidence of musical influence or interest: the very excellent colonial poet, Edward Taylor. Taylor was born in England, but the exact date and place are still largely matters of conjecture. He arrived in Boston in July of 1668 as a young man in his early twenties, and spent several days as the guest of Increase Mather. He was an orthodox Puritan minister,

who lived nearly sixty years in the frontier village of Westfield, Massachusetts, writing poetry until 1725 in the mannered style of the pre-restoration sacred poets. Though no imitator, he was really in the tradition of Donne and the Anglo-Catholic conceitists. His sole inspiration was a glowing, passionate love for Christ. . . . It is questionable, indeed, whether the depth of his poetic imagination and the vigor of his inventive fancy were equaled in verse by any of his countrymen until the nineteenth century.[35]

Taylor's verse is replete with musical images, metaphor, and similes of so profoundly musical a nature as to indicate that he was conversant with the art of string music as well as vocal. Though Taylor's conceits, like Donne's, are drawn from all of physical nature inclusive of man, the symbol of music seems to have satisfied in large part his attempts to express his feelings for God. Almost all passages dealing with music are at once fairly lengthy and technical.

Particularly is this instanced in the poem "An Ecstasy of Joy let in by this Reply return'd in Admiration":

> *Screw up,* Deare Lord, upon the *highest pin*
>> My soul, thy ample Praise to *sound*.
> O *tune it right,* that *every string*
>> May make thy praise *rebound*.
>
> But oh! how *slack, slow, dull?* with what delay
>> Do I this *Musick* to repare,
> While tabernacled in clay
>> My *Organs* Cottag'de are?
>
> Yet, Lord, accept this Pittance of thy praise,
>> Which as a Traveller I bring,
> While travelling along thy wayes,
>> In *broken notes I sing*.
>
> And at my journies end in endless joyes
>> I'll make amends where Angells meet
> And sing their *flaming Melodies*
>> In *Ravishing tunes most Sweet.*[36]

Here the metaphysical conceit of conceiving the human soul as a musical instrument is carefully carried out. However, the reader will be interested to note again that the relationship between singing and instruments is considered very close, for while stanzas one and two refer to stringed instruments and then to an organ (used to indicate a bodily part as well as the instrument), the last two stanzas make references only to singing. This confusion between instrumental and vocal music was natural throughout the century, since music was often marked indiscriminately for singing or playing.

Taylor, whose chief purpose in writing verse at all seems to have been that of proving his unworthiness in the sight of God, wrote another poem entitled "Our Insufficiency to Praise God suitably for his Mercy." Here the conceit works inward, from the tongue, to the songs of praise the tongue sings, to the tunes that make up the songs. When all these come together to glorify God, then, says the poet, we are become but "sounding organs" to thy glory:

Nor should all these Conspire in us, that we
    Could breath such Praise to thee, Most High:
    Should we thy *Sounding Organs* be
        To *ring such Melody?*
Our *Musick would the World of Worlds outring,*
Yet be unfit within *thine Ears to ting . . .*

Though e're *our Tongues* thy Praises due can fan,
    A Weevle with the World may fly,
    Yea fly away: and with a span
        We may out mete the sky.
Though what we can is but a Lisp, we pray
Accept thereof. We have no better pay.[37]

It is evident that Taylor succeeds in his effort to prove through musical images that any attempt to glorify God is too meagre. The very best that man can do is but a "lisp." Here the whole conceit is musical. In addition, the refrain endings, "Each man would sing . . . Each man would tune . . . Each song a world of music makes," borrow the repetitiveness of music. This poem does not reveal any extensive acquaintanceship with musical terms, but it is obviously musical in pattern. A far more musically-knowledged poem is titled "The Souls Admiration hereupon." The whole of the poem is quoted by way of illustration.

What! I such Praises sing? How can it bee?
    Shall I in Heaven sing?
What! I that scarce durst hope to see,
    Lord, such a thing?
    Though nothing is too hard for thee
    One Hope hereof seems hard to mee.

What! Can I ever tune those Melodies,
    Who have no tune at all?
Not knowing where to stop nor Rise,
    Nor when to Fall.
    To sing thy Praise I am unfit:
    I have not learn'd my Gam-ut yet.

But should these Praises on string'd Instruments
    Be sweetly tun'de? I finde
I nonplust am, for no Consents
    I ever minde.
    My Tongue is neither Quill nor Bow:
    Nor Can my Fingers Quavers show.

But was it otherwise, I have no Kit:
    Which though I had, I could
Not tune the strings, which soon would slip,
    Though others should.
      But should they not, I cannot play
      But for an F should strike an A.

And should thy Praise upon Winde Instruments
    Sound all o're Heaven Shrill?
My Breath will hardly through such Vents
    A Whistle fill:
      Which though it should, its past my spell
      By Stops and Falls to sound it Well.

How should I then, joyn in such Exercise?
    One sight of thee'l intice
Mine Eyes to heft: whose Extasies
    Will stob my Voice.
      Hereby mine Eyes will bind my Tongue,
      Unless thou, Lord, do Cut the thong.

What use of Uselesse mee then there, poore snake?
    There Saints and Angels sing
Thy Praise in full Cariere, which make
    The Heavens to ring.
      Yet if thou wilt, thou Can'st me raise
      With Angels bright to sing thy Praise.[38]

Here again the poet questions his ability to write in praise of God. Like Caedmon, he is almost afraid to trust that God can make a musical (poetical) creature of him. So humble is he that his "melodies," his poems, which "have no tune at all," are unmelodious because, says the poet, he has no sense of tune: he knows not when to rise (in the scale), nor when to fall (to lower the tone), nor even when to stop. He says he hasn't learned his gam-ut (scale)[39] yet. In short, he claims to be a pitiful beginner in his musical instruction.

The customary transference to instrumental music appears when the poet says that he cannot play for the glory of God, though others might, for he knows not how to tune an instrument, nor has he learned the "consents" (partials or steps upon them). His tongue cannot act as quill (for stringed instruments like the lute and clavichord), or bow, nor can his fingers trill (quaver).

He says further, that even if he could play, he has no "Kit" (the tiniest instruments in the violin family), and that if he had, he wouldn't know how to tune it. (Tuning, a problem to the musician at any time, was a genuine burden in Taylor's time when pitches were generally unestablished, strings poor, and pegs worse.) Even if the pegs didn't slip, he insists he could not play upon the instrument.

He proves his inferiority further by saying he can't play wind instruments either—he hasn't breath or training enough. But he knows he will be tempted to sing such praises, though hampered by his ignorance of music. Only God can raise him to the chorus of angels singing His praise. The relationship of poet to musician is borne out unchanged in the poem. It is a nice conceit, revealing how much a minister could know of the music of his day.

That a seventeenth century poet should so deliberately conceive musical analogies, and carry them through with such care, especially in a country where it was once commonly assumed music played a negligible role, proves musical knowledge was more common than we once thought. It is obvious that music was a part of Taylor's stock of association, upon which he drew readily in the creative process. The refrain device, unessential in poetry, except insofar as it is sung-verse as ballads are, looms large in Taylor's verse. It is characteristic of most of his musical poems. A typical example is that of "The Joy of Church Fellowship rightly attended":

> In Heaven soaring up, I dropt an Eare
>   On Earth: and oh! sweet Melody!
> And listening, found it was the Saints who were
>   Encroacht for Heaven that sang for Joy.
>   For in Christs Coach they sweetly sing,
>   As they to Glory ride therein . . .
>
> And if a string do slip by Chance, they soon
>   Do screw it up again: whereby
> They set it in a more melodious Tune
>   And a Diviner Harmony.
>   For in Christs Coach they sweetly sing,
>   As they to Glory ride therein . . .[40]

There are numerous musical references of the same nature in his other poems. It is interesting to note, however, that far and away the largest proportion of these references is found in the "Meditations." Music, as symbol, calls forth this type of verse:

Oh; that my Heart, thy Golden Harp might bee
   Well tun'd by Glorious Grace, that e'ry string
Screw'd to the highest pitch, might unto thee
   All Praises wrapt in sweetest Musick bring . . . [41]

Or he may use another instrument, after this fashion:

My Soule shall then in Lively Notes forth ring
Upon her Virginalls, praise for this thing.[42]

Taylor has passages like this one that sound very like some of the triumphal psalms:

God is Gone up with a triumphant shout:
   The Lord with sounding Trumpets melodies:
Sing Praise, sing Praise, sing Praise, sing Praises out,
   Unto our King sing praise seraphick-wise!
   Lift up your Heads, ye lasting Doore, they sing,
   And let the King of Glory Enter in.[43]

In the "Meditations," the most personal of all his poems, Taylor's religious excitement is so great, so fervent, that nothing, aside from the image of something capable of rising higher and higher toward God, will satisfy. In the musical images which occurred, the tightening of the string, the being played upon as an instrument of God, the rapturous singing forth of God's praises were all themes that could satisfy this God-intoxicated man. The "Meditations" have a headiness about them, an ecstasy that is like music. Taylor's own musical images at times are almost sensuous. He speaks of "heart-cramping notes of music [melody]," of strings which "inravish" with their melodies.[44] He speaks of blushing and trembling at angels' songs,[45] and he draws an apt comparison between wine and the sweet songs of the harp.[46] Part of Taylor's appeal, like that of any good poet, and most apparent in the metaphysical poets, is his tremendous physical responsiveness to spiritual experience.

One of the most typical uses of musical imagery Taylor made appears in "Meditation One Hundred and Ten":

The Angels sung a Carole at thy Birth,
   My Lord, and thou thyselfe didst sweetly sing
An Epinicion at thy Death on Earth.
   And order'st thine, in memory of this thing,

> Thy Holy Supper, closing it at last
> Up with an Hymn, and Choakst the foe thou hast . . .
>
> Joy stands on tiptoes all the while thy Guests
>   Sit at thy Table, ready forth to sing
> Its Hallelujahs in sweet musicks dress,
>   Waiting for Organs to imploy herein.
>   Here matter is allowed to all, rich, high,
>   My Lord, to tune thee Hymns melodiously.
>
> Oh! make my heart thy Pipe: the Holy Ghost
>   The Breath that fills the same and Spiritually.
> Then play on mee, thy pipe, that is almost
>   Worn out with piping tunes of Vanity.
>   Winde music is the best, if thou delight
>   To play the same thyselfe, upon my pipe.
>
> Hence make me, Lord, thy Golden Trumpet Choice,
>   And trumpet thou thyselfe upon the same
> Thy heart enravishing Hymns with Sweetest Voice.
>   When thou thy Trumpet soundst, thy tunes will flame.
>   My heart shall then sing forth thy praises sweet,
>   When sounded thus with thy Sepulcher reech.
>
> Make too my Soul thy Cittern, and its wyers
>   Make my affections: and rub off their rust
> With thy bright Grace: and screw my Strings up higher,
>   And tune the same to tunes thy praise most Just.
>   Ile close thy Supper then with Hymns most sweet,
>   Burr'ing thy Grave in thy Sepulcher's reech.[47]

It is evident here, as it is in most of Taylor's verse, that no such feeling for music in itself saturated his verse as saturated Milton's. Taylor's use of musical images is fairly limited and obvious. It can hardly be claimed that his verse is truly lyrical; it lacks the customary flow and easy movement of lyrical verse. There is in it oftentimes a stultification of the poetic line that results from an over-burdening of image and idea, and this frequently knotted texture is not relieved by his use of musical terms. The excitement (if religious fervor dare be called that) of the verse is heightened by musical references, but so is the confusion in many cases. The fact that common musical terms such as "sing," "hymn," "voice," and "melody" are a part of the poet's vocabulary too, sometimes results in a line of uneasy nebulousness. The last stanza of the poem just quoted serves by way of illustration:

Make too my Soul thy Cittern . . .
.   .   .   .
Ile close thy Supper then with Hymns most sweet,
Burr'ing thy Grave in thy Sepulcher's reech.

While five of these lines carry reference to music, lines like "And tune the same to tunes thy praise most Just" and "Burr'ing thy Grave in thy Sepulcher's reech" are not only obscure, they are almost meaningless. The impacted quality of such phrases leaves the reader confused, despite the clarity of the other images in the stanza.

Another reason for this evident confusion lies in Taylor's use of imagery. One of the criteria of successful metaphysical verse was the skillful extension of an image through a section of a poem, or through a whole poem. Music, since it includes the vocal as well as the instrumental, and since the details of each and the vocabulary belonging to each are full and rich, seemed ideally suited to the needs of a poet like Taylor whose poetic ideas were limited to one large theme: the worship of God. Instrumental and vocal music can be spoken of in detail since each contains many smaller divisions which in turn can be divided. Not only is the number of instruments great and various, but the methods of playing upon each are different. The latitude offered Taylor through musical conceits was necessary to his writing style. In addition, his stretching for the uttermost meaning in the analogy he has chosen made the imagery of music particularly welcome. The natural range of associations between music and the spirit was a further aid to him. However, in many of his poems, and "Meditation One Hundred Ten" is a suitable example, Taylor muddies up the clear stream of association between music and the spirit of God with many other associations at once subtler, often tenuous, and sometimes nearly lost through the passage of time. For instance, stanzas two, three, and four are clear and intelligible. The association of the Holy Spirit with the breath that will pipe through the heart of the poet and fill him with love of and songs for the worship of God is a plausible one. So with the hymns of the flaming trumpet and with the carols sung at the birth of Christ, the musical symbol is understood.

But stanza one vacillates between musical images, references to the meaning of the Holy Supper, and references to the enemies of Christ, without achieving anything like an harmonious arrangement of these disparate ideas. Actually the symbol of music has nothing to do with the last two references, which enter the verse almost obliquely. And stanza five makes a quick reference to the Last Supper as well as to the Grave and Sepulchre of Christ without clarifying the meaning in any way whatsoever.

It is true that there is nothing apparently difficult in the over-all impression the reader receives of the poet's desire to be made various instruments of the Lord's in order to worship him; it is only on a closer reading that the verse is found to have much underlying reference to the Holy Supper. Also vocal music impinges its vocabulary upon the verse in the Carole and the Epinicion. Unfortunately all these references not only meet within a line or two of each other, but they often meet within a single line—limits far too narrow for the resolution of such dissimilarities.

Matters such as these must have had their effect upon the popularity of the poet, and probably always will have. However, there is no denying to Taylor a genuine poetic gift, even if his technique suffered from time to time through this weightiness. On the whole he develops instrumental images more fully than other musical references, and here they are so clear that the rubbing the rust off the wires of affection with "thy bright Grace" seems particularly apt poetic symbolism. The poet has asked to be made a pipe of the Lord, a sweet trumpet, and a cittern. The whole poem is stretched upon the framework of music, and had any of Taylor's verses seen publication when they were written (1700-1729), they would have done much to dispel the notion that orthodox ministers of early New England regarded instrumental music lightly. It is pure conjecture what Taylor's musical education consisted of, but one thing is certain: music played an important part in his creative thinking.

III

Eighteenth Century American Poetry

COMPARATIVELY LITTLE ATTENTION has yet been paid to the lyrical murmurs in eighteenth century American verse. Traditionally the age is associated with the political satires of the Connecticut Wits, the prose of Washington, Franklin, and Jefferson, and the rather weighty volumes of Freneau's verse. Men's minds then were largely concerned with the formation of a state, and the poetry of the period, still accorded full recognition in anthologies, is that which concerned itself most ardently in that cause. Even songs were given over to this patriotic end, and many a poet who might have devoted himself to pastorals and lyrics wrote passionately vitriolic words to familiar tunes.

However, there is a considerable body of American verse in the eighteenth century that is lyrical. The poets who sustained this lyricism through the century were settled principally in two cities—Philadelphia and Boston. These cities were the chief musical centers of the period, and there grew up polite musical and literary cliques centered largely around the colleges and the theatres. One of the earlist of these in Philadelphia included Francis Hopkinson, Doctor of Laws, poet, and musician, and his friend, Dr. Benjamin Rush. Hopkinson, together with the youthful poets Thomas Godfrey and Nathaniel Evans, did much to uphold the Miltonic tradition in the age. Though each was fully aware of the writings of Pope and Dryden and could turn with equal ease to the writing of closed couplets, Evans[1] and Hopkinson seem to have been particularly adept at Miltonic imitations.

Musical influence can be traced in the century through the attempts of writers like Mather Byles to imitate and describe a fugue in verse.[2] Byles, who was a correspondent of Pope's and was considered something of a wit in his own right, wrote his "On a Fuguing tune of Hopkinson" to be published with the "curious little book of sacred music, called the 'New England Psalm Singer'," a book by the "fuguing composer," William Billings.[3] The interesting thing about this fugue as a poem is that Byles succeeds in handling musical description of a rather difficult nature. Dr. Byles revealed no little knowledge of the nature of the fugue in writing the verse, and it compares favorably with the poems of Hopkinson, who was certainly one of the most superior of poets in musical description. Byles's use of imagery here is much clearer than that of Taylor, who always used music for a "metaphysical conceit."

> Down steers the *Bass* with grave majestic Air,
> And up the *Treble* mounts with shrill Career;
> With softer Sounds, in mild Melodious Maze,
> Warbling between, the *Tenor* gently Plays:
> But if th' aspiring *Altus* join its Force,
> See! like the Lark, it Wings its Tow'ring Course;
> Thro' Harmony's sublimest Sphere it flies,
> And to Angelic Accents seems to rise:
> From the bold Height it hails the echoing *Bass,*
> Which swells to meet, and mix in close embrace.
> Tho' diff'rent Systems all the Parts divide,
> With Music's Chords the distant Notes are ty'd;
> And Sympathetic Strains enchanting winde
> Their restless Race, till all the Parts are join'd:
> Then rolls the Rapture thro' the air around
> In the full Magic Melody of Sound.[4]

Byles's handling of each of the different voices, and his description of the meeting of the high and low voices which are "ty'd" only through the harmony is a tribute not only to Hopkinson, but to Billings, who had adapted instrumental fugues for voices.[5]

In addition to this fugue, Byles also tried his hand at writing hymns after the fashion of Watts who was widely imitated in the century. His verses to Dr. Watts are fairly familiar. Less well-known is an excellent little lyric called "Hymn for the Spring."[6] Here the poet reveals a grace and musical sonorousness unknown to American verse in 1739. Byles's poetic nature had, quite surprisingly, its lyrical side.

The form of the hymn and the psalm continued to interest poets of the century. The Reverend Cotton Mather himself brought out a metrical version of the psalms, the *Psalterium Americanum,* in 1718. Even then it was little more than a curiosity since the taste for metrical psalmody was on the wane and the hymns of Watts were gaining popularity. The rise of polite literature in the eighteenth century in England made metrical psalmody seem crude. Poets wrote hymns as their predecessors had written metrical psalms. Even Addison and Pope turned out a hymn or so. Watts's hymns and psalms were first printed by Franklin in this country in 1729, but he complained that no one bought them. Not until 1741 was another edition published in Philadelphia, although one had been published in Boston in 1739.

During his two years here, 1739-41, George Whitefield did much to popularize the *Psalms and Hymns* of Watts. Jonathan Edwards, father of the revival of religious feeling, accepted singing as one of the greatest assets of the revival, and, though he was a Calvinist, approved of Watts's hymns so long as the psalms were "not set aside" as a result of such singing. Many church congregations split over the question of accepting hymns as part of the service.

From the mid-century on, the *Bay Psalm Book* suffered innumerable revisions and was adapted and expanded to meet the changing taste of the day. In the Episcopal Church, Tate and Brady, which had been standard, was replaced by the *Book of Common Prayer* in 1786. The Reverend John Barnard published in America in 1752 a new freer translation of the psalms which abandoned the "antiquated forms" of the *Bay Psalm Book.* The Reverend Thomas Prince, who seems to have had some literary taste, wanted a substitute for the *Bay Psalm Book* but was permitted only to revise it by his congregation. He included some of Watts's hymns. In 1785 Joel Barlow tried to edit a hymnal, but his critics felt that he revised Watts's Psalms "too freely." Timothy Dwight had better luck with his *Psalms of David,* which was accepted by the General Assembly of Presbyterian Churches. America, however, was no longer a provincial nation and religious verse was only a minor part of the total body of verse. By 1700 America was becoming a secular nation, interested in the ideas current in the eighteenth century world. This change was of course reflected in the verse.

Musical imagery in eighteenth century verse was bound closely to nature whenever the poem was a Miltonic pastoral imitation, since Miltonic pastoral imagery often revealed his sensitivity to music. Otherwise, music received a clarity of treatment in verse quite unlike that of the preceding period. Several laudatory verses *to music* were written, and each is characterized by a real understanding of eighteenth century musical techniques. The poems to music celebrate music. They do not use music as a means to another end.

One of the neglected forms of eighteenth century American verse was the cantata ode, often referred to as "libretto" verse. This form relied heavily upon music and demanded that the poet writing the "libretto" understand not only the form itself, but the difficulties of composing for such a medium. The form had startling popularity for public occasions, and most of the "lyrical" poets tried their hands at this form with varying degrees of success. Davenport wrote of it:

The most striking feature about the American ode in the eighteenth century was the frequency with which it was designed to be sung. Both the ode as simple lyric set to the tune of some already popular melody, and the more elaborate production intended to be staged at some particular celebration abound in great quantities. In almost every case the poet realized that there was a distinction between the sung ode and the simple song; the former was usually a more serious, a more universal and momentous production. But why some songs of the time were not called odes is difficult to fathom . . . Whatever may be the explanation for this, the situation makes it all the easier to say that the outstanding type of the form in this early period is the patriotic nationalistic ode intended to be sung. . . .[7]

This sung ode is the same one that had swept England shortly before. It pleased both the musical and the unmusical since the song itself was closely related to the oratorio, and thus to opera. It was a dramatic presentation with music on a scale suitably simple so that colleges and clubs could hold performances of it without elaborate preparations. The scores were not too difficult for the native composers of the period to write, and even the poets wrote with a modicum of success. That the verses are forgotten argues against any unusual beauty in them.

One of the chief musical figures of the day was Francis Hopkinson.[8] He excelled not only as harpsichordist and composer, but also as an American poet. His lyrical verse has lain too long neglected and deserves attention here because Hopkinson was even earlier than Lanier in working out theories of the relationship of music and poetry. His verses on music are among the best ever written on that subject. The now famous "Prologue in praise of Music: Ode on Music" (1754) reveals a clarity of conception and an alliterative pattern that forces the poem into musical channels.

> Hark! hark the sweet *vibrating lyre*
> Sets my attentive soul on fire;
> Thro' all my frame what pleasures thrill
> Whilst the *loud treble warbles* shrill,
> And the more *slow and solemn bass*
> Adds charm to charm and grace to grace.
>
> Sometimes in *sweetly languid strains*
> The *guilty trembling string* complains;
> How it delights my ravished ear,
> When the expiring notes I hear
> Vanish distant and decay! —
> They steal my yielding soul away.
>
> Neatly trip the merry dance,
> And lightly touch, and swiftly glance;
> Let boundless transport laugh aloud,
> *Sounds madly ramble mix and crowd,*
> 'Till all in *one loud rapture rise,*
> Spread thro' the air and reach the skies.
>
> But when you touch the *solemn air,*
> Oh! *swell each note* distinct and clear;
> In *ev'ry sound* let sorrow sigh,
> Languish soft, and sweetly die.
>
> So shall th' admir'd celestial art,
> Raise and transport my ravish'd heart;
> Exalt my soul and give my mind
> Ideas of sublimer kind.
> So great the bliss it seems to prove
> There must be music, too, above.
> That from the *trumpet's silver* sound
> Of wing'd arch-angels plac'd around
> Thy nursing throne—Oh! king of Heav'n!
> Most *perfect harmony* is giv'n!
> Whilst happy saints in *concert join*
> To make the music more divine,
> And with *immortal voices* sing
> HOSANNAHS to their heav'nly KING.[9]

This ode was written when the poet was seventeen, shortly after he began to study the harpsichord. It was dedicated to this instrument—a matter which makes much clearer the opening lines of the poem. A lyre, for instance, might set one's "attentive soul on fire," but one hardly associates it with "shrill warbles" and a "more slow and solemn bass." Hopkinson was poetically and musically justified in referring to the harpsichord as a lyre, since the instrument was strung in exactly that shape.

Something of the nature of the old instrument is revealed in this youthful poem, as well as the styles of music once so closely associated with the harpsichord. That the treble of the harpsichord was shrill there can be no doubt, and efforts to improve quilling of the instrument to soften the tone form a history in themselves.[10] The lower tones of the harpsichord were often difficult to hear, and large fiddles were used to second the tones in the orchestra. Therefore there grew up the custom of writing music of as slow and sustained a nature as possible for the bass.

The description of the sound of the strings of the harpsichord that the young poet offers in the next stanza is surprisingly apt, as those who have heard the instrument will admit. "The guilty trembling string" is a phrase that could never be applied to the pianoforte, because much of the pure string quality is dampened and controlled. The "expiring notes" are notes that "vanish" and "decay," not because they have been held by a pedal or damper, but because they are pure string tones which vibrate and gradually "expire." Finally, this stanza speaks of the "sweetly" languid strains. The pianoforte is not constructed so that it is considered a *sweet* instrument, though the melody, of course, might be considered thus. But the harpsichord was an instrument of a much wider variety and range of tonal possibilities. For this reason, for more than a century after the more accurate pianoforte was invented, the harpsichord was still the preferred instrument of many. Even today there are people who claim the sweetness of Mozart's music is lost through performance on the piano.

Hopkinson's descriptions of the "merry dance" wherein a great number of running themes "madly ramble mix and crowd," till they rise in one "loud rapture" again applies fully to the harpsichord and the other quilled instruments of the day on which fugues made a tremendous conclave of sound. The unstopped tones of each struck note would linger in the air, until, said the poet, they would mount the skies.

By way of contrast, the young poet moves from the dance to the solemn air—a kind of solo for the strings separately—a monophonic line.

The poem excels as verse about music in that the poet knows well the musical matters he mentions. At no place does the thought falter. When music has sufficiently exalted his soul, the poet turns his thoughts to heavenly music. And the ending of the poem is in every way as exactly conceived as the earlier parts. For a poet so young, Hopkinson revealed much of the true poet's touch in this poem.

The young poet showed no evident improvement over his earlier "Prologue in Praise of Music" when he wrote a poem on a similar subject in 1759. The poet's viewpoint, it is true, is different, in that in the later poem he is largely concerned with the effect of music upon the human soul. Perhaps here the very speculations of the young poet reveal greater maturity.

> When the *loud organ* fills the *sacred* choir,
> The pious soul is wrapt in holy fire;
> The *trembling isles the solemn airs resound,*
> And *list'ning angels* hang attentive round;
> *Harmonious strains* with high devotion join,
> And *sacred themes make music* more divine. . . .
> Such *pow'r hath music o'er the human soul,*
> *Music the fiercest passions can control;*
> Touch the nice springs that sway a feeling heart,
> Soothe ev'ry grief, and joy to joy impart,
> Sure virtue's *friends and music are the same,*
> And blest that person is that owns the *sacred flame.*[11]

This prologue was spoken by Mr. David Hallam to the audience gathered at College Hall in Philadelphia to see *George Barnwell* enacted. The evening's proceeds were to go to the purchase of an organ for the hall. Thus Hopkinson wisely dwelt here upon the virtues of music: that music might be expected to bring to the young who would hear it in College Hall spiritual comfort in the mitigation of profane love.[12] His ideas sound similar to those expressed in "Music hath Charms." Hopkinson's ideas were shared also by the Greeks who felt that music had every power over the human soul. *They* even went so far in the doctrine of "ethos" as to designate certain modal melodies for certain moods to excite certain responses. An unmusical man was a pariah indeed. But "blest," says Hopkinson, is the man who "owns that sacred flame."

Hopkinson continued in this poem to make a connection between music and the sacred, and the whole history of music proves that the association is a common one—to composers as well as poets. Music is traditionally regarded as an aid to virtue, as an awakener of the soul in man to better ends and ideals. Each of these two prologues is a tribute to music, but the later one has more timeless appeal.

One of the interesting strains revealed in the poetry of this fairly neglected eighteenth century writer is the Miltonic—a strain which is found in great quantity in all the verse of the minor lyricists. Some of the verse is simply in the pastoral tradition, and cannot, strictly speaking, be considered Miltonic. However, many of Hopkinson's poems are actual Miltonic imitations. His "L'Allegro" and "Il Penseroso" are quoted in part here to show how much like the original the poet could make them:

L'Allegro

Frolic, frisky, wanton, gay,
Round and round thee let them play . . .
As thou thus approach'st me nigher
Let me hear the *warbling lyre;*
Graceful use the *springy quill,*
Touch it with superior skill;
But not to such *soft languid airs,*
Soothing sorrows, soothing cares,
With which the *silly singing* swain
Proclaims imaginary pain. . . .

Il Penseroso

Vanish mirth, and vanish joy,
Airy pleasures quickly cloy;
Hence all ye bacchanalian rout,
And wine, and jest, and noisy shout;
And quips, and cranks, and gay grimace,
And wit, that wears a double face.
Hence ev'ry kind of jollity,
For you have no delights for me,
But welcome, welcome, melancholy;
Thou goddess sage, demure and holy! . . .

Nothing but the night-bird's cry,
Echoing thro' the vaulted sky;
Nothing but the ceaseless rill

Murmuring o'er its pebbles still:
Or the distant falling flood
Shakes the silence of the wood.[13]

The general quality of these imitations is high. Not only is the
pastoral element properly attended to, but there is real poetry in
many of the lines. The melancholy induced by the lines beginning
"Nothing but the night-bird's cry" is carefully borne out through
a series of scenes that regard nature with the eye usually associated
with poetry of a somewhat later date. Part of the pleasure these
imitations arouse, simply as imitations, lies in the apparent ease
with which the poet falls into the pastoral pattern and his own
interesting method of handling imagery to call up the contrasting
moods. It might be noticed that by the mid-eighteenth century, an
American poet was consciously referring to nature in a "romantic"
vein:

But hark! what voice so loud and shrill
From yonder dark romantic hill. . . .

There is, finally, a melodious quality in these verses that arises
from the ease with which the poet handles his rhyme and his
rhythms. At no point is there a sign of strain to express an idea
poetically. And there is only one spot that seems needlessly prosaic:

'Tis hers—that bird well known to fame,
The fond repeater of her name—

Hopkinson was often likely to fall into the Hellenic tradition.
Many of his poems have pastoral accouterments. And there is a
simplicity about his simpler pastorals that is song-like. "The
Hermitage," for instance, is such a song:

My muse delights in humble strains
    To sing the sylvan scenes,
Of rural prospects, flow'ry plains,
    And wide extended greens. . . .

Oft did this happy grove resound
    Strains sweeter far than mine;
Here sat the Bard, and here around
    Stood the indulgent Nine.

Poetic music from his tongue
    Harmonious roll'd away;
The birds in dumb attention hung
    To hear his softer lay.[14]

There are several songs in Hopkinson's *Miscellaneous and Occasional Writings,* printed by T. Dobson in 1792. They are true songs and reflect none of the elements one finds in Freneau and the Connecticut Wits—elements of wit and satire. They are much more akin to the songs of Ben Jonson.

Eight of these songs were written to be sung to his own music. They constitute probably the best of his writing. The simplicity of the songs themselves, the ballad-like ease with which the poet handles the repetition of key lines, and his undeniable ability to sustain a mood without interruption mark these as worthy of more attention than is ordinarily accorded his verse. Two of them follow:

Song III

Part I

Beneath a weeping willow's shade
   She sat and sang alone;
Her hand upon her heart she laid
   And plaintive was her moan.
The mock bird sat upon a bough
   And listn'd to her lay,
Then to the distant hills he bore
   The dulcet notes away.

II

Fond echo to her strains reply'd
   The winds her sorrows bore;
Adieu! dear youth—adieu! she cry'd,
   I ne'er shall see thee more.
The mock bird sat upon a bough
   And listn'd to her lay,
Then to the distant hills he bore
   The dulcet notes away.[15]

Song IV

O'er the hills far away, at the birth of the morn
I hear the full tone of the sweet sounding horn;
The sportsmen with shoutings all hail the new day
And swift run the hounds o'er the hills far away.
Across the deep valley their course they pursue
And rush through the thickets yet silver'd with dew;
Nor hedges nor ditches their speed can delay—
Still sounds the sweet horn o'er hills far away.[16]

The songs evidence one of Hopkinson's chief appeals as a lyric poet: his sibilants and liquids form a pattern of interlacing sounds that cannot help but effect a musical murmuring in the reading. In Song III, part I, for instance, alliteration, internal as well as at the beginning of words, is most noticeable. The letters most freely alliterated are w,n,b,p,s,l,h,d, and t. There is, in the first place, a close connection between the very letters alliterated. Then the poet so knits the stanza that every word is necessary to it; yet the image itself is simply one of loneliness for which the bird is the voice. Since the image is simple, there is a freeness and certain ease in the stanza resulting from what can be said of it. Part II of the song only tells what her song was, and then repeats the image of the mock bird who "bore the dulcet tones away." This repetitive device gives to the song form and finish as well as a certain plaintive appeal since only the most emotionally significant portion of the verse is repeated.

The same devices are apparent in Song IV where the longer anapestic line spaces the alliteration so that there is a springing, bounding return to certain key sounds, unlike the more closely knit alliteration of most lyrical poems. Lines three and four, as well as line eight, provide contrast in their more constant alliterations within the line. Their smoothness offsets the "hunt" measure of the earlier lines. Again the ease with which Hopkinson handles rhythms such as these is commendable. Here is a poet to whom the lyrical gift was given in a generous measure.

Another example of Hopkinson's use of alliteration is this stanza from his poem "On Disappointed Love."

> High rais'd in aether from her silver throne,
> The moon in melancholy mildness shone;
> Nor voice, nor sound disturb'd the mid-night hour,
> Save the sad south-wind murm'ring in the bow'r. . . . [17]

Here the mood is sustained by the smooth repetitions of s,m,n,l, and the sounds d,b, and th. Lines like "save the sad south-wind murm'ring in the bow'r" are built, undoubtedly half unconsciously, around s,m, and r. It may be that Hopkinson's musical ear led him unconsciously to this lyrical device. It may be that he deliberately studied lyrical verse to that end; but whatever the reason, the fact remains that Hopkinson's verse in its own day is unique in the degree and the success with which he used alliteration. And the pattern of his alliterations was not again so evident in American verse until the work of Poe.

Much has already been said of Hopkinson the composer. He has just claim to the title of first American songster; he may have written the first American opera in the *Temple of Minerva*. But he is best remembered in American literature for songs such as these quoted above, and those more popular ones which are still sung like "My Days Have Been So Wondrous Free" (1759); "The Garland" (1760); "My Generous Heart" (1788); and "Give Me Thy Heart as I Give Mine" (1789). These songs are still popular and find their way occasionally into concert programs.

Hopkinson wrote verse, however, of every type. He wrote hymns,[18] several elegies, among the most beautiful of which was that upon the death of his teacher, James Bremner. This elegy took the form of the cantata ode—a form unusually well suited, one might suppose, to the dual nature of Hopkinson's talents (since he was both librettist and composer).

Hopkinson was the most prominent of the cantata odesters in America, and only Robert Treat Paine exceeded his out-put, though Paine's odes were of a more flamboyant texture than Hopkinson's. The odes which Hopkinson wrote were literary, and celebrated events of the nature of the accession of George III and the death of George II. Hopkinson understood fully the nature of air, recitative, and chorus, and Davenport felt that he was writing in the tradition of Dryden and Gray. Of one unperformed ode he wrote:

It is built on the same model as the earlier specimens with a recitative, chorus, and airs. It is evident that these three poems were constructed along the same lines as Dryden's "Alexander's Feast" . . . and as Gray's "Ode to Music". . . .[19]

The poorer of the two poems Hopkinson left on the Georges was the "Ode Sacred to The Memory of his late Gracious Majesty George II," sung at public commencement at the College of Philadelphia, May, 1761. This was a true cantata ode:

Recitative
Why looks the visionary maid so sad,
Oh! why, *Britannia,* thus in sable clad?
Oh! speak the cause from whence such sorrows flow,
That, by partaking, we may ease thy woe.

Air
Lend, lend your tears, ye virgin train,
Let music swell her softest strain!

Oh! make the solemn dirge resound,
And spread religious sorrow round
With me the deep-felt loss deplore—
My son! my son! is now no more!

Chorus

Then let the solemn Dirge begin,
   Whilst we our voices join,
To swell the tend'rest note of grief,
   And mix our woe with thine!
             (A Slow Symphony)

Air

The glorious sun, *Britannia's* king,
Withdraws his golden light:
   His setting ray
   Glides swift away
And yields to conq'ring night.

Down in the deep and dreary tomb
His mortal part must lie;
   And ev'ry bell
   Now tolls his knell,
Tears flow from every eye. . . . [20]

Though the poem is quoted only in part here, there is enough for the reader to see that the poet made conscious effort to follow the approved pattern for the different portions of the cantata. The country that had done the most to further the development of the cantata ode musically, after its Italian inception, was Germany.[21] There was gradually shaped the notion that the epic element in the poem should be taken care of in the recitative. Lyric passages were to be handled as airs or arias, and purely dramatic elements were apportioned to the chorus. In addition the "symphony" often appeared as an instrumental interlude, to increase the effectiveness of the presentation.

It should be noted in Hopkinson's ode that the recitative section differs from the chorus in that the latter is used for lamentation, most effective with musical setting; whereas the recitative, with its foreboding, almost speech-like character, handles the fateful question. The air is reserved for the answer of Britannia, a solo sung to heighten the effect of the answer she must give. The second air, it should be noted, is much freer in its range of possibilities since the singer now simply turns to the various losses England will sustain. The distinction between the parts of this ode is not as evident as it might be, though it is still apparent. Hopkinson was trying his hand at the form for the first time, and though the general literary tendency of the day was dramatic, Hopkinson's genius was not. He certainly devoted himself to dramatic entertainments often enough, both as musician and as poet, but it is evident that his talents do not lie here when one compares his cantata odes with his pastorals, hymns, and songs. Even Paine excels Hopkinson in dramatic appeal.

The second of Hopkinson's odes came a year later at the time of the accession of George III. It too was performed at Philadelphia, and it is an improvement over the earlier one in variety and suitability for musical setting. However, Hopkinson's odes have a singularly sickly quality, even in a day when much uninspired verse appeared often on public programs. Unfortunately the music is no longer extant which may have enlivened verses like these:

The Ode
Bright ascending to the skies,
See *Britannia's* glory rise!
Cease your sorrows, cease your fears,
Night recedes and day appears;
Another *George* majestic fills her throne,
And glad *Britannia* calls him all her own.

Chorus
Let the tuneful chorus join
And high their voices raise,
To celebrate in notes divine,
The youthful monarch's praise.

Air I
Rejoicing science with each polish'd art,
Beneath his reign shall with success conspire
To form the manners, humanize the heart,
And virtuous thoughts, and virtuous deeds inspire.

Air II
. . .

Chorus, etc.[22]

The ode continues with another air and chorus, followed by two airs and a final chorus. The final lines of the chorus each time are repeated with the change of one word only. The ode is quoted in part here only to show how music affected the form of the verse

as well as its content. The prevailing mood is joyful, and thus
again the ode suffers from lack of contrast between air, chorus,
and recitative. The form of this ode is much like another that
remained unperformed, and it may be that though Hopkinson was
certainly well thought of as a composer, his odes were considered
too dull for public consumption. There are, extant of Hopkinson,
two additional unperformed odes—one simply designated "for public commencement at Philadelphia" (1763), and another an ode on
"Disappointed Love." The commencement ode was unperformed
because of a squabble over "grammar." At any rate the only ode
that gained for Hopkinson any measure of fame was his elegy on
James Bremner, which must have been recognized for its genuinely
mournful quality and its sincerity. Part of it is quoted here:

> Sing to his shade a solemn strain,
> Let music's notes complain;
> Let echos tell from shore to shore
> The swain of Schuylkill is no more. . . .

> *Air*
> From Scotia's land he came,
>   And brought the pleasing art
> To raise the sacred flame
>   That warms a feeling heart.
> The magic pow'rs of sound
>   Obey at his command,
> And spread sweet influence round,
>   Waked by his skilful hand. . . . [23]

Bremner had been invaluable as teacher and friend to Hopkinson,
and made notable contributions to the musical life of Philadelphia.

Hopkinson tried his hand at some seven odes, including one to a
lady on her birthday, one to science, and one for the Grand Federal
Processional, July 4, 1788. But, as poetry, they remain inferior to
the larger body of his work. It is somewhat strange that a poet so
equipped should lack the dramatic touch to the extent that Hopkinson did. His very nature was undramatic.

There is a considerable body of his verse which does find its way
into anthologies—his political ballads, his "Battle of the Kegs," his
"A Camp Ballad"—largely because it follows the more commonly
accepted pattern for eighteenth century verse. In addition to
these he left a great many verses in the sentimental tradition,
writing verses "To Rosalinda," "Verses Wrote in a blank book
which once belonged to Shenstone," "A Sentiment," etc.—verses

which are no better than any of that kind written in that day. He was a fairly prolific writer, and did not hesitate to try various styles. The most interesting thing about the total body of Hopkinson's work is how early signs of romantic interest appear in it. Of course he knew Shenstone, and was strongly influenced by Milton; still Hopkinson is more important in American poetry as a romantic figure than the publication of his satires would indicate.

Since he was a poet-composer, his tributes to music are of especial interest. In writing "Description of a Church," he left the following excellent tribute to the baroque organ:

> I trod—and started at the mighty noise;
> The hollow pavement lifted up its voice;
> The swelling arch received the rising sound,
> Responsive to the stroke the walls around . . .
> Thro' lengthen'd aisles prolong'd the solemn sound.
>
> Far in the west, and noble to the sight,
> The gilded *organ* rears its tow'ring height;
> And hark! methinks I from its bosom hear,
> Soft issuing sounds that steal upon the ear
> And float serenely on the liquid air.
> Now by degrees more bold and broad they grow,
> And riot loosely thro' the isles below;
> 'Till the full organ lifts its utmost voice,
> And my heart shudders at the powerful noise:
> Like the last trump, one note is heard to sound
> That all the massy pillars tremble round;
> The firm fixt building shivers on its base,
> And vast vibration fills th' astonish'd place. . . .
>
> But now the blast harmonious dies away,
> And tapers gently in a fine decay . . .
> 'Till grown too soft, too fine for mortal ear,
> The dying strains dissolve in distant air.
> Methought I heard a flight of angels rise,
> Most sweetly chaunting as they gain'd the skies:
> Methought I heard their less'ning sound decay
> And fade and melt and vanish quite away.
>
> Hail heav'n born music! by thy pow'r we raise
> Th' uplifted soul to acts of highest praise:
> Oh! I would die with music melting round,
> And float to bliss upon a sea of sound.[24]

There are few tributes to music equal to that of the last stanza. The poet achieves an image of the vaulted church, the organ, and the massy pillars that should not be undervalued because it is a tribute to music. In this verse, as in all his best work, Hopkinson revealed his really fine hand in handling alliteration. Not so obvious in this poem as to detract from the sense of the verse, the alliteration moves beneath the surface with subtlety and smoothness.

In all his lyrical verse, Hopkinson sought an undeniably musical combination of sounds. The pacing of alternate lines, resulting from differences in beginning consonants and syncopation of accents, is delightful. Yet Hopkinson moved in the traditional patterns and was no innovator metrically. He is a better poet than critics have recognized, and deserves a place before that of Freneau's in the history of the romantic movement in American poetry.

Another poet who evidenced some interest in music through his verse was the short-lived young dramatist Thomas Godfrey. Born in 1736 into the congenial musical atmosphere of Philadelphia, he was said to possess "a fine ear for music and an eager propensity to poetry."[25] His verse was first published in its entirety together with *The Prince of Parthia* in 1765, though his "Court of Fancy" was published separately in 1762. His is verse in the Spenserian-Miltonic pastoral tradition. It makes constant references to song, strains, and lyres. His chief verse form was the ode, though his "Ode to Wine" is actually a dithyramb in five parts. He was a close friend of Nathaniel Evans, another short-lived lyricist, and like Evans he left songs, six of them, replete with Green references to Thyrosis, Celia, Delia, etc. He wrote a paraphrase of the *First Psalm,* a poem entitled "Amyntor" which has alternate recitatives and airs, and a cantata ode on "Peace" in 1763. There is no record that the ode was performed or that music was written for it, though it was originally the hope of the poet that this should be done. Both "Amyntor" and the ode entitled "Peace" make dull reading, and do not succeed as well as Hopkinson's odes.

There are many laudatory references to music in Godfrey's verse. Typical of the references that Godfrey made to music was this one, which echoes ideas Hopkinson also expressed in his second "Prologue in Praise of Music":

Suddenly I heard soft sounds, a pleasing strain!
Music advanced, with all her heavenly train
Sweetly enraptured, then my pulse beat high,
And my breast glow'd with unusual joy.
'Tis harmony can ev'ry passion move,
Give sorrow ease or melt the soul to love;
Exulting pleasure to her call attends,
E'en stormy rage to pow'rful music bends.[26]

Apparently music came in for fulsome praise during the century. Godfrey's career was foreshortened by his premature death. He was still largely an imitative poet with a talent peculiarly suited to the pastoral tradition. It cannot be said that music influenced his verse to the extent that it did Hopkinson's, for instance, but few of his verses are written without some reference to music. The fact that the cantata ode interested him, in part because of its dramatic quality, revealed his interest in the use of music with poetry.

One of Godfrey's friends, Nathaniel Evans (1742-1767), also Philadelphia born and educated, was a romantic poet of no slight stature in this century. Though almost as capable at writing *vers société* and satires after the fashion of Dean Swift, Evans was an excellent imitator of Milton and did much to keep the Miltonic tradition alive during the century. He was keenly sensitive to the pastoral tradition in poetry, and his poetry, like that of Godfrey's, abounds in classical references to lyres, pipes, reeds, and singing swains. In a brief description of the nature of poetry and the poet, Evans has left us probably the earliest essay on the nature of romantic poetry in America:

There *is a pleasing* Je Ne scay [sic] quoi *in the productions of* poetic *genius, which is easier felt than described. It is the* voice of nature *in the Poet, operating like a charm on the soul of the reader. It is the* marvelous conception, *the* noble wildness, *the* lofty sentiment, *the* fire and enthusiasm *of spirit, the* living imagery, *the* exquisite choice of words, *the* variety, *the* sweetness, *the* majesty *of numbers, and the irresistable* [sic] magic *of* expression.

The Prose writer *may indeed warm his Reader with a* serene *and* steady *fire. . . .* But the Poet's *it is to* wrap him in a flame—*to dissolve him, as it were, in his own* rapturous blaze! The Poet's *it is to hurry him* out of himself. *. . . It is his, to exhibit to his mind, all the* novelty of this varied world, *to carry him back into the* darkness of antiquity, *or waft him forwards into the* vast sea of futurity—*and finally, to inspire him with* the patriotic glow, *or fire his soul with the* heavenly *ideas of* Moral Beauty, *and all the varied passions of* Love, Fear, Terror, Compassion. . . .[27] *Such is the genuine Poet . . . and the works of such have*

*been the continual delight of mankind, as they afford the sublimest
intellectual enjoyment. . . .*

  But it is rare, that such Natural Geniuses *are seen to arrive at this
envied height. Some* black obstacle *still clogs their wings, and retards
their progress—Frequently those to whom nature has been thus bounti-
ful, have not leisure to attend to the cultivation of their talents—
frequently, like the rose in the wilderness, they just bloom, and wither
away in obscurity; and sometimes, alas!,—the iron hand of* DEATH
cuts them SUDDENLY off, *as* their beauties are just budding forth
into existence, *and* leaves but the *FAIR PROMISES of FUTURE
EXCELLENCIES. . . .*

Here the pen was stayed, and death claimed the poet in his
twenty-sixth year.

It is almost impossible to determine from the meagre accounts
of the life of Evans just what his musical education, if any, consisted of. From the comments on music in his work, it seems that
the musical leadership Philadelphia claimed during his lifetime
left its mark upon him. He used music imagery much as Milton
did and was an ardent odester. The lyrical quality is strong in all
of Evans' verse and suggests that the references he made to music
were natural to one enamored of music. In his "Ode to a Friend"
he wrote:

> Thrice blest is he, whose placid birth
>   The warbling *Muses* hover'd round;
> Novice to all the ills of earth,
>   While wrapt in music's soothing sound. . . .[29]

The young poet in his sixteenth year wrote "Daphnis and
Menalcas," a poem in which he indicated his own high hopes for
his fame as the poet of Philadelphia. The poem also reflects how
early his pastoral imitations were begun as well as his interest in
couplets:

> Shall fam'd Arcadia own the tuneful choir,
> And fair Sicilia boast the matchless lyre?
> Shall Callia's groves resound with heav'nly lays,
> And Albion's poets claim immortal bays?
> And this new world ne'er feel the muse's fire;
> No beauties charm us, or no deeds inspire?
> O Pennsylvania! shall no son of thine
> Glow with the raptures of the sacred nine? . . .
> Fir'd with the thought, I court the Sylvan muse,
> Her magic influence o'er me to diffuse;

> Whilst I aspire to wake the rural reed,
> And sing of swains, whose snowy lambskins feed
> On Schuylkill's banks. . . .[30]

He continues in the same vein, and remarks of the music in the "feathered choir" that "each grove is music." But Daphnis grows sad. "The linnet's songs no more entice my ear."

> The sportful trouts may leave their wat'ry plains,
> To dwell in woods, and *tune spontaneous* strains;
> The *warbling linnets* may in rivers glide,
> And dash the bellows with the dolphin's pride. . . .[31]

There is no faltering in the pastoral conception of the poem as a whole, and it is quite excellent poetry when one considers the poet's youth. At the same age he wrote "a Rural Ode" which takes music in nature as a theme:

> In yonder gay-enamell'd mead,
>   The starling plumes his golden wings,
> Then tow'ring up the azure height,
>   He mounts sublime, and soaring *sings*.
>
> The yellow finch, and linnet blue,
>   In *mattins* wild salute the day,
> While their *sweet songs*, by *echo* caught,
>   In double-sounding notes decay. . . .
>
> Deep in yon old sequest'red grove,
>   Where the down-dashing torrents roll,
> Ascends on fancy's roving wing,
>   The rapture-breathing poet's soul.[32]

The poem reads somewhat like the early verse of Keats. It has a smoothness in "numbers" that again indicates a natural rhythmic awareness. Evans was an excellent songwriter, as the songs to Myra, to Sylvia and "Wild music sweetly floats along" prove. These songs are far removed from the main stream of eighteenth century verse and are closer to the songs of Jonson, Waller, and Herrick, than to Dryden or Pope.

Evans' Miltonic imitations, like those of Godfrey and Hopkinson, are usually reserved for "L'Allegro" and "Il Penseroso." His "Anacreontic Ode," for instance, is another "L'Allegro": his poem "To Melancholy" is also Miltonic:

> Hence with sorrow, spleen and care!
> Muse, awake the *jocund air*;

Wreathe thy brows in myrtle twine,
And assist the gay design;
Strike the trembling string with pleasure,
Till it found the enchanting measure.
Avaunt! thou fiend, pale melancholy!
We are mortals free and jolly. . . .
If *wine inspires the tuneful band,*
Who can the *glowing strain* withstand?
Floods of music, all divine,
Pour along in every line;
And the *wild Dithyrambic strain,*
Rushes thro' the poet's brain.
Alcaeus lov'd the purple juice;
Sprightly Flaccus felt its use;
And the sweet Anacreon,
Warbled best when *half-sea gone.*
Ivy-crown'd Bacchus hail!
And, o'er my *reeling* song prevail.[33]

.   .   .   .

Come, thou Queen of pensive air,
In thy sable, sooted car,
By two mournful turtles drawn—
Let me meet thee on yon lawn . . .
Quickly come, thou sober dame,
And thy musing Poet claim.
Bear me, where thou lov'st to rove,
In the deep, dark, solemn grove . . .
There, sweet Queen, I'll sing thy pleasures
In enthusiastic measures,
And sound thy praises thro' the lone vale,
Responsive to the hollow gale;
The murm'ring rills shall spread it round,
And grottoes the wild notes rebound. . . .[34]

As imitations, these may not be the equal of Hopkinson's, but they reveal a genuine understanding of the nature of pastoral poetry and some sympathy with Milton's subjects.

Evans was sympathetic to the musico-poetic traditions of the seventeenth century in other ways, too. He felt strongly the power of religion and thought the Psalms of David were divinely inspired. He wrote to urge young poets to seek themes from the Bible.

I have thus far premised, to induce, if possible, those youths among us, who have enjoyed the advantage of a liberal education, and have leisure for literary pursuits and a taste and capacity for poetry . . . to turn their talents towards such instructive performances. The Holy Scriptures are the true fountain from which to extract the richest draughts of poesy . . . witness the noble use the great Milton made of them in his marvelous poems. . . .[36]

He himself wrote paraphrases of Psalms 97, 145 (a kind of hymn of musical utterance), and 137.

Since Evans took holy orders, it is natural that many of the poems found in the 1772 edition are of a religious nature. One of the best of these is "On the Passion and Resurrection of Christ." In addition, among the fragments at the conclusion of the volume is found a series of early romantic verses like that "On Time," the "Introduction to a Night Piece," and the excellent "Sea-Piece." Moreover, he wrote a series of odes after the fashion of Pindar— a matter that also set him apart from the odesters of the period who were imitating Horace. He wrote, too, a cantata ode—the "Ode on the Occasion of the Peace"—which was performed at the College of Philadelphia, May 17, 1763. It was filled with references to music, and its general tenor was more lyric and poetic than dramatic and musical. It began:

> Come then, my friends, your *notes mellifluous* pour,
> And the *soft soul of harmony* explore;
> With *melting strains* the happy day prolong,
> What more enchanting than the *charms of song?* . . .

And near the end:

> Enough, my friends!—*ye sweeter numbers flow,*
> And let the *deep ton'd swelling organ blow;*
> Ye *tuneful quire, your dulcet warblings* join
> And sooth th' *attentive soul with harmony divine.* . . .[36]

The musical quality in the verse itself does not mean that it was particularly adapted to music. As a matter of fact, the poem has rather high literary quality for a cantata ode and probably reads better than it would have sounded. Unfortunately, Evans' experiments in poetic forms were only to last another two years, and in those last years, dating from the year of his graduation (1765) from the College of Philadelphia, he showed an increasing familiarity with the neo-classical couplet and satire.

Evans left a poem of some length to Benjamin Franklin "Occasioned by hearing him play on the Harmonica"; a portion is quoted here:

In grateful wonder lost, long had we view'd
Each gen'rous act thy patriot-soul pursu'd;
Our Little State resounds thy just applause,
And, pleas'd, from thee new fame and honour draws:
In thee those various virtues are combin'd,
That form the true preeminence of mind. . . .
Yet not these themes alone thy thoughts command,
Each softer *science* owns thy fostering hand;
Aided by thee, Urania's heav'nly art,
With finer raptures charms the feeling heart;
Th' *Harmonica* shall join the sacred choir,
Fresh transports kindle, and new joys inspire—

Hark! the soft warblings, sounding smooth and clear,
Strike with celestial ravishment the ear,
Conveying inward, as they sweetly roll,
A tide of melting music to the soul;
And sure if aught of mortal-loving strain
Can touch with joy the high angelic train,
'Tis this enchanting instrument of thine,
Which speaks in accents more than half divine![37]

The careful, almost meticulous use of couplets, artfully knit,
was a device up till now not wholly familiar to Evans. The ideas
he expresses here are not different from those in his earlier tribute
to music—the association of music with the divine, the speaking of
music to the soul, the "celestial ravishment of the ear"—but this
poem marks the first departure from the forms of the funeral ode
and elegy which were the delights of his early youth. Even when
Evans chose so romantic a subject as the "Aeolian Harp" some
quarter of a century before it began to loom large in the poetry of
the English romantic movement, his verse shows an unfamiliar
regularity of stanza, though scarcely any loss of lyrical flavor. One
can hardly doubt, in looking at the last verses of Evans, that he
was entering upon a period of imitation of neo-classical verse—
an imitation most unfortunate because it was unsuited to his
poetic genius. For comparison's sake, most of the "Aeolian Harp"
is quoted here:

Sweet Zephyr leave th' enamel'd plain,
    And hither wave thy gentle wing;
Would'st thou out-rival Orpheus' strain,
    O haste and touch this trembling string.

The balmy-breathing power obeys,
    'Tis his my slender *harp* to claim;

> He comes, and o'er its bosom plays,
>   And rapture wakes the slender frame!
>
> The tender, melting notes of love,
>   The soul in soothing murmurs steal;
> Low as the languor-breathing dove,
>   That, lonesome, coos her plaintive tale.
>
> Hark! what sounds of pleasing pain,
>   Deep as some bleeding lover's lay,
> Sad as the cygnet's moving strain,
>   When on the shore she dies away.
>
> A nobler gale now sweeps the wire,
>   The hollow frame responsive rings,
> Loud as when angels strike the lyre,
>   Sweet as the heav'nly chorus sings.
>
> And hark! the numbers roll along,
>   Majestically smooth and clear,
> Like Philomel's enchanting song,
>   The notes mellifluous pierce the ear.
>
> Thus as the varying accents flow,
>   Each passion feels th' accordant sound—
> *This* lifts the soul, *that* sinks it low,
>   We seem to tread on fairy ground.[38]

This poem is a kind of half-way mark on the road to efforts like "The Morning Invitation to Two Young Ladies at the Gloucester Springs" and other occasional verse. Though the imagery has lost some of its lushness, the poet still retains the alliterative quality that marked the earlier verse. The admirable variation of liquids and sibilants is well suited to a poem on music, but the enchanting, almost shimmering quality of his Miltonic imitations and early pastorals is gone. In many respects the pruning process resulted in a better poem here. In others, it but pointed in the direction of the doggerel that was characteristic of the poems of the last period of his life.

A subscription had already been taken for the printing of Evans' verse in 1766, but his death in 1767 prevented its publication. His poems were finally fully collected by a young woman correspondent and one of his early teachers. The volume is in itself one of the best proofs that the romantic and the lyrical found expression in eighteenth century America.

Robert Treat Paine, born Thomas Paine, Jr., in Boston, 1773, was one eighteenth century poet who succeeded in making a good living writing cantata odes for public celebrations.[39] He had, in addition, a genuine poetic gift.

His interests were always closely allied to the theatre, and his style, which at first reflected Pope's polished couplets, later gave way to the more dramatic forms of the cantata ode. Almost to his dying day he haunted the theatres of Boston. Strangely enough, he was one of the few poets who earned large sums of money for his verse, most of which was of an occasional nature.[40] He had a marked talent for languages and was an excellent Greek scholar. His Latin imitations brought him unusually high sums of money for the day—or any day. "The Ruling Passion," after the satires of Horace, Juvenal, Boileau, and Pope, sold for $1200, while his "Invention of Letters" brought him $1500. For one song, "Adams and Liberty," he received $750. It turned out to be the most popular song ever written in defense of Federalism.

Paine began writing for the *Massachusetts Magazine* shortly after his graduation from Harvard in 1792. At almost the same time his theatrical tastes developed. He attempted drama unsuccessfully, though he frequently wrote prologues and odes for the dramas of others. By 1808 he began collecting his verse, correcting and preparing it for publication, but again he dallied. On his death bed in 1811 he wrote that he had been "too negligent of . . . fame, in not publishing under my own eye;—God knows who will do it now."[41]

Paine wrote about eighteen odes and translated four of the odes of Horace and Sappho.[42] One of his early songs—"The Lass of Eden Grove"—illustrates the lyrical quality of his youthful period:

> In Eden Grove there dwells a maid,
>   Adorned by every grace;
> The pearls, that deck the dewy shade,
>   Fairer confess her face.
>
>   The sun has spots, the rose has thorns,
>   And poisons mix with love;
>   But every spotless charm adorns
>   The Lass of Eden grove.
>
> The sparkling, soft, cerulean eye;
>   Bright Virtue's starry zone;
> The smile of Spring's Favonian Sky;
>   These charms are all her own.[43]
> Chorus: The sun has spots. . . .

These songs of Paine's had surprising popularity. Again the names of the popular Elizabethan song writers come to mind in seeking parallels for his verse.

After 1792 his literary output was characterized by his prosodic ambidexterity. He wrote neo-classical and lyrical verses with equal ease, though the feeling of his poetry is Augustan. He wrote "Edwin and Emma—An *Epithalamium*"; "A *Monody* to the Memory of W. H. Brown"; and a most didactic poem, "Self-Complacency."

But he was also one of the first American poets to revive the essential song-form of the sonnet, with his "Sonnet to Eliza" and "Sonnet to Belinda." For this reason alone he is important in the history of American verse.

The influence music exerted on Robert Treat Paine was chiefly that of form. He wrote odes to be sung in cantata form, and songs to be sung as monodies. Many of his cantata odes were written for celebrations of the Massachusetts Fire Society[44] and were sung on such occasions. His "Fire" ode of 1809 illustrates how carefully he worked in connection with the orchestra and singers:

Grand Recitative

Bleak lowered the morn; the howling snow-drift blew;
    Rude piles of devastation smoked around;
While houseless Outcasts, shivering o'er the ground,
    Bade the sad phantoms of their Homes adieu:

Air

Ah! mouldering wrecks! ye flit in fearful trance,
    And the vision of frenzy recall,
When in horror we leaped, with a fugitive glance,
    From the flames of yon desolate Wall!
See, now, with blighting melancholy bare,
    Like the monument stone at a sepulchre placed
    It weeps o'er this ruinous waste,
As it totters and rocks in the air,
    In vain, sweet pleading Pity calls;
    Or the cry of shrill terror appals;—
Bending, beetling, crushing o'er the crowded way,
    Hark! it cracks! see, it falls!
And wretches forget all their griefs in dismay.

Recitative

    But lo! along its crumbling base,
    With vacancy's ecstatic pace,
All-reckless, a heart-broken mourner repair;

Grief has reason beguiled,
And with melodies wild,
Invoking her child,
She wanders like Hope, and bewails like Despair.

Air-Andante

My Boy beneath this ruin lies!
Lost William! hear a Mother's sighs!
Through blasts that freeze and paths that burn,
Thy tombless dust she comes to urn . . .

. . . .

Vain was thy Mother's frantick flight
To snatch thee from the Fiend of Night!
Thy Couch, alas! thy funeral pyre,
Mid shrieks of horror, sunk in fire!

Allegro Furioso

Now to clouds of purple light,
Where William sits, I'll steal my flight!
Cold is this crazy crust of clay,
He beckons to a warmer day!
Wealth! I'm a happier wretch than you,
And laughing bid the world, Adieu![45]

The merit of Paine's verse is highly questionable, and there is no doubt that his love for the sentimental drama of the day, which he saw with astonishing frequency,[46] often gave rise to mawkish verse. However, as one of the most successful poets in Boston, and certainly one of the most successful cantata ode writers, Paine's ode is worthy of some perusal. In the first place, beside the cantata odes of both Hopkinson and Evans, this ode is, even at first glance, much more dramatic, less abstract, and tells briefly a rather maudlin tale that would interest an audience. There is no chorus in Paine's ode that would center attention chiefly upon the music. The divisions are well contrasted, and the ode actually falls into only two parts—the recitative and the air. The recitative here is devoted to the setting—the ruins after a fire. It contains both the epic and dramatic aspects. The *Air* that follows relates the feelings of the outcasts who have leapt from the wall that is now crumbling. The *Recitative,* in a quickened line, tells briefly that one mourner, heart-broken, and oblivious to her surroundings, moves below the crumbling wall. The *Air-Andante,* probably sung exceedingly dramatically, tells the mother's story—or, rather, permits her to sing it dolefully. In the finale, marked *Allegro Furioso,* the flames leap up, and the mother dies, singing a sentiment that sounds like the exit line from any drama of the day.

It is obvious that a poem such as this would have more audience appeal than even the earlier "Spirit of the Vital Flame," written for the Humane Society in 1804, and superior structurally to this one. As poetry, the 1804 ode excels in conception and treatment. It contained an *Air-Adagio,* a *Recitative,* an *Air-Largo Maestoso:*

> Spirit of the Vital Flame,
> Touch with life his marble frame,
> From the day-star's radiant choir,
> Bring thy torch of quenchless fire,
> And bid a mother's hope respire!
>
> *Allegro*
>
> Hither, sparkling cherub, fly!
> Mercy's herald, cleave the sky!
> To human prayer, benignant Heaven
> The salient spring of life has given. . . .
>
> *Maestoso*
>
> Spirit of the Vital Flame
> Touch again his marble frame. . . .
>
> *Allegro Assai*
>
> Behold the quickening Spirit raise
> The trembling limb, the wandering gaze!
>   Instinct listens! Memory wakes!
>   Thought from cold Extinction breaks;
> Passion, motion, frenzy, fear,
> Religion's triumph, Nature's tear,
> Almighty Power, thy hand is here![47]

The use of tempo markings here is interesting and indicates, as does the 1809 "Fire" ode, that Paine recognized something more in musico-poetic union than the tripartite division of air-chorus-recitative permitted. He knew that rhythm and the tempos at which his verses were sung or spoken had much to do with their success. He was among the first to title his divisions in this fashion.

Paine wrote numerous songs; among the better ones were "Ye Yeomen of Hampshire" (1801) to the tune of "Adams and Liberty" with alternate aria and chorus; "Masonic Ode," sung in 1796; an "Ode" for the anniversary of the Sons of Pilgrims, sung to the tune of the "President's March" with alternate chorus; a "Song—The Green Mountain Farmer" (1798) on Washington's accepting command of the United States Army; an "Ode" written and sung at the anniversary of the Boston Female Asylum, 1802; an "Ode" on July 4, 1806, to celebrate the "Anniversary of American Independence" sung to "Whilst Happy in My Native Land"; odes for July 4, 1810; an "Ode for the Anniversary of the Faustus Association" (1809) to the tune of "Adams and Liberty"; and an "Ode for the Anniversary of the Eaton Fire Society" (1808) to the tune of "God Save the King."[48] These constitute the most musical portion of Paine's verse. The poems are uniformly mediocre, as one might almost expect them to be from the variety of occasions demanding his pen. The fact that they were all sung to familiar tunes probably was in their favor. They were certainly popular once. The tunes also had much to do with structure, since after all the verse was written with certain melodies in mind.

The cantata odes and the songs of Robert Treat Paine have fallen into critical neglect, which they probably deserve. They by no means constitute the whole of his poetic output. His neoclassical verse is as extensive as his libretto verse. He had no true poetic style, and in affecting all may be said to have succeeded at none. However, Paine was a favored poet in his own day, and his work did much to keep the tradition of musical influence alive in the century. With the neglect of libretto verse, one whole segment of American poetry has been disregarded. The eighteenth century lyrical poets who preceded Philip Freneau onto the literary scene have been, on the whole, shamefully neglected. Since these poets—Hopkinson, Evans, and Paine—did more to keep the strain of lyricism alive in the century than any other group of poets, since they carried on the Miltonic tradition, as well as the pastoral, to neglect them has meant that only partial light has been shed upon eighteenth century American poetry. Granted that these be the lesser lights, they did much to illuminate the quietly flowing lyrical stream that moved ever nearer the surface as the century waned.

It would certainly seem that Philip Freneau should find a place here because of the evident lyrical quality of some few of his verses. Unfortunately, Freneau devoted so large a portion of his poetic output to satire, invective, and political balladry that the slight body of his lyrical verse appears in startling contrast. His "Book of Odes," for instance, is a series of parodies and satires. However, his was a keen poet's ear for rhythmic and melodic patterns in verse, and had he not striven so valiantly for the title

"Poet of the American Revolution" in his youth, his very real poetic gift might be even more apparent. As it is, Freneau's more musical poems derive not from any conscious awareness of music, but from an inherent melodious quality which Coleridge found to arise from the alliterative pattern in poetry.[49] He liked the rhythms of Marvell and experimented freely in stanza form. In these respects he belonged more to the nineteenth century than to the eighteenth.

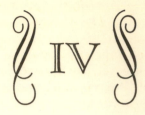

Nineteenth
Century
American Verse

THE NINETEENTH CENTURY WAS, artistically, a period of synthesis. The very essence of romanticism was the sense of exaltation that strained and burst the boundaries of the arts, often resulting in excesses less artistic than bizarre. Synaesthesia, the term used to define the artistic tendencies of the century, exhibited itself in color-hearing, tone-painting, and the efforts of the German philosophers to link abstract ideas with the newly developed "pure" or instrumental music. A. W. Schlegel went so far as to hope for statues that could become paintings, paintings that would be poems, and poems that should become music. Louis-Bertrand Castel anticipated the century with his scale of colors for each tone. Rimbaud *colored* all the vowels in his poetry in keeping with the idea that vowels are the most musical elements in a word, hoping thereby for stronger musical emphasis. Poets turned more strongly than before to onomato-poetic devices. Instrumental composers, writing to no given libretto or text, turned to program music, the tone poem, the symphonic poem, and impressionism. Franz Liszt took three of Petrarch's sonnets and composed instrumental music to them. Scott set the vogue for the revival of interest in the ballad. Thomas Moore wrote his simple songs to definite airs as Burns had done. Most interesting was the influence of philosophy on poetry, which led the poet to strive for the suggestive, the formless, and the abstract. Huneker wrote of the period: "Persons who hear paint-ing, see music, touch poems, taste symphonies, and write perfumes are now classed by the psychical police as decadent, though such notions are as old as art and literature."[1]

The merger of music and philosophy was one of the important syntheses of the age. Largely resulting from the increasing emphasis upon philosophy in German intellectual life, the association of music with the abstract and lofty had been directly inspired by the studies of Greek thought by men like Winckelmann[2] and indirectly by the growing popularity of instrumental or "pure" music. Novalis, Schlegel, Tieck, Schopenhauer,[3] and Nietzsche, all testified to the profound philosophical importance of music in the life of man. Interest in the abstract and the ideal was rampant not only during the romantic movement but throughout the century. Tieck felt so strongly about the place of music in the world that he wrote: "Never forget, when you would entrust a sentiment to words, to ask yourselves: what, after all, is there that can be said in words."[4]

Schlegel toyed with the idea that words themselves, stripped of their narrow meanings and properly chosen for the music of their sounds, could project the reader into the realms of the suggestive and the indefinite. This was an anticipation of the device Joyce employed in *Finnegan's Wake*.

This union of philosophy and music infected poetry, first the verses written as songs and later the whole body of lyrical verse of the period. The boundary between the definite and the indefinite faded as the poet strove for the suggestive and the abstract. The relationship of music and poetry was furthered by the constellation of poets and musicians who appeared almost simultaneously in England and Germany at the end of the eighteenth century. There was revived in the century an interest in music by the poets, and an equally intense interest in poetry by musicians, a creative duality of interest unknown since the Renaissance. But of the two arts, music was believed, by the German philosophers, to be the dominant one. Schopenhauer, writing in the *World as Will and Idea* (1818), said of words that they were "a foreign addition of secondary value."[5] Hegel and Nietzsche expressed similar ideas. Goethe composed so many of his verses either to tunes known to him or for music that it was said the music had produced the poetry.[6] Jean Paul and E. T. A. Hoffmann did much to merge the arts in Germany. Hoffmann filled his Gothic novels with musical settings, and Kleist, another dramatist, claimed that his dramas were composed musically, the protagonists acting as "voices" running contrapuntally rather than as figures. He thought "the secret of poetic form lay in counterpoint."[7] Coleridge,[8] Shelley,[9] and Keats[10] all came under the influence of music. Similarly, many American poets were fascinated by the possibilities of musical analogies.

Music and poetry in the era shared certain romantic characteristics, among them (1) nature worship; (2) Byronism; (3) symbolism, evident musically in Wagner's leit motif and Debussy's impressionism; (4) Gothicism; (5) expansion of forms; (6) emotionalism; (7) Shakespeare worship; (8) exoticism; (9) respect for personality; (10) varied rhythms; (11) dramatic intensity; (12) emotional autobiography (Berlioz, *Symphonie Fantastique);* (13) tonal coloring; (14) abstractness and indefiniteness.

The nineteenth century poet indicated his interest in music by (1) the composition of ballads and narratives to famous old folk tunes; (2) writing librettos of a nature suitable for musical settings; (3) writing a poem as a result of hearing a musical composition and trying to recreate it in words; (4) writing a lyric to a remembered melody; (5) attempting to equal within the range of poetry the musical qualities of sound associated with music; (6) attempting to capture some of the quality of abstractness associated with music which expresses the yearning for immortality of the human spirit; (7) breaking away from poetic patterns of too rigid a nature; (8) raising again the question of quantity in verse; (9) seeking to darken the tone of the verse and heighten the emotional quality of it; (10) sharpening the phrase, making deliberate use of parallelism, repetition, balance and contrast as well as building toward climaxes;[11] (11) borrowing musical forms such as the canon, the fugue, the round; (12) deliberately using onomatopoetic devices; (13) writing marginal directions outside the text of the poem as to the exact performance of the poem;[12] (14) using musical imagery; and (15) forming a melody from an alliterative pattern.

French and German poets of the century were particularly sensitive to musical possibilities in verse. Transcendentalism in Germany was fully aligned with music, and Paul Valery, writing in retrospect of the Symboliste movement in France, said:

We were fed on music and our literary minds only dreamt of extracting from language almost the same effects that music caused on our nervous beings. . . . Certain people who had preserved the traditional forms of French verse . . . purged their poetry of almost all those intellectual elements, which are outside the sphere of music. Others gave to all objects infinite meanings, implying some hidden metaphysic. Their means of expression was delightfully ambiguous. . . . Everything was allusion . . . further some . . . challenged the old prosody. For some color hearing and the art of alliteration appeared to have no secrets. They deliberately transposed orchestral timbres with verse. . . . Others cleverly sought out the naivety and spontaneous grace of old folk verse. . . . They saw order and perhaps truth in the cult of a unification of the arts.[13]

American poets who were near any of the great music centers of the nineteenth century, Boston, Philadelphia, and New York, evidenced no less significant response to music than poets anywhere else. As a matter of fact, America displayed an early interest in the musical possibilities of the language in the poetry of Edgar Allan Poe and considerable concern for the common metrical basis of the two arts in the work of Sidney Lanier. The nineteenth century saw in America a flowering of the lyric and song fully equal in quantity, if not in quality, to that of England and France. It also was the period in America when the symphony and the opera came into greatest popular acclaim. The effect of so much music upon creative personalities resulted not only in an early interest in the metrical basis of music and poetry, but also in considerable experimentation with poetic forms and a freedom in verse writing before the romantic period in music. No serious student of the arts could fail to recognize that the tremendous growth of musical interest among poets in the nineteenth century and the increasingly accelerated pace of that interest as the century waned have led in the twentieth century to a wide-spread acceptance of the role music plays in the creation of poetry. Almost every major nineteenth century poet gave some evidence of musical influence, directly or indirectly, upon his verse and some few not only turned to music for inspiration but held it to be an art superior to verse. Undoubtedly there were American poets who were not interested in music, but since the nineteenth century was essentially a lyrical, singing, romantic century, it is not surprising that great numbers of our most familiar poets made some obeisance to music. Though obviously it is impossible, within the limits of this study, to deal fully with all of the nineteenth century poets responding to music (only three of these are treated here in detail), it is possible to see one of the interesting poetic tendencies of the day. The poets who were musical or responsive to music usually fashioned their poetry in accordance with that interest, and lyricism abounded wherever this was true.

THE KNICKERBOCKER POETS

Massachusetts-born Richard Henry Dana, Sr., while no musician, proved to be a thoroughly romantic writer. In New York where opera flourished and Beethoven was often heard, Dana began the publication of *The Idle Man*. One of the founders of the *North American Review*, Dana published in 1833 a slight volume of verse and prose clearly marked by romantic elements. Though William Cullen Bryant's first mature volume of verse preceded this by some twelve years, Bryant was the younger, and it is partially due to Dana's early recognition of Bryant's talents that Bryant began his long association with the *North American Review*. It was Dana who first recognized the romantic element in Bryant. When the writer was yet unknown, Dana had expressed doubt as an editor that "Thanatopsis" could have been written on this side of the Atlantic. Dana's verse shows clearly the influence of Wordsworth and Coleridge, just as Bryant's does; and it is wholly different from the works of Timothy Dwight, Paine, and Hopkinson. Narrative poems like "The Buccaneer" reflect a Coleridgeian preoccupation with the same forces that the mariner faced. In "The Dying Raven," Dana expressed a "universal sympathy" for all living things, even for the bird he calls the *prophet*. "Thoughts on the Soul" is a good poem in the Wordsworthian mode, and "The Pleasure Boat" and "The Early Spring Brook" are both nature poems quite new to American literature.[15] The break with the preceding century is best illustrated in the comparative metrical freedom of the lines of "The Little Beach Bird":

> Thou little bird, thou dweller by the sea,
>   Why takest thou its melancholy voice?
>   And with that boding cry
>   Along the waves dost thou fly?
> O! rather, Bird, with me
>   Through the fair land rejoice!

> II

> Thy flitting form comes ghostly dim and pale,
>   As driven by a beating storm at sea;
>   Thy cry is weak and scared,
>   As if thy mates had shared
> The doom of us: Thy wail—
>   What does it bring to me?

III

Thou call'st along the sand, and haunt'st the surge,
   Restless and sad; as if, in strange accord
     With the motion and the roar
     Of waves that drive to shore,
One spirit did ye urge—
     The Mystery—The Word.

IV

Of thousands, thou, both sepulchre and pall,
   Old Ocean, art! A requiem o'er the dead,
     From out thy gloomy cells
     A tale of mourning tells—
Tells of man's woe and fall,
     His sinless glory fled.

V

Then turn thee, little bird, and take thy flight
   Where the complaining sea shall sadness bring
     Thy spirit never more.
     Come, quit with me the shore,
For gladness and the light
     Where birds of summer sing.[16]

This is an obvious metrical and stanzaic experiment. It has little to do with closed couplets, and reveals that the poet was choosing not only the subjects closely associated with the Romantic movement, but that he had also considerable ease in handling the flow of the numbers—a characteristic of lyrical poets. Dana was particularly interested in metrical freedom and urged his friend Bryant to write a treatise on versification:

I wish that your half a mind to write a book on English versification might become an entire one. . . . I should be glad to see such a work as you would write, illustrating your principles with such selections as you would make from our master poets and from the Greeks and Latins, where you wished to point differences or resemblances. We have no work deserving the name of a treatise on English prosody. Every departure from the ordinary rule is set down to neglect, or ignorance, or laziness; for instance, the trisyllable—with how much beauty you have used it (a little too frequently, perhaps, for what is peculiar!) How exquisite it is in Shakespheare, and how fine in Milton, I need not say. To me, *sometimes,* in an impassioned line, when Milton makes a break, the trochee following the iambus gives an abrupt, startling energy to the passage, which it would hardly have had if he had adhered to the common rule.[17]

The defense of metrical freedom Dana urged in this letter resulted in Bryant's discussion of trisyllabic feet in verse, a discussion based upon the practice of the great poets of all time.[18] Not only did Bryant write the work on metrical freedom, he practiced it in his verse, working "organically": that is, he let the poem take its shape or structure from the material with which he was working.[19] In this respect he followed Dana's lead.

Bryant, who was also Massachusetts-born, came from a musical family. His father was something of a violinist and made for himself a bass-viol on which to play.[20] When he first came to New York to live, Bryant lived with a family of famous Italian singers, the Garcias, in whose honor the first Italian opera house was built. He studied Italian[21] with Da Ponte, Mozart's former librettist who had taken up residence in New York. How much of the musical environment Bryant absorbed can be only conjectured. It may be assumed that his contact with music did have something to do with his being called our first "father of American song." American poetry in the past has been dated from the first volume of Bryant's verse.

Bryant's concern for stanzaic forms and metrical patterns interested the young Poe, who was to publish his first volume of verse in 1827—six years after Bryant's. Poe thought Bryant the most eminent poet America had produced in his lifetime.[22] Certainly Bryant was our first serious critic, and the melodious quality of his verse pleased Poe. His experiments in verse are an anticipation of Poe's. Leonard wrote of Bryant's poetic forms:

But the metrics alone do have their peculiarities . . . line endings like "and the green moss," caesuras at the end of the first and of the fourth foot, the tendency to repeat the same caesura and cadence through a succession of lines, a stanza group of five or more lines with full stop followed by a single line or so, inverted accent at the beginning of a line and a differentiated, strong cadence at the conclusion of the whole poem which gives the effect of a completion, not of a mere stopping— these are all contributing factors.[23]

It might be said too that his experiments with the six line stanza, as well as the five and ten line stanzas, in a day when Spenserian measure was virtually unpracticed, are signs of a genuine interest in poetic form. Bryant also used the sonnet when no one else in American literature was writing in that form, excelling in both the English style and a "hybrid form." Considering all these matters, Tremaine McDowell concluded that Bryant had an "unusual range" of "technical resources."[24] Certainly most critics have agreed that a combination of sound sense, metrical ease, and Wordsworthian simplicity and dignity has given Bryant's verse high rank in American letters.

Bryant was a frequent writer of hymns, and early in life was set at the task of rhyming books of the Bible. He wrote a "Forest Hymn," a "Hymn to Death," and a "Hymn of the Waldenses." He also wrote a series of songs using the repetend, among them the "Song of the Stars," "Song of Marion's Men," and the song-like structures of "The May Sun Sheds an Amber Light" and "Robert of Lincoln."[25] Much of Bryant's interest in hymnody and songs was natural to the temperament of the poet and the time, as well as to the Massachusetts environment in which he grew up. In his "Autobiography" he tells the story of how many a winter's afternoon was passed at the singing schools to which the boys came for recreation. The old "fuguing" tunes were sung, as well as the psalms, though it was the catchy quality of the former that appealed to the singers, Bryant wrote:

It often happened that the teacher was an enthusiast in his vocation, and thundered forth the airs set down in the music books with a fervor that was contagious. . . . In those days a set of tunes were in fashion mostly of New England origin, which have since been laid aside in obedience to a more fastidious taste. They were in quick time, sharply accented, the words clearly articulated, and often running into fugues, in which the bass, the tenor, and the treble chased each other from the middle to the end of the stanza. I recollect that some impatience was manifested when slower and graver airs of church music were introduced by the choir, and I wondered why the words should not be sung in the same time that they were pronounced in reading.[26]

There was a background of song and music in Bryant's life that admirably fitted him to work with metrics as Dana hoped he would. Dana wrote him:

To think of the infinite variety of sound that one with a bold mind and a harmonious ear may pour forth! It seems to me that versification has never been treated upon philosophically enough. . . . I began *too late*, and am too impatient, also, of the labor, or rather am not enough skilled to preserve all the meaning and strength, and give harmony too. Write such a work as I know you can write, and I promise you I will be your diligent pupil. . . . [27]

Though it cannot be claimed that the superiority of Bryant's verse depended upon his musical ear, there was certainly a connection between his feeling for words and his interest in music. He wrote of poetry that it was a wholly suggestive art, that it grew out of intense emotion, and that "the limitation of the power of language" was the chief magic poetry possessed since words themselves were necessarily suggestive.[28] He is important to this study because of his serious interest in prosody.

The other members of the Knickerbocker group, Paulding, Verplanck, and Sands, exhibited little of the nature of the lyricist in their work; Irving and Cooper devoted themselves to prose, and only Halleck, Drake, and Charles Fenno Hoffman revealed anything of the influence of music upon their verse. George Pope Morris, Samuel Woodworth, and John Howard Payne were, of course, song writers.

Fitz-Greene Halleck (1790-1867) was deeply interested in and indebted to the Scotch songsters whom he called most "tender and musical." He was a close friend of Joseph Rodman Drake, an accomplished flutist, and the two spent many a musical evening together.

Like Bryant, Halleck was a student of Da Ponte's, and was one of the celebrities at the Italian's funeral.[29] Halleck was a frequent admirer of opera and a lover of minstrelsy. Poe considered Halleck second only to Bryant in reputation and acclaimed "Marco Bozzaris," a "spirited" Byronic poem. The poems to "Burns" and on "Music" reveal the elegance which was characteristic of his best work. Bryant said of the lines on Burns that he was not sure that the verses were not "the finest in which one poet ever celebrated another."[30] He wrote further of Halleck:

Halleck's poetry, whether serious or sprightly, is remarkable for the melody of the numbers. It is not the melody of monotonous and strictly regular measurement. His verse is constructed to please an ear naturally fine, and accustomed to a wide range of metrical modulation. It is as different from that painfully balanced versification, that uniform succession of iambics, closing the sense with the couplet, which some writers practice, and some critics praise, as the note of the thrush is unlike that of the cuckoo. Halleck is familiar with those general rules and principles which are the basis of metrical harmony; and his own unerring taste has taught him the exceptions which a proper attention to variety demands. He understands that the rivulet is made musical by obstructions in its channel. You will find in no poet, passages

which flow with a more sweet and liquid smoothness; but he knows
very well that to make this smoothness perceived . . . occasional rough-
ness must be interposed.[31]

Even more musically aware than Halleck was Drake (1795-1820).
Remembered largely as the writer of the first "fairy" poem in
American verse, Drake was a musician of some ability,[32] the com-
poser of the popular song, "The American Flag," and a rather
prolific song writer. A picture of the surroundings in which "The
Culprit Fay" had its origins appears in Pleadwell's account:

> It was at Drake's rooms on the Bowery that his friends Halleck and
> De Kay often came to see him, and from this point they started their
> excursions into the country to Hunts' Point. Here they entertained
> their friends, Halleck with his stories and Drake with his flute, upon
> which he was an admirable performer, and with his singing; and here
> also in the space of three days Drake composed that brilliant improvisa-
> tion, *The Culprit Fay*.[33]

The resemblance between the opening lines of "The Culprit
Fay" and "Christabel" is at once apparent: a resemblance unmen-
tioned, though Drake's indebtedness to Moore, Allston, and Shakespeare is made much of.[34]

> 'Tis the middle watch of a summer's night—
> The earth is dark, but the heavens are bright;
> Nought is seen in the vault on high
> But the moon, and the stars, and the cloudless sky. . . . [35]

There is also a surprising resemblance to the poetry of Keats
and Shelley in "The Culprit Fay," though it was written in 1816
when neither Keats' nor Shelley's work could have been known
widely, if at all, in America. Drake was called the "American
Keats" and so great a poet as Poe, hearing of the reputation of
"The Culprit Fay" while it was still in manuscript, was anxious
to procure a copy at its first printing in 1835. Decidedly a lyrical
poem, "The Culprit Fay" seems by modern standards to be lacking
in originality since it borrowed its shimmering qualities from
many a poet, including Milton and Shakespeare:

> Hail the wanderer again,
>   With dance and song, and lute and lyre,
> Pure his wing and strong his chain,
>   And doubly bright his fairy fire.
> Then twine ye in an eerie round,
>   Brush the dew and print the lea;

Skip and gambol, hop and bound,
  Round the wild witch-hazel tree.
The beetle guards our holy ground,
  He flies about the haunted place,
And if mortal there be found,
  He hums in his ears and flaps his face;
The leaf-harp sounds our roundelay,
  The owlet's eyes our lanthornes be;
Thus we revel, dance, and play,
  Round the wild witch-hazel tree.[36]

Several of Drake's most charming poems are written to Scottish and Irish airs—the "Song" to the air "What ye wha" was obviously influenced by Burns, an early favorite of Drake's; the "Song" to the air "The Legacy" from Moore's *Irish Melodies;* the "Song" to the air "Peggy na Leven," an old favorite Irish song of Jeremy Taylor's; the "Song" from the air "Musette de Nina" from Dalayrac's opera, *Nina, ou La Folle par Amour;*[37] and several poems to Miss McCall, a fine singer of Irish songs. Drake had an evident love for the simple ballad. The lyric flavor in his poetry is found also in lines called simply "Stanzas." Almost all of his poetry seems to have been written to some musical pattern, and though there is no known music for "The American Flag," the spirited quality of the poem, its rousing metres, and its instant popularity indicate that the writer must have had some melody in mind. His sonnets are lyrics, and one of his lovely short poems, "The Song at Sea," is reminiscent of Jonson.

Charles Fenno Hoffman (1806-1884) was something of a lyricist, despite his addiction to adventure tales and his success with *Greyslaer,* a novel. One of the editors of the *Knickerbocker Magazine* in its earliest period, Hoffman was attacked in the English press for his lyrics, which they referred to as "Moore hocussed for the American market."[38] Hoffman's lyrics are little known today, overshadowed as they have been by the work of George Pope Morris, but one of the justly familiar and popular is "Sparkling and Bright."

Morris (1802-1863) was one of the most famous American song-writers in his day. He wrote the libretto for Charles Edward Horn's *Maid of Saxony* and compiled *American Melodies* (1840-41) which contained over two hundred American lyrics by different poets. Together with another song-writer, Samuel Woodworth, Morris edited the *New York Mirror.* His best songs, which were sung by Jenny Lind and Mme. Malibran, include the familiar "Woodman, Spare That Tree" and "By the Lake Where Droops the Willow." Stephen Collins Foster wrote his first published music for a lyric of Morris's in 1844. In his collected *Songs and Ballads* (1852), Morris devoted section one to "Melodies" and the latter section to the "Songs and Duets" taken from the *Maid of Saxony.* In the *Deserted Bride and Other Productions* (1853), he ridiculed the vogue for Italian opera in the New York of 1826.[39] Another close friend of his, Richard Storrs Willis, was the editor of *Church Music* and the *Musical World.*

Samuel Woodworth (1785-1842), whose "Old Oaken Bucket," like Wilde's "My Life is Like the Summer Rose," has had an admirable and enduring popularity, was closely associated with Willis and Morris on the *New York Mirror.* His poems were largely either ballads or songs for dramatic production. They were collected in 1826 in *Melodies, Duets, Trios, Songs and Ballads,* which went through several editions.

John Howard Payne (1791-1852) wrote a memorable lyric, "Home, Sweet Home," in his *Clari or the Maid of Milan,* which had been set to music, like the rest of the opera, by Sir Henry Bishop. Payne also published a weekly journal, the *Opera Glass,* and of course his connection with the theatre needs no retelling. (He once played Romeo to Mrs. Poe's Juliet.) Thomas Dunn English has some claim to fame as a balladist, particularly for "Ben Bolt," which has some twenty-six musical settings.

The many songs and lyrics written by the Knickerbocker and New York poets in the nineteenth century cannot be listed here, nor is it possible within the limits of this chapter to offer a full discussion of each man's work, profitable though such a study might be. The concern here is only with the preponderant evidence that the New York poets knew music and that music entered into their writings in large measure.

The Southern Poets

Both the lyric and the ballad flowered in the South in the nineteenth century, particularly in the cultural centers of Charleston, Baltimore, Atlanta, and Richmond. In many ways, however, the influence of the eighteenth century, and of cavalier verse, lingered long in the South. But the nineteenth century Southern poets were given to an originality of form and line, a quality especially

evident in the poetry of both Poe and Lanier. Aside from these
two, the Southern poets evidencing some interest in music were
John Shaw of Baltimore (1778-1809); Dublin-born Richard Henry
Wilde (1789-1846), who adopted Georgia as his home; Edward
Coote Pinkney (1802-1828), who was born in London but lived
in Baltimore, when not in naval service; William Gilmore Simms
(1806-1858), the Charlestonian novelist; Thomas Holley Chivers
(1807-1858) of Georgia; Henry Timrod (1829-1867), the Charlestonian poet laureate; and Paul Hamilton Hayne (1830-1886),
Lanier's friend, who lived alternately at Charleston and Augusta.
In addition, Philip Pendleton Cooke wrote his *Froissart Ballads* as
tribute to the old minstrels. And James Mathewes Legaré of
Charleston wrote lines in *Orta Undis and Other Poems,* obviously
experimental in nature. In "To a Lily" the angularity of the lines
is somewhat subdued by the inner rhythms and cross alliteration:

> Soft are thy leaves and white: Her arms
> Boast whiter charms.
> Thy stem prone bent with loveliness
> Of maiden grace possesseth less:
> Therein she charms. . . .

John Shaw's verse, collected in 1810, contains many of the same
neo-classical elements that appear in the verse of Thomas Godfrey,
whose work it resembles in content and proportion of lyric and
ode. Shaw was a classicist and a translator, but he fell heavily under
the influence of the early romantic, Gray, whose "The Bard" and
pindaric odes he imitated. He was also a translator of Petrarchian
sonnets and Anacreontic verse. He left a series of songs on several
occasions, a collection of "Moorish Songs," a song sung at Annap-
olis, and several poems indicating great interest in sound, chiefly
those written to the cricket. At his best, his rhythms are regular
and pleasing as in:

> Tis dark and the thick clouds are rolling,
>   And chill is the comfortless breeze,
> And slow as it sighs through the forest,
>   It shakes the big drops from the trees. . . .[40]

or in one of his songs:

> Who has robb'd the ocean cave,
>   To tinge thy lips with coral hue?
> Who from India's distant wave,
>   Who, from yonder orient sky,
>   Stole the marking of thine eye?[41]

Aside from his songs, however, and a few references to "concert," "song," and "music," Shaw reveals little evidence of musical knowledge and the chances are that he was influenced by the song, as a poet, without knowing very much about music. At least the lack of rhythmic grace in the large body of his work would indicate this.

Richard Henry Wilde, on the other hand, certainly understood the nature of the song, which fact probably accounts for his interest in and his translations of Italian lyrics. Unfortunately, Wilde's verses remain uncollected, and his most famous and familiar work, "My Life is Like the Summer Rose," set to music about 1815, today represents the sum of his fame. The use of the refrain and the repetition of initial line to bind each stanza undoubtedly has much to do with the poem's nostalgic charm:

> My life is like the summer rose . . .
> . . . .
> My life is like the autumn leaf . . .
> . . . .
> My life is like the print which feet
> Have left on Tampa's desert strand. . . .

And then the closing line of each stanza, with its "But none shall weep . . . breathe . . . mourn for me," carries the repetitiousness native to the song.

Samuel Henry Dickson (1798-1872) of Charleston wrote one beautiful lyric, "I Sigh for the Land of the Cypress and Pine," in true ternary song form, with the return in the final stanza to the initial one. The poem is melodious with much cross alliteration. One stanza reads:

> The snowy flower of the orange there
> Sheds its sweet fragrance through the air
> And the Indian rose delights to twine
> Its branches with the laughing vine.

Certainly one of the most musical of Southern poets was Edward Coote Pinkney, who left sonnets, serenades, and songs with all the spirited rhythms and *joie de vivre* that typified cavalier verse. One of the loveliest of Pinkney's songs is the "Serenade," written when the poet was twenty, was set to music by one of the prominent music masters of the day, H. N. Gilles, and published with the music in 1823. The quality of the song is implicit in the lines:

> Look out upon the stars, my love,
>   And shame them with thine eyes,
> On which, than on the lights above,
>   There hang more destinies. . . .[42]

In one of his songs, set to music, the ballad quality prevails, and melody which arises from the combinations of liquid sounds is undeniable:

> Day departs this upper air,
>   My lively, lovely lady;
> And the eve-star sparkles fair,
>   And our good steeds are ready.
>
> Leave, leave these loveless halls,
>   So lordly though they be—
> Come, come—affection calls—
>   Away at once with me![43]

Pinkney's wife, Georgiana, was a talented harpist and was said to sing "divinely."[44] Many of his songs were written for her after his marriage at twenty-one, among them certainly N. P. Willis' favorite, "We Break the Glass," with its lovely image:

> And still it looks as when the hours
>   Went by like flocks of singing birds,
> Or that soft chain of spoken flowers,
>   And airy gems, thy words. . . .[45]

When Willis published Pinkney's *Poems* (1844), the song "Day Departs This Upper Air" was given musical setting. One of the most famous of his poems, "A Health," typifies his poetic style:

> I fill this cup to one made up of loveliness alone,
> A woman, of her gentle sex the seeming paragon . . .
> Her every tone is music's own, like those of morning birds,
> And something more than melody dwells ever in her words. . . .[46]

His ability to take a phrase and repeat it (and this is music's chief device and delight) appears in many of his songs and can be seen in "Those Starry Eyes":

> Those starry eyes, those starry eyes,
>   Those eyes that used to be
> Unto my heart, as beacon-lights
>   To pilgrims of the sea!—
>
> I see them yet, I see them yet,
>   Though long since quenched and gone. . . .[47]

While Pinkney's musical references are not exactly learned, they do prove that he knew something about music, particularly the song. For instance, he understands what constitutes a cadence, and how it depends upon the appearance of a leading note, as well as that it returns to the "home" key:

> List the last cadence of a lay,
>> That, closing as begun,
> Is governed by a note of pain,
>> Oh, lost and worshipped one. . . .[48]

However, many of his musical references are of this order:

> Our wedded souls, like pleasant sounds
>> In music softly blending,
> Together make a harmony
>> That should have known no ending. . . .[49]

But his odes and songs certainly reveal a keen interest in music and sound.

William Gilmore Simms left a tremendous body of verse, much of which reveals a love for and some knowledge of music. When his muse is properly attendant, his metres are true and pleasing, as in: *"'Tis True That Last Night I Adored Thee"*:

> 'Tis true that last night I adored thee,
>> But 'twas moonlight, the song, and the wine;
> The cool morning air has restored me,
>> And no longer I deem thee divine. . . .[50]

or as in "The Grape-Vine Swing":

> Lithe and long as the serpent train,
>> Springing and clinging from tree to tree,
> Now darting upward, now down again,
>> With a twist and a twirl that are strange to see. . . . [51]

The metres of "The Swamp Fox" are swift and measured so that the syllables are exactly suited to the regular beats he establishes:

> We follow where the Swamp Fox guides,
>> His friends and merry men are we;
> And when the troop of Tarleton rides,
>> We burrow in the cypress tree. . . . [52]

Simms was experimental with line length in a way that suggests the work of Lanier. His "The Lost Pleiad," for instance, is certainly marked by irregularity of line. Simms' musical references are marked by a knowledge and understanding of musical language. He wrote poems like "Dithyrambic" in which music plays a large part, as it does in numerous other songs and lyrics. His sonnets and canzones and his "Stanzas for Music" are dramatic and wild, offering possibilities for mood music. His songs, in general, follow the pattern of Pinkney's and Wilde's:

> The stars are high in heav'n, Love,
>   Look out, look out and see,
> The fairy time that's given, Love,
>   To light my heart to thee. . . .[53]

One collection of Simms' verse he titled *Areytos* (1860), which he explained was a Cuban musical term for songs. "It is quite as worthy of use as that of *lay, ballad,* canzone or sirvente. . . . The Provencal troubadour had none more appropriate . . . in all his melodious vocabulary. . . ."[54]

Simms' musical knowledge seems literary, however; that is, it seems to stem from having read of Greek music and its effect upon poetry rather than from a musician's understanding of music. In his "First Fruits—a Prelude" he made numerous musical references to "Lydian measures," which he understood, and to the doctrine of "ethos," the Creeks' idea of the value of music in the evolution of man's spirit. This sort of knowledge on the poet's part frequently led him into the use of such terms as "race of song," "starry harmonies," and "profligate melodist." He wrote songs like "My Forest Harp":

> Come, while the evening sets sweet and clear,
>   And the winds are hush'd and the air is balm,
> Sing me a Cuban Areyto, dear,
>   Of the vine, the orange, and the bending palm;
>   Paint me the scene
>   The sweet serene
> Of that clime of bliss ere the Spaniard came. . . .[55]

Scarcely a song or a lyric of any sort written by Simms fails to make reference to music. Lyrics like "Oh the Sweet South," or "Make Gay the Spear with Flowers" are very musical. A poem like "Eyes, Eyes, Ye Have Led Me to Pain!" illustrates his varied line lengths, enmeshed alliteration, and rhythms:

> Dusk and with Hesper,
>   South wind thou wakest!
> With wooing and whisper
>   Green leaves thou shakest!
> In the hush of the sunset hour,
> In the blush of the virgin flower
> In the bright sun-flush, in the soft shower,
>   Sweet South, thou wakest! . . . [56]

Simms wrote a "Battle Ode—A Tyrtaean—For Music," which certainly requires musical background; "Let the Bugle Blow," and imitations of birds in several songs, chiefly in "Coo! Coo! Te Weet Tu Whu!" He also wrote an echo song, a canzone "If thou Couldst See the Tears," "Battle Hymn," and several serenades. His poem, "The Bride of Christ," is filled with musical imagery. I think it cannot be doubted that his was a conscious effort to use music in poetry.

Thomas Holley Chivers wrote in his preface to *Virginalia* (1853):

> No poem can become the mediation of the revelation of the influx of the Divine Life of God into the soul, without the highest knowledge of the *true Art of musical language* . . . so does a full manifestation . . . of the passions and emotions of the soul depend entirely upon the Art displayed in its creation according to *certain musical laws,* by the Poet. . . . For as the irradiancy of a Diamond depends upon the diaphanous translucency, so does the beauty of a Poem upon its *rhythmical crystallization* of the Divine Idea. . . .[57]

These lines are a less rational echo or an equivalent of Poe's own theories in "The Poetic Principle," but they certainly illustrate why Chivers' verse often riots in sound rather than sense, and they also account for much of the iridescent quality of his rhythms. He wrote of the refrain to a poem: ". . . It is not only an ornament but an essence . . . a life—a vitality—an immortal soul,"[58] and he compares it to the wheels of Apollo's chariot which make "continual, ever-recurring Aurora chime . . . which is never lost, or dies away into an echo, but forever returns upon itself."[59] And he writes that he does not expect critics to understand what he is striving for in verse: "Old ears cannot hear New Music."[60]

Chivers' verse fairly bristles with references to music, usually of this nature:

A living music, voiceless, yet forever
   Speaking such words as tongue can never tell;
A heavenly Hymn, whose echoes shall die never,
   As long as this sweet Song shall say *Farewell;* . . .

Two of the golden strings of thy dear harp are broken,
   Leaving the harp-strings of thy spirit still complete;
Words in thy tongue have never yet been spoken,
   Yet, thy dear soul doth warble words most sweet
Whereon blest Spirits, from their bright abode
Make music such as please the very Ears of God.

Thou hearest the far-off, endless chiming
   Of the eternal music of the Spheres;
And knowest, by intuition, all the rhyming
   Of all the cycles of the rhythmic years. . . . [61]

These verses do not reveal the poet's knowledge of music; but that
he read much about it, thought about it, and heard what he could,
must be evident to anyone who has read his verse.

    Like Poe, Chivers wrote in terms of the cadence, rather than the
line, a fact which is typical of most musical poets. But in Chivers
the tendency toward jingling rhythms is carried to an extreme. In
"The Bells of Tontine" (1851) we hear a familiar music:

In this city, in the Palace,
Called the Tontine, kept by Allis,
Standing Eastward of the Eden of the Green—
Dwells the lady Ellen-Mary,
Who is of her charms so chary,
That opinions never vary,
Of her beauty in Tontine—
All agreeing she is Belle of this Tontine—
Cynosure of all the lesser lights that twinkle in Tontine.[62]

Whether this is poetry or doggerel, as stanza two continues, is a
matter of opinion. The poem certainly wheels onward to the end
lines of each stanza. Another familiar melody appears in the
cyclical rhythms of "Lily Adair":

On the beryl-rimmed rebecs of Ruby,
   Brought fresh from the hyaline streams,
She played on the banks of the Yuba,
   Such songs as she heard in her dreams.
Like the heavens, when the stars from their eyries
Were the groves by the Ouphantic Fairies

> Lit up for my Lily Adair—
> For my child-like Lily Adair—
> For my heaven-born Lily Adair—
> For my beautiful, dutiful Lily Adair. . . .[63]

Music is frequently identified with heavenly sounds in Chivers' verse. He speaks of "golden music on silver pages," of "beautiful Evangels," of "blowing through the clear-sounding trumpet of love." In his "Marcia Funebre" with its "Toll, toll, toll . . ." he attempts a parallel of "The Bells," Poe's essay in verse. Refrains are a portion of almost every song he writes, and he makes use of the Elizabethan "Heigh ho" in "First Love." His "Israfelia," he says, was written on first hearing Jenny Lind sing in Castle Garden in New York on January 10, 1851. He also wrote serenades, a "Hymn from the inner life" in which is displayed familiarity with such terms as "diapason," "burden," etc. The poem with the greatest number of musical references is "Uranothen," most of them being of a rather obvious literary nature. Chivers' rhythmic fertility is perhaps the strongest indication of his awareness of music. In the subsequent chapter on "Poe and Music," much of what is said of Poe is true of Chivers. When he wrote sincerely, as he did momently in "Dark Is My Soul Without Thee," the smoothness of his numbers indicates how just his rhythmic sense was.

Henry Timrod's verse, by contrast to Chivers', is more markedly reserved, and depends less upon verbal music, though he was capable of achieving it had he so desired. "A Summer Shower" reveals what this poet might do if he consciously desired to write only in musical sounds:

> . . . Patterning on the gravel,
> Dropping from the eaves,
> Glancing in the grass, and
> Tinkling on the leaves,
> They flash the liquid pearls as flung from fairy sieves. . . .[64]

Many of Timrod's verses were written to be sung and actually were sung. His "Hymn Sung at a Sacred Concert at Columbia, S. C.," his "Hymn Sung at Consecration of Magnolia Cemetery, Charleston, S. C.," his "Hymn Sung for the Anniversary of an Orphans' Asylum" are indications that committees evidently thought the Charleston poet familiar with music. The famed measures of "Carolina," with their three line stanza and refrain, are reminiscent of a familiar song:

> The despot treads thy sacred sands,
> Thy pines give shelter to his bands,
> Thy sons stand by with idle hands,
>   Carolina. . . .[65]

In addition to such romantic titles as "A Rhapsody of a Southern Winter Night," Timrod wrote lines of excellent tempo like these:

> Hark to the shouting wind!
>   Hark to the Flying rain!
> And I care not though I never see
>   A bright blue sky again. . . .
> There are thoughts in my breast to-day
>   That are not for human speech;
> But I hear them in the driving storm,
>   And the roar upon the beach.[66]

Perhaps the most interesting revelation of what music means in the creation of a poem appears in Timrod's "Vox et Praeterea Nihil."

> I've been haunted all night, I've been haunted all day,
> By the ghost of a song, by the shade of a lay,
> That with meaningless words and profusion of rhyme
> To a dreamy and musical rhythm keeps time.
> A simple, but still a most magical strain,
> Its dim monotones have bewildered my brain
> With a specious and cunning appearance of thought,
> I seem to be catching but never have caught.
>
> I know it embodies some very sweet things,
> And can almost divine the *low burden* it sings,
> But again, and again, and still ever again,
> It has died on my ear at the touch of my pen. . . .
> . . . .
> Oh give me fit words for that exquisite song. . . .[67]

Timrod is another poet, then, who would agree with T. S. Eliot, who said that poetry occurs to him first as a wordless melody and rhythm. One of Timrod's most familiar poems is his "Ode Sung on the Occasion of the Decoration of the Graves of the Confederate Dead at Magnolia Cemetery," 1867.

Paul Hamilton Hayne makes rather unimaginative references to music, but his lengthy correspondence with and devotion to Sidney Lanier, whose advice Hayne respected, indicates his consideration of the problem. Hayne wrote several songs, the best of which are certainly "Ho! fetch me the winecup. Fill up the brim!" and "Fly, swiftly fly. . . ." He was something of a master of alliterative patterns, as can be seen in "The Winter Winds May Wildly Wave" and "The Pine's Mystery," where lines like these appear:

> Passion and mystery murmur through the leaves
>   Passion and mystery, touched by deathless pain
> Whose monotone of long, low anguish grieves
>   For something lost that shall not live again. . . .[78]

In his song "O! Your Eyes Are Deep and Tender," the melodic pattern is smoothly achieved through alliteration.

Again like Lanier he discloses a certain felicity in the handling of unusual rhythms and line lengths. These can be seen in "Fire Pictures" and "A Lyrical Picture," as well as in many other poems. Hayne was a prolific poet who wrote occasional verse as well as poems like "The Broken Chord," and "The Rift within the Lute." The following lines from "Motes" illustrate his interest in metres:

> Up and down, up and down
>   In the air the sunshine mellows. . . .
>   Who can fold them,
>   Catch or hold them?
>   Evanescent,
>   Omnipresent
>   Shy eluders
>   Bold obtruders
> Past all joking, most provoking
>   Tricksy, whisky, frisky
>   Motes.[69]

MUSIC AND THE TRANSCENDENTALISTS

Not all of the poets who make up the group that had its meeting place in the environs of Boston were transcendentalists, and many openly declared their freedom from any such label. However, many American poets in the century were affected in some fashion by transcendentalism, and the poets who took part in the Brook Farm experiment were more positively affected than others.

Only recently has some effort been made to explore the relationship of music and transcendental thought in America. That such research should appear so tardily is difficult to understand, since German thought was permeated by music, and it is chiefly

German thought that instigated and supported transcendentalism in America. It was a part of the feeling, at the turn of the century, that the Germans had come closer to the eternal truths than had any other nation. And music was accorded so high a place in the Germanic scheme of nineteenth century thought that it was inevitable that the transcendentalists should share in that feeling. Those who felt a musical deficiency in themselves, as Emerson did, were almost apologetic, and took every opportunity to educate themselves in the mysteries of music, made still more mystical by the philosophical cloak that was wrapped around them. Music was the "purest," the most abstract and lofty of all the arts, and the transcendentalists around Boston involved themselves with deep philosophical questions as to the meaning of music to man. Many years after his stay at Brook Farm, George Curtis wrote: "The musical revival was all part of the new birth of the transcendentalist epoch. . . ."[70]

Boston, long one of the important American music centers, fostered the transcendentalists' love for music through the performance of the great works of Handel and Haydn after 1815. Oratorios were heard then that have rarely since been given. The early performances of the Handel and Haydn Society (1815) were, characteristically, carefully planned.

Brook Farm was a veritable hive of musical activity under the direction of John Sullivan Dwight (1813-1893) and Christopher Pearse Cranch (1813-1892), though to Dwight must go the chief credit for stimulating musical interest. McCusker wrote of music at Brook Farm:

Music of the best type played a conspicuous part in the life of the Brook Farm colony; and all around the neighborhood of the Farm "Mass Clubs" sprang up to sing the Masses of Mozart and Haydn with Dwight as leader.[71]

And Lindsay Swift wrote of the musical life there:

Attendance at concerts and lectures away from the farm was comparatively of infrequent occurrence; there was so much that was interesting in quality at home. Whenever such excursions were taken, the motive was usually something more serious than a search for pleasure. Nothing better evinces the fine zeal of these Brook Farmers—some of them simple folk enough—than their journeying to Boston to hear good music, and then walking back a good nine miles under the

stars and in the middle of the night, with an early morning's work
before them.[72]

It was Dwight who first started classes in singing at Brook Farm
which began attracting outsiders, and it was due to his patience
and actual creative interest in the growth of music at Brook Farm
that instrumental music developed on a plane that was high from
the beginning. Dwight was aided somewhat in his efforts by his
sister and a Swiss engineer, Jean M. Pallisse, violinist, as well as
by Cranch, when he visited the Farm. However, almost single-
handedly Dwight forced Boston into a recognition of the importance of instrumental as well as vocal music. He was a force
not only at Boston and Brook Farm, but also in the Saturday Club
and the Harvard Musical Society. He lectured many times in
New York where his musical ideas were well regarded, and the
numerous articles he turned out on music did much to further
the appreciation of the three great German composers—Haydn,
Mozart, and Beethoven. His translations of German poets, his
contributions to the *Dial,* and his efforts to keep the *Harbinger*
alive reveal his literary preoccupation. When he felt that the time
was ripe, he founded the music journal which bore his name from
1852-1881. He was music critic, moreover, for the concert season
beginning in 1865 and ending in 1881 in Boston. Most of his
friends—Emerson, Margaret Fuller, Holmes, Curtis, Cranch, and
Longfellow—contributed to *Dwight's Journal of Music: A Paper
of Art and Literature.* And he was the moving force behind the
Boston Musical Jubilee of 1852. He brought to Brook Farm the
piano virtuoso, Mrs. Graupner; the singers, Mary Bullard and
Signora Biscaccianti; and chamber music groups, often imported
from Boston. He also wrote reviews of Tennyson's poems in 1838
and of Schiller's "William Tell," and translated the minor poems
of Goethe and Schiller for George Ripley's *Specimens of Foreign
Standard Literature.*

Dwight was an admirer of Emersonian idealism and wrote in
1870:

It is a fact of some significance that the interest here felt in Beethoven
began at the same moment with the interest in Emerson, and notably in
the same minds who found such quickening in his free and bracing
utterance. It was to a great extent the young souls drawn to "Transcendentalism." . . . to escape spiritual starvation, who were most drawn
also to the great, deep music which we began to hear at that time. For

be it remembered, the first great awakening of the musical instinct here was when the C Minor Symphony of Beethoven was played, thirty years ago or more . . . which gave us some first glimpses of the glories of great orchestral music. . . . Then came the Brook Farm experiment. And it is equally a curious fact that music, and of the best kind . . . was one of the chief interests and refreshments of those halcyon days. . . . Then too, among the same class of minds (the same "transcendental set"), began the writing and the lecturing on music . . . treating it from a high spiritual point of view . . . and seeking . . . the key and meaning to the symphony. . . . Beethoven, above all, struck the key-note of the age. . . .[73]

Dwight was not alone in feeling that transcendental thought and music were closely allied in the writings of that day. Margaret Fuller, who is not ordinarily thought of as a poet, left a number of poems and references to music in her earliest book, *Summer on the Lakes in 1843.*[74] In addition, in her writings for the *Dial*, she fully seconded the efforts of Dwight to arouse the Bostonians to a high pitch of excitement over music. Like a true transcendentalist she wrote:

There is a musical element in the people; for there is certainly a religious sentiment . . . an inspiration and yearning of the heart for communion which cannot take place through words and thoughts, but only through some subtler medium like music. It is not nature's fault if we want the musical sense or organ. Slow but sure development under proper culture will prove this. . . . We should be taught the same reverence for Bach and Handel as for Homer. . . . Every opportunity of hearing good music is to be hailed as an angel's visit in our community. . . .[75]

That Boston could found, within a little more than a decade, two journals treating of music and poetry, each indebted to transcendental thought, is interesting. Margaret Fuller's "Lives of the Great Composers," which ran in every issue of the *Dial,* gave her a rare opportunity to do music criticism. She wrote regularly the columns devoted to "Concerts of the Past Winter" for the *Dial.* She was strongly influenced by German thought and spoke of music as a "heavenly influence." And she wrote:

Music is the great living, growing art . . . all that has spoken such divine words in the other arts, rushed here in great tides of soul. . . . We look out through this art into infinity. . . .[76]

The poets who made up the transcendentalist group showed

concern for music too, albeit a different kind of concern from that of the Knickerbocker group. The Boston poets had a regard for music that was tinged by a religious and/or philosophical approach. A profound respect for the meaning of music in the total scheme of things directed the pens of the transcendentalists.

Jones Very, "Emerson's brave saint," wrote for the *Dial,* July, 1842, a poem entitled "The Evening Choir." He also wrote a song to the tune of "Auld Lang Syne." Aside from several minor songs and many hymns, Very reveals little of the influence of music upon his verse, either through imagery or form.[77] The smoothness of his numbers, however, is certainly due to a "good ear," and he did write, like so many others, a "Birds of Passage" poem, and several verses to birds. Despite his extraordinary knowledge of Greek, however, there is little of the lyrical in his verse and much of the tempered quality associated with the classical period.

Emerson himself made numerous references to music in his verses, his essays, and in his private journals. It has long been the custom to account for Emerson's frequently discordant rhymes either as natural to a poet lacking a sense of music, or as a result of his theory that the organic structure of verse was unconcerned with the niceties of rhyme. That Emerson lacked a "nice" ear he readily admitted; but he could write metres as exact as any poet, on occasion. His metres anticipate Frost,[78] and seem strikingly modern rather than unpoetic. Carpenter made an astute statement when he recognized that Whitman followed Emerson in metrical practice as well as in theory.[79] Emerson's verse was, in every sense, experimental; not free verse, but a verse that took its shape from the content and was, in short, organic.

Emerson was, of course, widely influenced by the Germans, by Carlyle and Coleridge; as a result it was natural that music should creep into his references and poetry. He wrote in his journal in 1825 that he could tell whether music was good or bad largely by whether the transitions from piano to forte were smooth or abrupt. He admitted lacking a real ear for music.[80] But he was profoundly touched by great music, as he recorded upon his visit to Rome where he heard the *Miserere* performed in the Sistine Chapel, and the haunting, almost heavenly quality of it led him to write:

Surely it is sweet music, and sounds more like the Aeolian harp than anything else . . . out of the silence and the darkness rises this most plaintive and melodious strain . . . *"Miserere mei, Deus"* . . . the sight and sound are very touching. . . .[81]

Emerson heard the Urania group in church,[82] the quintettes in the town, the music boxes of the day, the ballad-singers and the organ-grinders;[83] he kept accounts of music in the journals and seemed particularly fond of organ music, which he felt had a curative quality to it; and he drew often upon musical imagery to explain his feelings.[84] In 1835 he wrote of music as one of the "mind's asylums":

So is music an asylum. It takes us out of the actual and whispers to us dim secrets that startle our wonder as to who we are, and for what, whence, and whereto. All the great interrogatories, like questioning angels, float on its waves of sound. "Away, away," said Richter to it; "thou speakest to me of things which in all my endless being I have found not and shall not find."[85]

He compared the philosopher and the musician, both of whom were working with a complex of ideas:

. . . as many emotions in the soul of Handel and Haydn are thousand-voiced and utterly incapable of being told in a simpler air on a lute, but just ride on the mingling of whirlwinds and rivers and storms of sound of the great orchestra of organ, of sackbut, dulcimer, and all kinds of music. As the musician avails himself of the concert, so the philosopher avails himself of the drama, the epic, the novel, and becomes a poet; for these complex forms allow of the utterance of knowledge of life by indirections. . . .[86]

Emerson frequently wrote of the salutary effect of great music upon the *soul* which led him to admire Beethoven. Of the meaning Beethoven's music held for man, he wrote:

Swedenborg taught *ab intra;* and in music, Beethoven, and whosoever like him grandly renounces all forms, societies and laws as impediments and lives in, on, and for his genius and guiding Idea. How great the influence of such! how it rebukes, how it invites and raises me! . . .[87]

But Emerson was a little disturbed by music, because he couldn't be certain that he heard in it what a true music-lover might be expected to hear.

I hear much that is ridiculous in music. You would laugh to know all that passes through my head in hearing a concert. Not having an ear for music, I speculate on the song and guess what it is saying to other people; what it should say to me. It is Universal and seems to hint at communication more general than speech, more general than music also. What mystic obscurities in every breast do these love-songs accost?[88]

Emerson watched the westward musical growth of America with interest. He wrote that he was glad to hear "music in the village under the fine yellow moon," and said that it is "a consecration, a beautifying of our place."

A bugle, clarionet and flute are to us a momentary Homer and Milton. Music is sensuous poetry.[89]

Speaking of poetry he wrote: "A man's style is his mind's voice. Wooden minds, wooden voices. Truth is shrill as a fife, various as a panharmonium."[90] In 1839 he spoke of hearing some vocal concerts, among them that of Jane Tuckerman, to whom he was particularly attracted:

... the wonderful talent of Miss Tuckerman, her perfect taste, the sweetness of all her tones, and the rich variety and the extreme tenuity with which she spins the thread of sound to a point as fine as a ray of light, make the ear listen to her with the most delicious confidence. Her songs were better with every repetition. I found my way about in the hollows and alleys of their music better each time. Yet still her music was a phenomenon to me. I admired it as a beautiful curiosity, as a piece of *virtu.* . . .[91]

He responded quickly to the music of the choir and the organ:

A fine melody again at the church. I always thank the gracious Urania when our chorister selects tunes with solos for my singer. My ear waits for those sweet modulations, so pure of all manner and personality, so universal that they open on the ear like the rising of the world.[92]

Certainly Emerson was extremely aware of music, and despite his personal disavowal of any talent for music, he was interested in it and had an almost creative response to it, finding some pleasure in its "hollows and alleys."

References to music in his essays are frequent and varied. He writes of Paganini[93] and Handel ("Does not the ear of Handel predict the witchcraft of harmonious sound?"),[94] and he said in the essay on "Love" that the poet who loves nature responds to music and poetry: "The heats that have opened his perceptions of natural beauty have made him love music and verse."[95]

The essay on "Heroism" contains frequent references to instruments, to flutes and flageolets, and Emerson uses these instruments

with that feeling for metaphor that is the particular mark of his
genius. In the single essay on "The Poet" he made references to
"key," to Orpheus, to the lyrical and metrical relationship; he
said: "We hear through all the varied music, the groundtone of
conventional life."[96] And he wrote:

> For poetry was written before all time was, and whenever we are so
> finely organized that we can penetrate into that region where the air is
> music, we hear those primal warblings. . . . The men of more delicate
> ear write down those cadences more faithfully, and these transcripts,
> though imperfect, become the songs of the nations.[97]

"What do we know of the mystery of Music?" he asked in "The
Senses and the Soul"; and he spoke further of the imperfect com-
munications of the ancient harper who opened "to a vagrant
audience his melodic thoughts."[98]

In his poetry, references to song and music are myriad. They
are usually of this type:

> Flowers they strew,—I catch the scent;
> Or tone of silver instrument
> Leaves on the wind melodious trace
> Yet I could never see their face.[99]

> To Ellen
> The green grass is bowing,
>   The morning wind is in it;
> 'Tis a tune worth thy knowing,
>   Though it change every minute.[100]

Other references are more learned as in "Merlin":

> Thy trivial harp will never please
> Or fill my craving ear;
> Its chords should ring as blows the breeze,
> Free, peremptory, clear,
> No jingling serenader's art,
> Nor tinkle of piano strings,
> Can make the wild blood start
> In its mystic springs.
> The kingly bard
> Must smite the chords rudely and hard,
> As with hammer or with mace;
> That they may render back
> Artful thunder, which conveys
> Secrets of the solar track,
> Sparks of the supersolar blaze,

> Merlin's blows are strokes of fate.
> Chiming with the forest tone,
> When boughs buffet boughs in the wood;
> Chiming with the gasp and moan
> Of the ice-imprisoned flood;
> With the pulse of manly hearts;
> With the din of city arts;
> With the cannonade of wars;
> With the marches of the brave;
> And prayers of might from martyrs' cave.[101]

Not only is the concept here based upon music, but the Emerson verse line attracts because nothing like it is seen again until the parallelisms of Whitman and Lanier, and the varied stanzaic forms of the latter.[102] Quantity, as well as stress, is at work here as can be readily ascertained by reading aloud the six lines and then noting particularly those that immediately follow. In "Bacchus" the poet says:

> Wine which Music is, —
> Music and wine are one, —
> That I, drinking this,
> Shall hear far Chaos talk with me. . . .[103]

And in "The House,"

> She lays her beams in music,
>   In music every one,
> To the cadence of the whirling world
>   Which dances round the sun. . . .[104]

The use Emerson makes of music in poetry is often that of synaesthesia—that is, music is mingled with other senses so that the effect is diffuse, suggestive, but at the same time pleasing because of the breadth of this suggestiveness. He does not limit himself to music as a symbol for only one thing in nature: his mingling of music and nature—that is sound and sight—makes for tremendous transcendental possibilities, since the musical term can be used in its limited or fixed sense while the associations with the term can be spread limitlessly. In "May Day" sound is omnipresent; and in "The Harp" he wrote:

> One musician is sure,
> His wisdom will not fail,
> He has not tasted wine impure,
> Nor bent to passion frail.

Age cannot cloud his memory,
Nor grief untune his voice,
Ranging down the ruled scale
From tone of joy to inward wail,
Tempering the pitch of all
In his windy cave. . . .

    Who is the Bard thus magnified?
When did he sing? and where abide?
    Chief of song where poets feast
Is the wind-harp which thou seest
In the casement at my side.

    Aeolian harp,
How strangely wise thy strain!
. . . .
From the eager opening strings
Run loud and bold the song.
Who but loved the wind-harp's note.[105]

"The Harp" is a poem erected upon his musical knowledge. Emerson not only recognizes here what happens to human musicians in most cases, but he also uses terms like "scale," "tone," and "tempering the pitch" in a musical sense and, simultaneously, in a much broader and more common sense.

On July 4, 1857, an ode of Emerson's was sung in Town Hall at Concord; his "Boston Hymn" was read in Music Hall on January 1, 1863. In "Voluntaries" he left a poem filled with musical images; he wrote "Merlin's Song," a "Song of Nature," and several odes. There are many poems that speak of "singing" or "song" and that carry some direct reference to music. Even a hasty glance through the Emerson concordance will outline for the reader the sheer numerical proportion of such references. Like Whitman, Emerson used music for symbol or metaphor and to express, through his sense of sound, the delight he felt in the natural world.

Transcendentalism spurred yet another writer and musician to turn his hand to verse. Christopher Pearse Cranch, close friend of Dwight and Margaret Fuller, wrote frequently for both the *Dial* and for *Dwight's Journal*. He was also often at Brook Farm, a visitor enjoyed both for his piano and his stories. Though never fully allied with transcendentalism, he shared many of the premises of the group. He was in close touch with George Curtis, during the latter's sojourns abroad, and the letters exchanged between the two on the musical world are entertaining and informative.

The Cranches spent over ten years in Paris after 1853 where they were in contact with a group of artists and writers who became their close friends: J. R. Lowell, the Storys, the Brownings, and Thackeray. Most of the letters of Cranch to Lowell, Curtis, W. W. Story, and Dwight are filled with references to music. He traveled with James Russell Lowell to Beethoven's grave and pursued music ardently abroad, to judge from his letters, which speak constantly of opera in Germany and Italy, of chamber concerts heard, and of artists met. Most of the Americans abroad during this period knew Mendelssohn, Mme. Clara Schumann, Jenny Lind, Ole Bull, the Garcias, Rubinstein, later hearing many of them in concerts in America.

Cranch followed musical circles as a flower follows the sun. From his earliest Richmond, Virginia, days, around 1836, he was seeking the company of the musical.[107] In Washington during the same year he wrote his good friend Dwight (their friendship lasted over fifty years) about a German minister in the city who introduced him to "the genuine air of the old ballad, the Erl-King."[108] In St. Louis, the story was the same. He played his flute—on which he was a fine performer—and tried hard to continue in the ministry for which he was trained. But his love for music and painting often led him astray. Louisville found him with pleasant and "musical folk," and in Boston in 1840 he was with the Pierians, "a musical society where we have flute music and singing."[109] In Boston he wrote of hearing the "sweetest tones of the violin, violoncello, oboe, guitar, and organ" and the "richest of singers of both sexes and the sublimest of choral and orchestral harmony."[110] "The music of harmony certainly seems to have descended this past winter upon the capital of Yankee land."[111] Cranch made several references to Dwight's courses of lectures on music and his musical criticism. The two men agreed that Ole Bull, while a great performer, was not a great composer—a judgment that time has verified.[112] In 1855, Cranch said: "I had the honor of writing the 'Farewell to America,' for young Jenny Lind . . . at her last appearance in this country. . . . Bayard Taylor had written her song of greeting."[113]

Before and after his European venture of ten years, Cranch joined musician friends for musical evenings and soirees in Boston at the home of Charles C. Perkins, where German and Italian compositions were heard.

The musical fare in Europe in the mid-nineteenth century was rich. But it was hardly less so at home in Boston. Story wrote to Cranch from Boston in 1855:

Speaking of music, there is good music here in the way of quartette and orchestra, and with little allowances all goes well; only there is the greatest bigotry in respect of the German school, and there are two cliques—one Italian and one German—who fight all day long, and one American headed by Fry and Bristow—who pitch generally into every one and strike out right and left. . . . Oh, little Peddlington; how charming are thy ways.[114]

Cranch's later Boston years found him close to John Knowles Paine, Samuel Longfellow, John Holmes, William James, and Frederic Hedge. When he died in 1892, he left in his letters and his correspondence with Curtis and Dwight a complete record of the musical life of that time.

This musical interest affected his poetry. He wrote *Satan: A Libretto* in 1874 with this introduction:

I call this poem a Libretto because, as in a Cantata, opera, or Oratorio, the Verses may suggest or accompany a music they only in part embody. A Libretto is too often a mere thread on which the composer strings his pearls,—a text for some work of art nobler than itself. While this poem makes no claims to be full-strung, it may perhaps serve to waken a few snatches of a music, containing some vital symbolic conceptions of the grandest of all harmonies—the Divine Order in Creation.[115]

The poem begins with a poetic overture, filled with references to music, and is followed by a chorus of World Spirits who discourse and sing. The second section concerns itself with a chorus of angels in Darkness with the same pattern of recitation and chorus. The poem reflects most of Cranch's religious beliefs as well as a rather labored conception of what constitutes a libretto. In *The Bird and the Bell with Other Poems* Cranch gave freer reign to his lyrical fancies. The form of his verse proved to be ballad-like and simple. None of his poems to music is superior, but many of his regular lyrical verses have a pleasant melodious quality to them. His use of alliterative devices is fairly obvious, and his best work has a sunny quality to it, akin to the verses of Longfellow.

On the whole, the effect of music on transcendental poets may be said to have been salutary. Part of the appeal of Emerson's verse lies in its suggestiveness, its depth, and the appearance of an abstraction caught in the form of an image which is constantly re-shaping itself through the lines of the verse. Music is most excellent as such a symbol since it has exact and abstract or denotative and connotative meanings.

Emerson's "bad ear" metrically was undoubtedly really the ear of a rebel with some of the love for irregularities that Dana and Bryant, as well as Poe, approved of. The rhymes which "fail" at certain points give a certain piquancy to an otherwise regular poem. They appear like sudden *minor* notes in music and temporarily suspend the listener between two melodic worlds before he is returned to the comparative regularity of exact rhyme. Emily Dickinson had the same feeling for "muted" tones in verse.

The transcendentalist poets brought music and religion closer together. They felt, with Dwight, that "Music must have some most intimate connection with the social destiny of man; and that, if we but knew it, it concerns us all."[116]

THE BRAHMINS

Another Boston group allied with the transcendentalists but actually much less closely bound to one another—the Brahmins—shared an interest in music. Longfellow, whose younger brother, Samuel, was so close a friend of Dwight and Cranch, was himself a capable flutist, and, as a young man, took his flute abroad on his trips through France, Italy, Spain, and Germany. He was very much interested in the songs and dances of every nation, and this interest, coupled with his language study and his indebtedness to the German romantics, influenced his verse. Longfellow had been criticized for his adaptation of verse to the known measure of the Kalevala, a criticism which he certainly answered fully in his own lifetime. He drew constantly upon the metres of the old songs he heard, on the ballad, on the hymn, and, naturally enough, upon the measures of the sagas he knew through his interest in the Scandinavian tongues. In his first volume of verse, *Voices of the Night,* he wrote to the simple measures of the psalm and hymn. His *Ballads and Other Poems* contained excellent poetry in more varied rhythms, and the verses of Coleridge seem also to have influenced him. Longfellow's reading was eclectic, and he had a very obvious interest in verse forms and stanzaic patterns. His choice of the older naive forms rather than the elaborately artificial structures of the Latinists was deliberate. He wrote, too, for the "ordinary man," and, in his way, succeeded perhaps better than Whitman.

Most of Longfellow's poems sound well. He necessarily depended much upon his ear, partially because he was a musician, and partially because his eyesight was very poor. Almost every poem of Longfellow's is filled with sound imagery. His poem the "Prelude" to "Voices of the Night" illustrates this. One section reads:

> A slumberous sound, a sound that brings
>> The feelings of a dream,
> As of innumerable wings,
> As, when a bell no longer swings,
> Faint the hollow murmur rings
>> O'er meadow, lake, and stream.[117]

The whole poem is filled with sound imagery. Longfellow also used much repetition in his song-verse as in "The Rainy Day," "Excelsior," "The Old Clock on the Stairs," to name a few. He usually handled rhythms with great facility, a facility that may have grown out of his extensive language training.

In "The Belfry of Bruges" there is, of course, musical imagery. His "Carillon" verifies that Longfellow, like Poe and sundry other poets, was fascinated by the sound of the bells—well cast. In "The Arsenal at Springfield" the poet's ability to see something of music in an arsenal reveals how harmoniously disparate ideas can be treated:

> This is the Arsenal. From floor to ceiling
>> Like a huge organ, rise the burnished arms;
> But from their silent pipes no anthem pealing
>> Startles the villages with strange alarms.
>
> Ah! what a sound will rise, how wild and dreary,
>> When the death-angel touches those swift keys!
> What loud lament and dismal Miserere
>> Will mingle with their awful symphonies![118]

In "Nuremberg" he celebrated Hans Sachs and the Meistersinger; throughout "Evangeline" music imagery and the sense of sound are very pervasive; references like this abound in the poem:

> Homeward she walked with God's benediction upon her.
> When she had passed, it seemed like the ceasing of exqui-
>> site music.

Poems like "Seaweed" and "My Lost Youth" are memorable for the handling of rhythms. Certainly some part of Longfellow's appeal is traceable to the easy, swinging line he achieves. In

Hiawatha, he made use of the line of the old Finnish Saga and that of the American Indian—made known through Schoolcraft's work— at a time when Whitman was using a device surprisingly similar.

Longfellow was intimate with the great Norwegian violinist, Ole Bull. He became fully familiar with the Cremona violin and the compositions of Ole Bull which were, more often than not, based on old Norse melodies. In *Tales of a Wayside Inn,* the musician to whom he paid such tribute is, of course, Ole Bull:

> Fair-haired, blue-eyed, his aspect blithe,
> His figure tall and straight and lithe,
> And every feature of his face
> Revealing his Norwegian race;
> A radiance, streaming from within,
> Around his eyes and forehead beamed,
> The Angel with the violin . . .
>
> The instrument on which he played
> Was in Cremona's workshops made . . .
>
> And when he played, the atmosphere
> Was filled with magic, and the ear
> Caught echoes of that Harp of Gold
> Whose music had so weird a sound,
> The hunted stag forgot to bound,
> The leaping rivulet backward rolled,
> The birds came down from bush and tree
> The dead came from beneath the sea . . .[119]

When the musician tells his tale of "The Saga of King Olaf," in "each pause" he played on his violin an interlude:

> Fragments of old Norwegian tunes
> That bound in one the separate runes,
> And hold in mind in perfect mood,
> Entwining and encircling all
> The strange and antiquated rhymes
> With melodies of olden times . . .[120]

Much of the saga follows the metrical pattern of the song and the ballad with some attention to alliteration. There are many references to music, and at the close of the poem, an "Interlude" occurs filled with music.

In "The Spanish Student," in which is found much singing and several serenades and songs, occurs a discourse among the musicians and Chispa, a servant, straight out of Tudor drama:

Chispa

. . . what instrument is that?

First Musician

An Aragonese bagpipe.

Chispa

Pray, art thou related to the bagpiper of Bujalance, who
asked a maravedi for playing, and ten for leaving off?

First Musician

No, your honor.

Chispa

I am glad of it. What other instruments have we?

Second and Third Musicians

We play the bandurria.

Chispa

A pleasing instrument. And thou?

Fourth Musician

The fife.

Chispa

I like it; it has a cheerful, soul-stirring sound, that soars
up to my lady's window like the song of a swallow . . .[121]

There are innumerable passages in the rest of the play that
have reference to music. At the beginning of Scene III a song
(serenade) is sung. Most of the references follow this pattern:

Victorian

That was the first sound in the song of love!
Scarce more than silence is, and yet a sound.
Hands of invisible spirits touch the strings
Of that mysterious instrument, the soul,
And play the prelude of our fate. We hear
The voice prophetic, and are not alone.[122]

Longfellow left a poem to "Walter von der Vogelweide," a series
of fine sonnets, and several excellent sea-poems, with alliterative
lines like these:

Like the long waves on a sea-beach,
   Where the sand and silver shines,
With a soft, monotonous cadence,
   Flow its unrhymed lyric lines.[123]

He wrote a poem on "The Singers" and "A Christmas Carol," and
left an accurate reference to a Puritan song in *The Courtship of
Miles Standish:*

Heard, as he drew near the door; the musical voice of Priscilla,
Singing the hundredth Psalm, the grand old Puritan anthem,
Music that Luther sang to the sacred words of the Psalmist . . .
While with her foot on the treadle she guided the wheel in its
    motions.
Open wide on her lap lay the well-worn psalm-book of Ainsworth,
Printed in Amsterdam, the words and the music together.
Rough-hewn, angular notes, like stones in the wall of a church-
    yard,
Darkened and overhung by the running vine of the verses.
Such was the book from whose pages she sang the old Puritan
    anthem,
She, the Puritan girl, in the solitude of the forest,
Making the humble house and the modest apparel of homespun
Beautiful with her beauty, and rich with the wealth of her
    being.[124]

Longfellow left a poem on "The Poet and His Songs," his "Belfry of Bruges," together with numerous translations of songs by Provençal, Spanish, Italian, and German poets. These translations, as well as his interest in music—despite the fact that he was never a great lover of opera—affected Longfellow's verse forms. Odell Shepard wrote:

Longfellow's ability to sink himself and his own moods out of sight enabled him to excel as a translator and a narrative poet. . . . Even the more acute readers of Longfellow have seldom recognized that his sense of form was at all uncommon, partly because the simple stanzas and meters of his familiar works—most of them derived from the popular ballad, Protestant hymnology, and the Romantic poets of Germany— are seldom associated with this Latin trait. Close reading of even his feebler early lyrics will show, however, that they usually contain little that could be dispensed with. For all their apparent laxity or ease, they are likely to be succinct, though seldom terse or laconic. Nearly every-thing irrelevant has been pruned away.[125]

Music seems to have been Longfellow's chief pleasure and recre-ation. It is impossible to treat adequately here his musical knowl-edge. He heard all the virtuosi, knew the latest compositions, enjoyed the great composers' works of his time, was delighted with the songs and ballads of all nations. He was a friend of Dwight's and his poem *Hyperion* fairly exudes music. J. T. Hatfield, in his *New Light on Longfellow*, makes much of Longfellow's German period when music was dearest to him.

James Lightwood has made a rather extensive study of Oliver

Wendell Holmes' musical awareness.[126] I am indebted to him for much of this material. Holmes was quite interested in the violin, though he began the study of it relatively late. Morse, his biographer, said that he used to "shut himself in his study and fiddle away with surprising industry." If he never attained any great facility of execution, he fully understood and appreciated the merits of a good violin; and it is when he begins to discuss violins seriously that he reveals the instinct of a true musician. In this respect he reminds readers of Scott.[127]

Holmes made many references to music in the *Autocrat of the Breakfast Table,* and, when he spoke of music, accorded it an enviable place in the art world: "No one's eyes fill with tears over the inventor of the logarithm, but a song of Burns or one of Charles Wesley's hymns goes straight to the heart."[128]

Though he had a limited singing voice, Holmes so loved music that he wrote the lines for the Thomas Moore Centennial Celebration of 1879. (Moore had been a particular favorite of his.) He was familiar with the organ as well as the violin and ranked the "Marseillaise" as a song above "God Save the King." Both, he commented, were far superior as music to "Yankee Doodle."

He was interested in the hymn, and Sir Harry Lauder said of him that he thought he might have been the "greatest hymn writer in the world had he written more."[129] His hymn, "Lord of All Being," has been highly praised, and he was himself partial to the hymns of Watts and Wesley. He called the "Rock of Ages" our Protestant "Dies Irae."

Typical of Holmes' musical verse is "The Silent Melody":

> Sweet are the lips of all that sing,
> When nature's music breathes unsought,
> But never yet could voice or string
> So truly shape our tenderest thought,
> As when by life's decaying fire,
> Our fingers sweep the stringless lyre.[130]

Holmes left a paper on the origin of the octosyllabic couplet that called forth some discussion with Sidney Lanier, who read an account of his idea in a newspaper. Holmes' suggestion, like Emerson's, was that the true basis of the octosyllabic line lay in the human breathing pattern. Lanier agreed. He wrote Holmes:

I had expected to quote your observation in my *Science of English Verse,* and to discuss it at some length, as connected with a confirmation—or rather with an extension of its bearing—which had come within my own notice. This extension is: that the whole body of instrumental music . . . is found to be segregated into rhythmic divisions whose length varies only within just such limits as are determined by the breathing places in ordinary songs. . . .

It may interest you if I mention two, out of several important bearings of this fact when taken in connection with your own principle. One is: that, since these rhythmic divisions which we are in the habit of calling "lines" in *verse* prevail also in music, we are necessarily driven back to a common origin for this remarkable rhythmic determination of what would seem naturally the most *undetermined* and lawless of human feelings . . . and that common origin seems necessarily the *Song*. . . .

I feel sure that when the fact of tunes in ordinary speech—the fact that in all our every day talk we convey our meaning quite as much by tune as by articulate word—comes to be fully recognized, philology will find a new world for its investigations. . . .[131]

Holmes' interest in music metre accounts for his "fine feeling for rhythm."[132] He was also particularly sensitive to tone-color in verse, arranging his words with care within the line. Though much has been said about Holmes' interest in music, much more could be said outside the limits of this chapter.

Another musical Brahmin was James Russell Lowell. His musical interests increased with his love for verse, and it is evident that Lowell often turned to music for "ideas" and "terms" in his verse.[133]

Brought up in a musical family, Lowell "could discuss with a partner in a dance the moral significance of the Fifth Symphony of Beethoven in comparison with the lessons of the Second or the Seventh."[134] Though he claimed to have "no ear for music," he loved to sing and frequently wrote songs. He was the leader of groups of young people in "musical evenings."[135]

He left among his prose writings an essay on "Song-Writing":

The songs of a nation are like wild flowers pressed . . . between blood-stained pages of history. . . .

A good song is as if the poet had pressed his heart against the paper . . . The best part of a song often lies not at all in the words, but in the metre, perhaps, or the structure of the verse, in the wonderful melody which arose of itself from the feeling of the writer, and which unawares throws the heart into the same frame of thought. . . . In a good song, the words seem to have given birth to the melody, and the melody to the words. . . . All our sympathies lie in such close neighborhood, that when music is drawn from one string, all the rest vibrate in sweet accord. . . .[136]

And in an essay entitled "Getting Up," he wrote:

I always have loved the organ, because it seemed to have more depth and majestic vastness than any other instrument; and often, when I am listening to the silvery notes of the orchestra at a concert, I have wished that the great organ would burst forth, without the touch of any hand, and drown all other sounds in its heavy sea of harmony. . . . But in the great soul and spirit of music, even in its gentlest tones, I cannot tell what I saw and heard. It was Beethoven. . . .[137]

Lowell's musical interest is reflected in his verse. He wrote a "Sonnet on Hearing a Sonata of Beethoven's Played in the Next Room," a poem "To a Lady Playing on a Cithera," some poems on "Remembered Music," and several musical poems variously titled "The Singing Leaves," "The Finding of the Lyre," "The Serenade," and "Music." In addition there are numerous musical allusions and metaphorical constructions dependent upon music in his verse. H. T. Henry wrote:

It will be, I think, well within the mark to assert that in no other writer of any generation who has not written professedly on musical topics, will so many musical ideas and expressions be found . . . to him life and nature are musical symbols of the unheard music hereafter.[138]

Lowell's recognition of the fact that critics should know music in order to judge adequately the work of poets is evident in his own criticisms of Milton and Shakespeare. His use of apt musical terms in criticism shows the range of his critical vocabulary to be beyond that of most poet-critics. Certainly Lowell's musical knowledge astounds, and does so all the more because he is not ordinarily thought of as a lyrical poet. H. T. Henry is quite right in claiming for Lowell unusual musical sensitivity.

Though this brief survey of the period up to approximately 1880 may not satisfy the reader as to the effect of music upon the actual creative power of the poet, it should serve to indicate that musical knowledge and appreciation were widespread among nineteenth century American poets. To show how fully music influenced some of the major poets, the following pages are devoted to a discussion of its effect upon the work of Poe, Whitman, and Lanier.

Poe and Music

POE IS ONE OF THE MOST MUSICAL poets America has produced.[1] Not only are his verses exceedingly melodious, his rhythms fluent, and his phrasings memorable and haunting, but his poems derive much of their tone and effect from his interest in music. That he wrote deliberately to musical principles has not been widely recognized, nor has much been said of the fact that a large portion of his critical writings was given to a discussion of the relationship of music and verse; yet most readers have been sensitive, to some degree, to the inherent music in his verse, though few have realized how consciously he actually strove to imitate music.

Poe's personal interest in and talent for music were hereditary. His maternal grandmother, Elizabeth Arnold, was one of the most famous vocalists at Covent Garden Theatre Royal.[2] She was also related by marriage to Samuel Arnold, the greatest English composer of her day.[3] On her American tour, one Boston newspaper carried the following account of her concert:

We have had the pleasure of a complete fruition. . . . The theatre never shook with such bursts of applause. . . . Not a heart but was sensible of her merits; not a tongue but vibrated in her praise; not a hand but moved in approbation. Nor did these expressions of satisfaction die with the evening; her merits have since been the pleasing theme of every conversation.[4]

Poe's mother, Elizabeth Poe, was a much finer actress and singer than has been customarily recognized.[5] At the height of her career she was one of our leading actresses, and she was equally fine as a vocalist in the light operas of the day. Her phenomenal memory often enabled her to play different parts in an evening. Although she died early, her fame was wide-spread. The *Boston Gazette* wrote of her in 1808:

> She has supported and maintained a course of characters more numerous and arduous than can be paralleled on our own boards during any one season. Often she has been obliged to perform three characters in the same evening; and she has been perfect in text and well comprehended the intention of her author . . . she has succeeded in the tender personation of tragedy . . . her conceptions are marked with good sense and natural ability.[6]

At the height of her career she played Juliet to John Howard Payne's Romeo. Poe kept her copy of *Tamerlane* and collected many of the songs that she made popular in her day. There is now a fairly complete collection of this sheet music at the Poe house in Philadelphia.

Like his mother, whom he never ceased to admire,[7] Poe was a precocious child.[8] He inherited not only her musical talent, but her phenomenal memory. He spent many evenings in the Allan house entertaining guests with his recitations and fine singing. As a youth, he had access to the scores of popular songs and miscellanies that the Ellis-Allan Company stocked and sold, and oftentimes when he was supposed to be working for the company he was found poring over these volumes. Whitty suggests that Poe learned from these songs the use of the repetend in verse.[9]

From 1815-1820 Poe was in England and Scotland where he must have heard not only the newly organized (1813) London Philharmonic, but also Scotch balladry[10] and the skirl of the bagpipes. He was spoken of as "beautiful, sad, silent, and fond of music and . . . sketching"[11] and as a youth at West Point he served as drum major for the band.[12] He was exceedingly fond of church music, and there is a story current in Richmond, Virginia, that he forgot himself one morning at church during the choral offering and stood transfixed before the choir, absorbing the music.

Poe excelled, significantly, in languages throughout his school life. As a boy his marks in French were unusual. He apparently read French purely for pleasure before he entered the University of Virginia, at seventeen, in 1826. He registered for both ancient and modern languages and excelled at both. Jefferson had stressed the learning of Greek at the University[13] and it is not unlikely that Poe's study of it, coupled with the teaching he had received at Joseph H. Clarke's English and Classical School in Richmond, gave him the ease in the handling of Greek and Latin which he claimed. Poe was early interested in metrics and made extensive studies of prosody, according to his own claims, in many languages.[14] His grades in Latin, Spanish, French, and Italian were excellent. If he had not left the University of Virginia there is reason to believe that Poe might have become another professor of languages and thus his career might have paralleled Longfellow's in more ways than the poetic.[15]

In his adult life, Poe had a rich baritone voice,[16] and tradition has it that he was something of a flutist.[17] His wife, Virginia, was musical,[18] and her fatal illness was ascribed in its day to the rupture of a blood-vessel while she was singing. Her harp stands in the little bedroom at the Poe house in Philadelphia. Shortly after their marriage, Poe attempted to teach her music. He bought at this time a piano so that she could have the advantages of a well brought up Southern girl.[19]

Poe's speaking as well as his singing voice has been frequently praised. It was said that he literally sang his more musical poems, and his voice is spoken of variously as "low," "musical," and "exquisitely expressive."[20] It was capable of the finest modulations, and his recitations of "The Raven" and other verses were thrilling.

Apparently he could read music because he was familiar with the musical staff and with musical terms. His extraordinary musical sensitivity led him to a comparison of the buzz of the gnat ("which never rose above second A") with the color orange.[21] It seems quite likely, from this reference, that Poe was endowed with what musicians frequently refer to as "perfect pitch." In other words, Poe may have been, and probaby was, so well endowed musically, that he could hear any pitch and name it correctly. Sarah Elmira Royster said of him that as a youth he was passionately fond of music,[22] and the references to music in his critical writings bear out the supposition that he had a genuine interest in music.

That Poe was thoroughly familiar with concert music is proved by his letters, tales, and critical essays. He heard and knew opera,[23] and since he excelled in Italian at college, it is quite possible that he was one of the comparatively few Americans hearing Italian opera in New York who understood both the words and the music. He was fond not only of the theatre, but also of the concert hall, of chamber music and, most of all, of vocal music.[24] He frequently wrote music criticism, and he discussed with ease the music of

Mendelssohn and Mozart.[25] His comments on the concerts that he heard and the great singers, such as Malibran and Pico, are not inferior in quality to those of contemporary music critics.[26]

His love for the verses of Burns, Moore, and Byron certainly stemmed from his musical responsiveness. He called music a passion of his and wrote in a letter to Lowell:

I am profoundly excited by music, and by some poems—those of Tennyson especially—whom, with Keats, Shelley, Coleridge (occasionally) and a few others of like thought and expression, I regard as the *sole* poets. *Music is the perfection of the soul, or idea, of Poetry.* The *vagueness* [and] exultation arous[ed by] a sweet air (which should be strictly indefinite & never too strongly suggestive) is precisely what we should aim at in poetry. . . .[27]

Here Poe clearly showed that both poetry and music were exciting to him, and he listed among his preferred poets those who had adhered most closely to musical forms and expressions.[28] Poe also indicated the typical nineteenth century preoccupation with the matter of music's vagueness, and the feeling that poetry should strive for the same end.

In addition he shared his century's feeling for the greatness of music and its effect upon the soul of man. He said, "It is in music, perhaps, that the soul most nearly attains the great end for which when inspired by the Poetic Sentiment it struggles—the creation of Supernal Beauty."[29]

He spoke of being able to hear the sound of darkness,[30] and this acute sensitivity led him to talk of the sense of sound in terms of his other senses. In this respect too he belongs to the century in which the arts merged.

This extreme consciousness of music crept into, nay, permeated his creative thinking. He wrote:

The great variety of melodious expression which is given out from the keys of a piano, might be made, in proper hands, the basis of an excellent fairy-tale. Let the poet press his finger steadily upon each key, keeping it down, and imagine each prolonged series of undulations the history, of joy or of sorrow, related by a good or evil spirit imprisoned within. There are some of the notes which almost tell, of their own accord, true and intelligible histories.[31]

It was inevitable that music should find its way into his writing. Some indication of the extent of Poe's knowledge of music can be gained from musical references in his critical essays and his famous tales. Almost unconsciously he drew sometimes upon music to explain a critical point or to set the atmosphere for a scene in a tale. Most of these tales in which musical references abound are mood studies, taking their color from the settings—largely psychological—that he provided. His use of music is like E. T. A. Hoffmann's, and it is often from the musical passages that the reader receives a clue to a situation or a change in it. For instance Poe wrote of Roderick in "The Fall of the House of Usher":

His long improvised dirges will ring forever in my ears. Among other things, I hold painfully in mind a certain singular perversion and amplification of the wild air of the last waltz of Von Weber.[32]

. . . .

I have just spoken of that morbid condition of the auditory nerve which rendered all music intolerable to the sufferer, with the exception of certain effects of stringed instruments. It was, perhaps, the narrow limits to which he thus confined himself upon the guitar, which gave birth, in great measure, to the fantastic character of his performances . . . (he not unfrequently accompanied himself with rhymed verbal improvisations), the result of that intense mental collectedness and concentration to which I have previously alluded as observable only in particular moments of the highest artificial excitement. The words of one of these rhapsodies I have easily remembered. . . .[33]

In "The Masque of the Red Death" music is used suggestively.[34] "The Island of the Fay" is the vehicle for Poe's short discussion of the role of the audience in music. He makes the point that the "higher order of music" is most "estimated" when the hearer is alone. "The proposition will be admitted at once by those who love the lyre for its own sake and for its spiritual uses."[35] In "The Assignation" music combines with rich draperies and perfumes for effect.[36] From "Dr. Tarr and Professor Fether" comes a reference to a young woman's being seated at a piano playing an air by Bellini.[37] Music, in this tale, offers an indication or anticipation of the insanity of the members of the orchestra made up of players on fifes, fiddles, trombones, and drum, and the insanity of the hearers who expressed no concern over the discordant quality of the music. In "Shadow" Poe speaks of the hysterical company who

sang the songs of Anacreon—which are madness . . . I, Oinos, . . . sang with a loud and sonorous voice the songs of the son of Teios. But gradually my songs, they ceased and their echoes . . . became weak. . . .[38]

In "The Domain of Arnheim" Poe wrote that Ellison became neither musician nor poet "although no man lived more profoundly enamored of music and poetry."[59] Typical of Poe's musical passages in prose is that of "Eleanora":

> . . . and the lulling melody that had been softer than the wind-harp of Aeolus—and more divine than all save the voice of Eleanora, it died little by little away, in murmurs growing lower and lower, until the stream returned at length, utterly into the solemnity of its original silence. . . .[40]

"The Spectacles" sketched a picture of attendance at an opera to which "my friend" who was a *musical fanatic* gave "his undivided attention" for two hours. Later he heard singing "never excelled in any private circle out of Vienna." When Lelande sang,

> The impression she produced upon the company seemed electrical. . . . I know not how to describe it. . . . It is beyond the reach of art to endow either air or recitative with more impassioned *expression*. . . . Her utterance of the romance in Othello—the tone with which she gave the words *"Sul mio sasso"* . . . is ringing in my memory yet. Her lower tones were absolutely miraculous. Her voice embraced three complete octaves, extending from the contralto D to the D upper soprano, and, though sufficiently powerful to have filled the San Carlos, executed, with the minutest precision, every difficulty of vocal composition—ascending and descending scales, cadences, or *fiorituri*. In the finale of the Sonnambula, she brought about a most remarkable effect at the words:
>
> > *Ah! non giunge uman pensiero*
> > *Al contento ond'io son piena.*
>
> Here, in imitation of Malibran, she modified the original phrase of Bellini, so as to let her voice descend to the tenor G, when, by a rapid transition, she struck the G above the treble stave, springing over an interval of two octaves.[41]

This single passage from the prose tales should prove that Poe understood much about vocal music. Not only does he know what Bellini originally intended to have sung, but he recognized the modification of the aria as Malibran performed it. In addition, he referred again to the exact range of the voice that was used, indicating that he knew contralto and soprano ranges, as well as the exact notes that were sung. Obviously he was either looking at a score (which would seem to be the case, unless he had "perfect pitch") or else he was using a libretto and recalling the ranges. It can hardly be doubted that Poe was familiar with the aria from "Sonnambula," as well as with such musical terms as appear here, among them *fiorituri*.

It is both impractical and impossible, within the limits of this chapter, to enumerate or to make a study of the numerous references to music in Poe's tales. However, the reader can see from these references that Poe knew music.

He was particularly sympathetic to the poetry of the song poet. In criticizing the work of his contemporaries, he showed concern for the difficulties that such a poet faced. He understood that such verse must be judged by something beside the rule of thumb, metrically and textually. His own criticisms of George Pope Morris bear out this point. He said of musical verse that it was beyond ordinary critical judgments and that the very vagueness of it was its chief charm. He wrote:

In this ultimate destination of the song proper, lies its essence—its genius. It is the strict reference to music—it is the dependence upon modulated expression—which gives to this branch of letters a character altogether unique, and separates it, in great measure and in a manner not sufficiently considered, from ordinary literature; rendering it independent of merely ordinary proprieties; allowing it, and in fact demanding for it, a wide latitude of law; absolutely insisting upon a certain wild licence and *indefinitiveness*—an indefinitiveness recognized by every musician who is not a mere fiddler, as an important point in the philosophy of his science, as the soul, indeed, of the sensations derivable from its practice. . . .[42]

Poe recognized the qualities which both Whitman and Lanier later explored, the necessary "wild licence" and the necessary "indefinitiveness" that a lyric poem must have in order to offer to the musician latitude in which to work. He said further:

The sentiments deducible from the conception of sweet sound simply are out of the reach of analysis. . . . Our impressions of harmony and melody . . . are more readily analyzed; but one thing is certain, that the sentimental pleasure derivable from music is nearly in the ratio of its indefinitiveness. Give to music any undue decision, imbue it with any very determinate tone, and you deprive it at once of its ethereal, its ideal, and, I sincerely believe, of its intrinsic and essential character. You dispel its dreamlike luxury . . . you exhaust it of its breath of faery.[43]

He deplored program music because he felt that it was an effort on the part of the composer to give finite meaning to music. He commented caustically on the compositions of those who were following this trend, showing his preference for Mozart.[44]

Poe felt that it was the union of music with verse in the older naive forms, with their lack of scrupulousness "about niceties of phrase" which "imparts to all songs, richly conceived, that free affluent, hearty manner." The best examples of this style, he felt, appeared in the old English carols and ballads.

Wherever verse has been found most strictly married to music, this feature prevails. It is thus the essence of all antique song. It is the soul of Homer. It is the spirit of Anacreon. It is the genius of Aeschylus. . . .[45]

He defended the song-poet from criticism for the form of his conceits, pointing out that if they weren't so clearly etched as some critics might prefer, they were in the best tradition of Donne and Cowley:

These views properly understood, it will be seen how baseless are the ordinary objections to songs proper, on the score of "conceit" . . . or of hyperbole, or on various other grounds tenable enough in respect to poetry not designed for music. The "conceit" . . . which some envious rivals of Morris have so much objected to—
         "Her heart and morning broke together
            In the storm—"
this "conceit" is merely in keeping with the essential spirit of the song proper. To all reasonable persons . . . the fervid, hearty, free-spoken songs of Cowley and of Donne . . . abound in precisely similar things; and . . . they are to be met with, plentifully, in the polished pages of Moore and of Béranger, who introduce them with thought and retain them after mature deliberation.[46]

This is possibly the first defense of the right of the songwriter to make use of conceits of a heightened emotional nature to secure an effect through a "conceit" that the musical background helped make understandable. Poe's attitude toward the songwriters is illustrated by this statement, and a very significant one it is:

Morris is, very decidedly, our best writer of songs—and, in saying this, I mean to assign him a high rank as *poet. For my own part I would much rather have written the best song of a nation than its noblest epic.*[47]

There is no doubting from this final statement where Poe's poetic alliances lay. He may not have been a songwriter himself, but his sympathy and respect for lyrical poets writing songs is something new in American criticism and probably grew out of the fact that he himself was a creative artist, a poet. Unfortunately too many critics are not.

Poe's statements about the relationship of the poet to the world sound surprisingly like those of Emerson and Whitman. Here is the poet's realization that poetry occasionally offers glimpses of that more eternal beauty:

He who shall simply sing . . . of the sights, and sounds and odors, and colors, and sentiments, which greet *him* in common with all mankind—he, I say, has yet failed to prove his divine title. . . . We have still a thirst unquenchable, to allay which he has not shown us the crystal springs. This thirst belongs to the immortality of Man. . . . And thus when by Poetry—or *when by Music, the most entrancing of the Poetic* moods—we find ourselves melted into tears, [it is] not . . . through excess of pleasure, but through a certain petulant, impatient sorrow at our inability to grasp now, wholly, here on earth, at once and forever, those divine and rapturous joys, of which *through* the poem, or *through* the music, we attain to but brief and indeterminate glimpses. . . .[48]

This quotation from "The Poetic Principle" reveals Poe's awareness of the religious import of music and of the relationship of the soul of man to poetry and music that transcendentalists, and Emerson, would not have found foreign to their own thinking. Poe wrote that the struggle to attain "supernal loveliness" has given the world all that it has of the "Poetic Sentiment," which is his term for the creative impulse. This poetic "sentiment is always found in an *elevating excitement of the soul,* quite independent of that passion which is the intoxication of the Heart, or of that Truth which is the satisfaction of the Reason. . . ."[49]

Thus poetry, according to Poe's premises, will neither please the passions nor satisfy the intellect. Poetry will have no commerce with social problems, nor will it simply please the sensuous, the sensual, the amorous. Rather, says Poe, poetry will elevate the *soul* and excite it as music excites and elevates. He wrote:

It is in Music, perhaps, that the soul most nearly attains the great end for which, when inspired by the Poetic Sentiment, it struggles. . . . It may be, indeed, that here this sublime end is, now and then, attained in fact. We are often made to feel, with a shivering delight, that from an earthly harp are stricken notes which cannot have been unfamiliar to the angels. . . .[50]

Poe also recognized the long historical parallel between music and poetry, and he did not hesitate to acclaim the union of the two:

There can be little doubt that in the union of Poetry with Music in its popular sense we shall find the widest field for the Poetic development. The old Bards and Minnesingers had advantages which we do not possess—and Thomas Moore, singing his own songs, was, in the most legitimate manner, perfecting them as poems. . . .[51]

Other American poets before Poe may have felt as strongly about the importance of music in verse; but if so, they wrote comparatively little about it. Poe accorded music not only an important place in the creation of poetry, he said of it:

Contenting myself with the certainty that music, in its various modes of metre, rhythm, and rhyme, is of so vast a moment in Poetry as *never to be wisely rejected*—is so vitally important an adjunct *that he is simply silly who declines its assistance,* I will not now pause to maintain its absolute essentiality.[52]

No other American poet had spoken more strongly of the assistance that he felt music offered verse. Until Poe, no American poet had attempted so consciously to embody in verse the characteristics of the song. And no other American poet seemed to have realized the tremendous impact of music upon versification—upon "metre, rhythm and rhyme."

Critical theories such as those Poe held were bound to find their way into his practice. The resultant musical quality of his verse has misled many a composer who felt that his poems would make excellent vehicles for musical settings.[53] Poe, however, was not a songwriter, and as a result, the efforts of the composers were wasted. All musical settings were inferior to the poems themselves. These possess an innate melody and harmony and a varied metrical pattern lost when set to music. Poe's theories resulted in a type of verse that challenges music on its own grounds.

II

The relationship between music and metrics fascinated Poe long before Sidney Lanier began to write on versification. Poe was a prosodic experimentalist, and he had the musician's recognition of quantity in verse. Like the minstrels, minnesingers, and the Renaissance figures—Ronsard, Campion, Spenser, and Jonson, among others—Poe subscribed to the thesis that until quantity was recognized again in verse, the more musical poets would be damned on premises they never accepted to begin with. It is well to look at his ideas on prosody in some detail, for it is here, he claimed, that his debt to music was greatest. And it is as a metrist that Poe is most memorable. He was rebellious, as all of the essentially lyric poets have been, against the syllabic system with its consequent stereotyped patterns of "feet," "longs" and "shorts." Like all of the lyrical poets, his verses were free from the tedious necessi-

ties which bound the poet of a poorer ear to exactly numbered
syllables. He knew the varied metres of the musician, the subtleties
of accents crossed, and syllables robbed of time values, and the
irregularities which tantalize the reader and open up to him new
metrical horizons. In 1838, in his twenty-ninth year when his poetic
conceptions were clearly formulated, Poe wrote to a critic concerned about his metrical "irregularities" that they were deliberate.
Though he praised the poems sent to him, as examples of metrical
propriety, he defended his own prosodic practice as more advanced:

I find that versification is a point on which, very frequently, persons
who agree in all important particulars, differ very essentially. I do not
remember to have known any two persons to agree, thoroughly, about
metre. I have been puzzled to assign a reason for this—but can find no
one more satisfactory *than that music is a most indefinite conception.*
I have made prosody, in all languages which I have studied, a particular subject of inquiry. I have written many verses, and read more than
you would be inclined to imagine. In short, *I especially pride myself
upon the accuracy of my ear—and have established the fact of its accuracy*—to my own satisfaction at least, *by some odd chromatic experiments.* . . . Your own verses . . . are absolutely faultless . . . "without
the intervention of any discords." I was formerly accustomed to write
thus, and it would be an easy thing to convince you of the accuracy
of my ear by writing such at present—but imperceptibly the *love of
these discords* grew upon me as my love of music grew stronger, and
I at length came to feel all the melody of Pope's later versification, and
that of the present T. Moore. . . .[54]

Poe's rather startling statement, that prosody is in a state of confusion because "music is a most indefinite conception," should
not be overlooked. The poet, almost unconsciously, speaks of
metre and music interchangeably, and he earlier indicated that
he thought any discussion of metre which left out music "simply
silly." His reference to "some odd chromatic experiments" which
established the "accuracy" of his ear is also an interesting one, for
the poet was undoubtedly referring to speech sounds. The idea
that Poe may have experimented with speech sounds or tones is
most significant, since his verse reveals an unusually pleasing combination of these tones. A "chromatic" experiment would involve,
in music, a movement of a half step, up or down (or higher and
lower), from a given tone; in speech it might be like moving
around the sound of the letter A, with à, ä, a, and hence to ē, and
so on, working with back and front vowel sounds involving differ-

ences of pitch of less than a half step. And it is very likely that this is what the poet meant, since in this phrase he is only defending his *ear* which would consider speech tones. However, these "chromatic" tones are also involved in *rhyme* words, a skillful use of which could result in pleasing "discord"—discord which we have come to recognize as "modern" in verse as well as in music. Discord or dissonance in both cases results from a close juxtaposition of sounds too "near" each other when sought in harmony. And harmony suggests either simultaneous sounding of two or more notes, or the creation of a similar effect by the sounding of one note in the memory, either through repetition or position of that note, while another one is struck in the same "harmony." In poetry, as in song, this harmony occurs between the rhyming tones.

Poe felt that in his day no competent work on prosody had been written,[55] and he set about to remedy that failing. He was the first American prosodist to seek musical analogies to prove his quantity theories. He took issue, in "The Rationale of English Verse," with the writer who felt that rhythmic "harmony" was achieved in verse by the *regular* alternation of *syllables differing in quantity*. Poe denied that there was any "essentiality" of alternation of syllables short and long. Here he demonstrated his radical departure from ordinary prosodic thought, such as Saintsbury advocates. For he says, directly opposing Saintsbury's strictures on the foot as the *sine qua non* of verse, "I deny the necessity of any regularity of feet and, by consequence, of syllables. . . ." More than that, he felt that "melody" in verse was ignored, while "harmony" was stressed.[56] He was, in short, interested in the musical pattern *within* the *line*—and not just in the close of each line. Like earlier lyrical poets, Poe recognized "quantity" in verse.

The fact is that *Quantity* is a point in whose investigation the lumber of mere learning may be dispensed with, if ever in any. *Its appreciation is universal*. It appertains to no region, nor race, nor era in especial. To melody and harmony the Greeks hearkened with ears precisely similar to those which we employ for similar purposes at present. . . .[57]

His recognition of quantity did not lead him into a very clear or detailed analysis of it. He seems to have used the term quantity not only in the older, accepted sense of a reference to the length of syllables in classical poetry, but also to mean a system of prosody based not exclusively upon accent and syllable length but upon groupings of equal units of *time*. His ideas here are actually more suggestive than conclusive.

Largely opposed to the drawing of "rules" from some classical work and judging all later poems by these rules, Poe advanced his own theory as to what a "long syllable" was. It was a syllable, not long because of the vowel, but long because of the consonants that made it easy or difficult of enunciation. "The *natural* long syllables are those 'encumbered'," and "the *natural* short syllables are those unencumbered by consonants."[58] He said, however, that for "purposes of verse we suppose a long syllable equal to two short ones: and the *natural deviation* from this relativeness we correct in *perusal*." And, he adds, very significantly, that "the more closely our long syllables approach this relation with our short ones, the better . . . will be our verse."[59] He also felt that the poetic "line" grew out of a natural desire to place limits and to "define" the succession of feet; that these lines gradually developed in exact proportions to each other (equality); and that rhyme arose from the necessity of "defining these lines to the ear. . . ."[60]

Like Bryant, Poe objected strenuously to the idea of a *regular* succession of feet of a certain character, and to the explanations of the unpoetical that variations within the feet themselves could be solved by a *synaeresis* or *blending* of the offending syllables to re-establish metrical sameness. Poe explained the true poet's "irregularity" to be deliberate, an effort for "the relief" of monotony.[61]

. . . men soon came to see that there was *no* absolute *necessity* for adhering to the *precise number of syllables, provided the time required for the whole foot was provided* inviolate. . . .[62]

Since, as Poe said, the effect of variation is pleasing to the ear and deliberate, why destroy the effect by blending the offending syllables into the unity of the one desired simply to maintain some tight metrical pattern? His argument, like Bryant's, is quantitative.

Of course, there must be *no* blending. Each syllable must be pronounced as distinctly as possible (or the variation is lost), but with twice the rapidity in which the ordinary syllable is enunciated.[63]

In these quotations Poe came nearer to an explanation of what he meant by quantity in verse. It is the *time* unit that is of importance, not the number of syllables per line. *Synaeresis* belonged to the syllable counters of the eighteenth century when poetry was largely divorced from music.

The quantity principle belongs, of course, to music, where a rhythmic notational system and the measure have long been set up to establish units of time. Metre is established for a given song or piece of music—established fundamentally as a two beat or a three beat measure. Within each measure (supposedly the musical equivalent of a foot), the two or three beats must persist, but the rhythmic or metrical patterns possible within the measure are nearly unlimited. In music the only limitation placed on the rhythmic pattern is the limitation of the ear. Therefore the rhythmic pattern must be discernible, memorable, and/or suitable to the tone and mood of the melody. It must be repeated enough times to establish itself as the rhythmic pattern. Here verse pattern is again analogous to music. For in music any given musical note can be replaced by two, or three, or more notes, provided they are exact substitutes in *time* value and are played or sung in the equivalent space of time of the original note. There is no blending here, because, as in verse, variety makes for interest. To illustrate:

In poetry substitutions of syllables within an equal unit of time, improperly called the *foot,* are common among the more musical and lyrical poets who enjoy rhythmic variety and syncopation. Once a pattern in music has been established, notes can be syncopated against it effectively because in music the strong stress occurs always with the *first* beat of the measure—a practice in poetry that would result in an endless succession of trochees and/or dactyls.

Poe cautioned the versifier, however, against too many rhythmic variations of a poetic line, for the presence of too many foreign rhythms might tend to confuse the ear. He also cautioned the writer against *beginning* his verse with a "bastard" foot of the "rhythm intended," since again the reader (hearer) is "thrown off" by the rhythm. He believed that the rhythm should be "commenced and continued, *without variation,* until the ear has had full time to comprehend what is the rhythm." This establishes for poetry where the strong stresses will appear and gives balance to the poetic line. Poe felt that the rhythmic pattern should be so obvious and of such a nature (so planned) that *"any* ordinary reader *can* read it properly." "It is the business of the poet to so construct his line that the intention must be caught *at once,"*[64] though variation is possible in the next line.

He said that there were only these six feet in verse and that all poetry could be scanned by them: the spondee, the trochee, the iambus, the anapest, the dactyl, and the caesura. This last he quite rightly called a foot, or a unit of time, "the most important in all verse," consisting of a "single *long* syllable, *but the length of this syllable varies.*" He recognized in poetry the "human enjoyment of equality and fitness" which is achieved through "rhythm, metre, stanza, rhyme, alliteration, the refrain," and other similar designs.[65]

Poe's use of the term "caesura" seems a little suspect. Usually the caesura appears in verse at the end of a line or at about the middle of the line, at which time it means the extension of that syllable for the remainder of a foot. In music it means the direct hold over a note that breaks the established rhythmic pattern *anywhere* in the musical line; and it is less a rhythmic marking than a climactic marking. Poe recognized the caesura not only in the middle of the line, but at any interval and at the end in verse: thus he is continuing to talk of prosody and poetry in terms of music.

Perhaps the most interesting aspect of all in "The Rationale of Verse" was his rather futile attempt to formulate for prosody a new method of annotation or metrical marking. Based upon the somewhat questionable theory that all short syllables are the one half of long syllables, the notation was so well conceived that Poe felt its acceptance would obviate any future doubt as to the proper scansion of a given verse line. His claim was that his system was not only more accurate than ordinary methods of scansion (because it concerned itself with the quantities of syllables) but that it solved, simultaneously, the problem of both light and heavy stress and long and short syllables. In actuality, the system, once it is grasped, does save time in writing out accentual markings. It errs in principle, however, as Lanier remarked: Poe does not make clear that heavy stress and long syllables do not always fall together.

The naturally long syllable according to Poe's theory would have no mark. The short syllable, the half of the long syllable, would have a 2 placed beneath it like the bottom half of a fraction. Thus an iamb (which is as much a matter of stress as quantity) would read (control). A trochee would be marked (manly). A dactyl

    2   2

would be marked (happiness) and an anapest (in the land). In a

          2 2   2 2

varied foot of any sort where three shorts deliberately replace a

long, a "bastard" dactyl would be marked (flowers ever), indicat-
3 3 3
ing that three syllables must be given in the space of time previously allotted to two. In music this rhythm, which is dearly loved,
is a kind of syncopation. No wonder Poe's poetry is rhythmically so
precise and yet so provocative. Poe demonstrated his system on the
musical verse of C. P. Cranch, which he admired. Cranch was frequently criticized for "irregularities" which Poe felt were natural
to a musical poet. He made use of the "quick trochee" at the
beginning of a poem which Poe marks with a 6 and Lanier would
have marked as a triplet:

3/2

Many are the/ thoughts that/ come to/ me
6 6   6   2   2
In my/ lonely/ musing/
2   2   2

3/2

And they/ drift so/ strange and/ swift
2   2   2
There's no/ time for/ choosing/
2   2   2

3/2

Which to/ follow/ for to/ leave
2   2   2
Any/ seems a/ losing./
2   2   2

Poe asked, after marking the Cranch poem by his method, how
ordinary methods of scansion could have handled the "shorts,"
"since they must be understood as expressing, all of them, one and
the same thing . . . they express indeed 'short' but this word has
all kinds of meanings." He said ordinary prosodical markings
leave to the conjecture of the reader when the short syllable is
one-third, one-fourth, one-sixth, or one-half the length of the long
syllable, while, he said, "the *long*, itself, in the books, is left unde-
fined and undescribed." It is, of course, true that the reader is left
in a quandary by ordinary methods of scansion. Still Poe forgets
that there is hardly any absolute time ratio set up in the minds of
readers. A good reader will catch, through the eye and the ear, the
rhythmic pattern of *his* scansions, but the poorer or more un-
rhythmical reader will not. How long, in the first place, is the *long*
which is to be used as a measuring rod for the other syllables?
The iamb, having a short syllable of ½ of long, would seem to

have a shorter "long" syllable *in point of time* than the anapest
with its two short syllables, each ½ of "long." This seems to be a
fundamental error in Poe's scheme—not from what he implies, but
from the notation system itself which is saying in musical values
that $\quad$ ♩ ♩ = ♪♪ ♩ $\quad$. On a purely mathematical basis, such a
means of marking the feet would mean that they were hardly
interchangeable in point of time, which is not true—nor did Poe
believe it was true.

One of the significant recognitions of the alliance of sound and
rhythm that Poe made came in his statement that *alliteration* and
the rhythmic pattern, since they were going on simultaneously
within the syllables, often impinged upon each other. I believe
this is the first time that such a recognition of a common phenomenon was made in verse. Since alliteration forms a melodic pattern
of sound, while rhythms are carrying on their metrical pattern, it
can readily be seen that lyrical poetry is very like music.

Poe's metrical skill earned him the epithet "jingle man" from
Emerson. It is feasible that a poet so conscious of metrics and
melody as Poe, and possessed of a mind as analytical as it was
fanciful, should experiment in his own verse.

Professor Fagin wrote recently of Poe's rhythms:

Iambs, trochees, dactyls, anapests, spondees, long vowels and short
vowels, alliteration and assonance, and medial and terminal rhymes
were, for him, more than devices for adornment, more than mere
frills; they were means by which the poet approaches as closely as
possible to music.[66]

And Thomas Hardy once said that Poe was the first to realize to
the full the possibilities of the English language in thought and
rhyme.[67] Poe counseled "the use of modifications of meter, rhythm,
rhyme and an ordered use of the refrain." He felt that in this way
the poet can "simulate" the proportion and also, at the same time,
the indefinite quality of music.[68]

Poe's rhythms are deliberately as marked as are those of music.
There is no doubt of his belief that the rhythm of a poem must
appear unmistakable to the reader. Through constant repetition
of the main metrical pattern, the rhythm is established. When any
variation of the pattern is found, Poe repeats that variation until
it too is familiar to the reader. He insisted upon the perfect time
unit just as the musician must have a perfect measure. But Poe
did not mind if one foot was iambic and another trochaic so long

as the effect did not interfere with the rhythmical sense of the whole. His repeatedly stated theory—rhythm is best sensed in a poem when based upon an exact ratio of one to one-half in long and short syllables—is demonstrated in the exactness of his own metrics, where words have values like notes in music. He also treated words as if they were combinations of syllables, more so than had previous poets, so that he could work with a series of syllables much the same as the musician works with a series of notes. With these syllables, Poe worked out refreshing metrical ideas, just as Byron, Tennyson, Chaucer, and the Old English poets had. It was for this reason that he desired a better system for marking prosody.

One of the most interesting phases of Poe's poetic technique is his rhyme. Richard C. Pettigrew denies Poe any claim to poetic genius, on the ground that his vowel rhymes are irregular and often identical.[69] He feels, as Professor Tucker once had, that such rhymes are a genuine limitation on Poe's part, and he makes much of the fact that Poe slipped into "stereotyped" rhyme words. He speaks of the "poverty" of his rhyme, since Poe had few rhyme words, and they were so often repeated. The only rhyme scheme that Poe used of which Pettigrew approves was *rime riche*—a system of rhyming which seems to be not only out of keeping with the general tenor of his verse, but which marks the period of the younger Poe when a kind of pseudo-punning pleased him. In defense of Poe's limited rhymes, much can be said.

Only recently has it been discovered that the human voice in reading or speaking verse unconsciously returns to the same pitch on each rhyme word, even though it is sometimes necessary for the voice to skip as many as five or six tones to reach the pitch of the original rhyme word.[70] This discovery links poetry still more closely to music, for in song the voice returns for the ends of phrases either to the key tones or to tones that are a part of the harmonic structure of the original. One of the chief assets in music is the reappearance of certain notes in various patterns. Beethoven's *Fifth Symphony,* for instance, is always recognized by the appearance of four notes in a given rhythmic pattern. Any fully familiar song like "America" or "Yankee Doodle" will illustrate the point that the voice repeats constantly and always moves in the direction of a certain key tone or set of tones. So it is with Poe's rhymes; that half their charm is derived from this very "poverty" that Pettigrew condemns.

It should be pointed out that Poe is one of the few poets not afraid to use identical rhyme. As a matter of fact he so frequently makes use of it that it might be considered a characteristic of his verse. (In music a return to identical tones in harmony is a "modern" touch.) In the first stanza of "The Raven," for instance, *door* is repeated in the fourth and fifth lines to rhyme with *lore* of the second line and *more* of the sixth. Throughout the rest of the poem that rhyming pattern is followed, though the other words in the lines which admit of the exact duplication of the final word differ. This is a parallel to music, where a phrase comes repeatedly to an identical ending, though the note pattern up to these points may be very different. In "Lenore" the final two lines are exact rhymes. "Ulalume" is filled with identical rhyme: the first stanza has only two rhyme tones, o and e:

> The skies they were ashen and sober;
>> The leaves they were crisped and sere—
>> The leaves they were withering and sere:
> It was night in the lonesome October
>> Of my most immemorial year;
> It was hard by the dim lake of Auber,
>> In the misty mid region of Weir—
> It was down by the dank tarn of Auber,
>> In the ghoul-haunted woodland of Weir.
>
> Here once, through an alley Titanic,
>> Of cypress, I roamed with my Soul—
>> Of cypress, with Psyche, my Soul. . . .[71]

In addition to identical rhyme, Poe made use of feminine rhyme. He was fond of three syllable words which rhymed in their final syllable with a one syllable word.[72] He was as careful to establish the pattern of his rhymes in a poem as he was to establish its rhythm. He used medial rhyme as well as end rhyme, and rhyme frequently within the body of a line but placed in no conspicuous position, as can be seen in "The Raven." His rhymes became so complex that they encroached on his alliterative patterns. If alliteration, at which he excelled, is the melody of verse (and it was his "melody" that Poe was most proud of), then again Poe exhibits his abilities as a musical poet, for melody is non-existent in music unless it is bound to the rhythmic pattern.[73] It is the rhythmic pattern in music that gives the melody its character. Just as

depends as much upon the note *values* as upon the *pitch* of the tones, so "The Raven" depends upon the internal *rhyme* as well as *alliteration* for its effectiveness.

A study of Poe's metrical patterns indicates the variety of metrics he made use of in a single poem. His feet are always equal units in time, and he was fond of what might be termed waltz time or three beat time, indicated by the iambic pattern. His poems often began with an upbeat: an iambic foot. One of the simplest of his poems, "Hymn," will illustrate this:

> At morn—at noon—at twilight dim—
> Maria! thou hast heard my hymn!
> In joy and woe—in good and ill—
> Mother of God, be with me still!
> When the Hours flew brightly by,
> And not a cloud obscured the sky,
> My soul, lest it should truant be,
> Thy grace did guide to thine and thee;
> Now, when storms of Fate o'er cast
> Darkly my Present and my Past,
> Let my Future radiant shine
> With sweet hopes of thee and thine.

The "Hymn" falls into almost perfect four line stanza form. But more important is the smooth shift from the iamb to the varied rhythms of line four. Line five begins a trochaic pattern, quickly altered in six to iambic. Lines nine and ten show metrical variation—nine with a trochaic pattern and ten with "Darkly my," equivalents in time value, though customarily calling for a heavy "accent" on the first syllable. Here Poe's quantity system would help, for "dark" is longer by standard prosodic systems in point of time than *ly* and *my,* though in a quantity system it would be only equally as long. Ordinary prosodic scansion would not indicate the equality of the syllable, though the reader might unconsciously read it that way because of his natural rhythmic sense. Here is obvious metrical variation, yet so smoothly accomplished that one is scarcely aware of it.

"To Helen" illustrates further his metrical dexterity.

> Helen, thy beauty is to me
>   Like those Nicéan barks of yore,
> That gently o'er a perfumed sea,
>   The weary, way-worn wanderer bore
>   To his own native shore.

On desperate seas long wont to roam,
   Thy hyacinth hair, thy classic face,
Thy Naiad airs have brought me home
   To the glory that was Greece
   And the grandeur that was Rome.

Lo! in yon brilliant window-niche
   How statue-like I see thee stand,
   The agate lamp within thy hand!
Ah! Psyche, from the regions which
   Are Holy Land!

This poem, one of his best, is yet most difficult to read well. Poe must have learned from the writing of the poem the meaning of the "caesura" and that the first word in the line hardly established much of a rhythmic pattern if it was, in value, a "caesura." The first word "Lo" of the final stanza balances in time value the word "Helen" which opens the poem. The variation of the last two lines of stanza two in no way destroys the musical rocking motion of the iambs and the lulling rhythmic flow. By the skillful substitution of two shorts for a long, there is some cross rhythm bordering on syncopation, that is aided by the impression of a legato through the careful spacing of syllables in that section of the poem.[74] The strophes are simple in form and almost naive in their rhymes. If *they* hadn't been so carefully planned, the effectiveness of the poem would be lost. Almost more than any of Poe's verse, *this* poem, because of its rhythmic fluctuations and perfect cadences, its use of the caesura and its alternate catching and releasing of time at unexpected intervals, might be set to music. It owes its success, not only to the occasionally varied rhythms which border on syncopation, but also to the smooth alliterative quality and spacing of the vowels and consonants which form above the rhythm a legato pattern.[75] The poem is not crowded with syllables and for this reason the resonance of the vowels prevails over the rhythmic patterns. It is justly considered among his best poems.

The poem "The Bells" best illustrates Poe's metrical virtuosity. Here his fortunate use of rhyme is the metrical key to the reading of the various lines. Even the most unmusical reader is forced by this poem's structure to some realization of the meaning of his metrics. Each line, whether it is directly followed by a line that rhymes with it or not, has a metrical parallel already established. Only for a moment does the reader hesitate over the length of "Silver Bells" in section one. Then he reads the third line which immediately gives a clue to the length of the preceding line and to the lengthening of bells. The poem is most rhythmical in that, though each foot is perfectly equal in time to every other, the poet has offered a variety of metrical patterns within each phrase. Whenever lines of verse are as carefully conceived and as tightly drawn as these lines are, music (mere music) is never extrinsically necessary. Musical settings of poems like "The Bells" are exceedingly flat.[76] And it is the popularity of regular and easily appreciated rhymes and rhythmic patterns like "The Bells" which gives Poe much of his fame. He was a skillful metrist.

An analysis of the first section of "The Bells" reveals the perfect rhythmical structure of the lines.

> Hear the sledges with the bells—
> Silver Bells!
> What a world of merriment their melody foretells!
> How they tinkle, tinkle, tinkle,
> In the icy air of night!
> While the stars that oversprinkle
> All the heavens seem to twinkle
> With a crystalline delight;
> Keeping time, time, time,
> In a sort of Runic rhyme,
> To the tintinnabulation that so musically wells
> From the bells, bells, bells, bells,
> Bells, bells, bells—
> From the jingling and the tinkling of the bells.

It would be well-nigh impossible to shorten or lengthen any syllable in this poem; obviously the principle of prosodic scansion is *quantity,* a principle which Poe felt no one could question. Scanning by a "foot" system alone would be impossible. Because he constructed carefully, with exact and interesting metrical precision, most people will read "The Bells" with rhythmical accuracy, aside from minor heresies. What will be missed by the ordinary reader is the variety of subtle *tonal* inflections. However, even a glance will prove that the poem owes its characteristics to the presence of *e, i, l, s,* and the dentals *k* and *t.* The repetition of identical pitches through repetition of identical words, as well as by certain alliterative units and end rhyme, might be thought wearisome were it not for the fact that this repetition is a deliberate artistic device.[77] Like a musician, Poe offers limited themes with unlimited variations. He demonstrates what less analytical persons have felt impossible: that *repetition* in verse can be no less extensive than in music. Most verse is not capable of such an analogy to music because it usually bears intellectual freight that cannot be repeatedly unburdened.[78] But Poe's verse shows "the word resolved into tone." What could be more rhythmical than "The Bells"? And how clearly the poem demonstrates his quantity theory, where equal units of time, not foot regularity, must prevail:

> Keeping time, time, time,
> In a sort of Runic rhyme;
> To the throbbing of the bells—
> Of the bells, bells, bells—
> To the sobbing of the bells,
> Keeping time, time, time,
> As he knells, knells, knells,
> In a happy Runic rhyme,
> To the tolling of the bells—
> Of the bells, bells, bells, bells—
>   Bells, bells, bells—
> To the moaning and the groaning of the bells.

If his "harmonies" (his rhyme words) here are few, his melodic pattern repetitious, and his rhythms swinging with rare and delicate monotony, the effect is one he consciously set out to create.

Even Poe's stanzas indebt themselves to music, for though he shared the feeling that a stanza is formed organically, he called the stanza actually an "arrangement of metres into masses"—and thereby places the form of the stanza on a rhythmic basis and not an intellectual one. This concept—that rhythm shapes the stanza structure—can be seen at work in "Israfel":

> In Heaven a spirit doth dwell,
> "Whose heart-strings are a lute";
> None sing so wildly well
> As the angel Israfel;
> And the giddy stars (so legends tell)
> Ceasing their hymns, attend the spell
>   Of his voice, all mute.

This is typical of Poe's arrangement of "metres" into "masses." Here the first two lines establish a common rhythmic unit, as do the next two. However, the idea of Israfel's appeal, even for the stars, is an additional thought which suspends the rhythm of the last two lines before the final phrase ending "all mute." Here "all mute" must be extended in point of time, to equal the time value of the first two lines, and in order to achieve a cadence. The prolonged final tones give a sense of finish to the stanza. This stanza may have occurred first to Poe as a complete rhythmic unit, rather than as phrases or as an idea. T. S. Eliot said that poetry occurs to him *first* as rhythms, and that it often does also to his poet friends.[79] The metrical variety in this first stanza is most pleasing. Poe's interpolated phrasings, such as "so legends tell," lend variety to his stanza structure.

"Israfel" is a fine example of Poe's technique. Not only are there many references to music, and music used as actual image, but there is also evidence of "logical" thought in the verse. For instance, stanza two is made up of lines that form themselves into poetry despite an obvious prosaic quality. The stanza depends upon the use of participial phrases and an interpolation of information about the Pleiades. It is followed by a stanza that is linked to it by "and" and falls back into the more lyrical pattern. It is only in stanza four that the thought, or rather, logic of the arrangement falters, largely because Poe shifts his train of thought in the poem. The final three stanzas are smooth enough in transition and rhythm. These stanzas, like the rest of the poem, exhibit how freely Poe constructs his lines—that is, with what variety—but also how he always directs the line to a perfect rhyme ending. Each line is always proportionate in point of time to the rhythmic pattern he has once established. Undoubtedly the most perfectly conceived stanzas Poe wrote occur also in the famous "To Helen," where every line, irrespective of its given rhyme ending, pushes steadily forward to the last phrase in the stanza.

Many of Poe's verse forms are derived from those which were allied with music. He did not know, however, or did not care for, the French song forms which were revived later in the century. When he did not write sonnets or hymns, his verse forms are termed, unfortunately, "irregular." It was one of Werner's chief concerns that Poe wrote more regular stanza forms in his youth than he did as his poetic skill increased.[80] Werner came to the rather strange conclusion that, since Poe's practice was to write irregular stanzas, he was incapable of writing regular ones. Fortunately Poe has left ample evidence of his ability to write regularly. Actually he was something of an experimenter in metrics, and, according to his definition of the stanza, he was also original in his stanzaic patterns. However, he left some verses in familiar stanza forms. He left a *"Hymn"* not unlike Pope's in its simplicity and sincerity, but briefer, and written to "Maria"—the Mother of God. (The hymn *is* a verse form with characteristics peculiar to its form.) He left, in addition, a "Bridal Ballad," a sonnet—"To Science," a *"Song"*—obviously the earlier version of the "Bridal Ballad," a *"Hymn* to Aristogeiton and Harmodius," and "A *Paean"*—also quite obviously an early form of "Lenore." In most of his other verse, Poe experimented with forms of his own, usually making use of the refrain. In "To Isadore" his alternation of lines in his ten line stanza is unique. Lines one and four rhyme as do lines two, three, six, and ten. Lines five, seven, eight, and nine also rhyme. Thus Poe achieves a unique inter-locking stanzaic pattern. He was perhaps overly fond of varying his stanza length and of varying the length of his lines.[81] "Eulalie" is an example of this variation carried to an extreme; yet "Eulalie" also contains Poe's most interesting variation of the refrain stanza. Stanzas even in "Annabel Lee" vary from six to eight lines. The happy variation of "The Bells" takes the reader from a stanza of fourteen lines to one, at the close, of twenty-four lines. Stanzas in "Ulalume" vary from nine to thirteen lines. Of them all, "The Raven" has the most exactly conceived stanzaic form—five lines, unvaried, and the refrain. Poe was especially partial to the five and seven line stanza, probably because it gave him at least a quatrain plus a chance to repeat a line with some little variation in it after the fashion of music. The poem "To My Mother" is a sonnet, just as "An Enigma" is one. The forms of Poe's stanzas may seem quite different from those of other poets, but they do not suffer from formlessness for this reason. If anything they are more tightly conceived than the "standard" forms, and one is frequently aware of the writer's interest in the shape of the verse he is creating.

III

Poe's imitation of music extended beyond the realm of metrics, however. He constantly expressed his belief that *verse* is *inferior music*. One of the important qualities he "borrowed" from music was that of indefinitiveness: this in spite of the fact that his poems are often imagistic. He praised Tennyson, Homer, Aeschylus, and others for the suggestiveness and indefinitiveness of their writing.

. . . the sentimental pleasure derivable from music is nearly in the ratio of its indefinitiveness. Give to music any undue decision—imbue it with any very determinate tone, and you deprive it, at once, of its ethereal, its ideal, and, I sincerely believe, its intrinsic and essential character. You dispel its dream—like luxury; you dissolve the atmosphere of the mystic in which its whole nature is bound up; you exhaust it of its breath of faery. It now becomes a tangible and easily appreciable thing.[82]

This quality of indefinitiveness which Poe admired in music and verse he sought to capture in his own poems. Like Tennyson's verse, his is sometimes narrative verse, but it also, like Tennyson's, possesses a provocative quality of mystery and a nebulousness *consciously striven for*.[83] "The Raven," "The Haunted Palace," "Helen," "Ulalume," "Lenore," "Al Aaraaf"—all are consciously tinged with this quality. His earliest published poem, "Tamerlane," is free from this since it is a record, essentially, of Poe's unconscious rejection of love to follow the "inner light." "Al Aaraaf" follows the Greek mode in its treatment of ideal beauty, goddesses, and spirits—a treatment common also to Keats and Shelley. This quality of suggestiveness in Poe is nowhere better exemplified than in "Ulalume." Throughout this poem the reader (hearer) realizes that some tragic happening, *perhaps* death, is associated with this "ghoul-haunted woodland of Weir," but even when the name of "Ulalume" the "lost" has been read on the tomb, the reader (hearer) can never be quite certain as to why Psyche is agonized and why Astarte appears. The effectiveness of the poem is in direct proportion to its suggestiveness. This is what Poe desired.[84] He hoped that poetry like music would stimulate the imagination, send it in search of unknown worlds. Professor Fagin has quoted Edward Shanks to the effect that "Ulalume" is as much and as little autobiographical as a nocturne by Chopin. Shanks said that he found reading "Ulalume" "a peculiar and exciting experience," although not necessarily an "intellectual one."[85] Critics have long condemned Poe for this lack of intellectual appeal and his unconcern with social problems. Quite frankly Poe thought of verse as the "rhythmical creation of beauty" and it is to the discredit of the critic to judge a man's work by something he admittedly had no interest in. Poe belonged to the art-for-art's sake school and was the first great American poet to strike out independent of any social message or concern for God or man.

The subtlety of Poe's mind was suited to the suggestive. In addition, he had a wide range of associations,[86] and these very

associations and this very subtlety gave to his verse its indefinitiveness. In the more famous of the two poems entitled "To Helen,"
some of the suggestiveness of the poem grows out of Poe's conscious
associations of the purely sensuous with classical knowledge: for
instance, the comparison of the ideal beauty of Helen to the
"Nicéan bark" presupposes some knowledge of what a Nicéan
bark is;[87] the "perfumed" sea is an image mingling the scent of the
woman with the concept of the boundless waters he travels in
search of the ideal; the "hyacinth" hair intensifies this same sensuous image[88] and is coupled with the assumption of knowledge of
"naiad airs" and of past classical glories. Through it all run the
emotions of the dejected poet—this "weary, way-worn wanderer"
who roams on "desperate seas"—at last brought safely to harbor (to
ideal beauty). The final image shows fulfillment by merging the
concept of a beautiful woman standing like a Greek statue of
welcome, holding an "agate" lamp, with the concept of the soul
itself beckoning and lighting up the only realm—the Holy Lands
(Beauty)—to which the poet is a pilgrim. The quest for ideal beauty
has perhaps never been more beautifully or briefly told. Yet the
poem is elusive. The hearer can move into realm on realm of his
own making. It is a haunting melody which echoes long in the
corridors of the mind; this melodic quality is characteristic of the
best of Poe's poetry.

G. B. Shaw has said that "The Raven," "The Bells," and "Annabel Lee," were "as fascinating at the thousandth repetition as at
the first."[89] No narrative poem or piece of program music could
bear so many readings unless it permitted to the reader much latitude—was suggestive. The human mind is not always pleased by
repetition of the familiar but the arts are suggestive and speak of
abstract things.

This quality of indefinitiveness that Poe borrowed from music
accounts for the difference between his poems and those, for instance, of Thomas Holly Chivers, who used a similar metrical
technique. Poe's verse appeals on the very basis of this suggestive,
"borrowed" quality. It not only *sounds* melodious, but like melody
it delights in subtle movements and changes in association. This
indefinite nebulous quality which marks his verse had its source
in music.

Poe was far too aware of the significance of music in poetry to
believe that simply using musical terms was an end in itself.
However, he frequently made reference to music and sound, and

some of his musical terms appear in the next few pages to illustrate his practice.

In "The Haunted Palace" Poe pictures the "Spirits moving *musically,*" to a *"lute's* well-*tuned* law," and "A troop of Echoes, whose sweet duty was but to sing" to indicate that the monarch Thought was in control. But later in the poem when "evil things" appear—"Vast forms, that move fantastically to a *discordant melody*"—he indicates by the words "discordant melody" that Thought is no longer monarch. In "The Conqueror Worm" the angel throng sees "A play of hopes and fears, while the orchestra breathes fitfully *The music of the spheres.*" This is, of course, one of the oldest musical references. In "The Sleeper" an "opiate vapor" "exhales" from the moon and "steals drowsily and musically into the Universal valley."[90] "Musically" here is more exactly used than it seems to be, for the poet has the vapor falling "drop by drop"—note by note![91]

In his earliest poems, "Tamerlane," "Al Aaraaf," etc., Poe's musical references are more frequently made to the music in and of nature than otherwise. In "Al Aaraaf":

> Oh nothing earthly save the thrill
> Of *melody* in woodland rill;
> Or (*music* of the passion-hearted)
> Joy's voice so peacefully departed
> That, like the *murmur* in the shell,
> Its *echo* dwelleth and will dwell.[92]

His feeling for the music of nature is further illustrated in the same poem when he wrote:

> *Sound* loves to revel in a summer night:
> Witness the *murmur* of the *grey twilight*
> That *stole upon the ear,* in Eyraco,
> Of many a wild star gazer long ago—
> That *stealeth ever on the ear* of him
> Who, musing, gazeth on the distance dim,
> And sees the darkness coming as a cloud—
> Is not its form—*its voice*—most palpable and loud?
>
> But what is this?—it cometh—and it brings
> A *Music* with it—'til the rush of wings—
> A pause—and then a *sweeping, falling strain. . . .*[93]

There are several songs in "Al Aaraaf"; the first song of the Goddess has this clothing of abstractions in musical terms:

> A *sound of silence* on the *startled* ear
> Which dreamy poets name *"the music of the sphere."*
> Ours is a world of words: Quiet we call
> "Silence"—which is the merest word of all.
> All Nature speaks, and ev'n ideal things
> Flap *shadowy sounds* from visionary wings—
> But ah! not so when, thus, in realms on high
> The *eternal* voice of God is passing by. . . .[94]

These "unheard" songs of which Poe is speaking seem to him much greater than those which he can hear. The "sound of silence" is an example of Poe's ability to mix senses and abstract thought in a single phrase without belaboring the idea, as a metaphysical poet sometimes does.[95] Sound certainly plays a great part in "Al Aaraaf":

> Young flowers were *whispering in melody*
> To happy flowers that night—and tree to tree;
> Fountains were *gushing music* as they fell . . .
> Yet *silence* came upon material things—
> Fair flowers, bright waterfalls, and angel wings—
> And *sound* alone that from the spirit sprang
> *Bore burthen to the charm the maiden sang.* . . .[96]

The most famous section of that song was completely associated with music:

> Ligeia! Ligeia!
> My beautiful one!
> *Whose harshest idea*
> *Will to melody run* . . .
>
> Ligeia! wherever
> Thy image may be,
> No magic shall sever
> *Thy music* from thee.
>
> Thou hast bound many eyes
> In a dreamy sleep—
> But the *strains* still arise
> Which *thy* vigilance keep—
>
> The *sound* of the rain
> *Which leaps* down to the flower,
> *And dances* again
> In the *rhythm* of the shower—
>
> The *murmur* that springs
> From the growing of grass

> Are the *music* of things. . . .
> Go! breathe on their slumber,
> All softly in *ear,*
> The *musical number*
> They slumber'd to hear. . . .[97]

In "Tamerlane" Poe wrote of

> The *undying voice* of that dead time,
> With its *interminable chime,*
> *Rings,* in the spirit of a spell,
> Upon thy emptiness—a *knell.* . . .[98]

And he spoke of the "trumpet-thunder's roar" and the "battle-cry of victory." In one of the best stanzas ever written by an eighteen-year-old poet, he again makes reference to music:

> O human love! thou spirit given
> On Earth of all we hope in Heaven!
> .   .   .   .
> Idea! which bindest life around
> With *music of so strange a sound.* . . .[99]

So typical of Poe are the elusiveness and the indefinitiveness in the parallel of the idea of love, which surrounds life, to music that it can be assumed the effect was deliberately sought.

In others of his early poems, Poe pictures Romance as loving to "nod and sing" and acknowledges his earliest familiarity with Romance. But with the passing of years, the poet comes to feel "that little time with lyre and rhyme" is forbidden and counts that his heart must be fully aroused in order for him to write sincerely.[100] In "To—" Poe says:

> The bowers whereat, in dreams, I see
> The wantonest *singing birds,*
> Are *lips—and all thy melody*
> Of lip-begotten words. . . .[101]

In "The Lake—To—" he speaks of the power the wind had to arouse him to the "terror of the lone lake":

> And the mystic wind went by
> Murmuring in melody. . . .[102]

This is a typical Poe reference, especially in his early verse. When he wrote "In Youth I have Known One" he spoke of that object "hid from us in life—but common—which doth lie, Each hour before us," but which only bids us awaken with a strange sound—*"as of a harp-string* broken."[103] In "A Paean" in his funeral songs he speaks:

> Thus on the coffin loud and long
> I *strike*—the *murmur sent*
> Through the gray chambers *to my song,*
> *Shall be the accompaniment.*[104]

Sections four and five of the poem "To Isadore" contain much music:

IV

> Like *music heard in dreams,*
> Like *strains of harps* unknown,
> Of *birds* forever flown—
> Audible as the *voice of streams*
> That *murmur* in some leafy dell,
> I *hear thy gentlest tone,*
> And *Silence* cometh with her spell
> Like that which on my *tongue doth* dwell. . . .

V

> In every valley *heard,*
> Floating from tree to tree,
> Less beautiful to me,
> The *music of the radiant bird,*
> Than artless accents such as thine
> Whose *echoes* never flee!
> Ah! how for thy *sweet voice* I pine:—
> For uttered in thy *tones* benign
> . . . . this rude name of mine
> Doth seem a melody![106]

Poe's use of the words "music," "song," "murmur," "melody," "harmony," and "voice" is not original. It is the significance the poet gives to the place of music in the scheme of things in his verse that is worthy of notice. All that he seemed to care for is bound up in music: the poet is exemplified in the musician; the creative power, in the harp-strings of the heart; love is bound to life through music; the dead are honored by music; nature is alive with music which exerts on the youth a salutary influence; a man is aroused to feelings of love by music. To read Poe's verse is to be assured that for him music possessed a power beyond that of other influences in this life. His most exalted tributes were made to music.

Alliteration is characteristic of musical poets, who use it with more skill and variety than do poets with less ear for verbal melody. With Poe, alliteration is a trade-mark, and it is this quality of his verse, coupled with a certain metrical virtuosity, which has gained for him fame.

The appeal of "The Bells" does not lie so much in the use of words suggesting music as it does in the words that were chosen for syllable sound. "Bells" are, of course, musical. So is their "welling" and their "jingling" and "tinkling." The "liquid ditty" which floats from the wedding bells to the turtle-dove is a musical reference. The "ringing out" of music and the "euphony" that "voluminously wells" "from out the sounding cells" as well as the "swinging and the ringing" and "the rhyming and the chiming" of the bells again are musical conceptions. The idea of discordant music is revealed in words like "turbulence," "clamorous," a "deaf" and "frantic fire," "clang and clash and roar," "palpitating Air," "twanging," "clanging," and "jangling," "clamor and clangor." Typical *sound* relating to bells is that of "tolling." In this fourth section Poe speaks of the "melody" of the bells, how it "rolls" and "swells."

Poe's avowed purpose in verse was to elevate the soul and to excite it. In this poem his coloring of the vowels by carefully chosen consonants like the *k* sound in "tin*k*le," "over-sprin*k*le," "*c*rys*t*alline," "runi*c*" and "Musi*c*ally" lends a delicate, brittle quality to stanza one. The consonant coloring here contrasts with that in stanza two where consonant colorings *m* and *n* of vowel sounds *o, oo,* and *u* sound smooth and round—legato—by comparison. In stanza three, consonants *t* and *k* again change the character of the verse, but here only because the poet has spaced the consonants widely, unlike those of stanza one. The final stanza has interesting contrasts between the consonants *w, s, m, n* and *l* and the vowels *e, o* and *i*. The liquid sounds bind together all the words in a line and lend themselves to a deepening of the tone. There is a sonority in *m*oaning, *tolling,* and *r*olling. The successful writing of a poem such as "The Bells," wholly dependent upon *sound* as it is, is a prosodic feat, metrically and musically.

"The Raven," for all its showiness, is like a piece of program music, complete in its harmony, rhythm, and melody.[106] There is no better example of his use of both overtly rhythmic and melodic (alliterative) material than "The Raven." By contrast, "To Helen" contains many subtle alliterations and much assonance, largely vowel repetitions, and the lines, though perfect, are not overpowered when music is added to them. Even a moment's study of "To Helen" will reveal the richly suggestive imagery and the interweaving of various pitches from the variety of assonance and alliteration. The *rhyme* words, dependent upon vowel sounds *o* and *e,* almost exclusively in stanzas one and two, and raised to *a* and *i* in the final, are used as much in the melodic pattern within the line as they are in the harmonies at the end. In stanza one *e* vowel sounds appear eleven times; *o* vowel sounds, nine; and *i,* eight. In stanza two, *a* sounds appear eleven times; *u* sounds, eight; and *e* and *i* sounds, seven; with *o* appearing six times. In the final stanza *a* sounds are heard eleven times; *i,* twelve. The use of the same pitch-tones in formation of melody line as in the harmonics themselves makes for a very pleasing (harmonious), song-like, and compact piece of verse. The whole matter of speech-tones needs further exploration. A pattern of Poe's use of vowels and consonants can be constructed on an enlarged staff and by following alliterations, the melody established. This necessarily calls into use the phonemic alphabet.

The alliteration in "The Raven" does not depend solely upon repetition of the consonant or vowel at the beginning of the word. This poem is filled with interlocking alliteration (syzygy) within the body of the word, just as music does not repeat *like* tones except when they occur on the first beat of a measure.

> Once upon a midnight dreary, while I pondered, weak and weary,
> Over many a quaint and curious volume of forgotten lore—
> While I nodded, nearly napping, suddenly there came a tapping,
> As of some one gently rapping, rapping at my chamber door—
> " 'Tis some visitor," I muttered, "tapping at my chamber door—
> Only this and nothing more."
> Ah, distinctly I remember it was in the bleak December,
> And each separate dying ember wrought its ghost upon the floor.
> Eagerly I wished the morrow;—vainly I had sought to borrow
> From my books surcease of sorrow—sorrow for the lost Lenore—
> For the rare and radiant maiden whom the angels name Lenore—
> Nameless *here* for evermore.

Gay Wilson Allen has suggested that a study be made of the initial consonants in Poe's verse. An overall study comparing Poe's use of consonants with that of other poets has revealed that Poe used the consonants *n, t, th* and *l* much more frequently.[107] From Werner's table, though, we learn an important thing about Poe: that he made more frequent use of these consonants *everywhere*

than the other poets did.[108] Since Poe's reiteration of consonants
occurs as often within the word as at the beginning, a new study
of initial alliteration would not have much value.

Certainly one of Poe's most perfectly achieved poems is "Annabel Lee." Not only are all of the devices which Poe handled earlier
used superbly well, but in addition certain key *words* carried in
the memory from line to line give unity to the stanza. In stanza
one, "maiden" is repeated in the third and fifth lines and the last
line carries the germ for the next stanza in "love." The second
stanza repeats the idea of the "kingdom by the sea,"[109] the fact that
they were both "children," and repeats, with variation, the concept
of "love." The third stanza concerns itself with the *reason* for the
death of Annabel. The fourth repeats that concept. The fifth
repeats the idea of love triumphing and the youth of the two as
well as the idea that their souls cannot be separated. In the last
stanza the melodic pattern (alliteration) of vowels and consonants
is excellent.

> For the moon never beams, without bringing me dreams
>   Of the beautiful Annabel Lee;
> And the stars never rise, but I feel the bright eyes
>   Of the beautiful Annabel Lee.
> And so, all the night-tide, I lie down by the side
> Of my darling, my darling, my life and my bride,
>   In the sepulchre there by the sea,
>   In her tomb by the sounding sea.

The melody of the words themselves is freer here, more like to that
in the famous "To Helen." This poem illustrates every device
that Poe used to make his poetry musical.

The question of "tone" in Poe's verse has been largely answered.
He wrote generally in what we designate as minor mode. But just
like a movement in music, a Poe poem has within its stanzaic
range many variations of this prevailing tone or mood. In music
the notes in the modes (or moods) of major and minor are identical. It is only in the combinations of the notes and in the leading
tone itself in the scale that the true nature of the mode is established. Usually it is not certain until that leading note is sounded
that the mode is to be minor. Poe's verse is parallel to music in this
characteristic. His poems do not call upon any different combination of sounds in his lighter moments; but he does establish the
mood by the repetition of a single word, or by placing that word
in such a position in the text that when the reader (listener) hears

it, he is certain of the mood of the verse. Poe could color, alternately, the tone of any stanza, just as in music a poignant quality often is achieved by a wavering between the two moods (modes), now suggesting one and now the other. The fourth section of "The Bells" is an excellent example of a mournful mood broken in upon.

Poe's conceptions of the climax are bound up in his desire to parallel in poetry the indefinitiveness and excitement of music. The reader is uncertain throughout a Poe poem that the climax will be what is hinted at almost from the beginning. Stanza after stanza increases the reader's interest, and though he is almost sure of the meaning, it is this anticipation of the climactic word or phrase that gives him the pace of Poe's verse. Like in a song or a symphony, Poe's climax is not operatic in its construction, that is, it is not mechanically or artificially contrived. The *last* line of a poem is not necessarily the climactic point. More often the climax is reached in the next to the last stanza, or before the last few lines, so that the climax or resolution itself can be artistically treated. Sometimes a complete verse is reserved for that resolution. To illustrate briefly: "Ulalume," one of the most suggestive of his poems, comes to a climax with "'Tis the vault of thy lost Ulalume!" The last stanza then devotes itself to the explanation that one year ago he had brought his dead lover there. The sense of dramatic climax in "The Raven" is excellent, and all the more fitting since the poet occasionally renders the tragic mood macabre by alternating the feeling of fear with a realization of humor in the raven's appearance. Thus the reader lives constantly in periods of alternate quiet and storm. Once the signal is given, however, for the last climactic climb, with the reference to the "velvet-violet lining with the lamp-light gloating o'er, *She* shall press, ah, nevermore!", the poet's rising hysteria is admirably sustained through four stanzas, coming to a climax in the fourth with the lines:

> Leave no black plume as a token of that *lie* thy soul hath spoken!
> Leave my loneliness unbroken!—quit the bust above my door!
> Take *thy beak from out my heart,* and take thy form from off
>   my door!
>
> Quoth the Raven, "Nevermore."

The final stanza simply repeats the idea of a future with the Raven's Eternal presence. Though Poe has made "nevermore" the climax of each stanza, there can be no doubt that these minor climaxes do not interfere with the rising line of the last four stanzas where the feeling of the medial lines far overpowers the bird's reply and pushes the poem forward.

It is hardly necessary here to belabor the use Poe has made of balance in his lines and of the refrain. These are most obvious in even a cursory reading of his verse and both are elements as common to later poets as they earlier were to Poe, though his refrains have more subtle variations than most writers allow.

There is another respect in which Poe's verse is indebted to music which goes beyond, though based upon, metre and alliteration. This is in the unique spacing of sounds in a verse line, the thickness or thinness of their settling, coupled with various combinations of sounds within words and phrases. These give to a particular line its character, whether legato or staccato, depending upon whether i's and k's or liquid combinations are used. Since this effect has to do with the style and movement of a line, with the tone of the whole, Poe's acute consciousness of it gives high lustre to his best poems.

Surely it must be admitted that if there is in Poe's verse any superior merit, any quality that separates his verse from that of his contemporaries in verbal melody, rhythmic flow, and a certain fascinating "tone," that superiority and that originality result from his understanding and love of music.

Walt Whitman and Music in *Leaves of Grass*

FEW MEN WITH A CONSCIOUS poetic theory have published less about their stylistic intentions than Whitman. That he had poetical principles and a *biographia litteraria* is obvious. He deliberately eschewed rhyme, he quite as deliberately eschewed the accepted poetic forms, themes, and metrical patterns. He made few references to his reading in his verses, shied away from any learned allusion to the classical, and deliberately wrote in the language of the common man in a most uncommon fashion—just as Wordsworth had.[1] He used his words loosely (poetically) and his lines still more loosely. He was apparently deliberately formless and redundant. He wrote poetry like prose—symphonic prose—and he sounded in his own day like a minor Biblical prophet. Nothing he ever wrote was either polished or elegant; yet his best works have undeniable power and greatness. Something in the way of a clue to this highly unique poetic style was offered by Whitman himself when he said to some friends: "I know from the way you fellows talk of it that the music of Wagner is the music of the 'Leaves'."[2]

Within the last thirty or so years readers have become increasingly aware of the presence of music in *Leaves of Grass*. Louise Pound made the pioneering effort in this direction, pointing out that the references to opera in Whitman's verse were neither accidental nor unlearned.[3] Calvin S. Brown devoted a chapter in *Music and Literature* to a discussion of musical form in "When Lilacs Last in the Dooryard Bloom'd."[4] Robert D. Faner, in a doctoral

161

dissertation, discussed "Operatic Music and the Poetry of Walt Whitman."[5] Many critical studies now mention Whitman's interest in music, and the recent translation of Frederick Schyberg's *Walt Whitman* reveals that he thought the influence of music on Whitman not inconsiderable.[6] Moreover, articles dealing with Whitman's poetic techniques always hover very close to a recognition of a parallel between these techniques and those of music.[7] Despite this recent concern and excitement about music in Whitman's verse, however, these studies have been regarded as interesting but hardly revelatory. This opinion may grow as much out of the manysidedness of *Leaves of Grass* as it does from the fact that Whitman's synthesizing powers were so great they have defied a careful analysis. At any rate, critics seem to have accepted the idea that Whitman knew something about opera and that he made the overtures to music that so many lyrical poets of the nineteenth century had made. More than this they seem unwilling to admit.

The purpose, then, of this chapter is to bring together evidence that *Leaves of Grass* differs in style and form from other poetry largely because of its imitation of music. Most of this evidence derives from his published texts; some of it is material from his notebooks that has been overlooked, largely because it did not seem of importance.[8] But all of the evidence points in the direction of the parallel that Whitman was consciously or perhaps unconsciously seeking for his verse in music. This parallel he found in the forms of the opera and the symphony—insofar as such grandly conceived works as a symphony or an opera in the nineteenth century can be said to retain "form." His lengthened, Germanic-sounding lines, which move through a series of phrasal units in search of a subject, have been indiscriminately dubbed "symphonic" and "polyphonic" as well as "contrapuntal," without much regard for the exact meanings of these terms. His references to music are often knowledged and occasionally symbolical; more often they refer to a musical form. Some of the finest Whitman poems *sound* so strongly of music that they have sent critics in search of a suitable musical parallel. Moreover the diffuse, mystical, suggestive quality of his verse indebts itself to music. But where Poe imitated the *song* and borrowed from it, Whitman turned to the more popular late nineteenth century musical forms of opera and symphony, and the difference in the style of the two poets can be traced to this choice of musical form.

It has hardly yet been realized how much of music Whitman

actually understood. His references to music do not reveal a patently technical knowledge thereof; therefore in the past it has been assumed that he had none. This assumption is ill-founded, as it does not take into consideration the fact that he never made any kind of learned allusions to any phase of life he thought would not be understood by the common man. His interest in music was life-long, and because of his fortunate residence in New York and environs, he had unusual opportunities to hear opera. There was some musical talent in his family, for his brother Jeff was a violinist.[9] That Whitman read music and had knowledge of the staff is evidenced from a statement that he made later in life about Poe's verse. He spoke of it as being written always in a certain range—from lower b to g.[10] As a newspaperman and journalist he took advantage of free tickets to hear most of the concerts of his day.

Though his life-long devotion to opera has been often noted, it is seldom pointed out that in writing of the opera his interest centered as much upon the symphony orchestra as upon the chorus. In a section from "A Visit to the Opera"[11] he wrote:

What honeyed smoothness! How exact! How true and clear! How inimitable the manner of the conductor, quietly signing with slight waves of his wand, to the right or the left. How delicious the proportion between the kinds of instruments—rarely met with in ordinary bands, but here perfect. — The violins, the bugles, the flutes, the drums, the bass-fiddles, the violoncello — all, all so balanced and their results merging into each other.

Now a rapid passage full of semiquavers given without the least discord by fifteen or twenty violins. — Now the clear warble of the flute — and now a passage in which advances the elephantine tread of the trombones. — Now a solo on the fagotto, relieved by the low, soothing, gulping notes of the base-viols. — And now, a long, tumultous, crowded finale, ending with a grand crash of all the instruments together, every one, it would seem, making as much noise as it possibly can — an effect which we perceive you don't like at all, but which we privately confess in your ear is one of the greatest treats we obtain from a visit to the opera.[12]

Not only was he a lover of opera, but of chamber music, symphonies, and soloists as well. Huneker recorded seeing Whitman often at the Carl Gaertner string quartet concerts;[13] and Whitman himself spoke of the opera he heard while working briefly in New Orleans, which had one of the finest operatic seasons in nineteenth century America. Among the great vocalists of the day that he preferred were Grisi, the tenor Mario, the baritone Badiali, whom he called the "finest in the world," the bass Marini, the tenor Bettini, and Jenny Lind and Adelina Patti, neither of whom, however, had thrilled him as much as Alboni.[14]

Of Marietta Alboni he wrote significantly that she had "touched and inspired him" and that she was the "sister of loftiest Gods."[15] He heard her every time she came to New York and said that her "glorious, golden, soul-smiting voice" had so "deeply penetrated" his spirit that he had never been able to forget her tones and never wished to "since they had been to him the unconscious inspiration of much poetry."[16] He wrote further that he heard the lines of his verse in her voice. His indebtedness to her, which was obviously great, gives us some insight into his creative processes. Holloway recorded that Whitman often used to write his verses with Jeff playing in another room, and claimed that Whitman could hear a concert and be "haunted by it for a month."[17] Moreover, he said Whitman wrote many poems "to the inspiration, if not the tune of the opera"—a most significant statement.[18]

Of the operas he heard Whitman wrote:

> I heard, these years, well render'd, all the Italian and other operas in vogue, "Sonnambula," "The Puritans," "Der Freischutz," "Huguenots," "Fille d'Regiment," "Faust," "Etoile du Nord," "Poliuto," and others. Verdi's "Ernani," "Rigoletto," and "Trovatore," with Donnizetti's "Lucia" or "Favorita" or "Lucrezia," and Auber's "Messaniello," or Rossini's "William Tell" and "Gazza Ladra" were among my special enjoyments. . . .[19]

Whitman's interest in opera was obviously not a passive one. He read carefully the librettos themselves, and their impassioned human quality had much effect upon him. He wrote:

> For theatricals in literature and doubtless upon me personally, including opera, have been of course serious factors. . . . *I was fed and bred under the Italian dispensation, and absorb'd it, and doubtless show it.*
>
> As a young fellow, when possible I always studied a play or libretto quite carefully over, by myself, (sometimes twice through) before seeing it on the stage. . . . We had some fine music those days. . . .[20]

There are unmistakable signs in Whitman's verse that he had absorbed much of this "Italian dispensation." Italian opera is characterized chiefly by its emphasis upon *bel canto* and the display of artistry—no matter how lengthy—that the singer is capable of.

The Italian libretto itself is often poor enough, and at times plot and background music only make-shift, but the solo arias are masterpieces of technical and emotional skill.

On the other hand, the "Italian dispensation" is a highly dramatic one, and high tragedy is intimately associated with Italian opera. The vibrant emotions of hate, love, grief, and despair nowhere seethe so violently as in Italian music. Always there is the *grande passione,* the heroic type, and the emphasis upon the beautiful voice. This pride, this emotional warmth can be traced in many of the poems that make up *Leaves of Grass.*

Whitman was also a great lover of chamber music and wrote of a string performance of the Beethoven Septette:

Never did music more sink into and soothe and fill me—never so prove its *soul-rousing power, its impossibility of statement.* . . . I was carried away, *seeing, absorbing many wonders.* . . . *I allow'd myself, as I sometimes do, to wander out of myself.* . . .[21]

In writing of this Septette he compared "Nature laughing on a hillside in the sunshine" to a "horn sounding through the tangle of the forest and the dying echoes; soothing floating of waves"

but presently rising in surges, angrily lashing, muttering, heavy; piercing peals of laughter for interstices; now and then weird, as Nature herself is in certain moods—but mainly spontaneous, easy, careless. . . . The conceit came to me of a copious grove of singing birds, and in their midst a simple harmonic duo, two human souls, steadily asserting their own pensiveness, joyousness. . . .[22]

However his tastes were eclectic and he wrote of martial music that it "made my heart jump,"[23] and said of a simple performance given in a hospital for the wounded soldiers: "I received as much pleasure under the circumstances . . . as I have had from the best Italian compositions, express'd by world famous performers."[24] He knew the music of the fashionable ball and spoke familiarly of the polka and the waltz.[25] He was a lover of the minstrel show and he said that he often saw Jim Rice, the original Jim Crow. He enjoyed a good balladist like Edwin as much as a first rate singer, and his enjoyment of bands and popular music was great. However, his closest association with music came through the human voice, and he loved to sound a sonorous phrase himself. He wrote:

I sometimes wonder whether the best philosophy and poetry, or something like the best, after all these centuries, perhaps waits to be rous'd out yet, or suggested, by the perfect physiological human voice.

. . . Beyond all other power and beauty there is something in the quality and power of the right voice (*timbre* the schools call it) that touches
the soul, the abysms. . . .[26]

He wrote many tributes too to the power of pure rhetoric since
it, as well as music, depends upon the power of the human voice.
Most of his tributes to great actors and actresses praise the quality
of their voices as well as their acting. He lived in a day when
eloquence and oratory roused men's souls, and he himself was
apparently something of a student of the human voice, for it is
said his own power in delivering lectures was "magnetic," and
certainly his written lines have a round oracular flavor.[27]
Among the many sounds to which Whitman was responsive, the
sounds of nature take precedence over all others. Most of his prose
writings are dotted with references to the music of nature. Sometimes even a great symphonic work or operatic work sounded so
like some aspect of nature to him that he compared the music to
nature, much as Poe did in his verse. On the other hand, his discussions of bird calls and the various insect and animal sounds drew
heavily upon the vocabulary and general knowledge of the true
music-lover. The chief sound in nature that inspired Whitman
was the song of the bird, and more particularly that of the hermit
thrush. His sense of hearing was unusually keen to musical sounds
and he wrote:

. . . and ever, mix'd with the dual notes of the quail, the soughing of
the wind through some near-by pines.
As I rise for return, I linger long to a delicious song - epilogue (is it
the hermit thrush?) from . . . off there in the swamp, repeated leisurely
and pensively over and over again. . . .[28]

He speaks of the "quawk [*sic*] of some pond duck," "the song
of the first cicadas," and he said the sound of the morning and
evening warble of the birds was "delightful." His description of
the sound of the locust might be compared to that of the pronouncements of music critics on a singer:

A single locust is now heard . . . a long whirring, continued, quite
loud noise graded in distinct whirls, or swinging circles, increasing in
strength and rapidity up to a certain point, and then a fluttering, quietly tapering fall. Each strain is continued from one to two minutes.
The locust song is very appropriate to the scene — gushes, has meaning,
is masculine, is like some fine old wine, not sweet but far better than
sweet. . . . Let me say more about the song of the locust, even to repe-

tition; a long, chromatic tremulous crescendo, like a brass disk whirling round and round, emitting wave after wave of notes, beginning with a certain moderate beat or measure, rapidly increasing in speed and emphasis, reaching a point of great energy and significance, and then quickly and gracefully dropping down and out. Not the melody of the singing-bird — far from it; the common musician might think without melody, but surely having to the finer ear a harmony of its own. . . .[29]

Passages like these, his numerous other prose references, as well as his essay on "A Visit to the Opera," unpublished, prove that Whitman's disavowal of musical knowledge is in line with his disavowal of other kinds of knowledge: a form of modesty that he affected or felt when speaking to his friends. He said of music that it was an art of which "he knew nothing" though "it served him as a sounding background for his pencilled improvisations,"[30] a statement of great significance.

He wrote further of the "wild flageolet-note of the quail," of the "roulading of the russet-back thrushes," of the "accompaniment" of autumn leaves, dry air and crows cawing, of the "liquid mystic theme of the sea" with "rustle and hiss and foam, and many a thump as of low bass drums." He wrote constantly of

the blue birds, grass birds and robins . . . the noisy, *vocal*, natural *concert*. For *undertones*, a neighboring wood-pecker tapping his tree, and the distant *clarion* of chanticleer. . . .[31]

He loved the drone of bees, and suggested that their "musical drone" serve as the background in some musical composition—a bumble-bee symphony.[32] This responsiveness to the music in nature is so keen and so passionate that it can only be called the response of a lyrical poet. There is a raptness, an almost unbelieving wonder in Whitman's worship of nature.

Just as Poe allied music to supernal beauty, conceived of it as the most perfect expression of man in his attempts to achieve immortal, divine, and spiritual loveliness, Whitman saw in music an alliance with poetry which expressed the *divinity* of all nature. Looking on a winter day, for instance, "grim—yet so delicate-looking, so spiritual—striking emotional, impalpable depths, subtler than all the poems, paintings, music, I have ever read, seen, heard," he added an interesting comment as to why nature took on this subtle quality of the spiritual: "yet let me be fair, perhaps, it is because I have read those poems and heard that music."[33]

And he wrote, after the fashion of other poets of his century: ". . . all words are mean before the language of true music."[34]

Unfortunately, Whitman's poetic creed did not permit him to *say* how much music influenced his verse. His life-long purpose in this "experimental" verse,[35] the *Leaves of Grass,* was to be *suggestive,* and to delete from it all of the purely *personal* experiences that the common man might not have had. But that he himself knew he owed the inspiration of his style to music there can be no doubt, for late in life he wrote that he would always remember his indebtedness to Mme. Alboni and to Verdi. And Rooney wrote, in "Whitman and Alboni":

Those readers who possess a musical mind cannot fail to have been struck by a peculiar characteristic of some of Whitman's grandest poems. It is apparently but only superficially a contradiction. A fault that critics have most insisted upon in his poetry is its independence of, or contempt for the canons of musico-poetical art, in its intermittent irregular structure and flow. Yet the characteristic alluded to which always impressed me as inherent in these — especially in some of the Pindaric "Drum Taps" — was a sense of strong rhythmical, pulsing musical power. I had always accounted to myself for this contradiction, because I . . . supposed this poet's nature to be a large one, including many opposite qualities; and that . . . a great poet's mind could not be thought of as an imperfect, one-sided one, devoid of any comprehension of or feeling for musical art. I knew too that Whitman was a sincere lover of Art. . . . Therefore on a certain Olympian day . . . I told Whitman of my belief in the presence of an overwhelming musical pulse behind an apparent absence of musical form in his poems. *He answered with as much sincerity as geniality that it would indeed be strange if there were no music in the heart of his poems, for more of these were actually inspired by music than he himself could remember . . . enthusiastic moods awakened by music in the streets, the theatre, and in private, had originated poems apparently far removed from the scenes and feelings of the moment. . . .*[36]

I think there is little doubt that the unusually fine musical background which Whitman as a listener possessed, coupled with evidence that there was musical talent in his family, had a definite effect upon the style of *Leaves of Grass.* He called his poems "songs," "hymns," and "chants" and spoke of himself constantly as a singer, much as Beethoven spoke of himself as a poet. Music is the only art that he consistently makes references to in his poetry, and his constant devotion to this art, by his own statements, acted as a yeast to the poetry of *Leaves of Grass.* Music was the only art

Whitman acknowledged to be greater than poetry, and it was natural in seeking some parallel to amplify the meaning of the *Leaves* that he should turn to music. He wrote of listening to a song:

Listen. Pure and vast, that voice now rises, as on clouds, to the heaven where it claims audience. . . . Ah, welcome that I know not the mere language of the earthly words in which the melody is embodied; *as all words are mean before the language of true music.*[37]

The most serious indictment of Whitman's poetic genius was once based upon his apparent lack of concern for form of any kind either in individual stanzas or in whole poems. More recently, Whitman scholars, notably Schyberg, have dealt with the various revisions of *Leaves of Grass* and have found that the poet made regular efforts to shape his expanding book. Unfortunately the key or clue to the lines upon which *Leaves of Grass* was repeatedly reorganized remains undiscovered. Most critics today have concluded that Whitman was following the pattern of his life in the over-all organization of the *Leaves,* and therefore that the form of the book is, in that sense, organic. I assume these critics to be, on the whole, correct; however, a truly organic arrangement of a man's life in poetry would be a chronological one. In *Leaves of Grass* there are some conspicuous lapses from that arrangement which suggest other principles at work.

There is, for instance, an interesting underlying linkage of musical terms in *Leaves of Grass.* These terms appear most obviously in the earliest and the last poems Whitman wrote, and indicate to the observant reader that the poet actually was seeking to bind his poems together somehow after the fashion of music, and, more particularly, after the fashion of symphonic or operatic music in its instrumental as well as vocal phases. Within certain of the poems, the poet so strongly stresses the importance of music that he quite astonishes the reader with his purpose. Though there are some exceptions, on the whole these earlier musical references are suggestive, and the later ones more detailed and exact, as though the poet desired the reader suddenly to understand the basis of organization of the poem. In addition, certain of the poems reveal a lyricism and an emotional power and fervor undoubtedly dependent upon music.

Proof for theses such as these must come from an analysis of this carefully synthesized poem or book of poems. To get at Whitman's theory of organization is more difficult than one might suppose it to be. Here form—if it can be called that—is so dependent upon content that it is impossible to speak of the one except in terms of the other. It is therefore helpful that the poet's creative process itself comes under examination, and in such an examination, Whitman's notebooks are of great value.

Whitman notebooks at Duke University, which have been recently printed, provide some interesting evidence that poetic forms were of interest to Whitman and that these forms rest heavily upon music.

Whitman's notebook collections of admonitions to himself and articles of interest which he had cut from newspapers often contain ideas for poems. In one volume three single columns of words are revealing:

poemet	warble	
leaf	carol	
chant	cavatina	
song	ballad	
poem	thought	melange
psalm	caprices	canticle
hymn	fantasia	songlet
	capricia	

sonnet-trio
sonnet-quinto
sonnet-duo   [38]

Here the poet struggles with the names and forms of the poem to be written and runs through those suggested by music. In another catalogue appears this notation in a big scrawling hand with the familiar finger pointing to indicate that Whitman wanted particularly to remember it:

Theme for poem
An Opera
an opera in a Dream
Different singers and characters
the suggestions, associations
Some old song? hymn? Rock me to Sleep Mother?
With its memories, associations
of where I last heard it
in Hospital
Some typical appropriate? *tune*
or? hymn—or? something played by the band (some Dirge or? opera)
passage or Dead March

Calling up the whole Dead of the War
The March in last act of *La Gazza Ladra* [39]
verso
One stanza must describe a strong triumphal
instrumental and
vocal *chorus*
as of *triumphant man*—triumphant
over temptation and all weakness. . . . [40]

It seems that the key to Whitman's creative technique lies in a search for a musical analogy. The above references reveal that the finished poem was undoubtedly "Drum Taps"—but it also settles forever the question of whether or not any of Whitman's poems *could* have been written with specific music in mind. In his search for this music, Whitman turns over various familiar hymns, band music, and songs, and seems to decide upon the dead march in the last act of *La Gazza Ladra*.

In addition, the writing on the reverse side indicates that in a given stanza Whitman planned exactly for the effect of music—that the many voiced polyphonic, or, if you will, *symphonic* cast of his verse has some actual musical basis. He *did* apparently describe vocal and instrumental choruses and knew well the technique of so doing.

There are several scraps of ideas—lists to be left to other poets of ideas to be explored, all involving music.

National hymns, real American music. . . .
Songs (written from the voice) (with notes)
with dramatic action, as for instance a song
describing the cutting down of the tree by wood-cutters in
    the west
the pleasures of a wood-life, etc. . . . [41]

In yet another place is found a notation:

Poem of Musicians
Tenor, soprano, baritone, basso. . . . [42]

And the crossing out of *poem* and the substitution of *song* in each of these lists indicates what he thought the nature of poetic expression was:

Song of Songs
The (poem) song of Democracy
of the Future—the (Poem) Song of Women—

(Poem) Song of Young men—the (Poem) Song of Life
here not elsewhere—the (poem) Song. . . .[43]

In deleting the word *poem,* Whitman also suggests how emotional
the power of the writing is to be. A poem is one thing, a song
quite another. His songs have a pulsing life in them too passionate to be titled poems. In his last work he puzzled over various
titles—all trial titles for "Sands at Seventy."

> Carols Closing Sixty-nine
> Carols at Candle-light
> Carols at entering Seventy[44]

Another of his more interesting listings follows:

Poet, bard, minstrel
Songster and Songstress
Rhymester
Versifier
Jongleur
Troubadour
Singer
mystic-singer
ballad-
Prose-
froth-
thrift-
moral-   cant-singer
song-   head-
droll-   heart-
fable-   [Penciled in:]
love-   The singers do not live long—only the poet
Wisdom-   lives long. The singers are—and in most ages
sea-   plentiful but vast and rare is the day and
wit-   divine the place that brings forth a poet. Not
Passion- every century, not every five centuries contains
parlor-   such a day, nor does every nation hold such a
echo-   place. These may have terrible names, but the
golden-   name of each of them is one of the singers.
silver-   The name of poet is reserved until it is taken by
(Burns, born 1759, died 1795 aged 36)[45]

He wrote in another place of:

Religious Canticles—"Hymns of ecstasy and religious fervor"
An after-thought of Two
and After-Songs

Banjo-song
Of Death—the poem of Immortality and Ensemble.[46]

Again it should be obvious that Whitman's thoughts—the
thoughts of an old man often concerned with death—were still running along musical lines. Even the rather amusing lengthy list on
the left, straining to include all phases of life, is revelatory. But
there are still other passages in the Notebooks that are worthy
of notice.

Sometimes even the clippings that Whitman kept in his Notebooks, and annotated, offer evidence of his genuine concern for
musical form. For instance, an article from the *American Messen-
ger* entitled "The Unity of the Bible" has the following passage,
underlined by Whitman, which is of great importance.

As in Beethoven's matchless music there runs *one idea, worked out
through all the changes of measure and of key, now almost hidden,
now breaking out in rich natural melody, whispered in the treble,
murmured in the bass, dimly suggested in the prelude,* but growing
clearer as the work proceeds, winding back until it ends in the key in
which it began, and closes in triumphant harmony, so through the
whole Bible, there runs one great idea—man's ruin by sin, and his
redemption by grace, in a word, Jesus Christ, the Saviour. . . .[47]

Before this clipping and its underlined passages, Whitman himself
wrote this note:

My poems, when complete, should be a Unity in the same sense that
the earth is, or that the human body or that a perfect musical composition is. . . .[48]

And at another point he reminded himself that his poems
should be

Hasting, urging, restless,—no flagging, not even in the "thoughts"
or meditations . . . to be perceived with the same perception that enjoys music . . . free and luxuriant. . . . As in Beethoven's.[49]

Here, then, is the chief explanation for the turbulent movement
in Whitman's verse, its pushing forward, its sense of unimpeded
flow. Characteristics of his verse were to be deliberately thought
out and deliberately followed. His poetry is "to be perceived with
the same perception that enjoys music."[50] It is to treat of the
"idea" after the fashion of the symphony, and it is to be unified
in that same sense. The great idea is to be suggested through the
prelude, (a term which is used interchangeably in Whitman's

verse with the word overture—each suggesting the setting of a mood for a long work to follow). In the case of the symphony, most of the themes to be used later are suggested in the prelude; in opera, the overture is a kind of medley of all the arias and entr'acte music that will be fully developed later.

Whitman's mention here of Beethoven and his music is significant, for Beethoven's name was magic to the nineteenth century. It was Beethoven who was truly the first great romantic composer, and his Third Symphony, with its announcement of freedom for music, thrilled poets as well as musicians throughout the western world. The fact that Whitman made reference to Beethoven's music, and almost to the specific familiar musical composition, is revealing. Why he drew a line through the name can only be conjectured. Perhaps he did not want so specific a reference to appear in his notebooks; perhaps no single composition came to mind as a parallel to the *Leaves of Grass*. On the other hand, perhaps one did, and he felt that the mention of it would limit *Leaves of Grass* in the minds of future readers if they tried to fit an exact parallel to his poetry.

At any rate, there is an interesting relationship between the work of Whitman and Beethoven which merits attention. Both men were unusually fond of nature and responsive to it. Both were expressing fully and freely for the first time in each medium the human personality apart from the traditional art forms into which such expression had previously been cast. Beethoven announced a freedom for music in his over-riding of sonata form, in his lengthening of the symphony and handling of the phrase, and in his method of treating themes freely and organically—a freedom which has given rise to the term "germ motif" to suggest the "growth" pattern of themes in his symphonies. It was Beethoven who first celebrated in music the heroic in man, and who in music consciously dealt with the problem of man's destiny. It was Beethoven who celebrated democracy and the common man in the "Eroica" and the "Fate Symphonies," and who celebrated in his Ninth "Choral" Symphony the triumph of man and the triumph of good (or joy) on earth. It was Beethoven who first made the symphony an organic whole, a unity to which the movements were but passing moods in a larger whole. It was Beethoven who discarded the elegance, the polish, the suavity of the suite and the sonata and gave emotional depth and color to the symphony. And it was his work which most fully inspired the nineteenth century poets— just as he had found inspiration in Shakespeare. Beethoven's was the seminal musical mind of the century, and it is no accident that Whitman mentions his name. No other musical figure placed so much emphasis upon the individual—and, through him, all humanity—as Beethoven did. The overpowering sense of sincerity in Beethoven's music has a speaking quality to it. Whitman's poems seem often but the verbalizing, the pencilled improvisations of Beethoven's music.

All that was grandiose and heroic found its way into Beethoven's music—but his favorite themes, like Whitman's, were nature, fate, war, death, and the triumph of the individual.

His reforms of the symphony were numerous—and all organic. He made the second movement of the lengthened symphony a movement of tragic significance, often a funeral march. On the other hand he lightened the third movement. Most important of all was the unity of tone in a Beethoven symphony, a unity maintained through joy and sadness, through mighty struggles of the soul and spirit. Contrasting moods were evident in the various movements of his symphonies, but through all ran the undertone, the musical character he established.

The most interesting parallels that Whitman's poetry has to Beethoven's music are the long poetic lines, made up of various separate themes, their treatment, and their organization. These long lines differ as much from lines of earlier poets as Beethoven's "free" musical structure differed from the structure of earlier musicians. Faner, in his dissertation, wrote astutely of them:

Today, understanding Whitman's method and his desire for organic structure, readers can detect these themes and derive pleasure from the way they are combined. Perhaps, however, even for today's readers, the poem might have been improved if the themes had not been blended quite so completely, if there were more contrast between them, for example. . . .
With all of its revisions, the poem remains what it was at first, a fabric of themes woven and interwoven . . . they are simply ideas which the poet presents, temporarily abandons for other ideas, and returns to for development. Thus an idea is not exhaustively treated upon its first appearance. . . . It was Whitman's plan to give the reader a sense of the growth of an idea, its organic expansion, by allowing it to develop beside and in the midst of other ideas. Each time it reappears it has taken on new meanings and significance. As all the ideas are woven together and blended, all seem to grow and, in the mind of a sensitive reader, do grow. Occasionally the theme will be clearly stated, only, at its next appearance, to be exemplified and not stated at all.[50]

The parallel here to music is rather obvious, especially to music such as Beethoven wrote. The blending of themes, the appearance, reappearance, and fuller development of them is typical of all romantic music, first "freed" by Beethoven from strictly defined patterns. Of the technique that Beethoven developed Sir Hubert H. Parry wrote:

Before Beethoven, the development of a long work was based upon antithesis of distinct tunes and concrete lumps of subject representing separate organisms, either merely in juxtaposition, or loosely connected by more or less empty passages. There were ideas indeed, but ideas limited and confined by the supposed necessities of the structure of which they formed a part. But what Beethoven seems to have aimed at was the expansion of the term "Idea" from the isolated subject to the complete whole; so that instead of the subjects being separate, though compatible items, *the whole movement, or even the whole work, should be the complete and uniform organism which represented in its entirety a new meaning of the word "idea" of which the subjects, in their close connection and inseparable affinities, were subordinate limbs.*[52]

This sounds startlingly like what Faner wrote of Whitman; yet there is scarcely any connection made by Faner between the two men, and it is doubtful that he had ever read Parry on Beethoven. Parry wrote further of Beethoven's handling of themes as

. . . so continuous and unified that we are barely conscious of the passage from one theme to another. Sometimes the structure is so closely knit that even the searching eye of an analyst is defied.[53]

This quality of diffuse and merging themes was the ear-mark of the Beethoven "germ" symphony, and thus of almost all the later symphonies of Brahms as well as the operas of Wagner. Whitman's verse lines in this respect are "symphonic"—that is, they follow the lines of the symphony in merging and blending ideas—in treating them "suggestively."

Any reader of Whitman's verse will recall the merging of one idea into another. Sections 5, 6, and 7, for instance, of "Song of Myself" well illustrate the point, though no better than other sections that might be chosen.

The Whitman themes, variously recorded as themes of love, religious awareness, death, sex, nature, democracy, positivism and personality, appear at almost any point in the poem, and move generally with a rush and impetuosity closely associated with music.

It is the fusion of these many themes, together with the large and grandiose aims of Whitman's verse, which makes *Leaves of Grass* seem symphonic. Whitman likened his themes to the mighty rush and undulation of the sea, just as Beethoven's music first suggested strongly the same parallel. To watch the interweaving of these suggestive and frequently viable themes in his verse is to be aware of a certain polyphony—a many-voiced effect unknown before to American poetry. And the lines, like waves of music, have their successions, their recessions, and their repetitiveness of ideas.

These ideas, according to their strength, their frequency of repetition, and their significance in the poem as a whole, become themes. And as the reader becomes conscious of them as themes, he awaits the various treatments which signify that the theme is about to be introduced. Oftentimes Whitman uses what might be termed a leitmotif—a symbolical suggestion of certain themes. Ideas such as democracy have many voices.

These ideas (themes) form symphonic cadence. As themes they are handled as a composer would handle them, and the lines form poetic divisions (stanzas) much as romantic music reaches sectional climaxes and conclusions. These themes are repetitive and suggestive, and gain in treatment from amplification, diminution, and inversion just as musical themes do.

Amplification of a theme is Whitman's chief technique in *Leaves of Grass*. The same theme appears in many voices—like his conception of democracy. Never does Whitman say, specifically, "this is what I believe democracy to be." By all-inclusive gestures, he creates the effect of the emotion aroused in free men permitted life in a free land. This repetitive tossing about of a Whitman theme (idea) is a musical device and arouses an emotional response in the reader (hearer) akin to music. There is also a "cyclical" unity in a Whitman theme. The theme sometimes appears near the end, in a different form, as often as at the beginning. Actually the unity of *Leaves of Grass* is the same as that of the symphony, no longer dependent upon pretty melodies but fascinating in its grandeur and its *treatment*. In Whitman's poems much of our interest lies in *how* next he will say to us a familiar thing.

Sculley Bradley felt that Whitman's verse took its "organic" structure from the German romantics, though he was unable to say just how Whitman absorbed it. Coleridge and Emerson were conscious of this same principle, and both absorbed much of the

German tradition. That Whitman's organic structure in poetry originated in the music of Beethoven has hardly been recognized. E. T. A. Hoffmann, in a criticism of Beethoven, wrote of the apparent unity of a Beethoven work:

> No doubt the whole rushes like an ingenious rhapsody past many a man, but the soul of each thoughtful listener is assuredly stirred, deeply and intimately. . . . The internal structure of the movements, their execution, their instrumentation . . . everything contributes to a single end; above all it is the intimate interrelationship among the themes that engineers that unity which alone has the power to hold the listener firmly in a single mood.[54]

Hoffmann was one of the first of many German and English poets who fell under the sway of Beethoven's music.

In the respects mentioned above, Whitman's verse seemed indebted to the larger instrumental forms such as the symphony and quartet, rather than the vocal form of opera, though he often employed in his verse the exact terminology of opera. Whitman and Beethoven were both iconoclasts striving for a sincerity of expression unknown before. Both were suggestive, mystical and indefinite in their creative ideas. Both had too much to express to use the simpler forms of their day. Each came to slow creative maturation. Each stamped upon his art an image of the heroic, the grandiose, and the positive. Each came late in life to a spiritual awareness which led Whitman to prophesy that his work would be more understandable to later generations, just as Beethoven had foretold the same about his work. Whitman wrote:

> . . . a poem which more familiarly addresses those who will, in future ages understand me,
> (Because I write with reference to being far better understood then than I can possibly be now. . . .)[55]

There is certainly some unrecognized—or deliberately ignored—debt or parallel to the music of Beethoven in Whitman's verse.

In addition to the expansiveness and omniscience of the poet's point of view which marks *Leaves of Grass* as symphonic, the feeling or impression that flows from the lines of any single poem in the volume is that ideas or suggestions are undergoing a treatment similar to themes in music. It was Whitman's particular genius to sound in verse a unity through variety, an effect that Emerson understood and considered the very essence of music.

Whitman's verse parallels music not only in the treatment of the line and the phrase, but also in the "stanza" and its formation. His verses, for this reason, are frequently referred to as symphonic or polyphonic. It is this many-themed quality that accounts for the success with which the poet is able to merge ideas from line to line, since any single theme in a line can be seized upon and treated in the following lines. Actually it is an error to confuse a symphonic line with a polyphonic one, though literary critics have chosen to use the terms indiscriminately. Musically, polyphony indicates a series of independent voices moving simultaneously in melodic lines that may at times intersect but never merge. The symphonic line carries also the idea of many sounds or voices, but these are inter-related either through melody or harmony and sometimes through both. More often the symphonic line is unified in melody—that is, all voices or instruments are contributing to a single effect. In one sense—the largest sense—the whole of *Leaves of Grass* might be considered thematically polyphonic, since its chief themes are often "running" separately; yet since all these ideas merge in the over-all hearing to one mighty theme—the triumph of the individual—*Leaves of Grass* may be rightly termed only symphonic.

Whitman's symphonic treatment of voices can be seen in the familiar catalogue system wherein the poet has a single idea which he expands through many facets of human experience, much as in the symphony where a musical theme is first plainly stated and then treated by the various instruments, taking on the colors and timbre of those instruments, though with few melodic and rhythmic changes. In "Song of Myself" Whitman treats symphonically (that is, he develops his ideas by stock means), rising to a not inconsiderable climax, the demonstration of the truth that all men share in the positive forces of life, a demonstration which explores as many facets of human experience in fifty-two sections as the poet can think of.

The development section of a Whitman poem usually follows this pattern, with lines like:

> I am of old and young, of the foolish as much as the wise . . .
> Maternal as well as paternal, a child as well as a man. . . .

These are obvious parallelisms, but they become much more than that. In the working out of the poem, these many expressions, these references to the soul as well as the body—to the one as much as to the other—fuse in the reader's memory and are remembered voices. Though all play the same theme, their ways of sounding that experience differ.

Polyphony in verse, on the other hand, is seldom achieved without considerable creaking of machinery and much loss of artistic flavor. Whitman's remarkable poem, "When Lilacs Last in the Dooryard Bloom'd," is an excellent example of three voices of the senses—the song of the thrush, the light of the star, and the fragrance of the lilac—running polyphonically. These three voices are thought of as moving continuously throughout the poem, even though the poet turns to them separately only one at a time. Insofar as they are all symbols of death triumphant, they are symphonic.

In the long, lazy, seemingly loose Whitman poetic line is found a further parallel to the symphony, for this line is no more the taut song line of earlier poetry than the line of the symphony is that of the song. Words in verse form phrases just as notes do in music. So it was that in music the verse of the ordinary song line rhymed at given points, usually on the second and fourth lines, or, to speak musically, at the close and half close where notes were sounded in a common harmony. At any rate, it was the *end* of the song line that was of importance. Not so with the new Whitman verse line and the symphony. The memorable quality of the symphony is its introduction at once of musical phrases that will be treated and repeated throughout the rest of the movement. The emphasis is upon the beginning of the musical line and not the close. So Whitman's lines depend upon a "germ" idea immediately stated—and take their final effect from the treatment of that idea.

> I celebrate myself, and sing myself,
> And what I assume you shall assume,
> For every atom belonging to me as good belongs to you. . . .

In addition it is the repetition of *initial* words and phrases that give unity to the Whitman verse lines: the repetition of "O," "And," "With," "As," etc.

In Whitman's verse there is no definition to the ear of the end of a line every four measures or four feet. His technique differs as widely from the song-form of Poe's verse as it would be possible to imagine, and he wrote:

I know well enough . . . especially in verbal melody and all the conventional technique of poetry, not only the divine works that today stand ahead in the world's reading but dozens more, transcend . . . all I have done, or could do.[56]

But this realization on his part did not prevent his verse from being musical. Just what the appeal of music is has never been recorded. That it appeals primarily to the emotions, but also to the mind, is certain. Of all forms of music, because it is the most indefinite and cannot tell a story as opera or the song does, instrumental music speaks more directly to our thoughts, and pleases by a discourse with some unidentifiable phase of our being. In the same fashion Whitman's verse rolls over the reader in torrents of emotion that are elusive, not capable of being fully identified, and moves with a rapidity akin to thought. This technique of Whitman's is almost an externalization of the stream-of-consciousness approach, though it differs in that the artist here is consciously creating an effect upon the reader. Whitman hoped that his poem would have one end: to awaken mankind to the heroic and the positive aspects of life. He wrote of music:

> All music is what awakes from you when you are reminded by the instruments,
> It is not the violins and the cornets, it is not the oboe, nor the beating drums, nor the score of the baritone singer singing his sweet romanza, nor that of the men's chorus, nor that of the women's chorus,
> It is nearer and farther than they.[57]

And so no exploration of the Whitman phrase, the verse line, even the form of the poem will explain the music of the *Leaves*, but knowing that he was consciously and unconsciously imitating music helps in a fuller understanding of the style of the *Leaves*.

During the last twenty years of his life, Whitman busied himself with the re-arrangement of the poems that make up *Leaves of Grass*, though there is some evidence as early as 1860 that the poet was concerned with the forming of the book. "Song of Myself," which dominated the first edition, remained the dominant poem in the final one, despite additions like "Drum Taps." The "Inscription" grew and changed. "From Paumanok Starting" acquired a more logical position. By 1876 the 1860 poems had been rearranged and divided into "Sea Drift" and the more personal "Children of Adam" and "Calamus" poems by the poems from the 1856 edition. The later poems—those written after 1871—on the whole, developed the "Whispers of Heavenly Death" motif in

"Passage to India" and "The Mystic Trumpeter." It is true that Whitman wrote in his later days several poems that were fit for the mood and tenor of the earlier sections—poems like "Birds of Passage" (1881) and "Song of the Redwood Tree" (1873)—but most of his concern after 1871 was in the shifting about of some of the poems, the number having mushroomed from the original twelve to three hundred.

By 1871, when most of the great poems had already been written and only the parting songs in various forms were to be added, not only had the music of Beethoven fully penetrated American concert halls, but the music of Wagner and Brahms was also familiar. Whitman, who was prematurely aging, so that in his fifties he seemed already an old man, continued to find his chief pleasure in music. In order not to speak in the manner of extravagances— of "firsts" and "most importants" in influence, it may simply be said here that music had its effect upon the form that the book finally took. Operatic terms and references appear mixed with those of the symphony. The style of a given poem is sometimes that of the aria but, by and large, the symphony with its less defined lines, its different movements, its more organic growth, and its more direct appeal to the emotions resting upon a breadth of ideas (or sounds) seems a more logical parallel to the whole poem. But Whitman moved freely from instrumental terms to vocal ones in the poem.

Since the form of the symphony itself developed out of the prelude or overture, with its many suggested themes treated later fully in the opera, it is understandable that the "Inscriptions" should be thought of either as overture or as "prelude" to the rest of the *Leaves of Grass*. Such was certainly Whitman's intention. Through the "Inscriptions" are suggested themes which are worked out with singular energy later in the poem. Although the "Inscriptions" *prelude* the poetic text, they were added *after* the early editions and apparently placed at the beginning just because Whitman had some idea of suggesting, after the pattern of music, the ideas to be treated more fully later. The two long poems, "From Paumanok Starting" and "Song of Myself," are both earlier works than most of the other "Inscriptions." They were finally chosen to follow the "Inscriptions" because Whitman saw, as the structure of the poem kept changing, that the personal element which is strongly struck in "Song of Myself" was the key to the poem as a whole. For *Leaves of Grass* comes to veer in its implications with the changing circumstances and the life of the poet, and Whitman was wise to let the whole of his life, with its loss of buoyancy and its recovery of it in a firmer, deeper sense, write itself out.[58] "From Paumanok Starting" was not part of the 1855 edition, having first appeared in 1860, but the twenty-four "Inscriptions" which later preceded it point to it as the first of the actual chants.

Even a glance at the "Inscriptions" reveals the substance of all later themes: "One's Self I Sing," "Eidolons," "I Hear America Singing," etc. There is even an inscription "To a Certain Cantatrice"—obviously a reference to the influence of Marietta Alboni.

"From Paumanok Starting" is an introduction—the first poem to sound the true symphonic strain. Like an overture, it sings a portion of the themes to be treated and sets the tone of the poem. Its position is logical since the poet must account for a little of what preceded the thirty-sixth year—and it makes clearer the pronouncements of "Song of Myself" by indicating the plan of them. The music in "From Paumanok Starting" is symphonic and many themed. It reaches a climax, a stretto in which the voices fuse in a choral climax. That this is the first of the actual poems is indicated, after the brief personal résumé, by the line:

> Solitary, singing in the West, I strike up for a New World.

The themes which are struck up are grand ones:

> Victory, union, faith, identity, time,
> The indissoluble compacts, riches, mystery,
> Eternal progress, the kosmos, and the modern reports.
> This then is life. . . .
> How curious! how real!
> Underfoot the divine soil, overhead the sun.[59]

The positivism in these beginning lines is borne out by the metre, which is a series of hard-struck words accented on the first syllable. In the same drum-beat fashion is sounded "Americanos! conquerors! marches humanitarian!" and then the promise of the chants and songs that the poet will sing. He will use best the themes of Love and Democracy and Religion, he says, themes which have been a part of the poetry of all ages:

> O such *themes*—equalities! O divine average!
> Warblings under the sun, usher'd as now, or at noon, or setting,
> *Strains musical* flowing through ages, now reaching hither,
> I take to your reckless and *composite chords*, add to them, and
> cheerfully pass them forward.[60]

And then, speaking of the larger purposes of the whole poem, he wrote:

> And I will *thread a thread through my poems* that time
> and events are compact,
> And that all the things of the universe are perfect
> miracles, each as profound as any.
>
> *I will not make poems with reference to parts*
> *But I will make poems, songs, thoughts, with reference to*
> *ensemble. . . .*[61]

And he says that for Democracy a throat "is now inflating itself and joyfully singing"—not a "dainty" song, but one from a "bearded sunburnt" man singing lustily. This first of all songs sung is the "Song of Myself." It is at one with the personal poems that make up the first section or movement of *Leaves of Grass*—a section that includes "Children of Adam" and "Calamus." But of them all it is the one most truly symphonic, the most positive, the most dynamic. He wrote:

> With music strong I come, with *my cornets and my drums,*
> I *play not marches* for accepted victors only, I *play marches*
> for conquered and slain persons. . . .
>
> I *beat and pound* for the dead,
> I *blow through my embouchures* my loudest and gayest for
> them. . . .[62]

In a long section (26) Whitman reveals his responsiveness to music, its almost physical effect upon him—the dizzying emotional response he feels, and how best of all is the chorus of grand opera. But this section is only a momentary interlude in the word symphony. The stream of on-rushing verbal music continues. There is a momentary breaking through of the human voice in the passage beginning

> Enough! enough! enough!
> Somehow I have been stunn'd! Stand back!

And again the poet launches himself into a catalogue of the forces which surround him. After a truly staggering working out of his ideas,[63] section 42 says:

> Now the *performer* launches his nerve, he has *pass'd his*
> *prelude on the reeds within.*
>
> *Easily written loose-finger'd chords—I feel the thrum* of your
> *climax and close.*

> *My head slues round on my neck,*
> *Music rolls, but not from the organ. . . .*[64]

There is a last briefer repetition of the mood that might well be called the "omnivorous." The mood changes a final time and the poet says: "It is time to explain myself—let us stand up."[65] This latter section is, of all the poem, the most abstract, the most appealing in its sweep, in its attempt to make understandable a soul, in its attempt to prove the immortality of the human by sheer positive assertion; and so excellently is the poem conceived that the reader is carried away with the rush and personal courage in it; he believes he is reading great truths. Nowhere else is the oracular and eloquent quality of Whitman's verse so apparent. The poet's treatment of nature is dignified and grand, never for a moment lapsing from a lofty and prophetic tone.

"Song of Myself" is a word symphony. Its constant harping upon certain strings, its repetitiveness, and its absoluteness all liken it to music. Its grappling with love, time, death, and immortality is also symphonic, and just as no composer can write a symphony of any merit if it is dull, qualified, faulty or false in tone, so the symphonic poet must be sincere and human almost to a fault. For all of the use of the "catalogue" system that Whitman makes, the rhythmic movement forward is unimpeded, and there is a sweep and finality in this that parallels the symphony. Never before had such a torrent of free emotion poured forth from a single verse; never had there been so heady and intoxicating a song as this. Whitman vented in a hundred places, by appeals to the senses, the guards of propriety, and the rush and fervor of that tapped emotional stream embarrassed many of his readers much as the music of Wagner once embarrassed music critics. Music rolled from a "living instrument," and the myriad emotions that are separately treated find their union in the omniscient poet of "Song of Myself."

The finale of "Song of Myself" is sounded in the rather quiet form of address made to death, the lifeless, and life itself, in which the poet points out the plan of life:

And whoever walks a furlong without sympathy walks to his own
  funeral drest in his shroud. . . .
And as to you Death, and you bitter hug of mortality, it is idle
  to try to alarm me. . . .
And as to you Corpse. . . .
And as to you Life. . . .

All of these lead to the lines:

> Do you see O my brothers and sisters?
> It is not chaos or death—it is form, union, plan—it is eternal life—
> it is Happiness.[66]

One of the strong assurances of artistic sensitivity in Whitman can be seen in the finales of the long poems. His device of sounding that ending by anticipation through a series of direct addresses, linked by a series of "ands" which force some conclusive statement, is excellent. The powerful feeling of the long poems is such that, like the symphony, a properly *extended* ending is necessary and is announced by repetitive phrasings which are the winding up or writing out of the pent-up emotion.

> The past and present wilt—I have fill'd them, emptied them,
> And proceed to fill my next fold of the future. . . .
> Will you speak before I am gone? will you prove already too late? . . .
>
> The last scud of day holds back for me,
> It flings my likeness after the rest. . . .
> It coaxes me to the vapor and the dusk.
>
> I depart as air, I shake my white locks. . . .
> I effuse my flesh in eddies, and drift it in lacy jags.
>
> I bequeath myself to the dirt. . . .
> If you want me again look for me under your boot-soles. . . .
>
> Missing me one place search another,
> I stop somewhere waiting for you.[67]

There is an appeal in Whitman's "Song of Myself" like that of the metaphysical poets—men who were also musical in their feeling, who drew upon nature for symbols, and who played with philosophical ideas with a two-fold approach. The finale of Whitman's song reveals this characteristic in large letters. The statement that "I too am untranslatable" reveals his larger kinship with nature and with music, with their indefinite and suggestive bigness. Incidentally, it should be noticed that the subsiding of the "Song" is only possible in instrumental compositions. Vocal art is more dramatic and cannot encompass it. The song has ended; here the symphony speaks, suggestively. This is what we find, then, of the form of the first poems. From the strategic placing of phrases like "I strike up for a new world," "marches humanitarian," and from the references to the "singing of the themes of all" there seems no doubt that Whitman was making strong musical analogies.

"Children of Adam," a personal analysis of a highly personal experience, departs somewhat—but necessarily so if the poet is to become the true singer for all humanity—from the symphonic, or the many-voiced. Since it is an extension of "Walt Whitman" the kosmos, it does belong in this first section or movement. Its theme is love—physical love—and the poem is an analysis of that love. The two poems—"To the Garden of the World," and "From Pent-up Aching Rivers"—act as preludes for the song proper, "I Sing the Body Electric." The themes to be dealt with are announced:

> . . . preluding,
> The love, the life of their bodies, meaning and being. . . .

and in "From Pent-up Aching Rivers":

> From what I am determin'd to make illustrious, even if I stand
>   sole among men,
> From *my own voice resonant.* . . .
> Singing the song of procreation,
> Singing the need of superb children. . . .
> *Overture lightly sounding the strain anticipating.* . . .[68]

The symphonic treatment again appears in "I Sing the Body Electric." And then, for the first time, a series of short poems after the fashion of "Inscriptions" serve as a "bridge passage" to the "Calamus" poems, important here only because they are part of the personal section of Whitman's life. Several of the poems have fairly regular stanza forms. The final "Calamus" poems reflect for the first time the minor mode—poems like "Of the Terrible Doubt of Appearances" and "Trickle Drops." The poet must turn now to fellow-humans for happiness, to comrades, to the singing of their songs; and sometimes even these fail:

> That may-be identity beyond the grave is a beautiful fable only,
> May-be the things I perceive, the animals, plants, men. . . .
> The skies of day and night . . . only apparitions, and the real
>   something has yet to be known. . . .[69]

"Trickle Drops" reveals the opening of his veins which

> Stain every page, stain every song I sing, every word I say, bloody
>   drops. . . .

and introduces a Whitman who is undergoing a kind of crucifixion, and his pages reveal how much it costs him. The "This mo-

ment yearning and thoughtful sitting alone" points up again his
loneliness, and in "Here the Frailest Leaves of Me" Whitman
shades and hides his thought which he no longer bravos forth but
permits to "expose me more than all my other poems." Nowhere
is one so well aware that who touches this touches a man. The
poet and prophet who sang in "Song of Myself" is revealed as
human. It is only through the love of comrades that he can sing;
he is no longer self-sufficient. The last of the 1860 poems is used
as introduction (as in a wider sense each in turn has been) to the
"Salut au Monde," the return of the poet, the prophet, the yea-
sayer, but this time singing of the World-brotherhood so carefully
suggested through "Calamus."

"Salut au Monde" announces the return of the strong influence
of music. It also announces a different cluster of poems, a new
movement, that relates to the universality of life and love in all
people. Musical passages like that of section three illustrate the
poet's ability to pile up lines like phrases in music, and also his
skill in concluding by an address to all people. The poem is
marked, as was "Song of Myself," by epanaphora and epanalepsis,

> I hear the Spanish dance with castanets in the chestnut shade,
>   to the rebeck and guitar,
> I hear continual echoes from the Thames,
> I hear fierce French liberty songs,
> I hear of the Italian boat-sculler *the musical recitative of old
>   poems.* . . .
>
> I hear the Coptic refrain toward sundown. . . .
> I hear the Arab muezzin calling from the top of the mosque,
> I hear the Christian priests at the altars of their churches,
>   I hear the responsive *bass* and *soprano.* . . .[70]

After this long catalogue of what the poet hears and sees, he
addresses all the people: "You, whoever you are." Of this cluster
of poems of occupations, expositions, etc., "Crossing Brooklyn
Ferry" is outstanding. The various themes merge in a symphony
of river, clouds, ships of Manhattan, brains, eyes, voices, flags,
cities, bodies, and the soul. The musical songs of the "Answerer"
are not to be missed.

> Time, always without break, indicates itself in parts,
> What always indicates the poet is the crowd of the pleasant
>   company of singers, and their words,
> The words of the singers are the hours or minutes of the light
>   or dark,

> But the words of the maker of poems are the general light and
> dark. . . .
> The singers do not beget, only the Poet begets,
> The singers are welcom'd, understood, appear often enough,
> but rare has the day been . . . of the maker of poems, the
> Answerer. . . .
>
> The singers of successive hours of centuries may have ostensible
> names, but the name of each of them is one of the singers,
> The name of each is, eye-singer, ear-singer, head-singer, sweet-
> singer, parlor-singer, love-singer, weird-singer, or something
> else.[71]

It was Whitman's dearest desire to be a complete singer, not just
the traditional idle singer of an empty day. He sought to celebrate
everything in his verse.

In "Song of the Redwood Tree," the mighty chant of the redwood, "its death-chant chanting" (n. b. the italicized passages),
Whitman uses various operatic devices, including the insertion of
a chorus of dryads joining with the "heirs and deities of the West"
in the refrain that the tree sings.

> Then to a loftier strain,
> Still prouder, more ecstatic rose the chant,
> As if the heirs, the deities of the West,
> Joining with *master-tongue bore part*. . . .[72]

This rising line, moving from a climax, comes to "A Song of the
Rolling Earth." Here the poet is obviously ending a movement,
a canto, a fitte. He concludes:

> No one can acquire for another—not one,
> Not one can grow for another—not one.
> The song is to the singer and comes back most to him. . . .
> I swear *I begin to see little or nothing in audible words*,
> *All merges toward the presentation of the unspoken meanings*
> *of the earth*,
> *Toward him who sings the songs of the body and of the truths*
> *of the earth*. . . .
> These to *echo the tones of souls* and the phrases of souls
> (If they did not *echo the phrases of souls* what were they then?). . . .
> Say on, sayers! *sing on, singers!*[73]

Love is the chief theme throughout "Birds of Passage," in "Song
of the Universal," "Pioneers! O Pioneers!" and "France." This
theme is sung by all nations and peoples:

And I guess some *chansonniers* there will understand them,
For I guess there is latent music yet in France, floods of it,
O I *hear already the bustle of instruments,* they will soon be
    drowning *all that would interrupt them.* . . .
It reaches hither, it swells me to joyful madness,
I will run transpose it in words, to justify it,
I will yet sing a song for you ma femme.[74]

"Birds of Passage" is rightly but a continuation of "Salut au
Monde" with its universal invocations. But "Sea Drift" is a different matter. Once again the *personal* experiences of the poet
impinge and are disclosed with a sincerity and an artistry that
make the lesson of love richer. "Out of the Cradle Endlessly Rocking" must surely have been one of the great 1860 poems written
as an improvisation of music. The pathos, the poignancy would
be almost impossible to achieve in the form of the aria unless the
poet had operatic music in mind, and almost certainly some particular operatic aria. The personal grief of the poet is most evident
in poems like "As I Ebb'd with the Ocean of Life" which indicates
that Whitman has lost touch with the great natural calm of nature:

But that before all my arrogant poems the real Me stands yet
    untouch'd, untold, altogether unreach'd. . . .[75]

This seems but the continuation in an even more intellectually
depressed but less emotionally concerned fashion of the feeling
not only for death, but that the poet has been fooling himself all
along.

I perceive I have not really understood any thing, not a single
    object, and that no man ever can. . . .[76]
Less positivism and more dependence now on the old primal forces.
I too am but a trail of drift and debris. . . .[77]

"Tears" is a perfect song, and of course invites comparison with
Tennyson's lyrics as well as with much of Poe's verse through the
use made of the reiterative devices. It is characterized chiefly by
a touch of impassioned sadness and by a subtle rhythmic pattern.
The beginning and end of the poem repeat the three beats—
"Tears! tears! tears!"—which are matched exactly in time (through
an admirable use of the caesura) with the line following.[78]

The separation of these poems from the others of the 1860 edition was wise artistically in that the poet separated the jubilant
mood of "Salut au Monde," with its cluster of poems, from the
vivid energy of "Drum Taps." It is also true that the poet felt a

loss of personal identity before the war which may be traced to the experience he tells of in "Out of the Cradle Endlessly Rocking." This experience could belong to the "Children of Adam," but actually the physical significance of the experience rightly belongs to the first section and its spiritual or psychological result to the period before the Civil War when not only was he personally depressed but also the political morality of his country appeared to him degraded. This is the mood of poems like "A Boston Ballad."

"Drum Taps" cuts like a whip-lash across the face of the *Leaves* and the excitement and pride Whitman felt in the sudden action for defense of the union sound clearly in "First O Songs for a Prelude."

First *O songs for a prelude,*
Lightly *strike on the stretch'd tympanum* pride and joy in my city,
How she led the rest to arms. . . .

How your *soft opera-music* changed, and the *drum and fife* were
    heard in their stead,
How you led to the war, (that shall serve *for our prelude, songs*
    of soldiers,)
How Manhattan *drum-taps* led. . . .

To the *drum-taps prompt,*
The young men falling in and arming. . . .

Mannahatta a-march and it's O to *sing it well!*
It's O for a manly life in the camp.[79]

His poem "Eighteen Sixty-One" is dedicated to the fighting man:

Saw I your gait. . . .
Heard your determin'd voice launch'd forth again and again,
Year that *suddenly sang by the mouths of the round-lipp'd* cannon,
I repeat you, hurrying, crashing, sad, distracted year.[80]

The three strophes of Beat! Beat! Drums! are held together by those repeated words, sounding in accent so much like the drumbeat in music. The whole of "Drum Taps" is given over to a variety of rhythms and stanza forms Whitman had not before used. In "From Paumanok Starting I fly like a Bird" the poet announces himself still as the poet of union:

To sing first, (to the tap of the war-drum if need be,)
The idea of all, of the Western world one and inseparable,
And then the song of each member of these States.[81]

And in "Song of the Banner at Daybreak" the poet says he will sing a "new song, a free song" made up of voices of the sound, the drum, the banner, the child, the sea, and the father. He says:

> Words! book-words! what are you?
> Words no more. . . .
> *My song is there in the open air* . . .
> I'll weave the chord. . . .[82]

But "Drum Taps" is representative of the war, with its fears of defeat and its hopes for victory. Death, suggested first in "Sea Drift," sounds again in "Drum Taps":

> Must I change my triumphant songs? said I to myself,
> Must I indeed learn to chant the cold dirges of the baffled?
> And sullen hymns of defeat?[83]

And, prophetically, he wrote in "Dirge for Two Veterans":

> I see a sad procession,
> And I hear the sound of coming *full-key'd bugles*,
> All the channels of the city *streets they're flooding*,
>   As with *voices and with tears.*
>
> I hear the *great drums pounding*,
> And the small drums *steady whirring*,
> And every blow of the great *convulsive drums*,
> Strikes me through and through. . . .
>
>   Now *nearer blow the bugles*,
> And the *drums strike more convulsive*
> And the daylight o'er the pavement quite has faded
>   And the *strong dead-march enwraps me.* . . .
>
>   O strong *dead-march you please me!*
> O moon *immense* with your silvery face you soothe me!
> O my soldiers twain! O my veterans passing to burial!
>   What I have I also give you.
>
>   The moon gives you light,
> And the *bugles and the drums give you music*,
> And my heart, O my soldiers, my veterans,
>   My heart gives you love.[84]

Here sound, imagery, sadness, strength, and Whitman's ever present love mix quite simply in the last stanza, and give to the poem a sense of completeness.

In "Lo, Victress on the Peaks" he speaks of singing of a "cluster containing night's darkness and blood-dripping wounds, and *psalms* of the dead." In "Spirit Whose Work Is Done" he addresses the spirit whose "sound of the drum, hollow and harsh to the last, reverberates 'round me" and whose "currents convulsive" will "scorch and blister out of my chants when you are gone."[85]

Just as the monument to the heroic in Napoleon was originally Beethoven's "Eroica Symphony," so it was that the finest poem Whitman wrote resulted from the worship of the heroic in Lincoln. Actually this poem is the natural culmination of "Drum Taps," though all the memories of Lincoln form a mournful funeral code of their own.

"When Lilacs Last in the Dooryard Bloom'd" is a poem of the senses—sight, scent, sound—and the soul. It is a poem which celebrates death victorious and, at the same time, celebrates the victory of the "sweetest, wisest soul of all my days and lands" over death, in the soul and the memory of the poet through the associations of sense. The spring always returning brings the memory of the lilac, the bird, and the western star. If the three symbols are regarded as symbols or leitmotifs for Lincoln himself, one gets for death ("lovely and delicate"), its symbol in the freshness and the richness of the lilac—signifying the corporeal, loving Lincoln, the human, the man. The "powerful western fallen star" is the Lincoln ideal, the "great star," the man become a symbol for shining, light-giving greatness. His death is anticipated in the falling and eclipse of the western star. The star not only announces the death of Lincoln, it brings knowledge of death for the first time fully home to the poet.

> A great star disappear'd—O the black murk that hides the star!
> O cruel hands that hold me powerless—O helpless soul of me!
> O harsh surrounding cloud that will not free my soul.

Whitman's ability to wander at will through a world of seeming reality and then quite suddenly confront the reader with the world of symbol (or the process in reverse) is nowhere better illustrated than in this poem. The third part of the leitmotif, the song of the hermit-thrush ("a shy and hidden bird") which finds its tally in the soul of the poet, is a song of the thought of mortality, of death, which the bird sings as a part of nature for which is developed the symbol of the sea, undulant, gliding, laving all the earth.[86] Death is represented by the bird's song as humanly sad but actually a deliverer.

The form of "When Lilacs Last in the Dooryard Bloom'd" has

long been a matter of interest, since there is so obvious a return to
the three symbols—bird, star, and lilac—and, since the poem has,
as a result of this mingling of senses, unusual artistic appeal, it has
been conjectured that Whitman may have been following some
musical form, either the sonata or the rondo. Each of these forms,
however, is, rightly understood, too narrow to superimpose upon
the poem: yet the form of the sonata is more formal and possible
than that of the rondo. For instance, sonata form contains within
its first section all of the material (main material, that is) to be
used in the development of the composition. A rondo uses only
one theme or phrase which is repeated throughout; sonata form,
however, demands rather rigid adherence to the stating of one
theme (subject) with a transition to a second: then a development
or "working out" section to be followed by a return to the first
and second subjects in their original forms (the recapitulation).
It is a misunderstanding of these musical forms which leads the
literary enthusiast to see them in Whitman's poem. However, what
Robert Haven Schauffler has designated as the "germ-motive" in
Beethoven's music *is* more applicable here. He says of the germ
motive, which became most apparent in Beethoven's work with
the Third or "Eroica" Symphony:

A germ-motive is a musical phrase which recurs, more or less disguised, in different movements of a composition to lend the whole
thematic unity.[88]

There is in this poem a kind of polyphony—that is, a simultaneous movement of voices, which is difficult to achieve in verse. Here
there is nearly a contrapuntalism. Is this a reminiscence, is it *now*
that the bird "warbles his song"? Or is it *"When* lilacs last . . ."?
Here are the experiences before the announcement of death that
the poet has, the sight of the western star "a month since" whose
"sad orb" was prophetic. There even now is the song of the bird
which the poet hears but cannot yet turn his attention to. He must
still pay his tribute to that black coffin which travels as surely as it
travels now in his imagination the length of America. That the
bird sings for all humanity the poet knows; still he cannot yet leave
the star and the lilac, signs of the hero's death:

Falling upon them all and among them all, enveloping me with
   the rest,
Appear'd the cloud, appear'd the long black trail,
And I knew death, its thought, and the sacred knowledge of death.[89]

And now with that knowledge, the song of the bird is tallied in the soul, and Whitman offers a most remarkable use of the note made manifest. No better effort has ever been made to translate into words the sad, rich song of the thrush at night. It combines simple dignity with lyricism. It recalls the scenes of the war. Though the poet returns to life, to the present, *always,* he says, the symbols of the lilac, the star, and the bird in the night will recall the dead to him, and especially "the dead I loved so well." Like the transcendentalist poets, Whitman was a symbolist who drew on nature and often imbued it with philosophical conceptions so that it was difficult to separate the finite from the infinite.

"By Blue Ontario's Shore" is the bridge between the deep sorrow which came of the war and Lincoln's death, and the late poems "Autumn Rivulets" and "From Noon to Starry Night." It is Whitman's prayer for the future of America, for bards and prophets who will be "good" for America. It is a warning to America to follow great men. It reveals, more than any of Whitman's verses, that the poet was beginning to step aside, that he was concerned with the type of person or persons to whom the torch he bore would be handed. The work is big, diffuse, and orchestral in the themes it handles: the soul of America, victory, Libertad, democracy.

A Phantom gigantic superb, with stern visage accosted me,
Chant me the poem, it said, *that comes from the soul of America,*
  chant me the carol of victory.
And strike up the marches of Libertad, marches more powerful yet,
And *sing me before you go the song of the throes of Democracy.*[90]

In section six of the poem "that comes from the soul of America," the poet speaks of:

Making its cities, beginnings, events, diversities, wars, *vocal* in him,
Making its rivers, lakes, bays, *embouchure* in him.

The poem is Janus-faced, looking back upon the victory of the war, and prophesying the growing age of the bard.

"Autumn Rivulets" is the first poem in the final and fourth long section or movement of *Leaves of Grass,* that section which deals with the spiritual side by symbol or suggestion as fully as the young poems dealt with the physical. The poet grows old but sees the new horizons open before him. The choral quality increases, music sounds most strongly, and the poet calls forth in these last poems all the triumphant joy and power of expression that are fitting to the climax, to the *tutti* in which *all* the instruments of the orchestra sound together in mighty finale.

One of the early suggestions of the spiritual life is made through music as the poet holds sea-shells "to the tympans of temples":

Murmurs and echoes still call up, *eternity's music* faint and far,
Wafted inland, sent from Atlantica's rim, *strains for the soul of the prairies,*
Whisper'd reverberations, chords for the ear of the West joyously sounding,
Your tidings old, yet ever new and untranslatable. . . .[91]

Falling between "Autumn Rivulets" and "Passage to India" is "Proud Music of the Storm"—the single poem that for sheer power and glory of vision is the equal of "Passage to India," if not its superior. Nowhere else in his poetry does Whitman reveal so fully his knowledge, his indebtedness to music. Nowhere else is there so rising a crescendo and so significant a revelation as to the meaning of music in his poems. The mingling of the music of nature with all of the music that Whitman has heard in concert opens the poem:

Strong hum of forest tree-tops—wind of the mountains,
Personified dim shapes—you hidden orchestras,
You serenades of phantoms with instruments alert,
Blending with Nature's rhythmus all the tongues of nations;
You chords left as by vast composers—you choruses. . . .

Passing through a rather lengthy list the poet says:

Now airs, antique and mediaeval fill me,
I see and hear old harpers with their harps at Welsh festivals,
I hear the minnesingers singing their lays of love,
I hear the minstrels, gleemen, troubadours, of the middle ages.

Now the great organ sounds,
Tremulous, while underneath, (as the hid footholds of the earth,
On which arising rest, and leaping forth depend,
All shapes of beauty, grace and strength. . . .
The strong base stands, and its pulsations intermits not,
Bathing, supporting, merging all the rest, maternity of all the rest,
And with it every instrument in multitudes,
The players playing, all the world's musicians,
The solemn hymns and masses rousing adoration,
All passionate heart-chants, sorrowful appeals,
The measureless sweet vocalists of ages,
And for their solvent setting *earth's own diapason,*

Of winds and woods and mighty ocean waves,
A new composite orchestra, binder of years and climes, ten-fold
   renewer,
As of the far-back days the poets tell, the Paradiso,
The straying thence, the separation long, but now the wandering
   done,
The journey done, the journeyman come home,
And man and art with Nature fused again.

Tutti! for earth and heaven;
(*The Almighty leader now for once* has signal'd with his wand). . . .

The tongues of violins,
(I think O tongues ye tell this heart, that cannot tell itself,
This brooding yearning heart, that cannot tell itself.)[92]

No other poet but Lanier has left us so knowledged and passionate a study of music. But more:

Ah from a little child,
Thou knowest soul how to me all sounds became music. . . .

And there follows a list of sounds musical to him: the mother's
voice "in lullaby or hymn," "tender voices, memory's loving
voices"; rain; growing corn; "sea-surf beating on the sand"; the
twittering of birds; the "hawk's sharp screams"; the "migrant wild-
fowl's notes"; "the psalm in the country church"; "the fiddler in
the tavern"; "the glee"; the sailor's song; lowing cattle; bleating
sheep and crowing cocks; "All songs of current land"—"German
airs of friendship, wine and love"; "Irish ballads, jigs and dances";
"English warbles"; "Chansons of France"; "Scotch tunes," and
"o'er the rest Italia's peerless compositions." He speaks of seeing
Norma stalk across the stage "with pallor on her face, yet lurid
passion"; of poor mad Lucia's eyes; of Ernani who, "walking in
the bridal garden," with his bride, "Hears the infernal call, the
death-pledge of the horn."[93] He hears the "clear electric bass and
baritone of the world; the trombone duo; Libertad forever!" and
by the Spanish convent walls, the "Song of the dying swan: Fernando's heart is breaking."[94] He hears the glad song of the "lus-
trous orb," "venus contralto. . . . Sister of loftiest gods, Alboni. . . ."
He then proceeds to list the "odes, symphonies and operas" he
hears: *William Tell,* the *Huguenots,* the *Prophet, Robert, Faust*
(Gounod's) and *Don Juan.*
   He hears the dance music of all nations, the waltz, the bolero,
the religious dances "old and new," the Hebrew lyre, the crash of

the crusader's cymbals, the chanting of dervishes, the religious
dances of Persians and Arabs, the modern Greeks, the wild Cory-
bantian dances, the Roman youths dancing to flageolets, the
sound of the muezzin in the mosque calling, of the Egyptian harp,
and the "primitive chants of the Nile boatmen," the ancient "imperial hymns of China," "the delicate sounds of the king (the
stricken wood and stone)," or the "Hindu flutes" and the "fretting
twang of the *vina,* and a band of bayaderes. . . ." "Leaving Asia"
he is called to Europe where the organ and huge bands and many
voices sound in Luther's "Eine Feste Burg," in Rossini's *Stabat
Mater Dolorosa* or in parts of the Mass, the *Agnus Dei* or *Gloria
in Excelsis Deo.*

> I hear the annual singing of the children in St. Paul's cathedral,
> Or, under the high roof of some colossal hall, the symphonies,
>   oratorios of Beethoven, Handel, or Haydn,
> The *Creation* in billows of godhood laves me.
>
> *Give me to hold all sounds, (I madly struggling cry,)*
> *Fill me with all the voices of the universe,*
> *Endow me with their throbbings, Nature's also,*
> *The tempest, waters, winds, operas and chants, marches and dances,*
> *Utter, pour in, for I would take them all!*[95]

In no other place in his poetry does Whitman make so indubitably plain what he knew of music, and how it inspired him. Perhaps
1871 was a year of more musical significance than others: it produced not only this great poem but "Passage to India," possibly
his high point of spiritual power. That Whitman, however,
wanted to say once and for all to the reader that it was music—all
kinds of music and not just opera—that had inspired him and was
vocal in him and sounded a symphony through him is most apparent. "Tutti for earth" and now for heaven too, he cries. Let us
sound the last and the greatest of the songs. Let this be the reader's clue:

> Then I woke softly,
> And pausing, questioning awhile the music of my dream. . . .
>
> I said to my silent curious soul. . . .
> *Come, for I have found the clew I sought so long. . . .*
>
> *A new rhythmus fitted for thee,*
> *Poems bridging the way from Life to Death, vaguely wafted in*
>   *night air, uncaught, unwritten,*
> *Which let us go forth in the bold day and write.*[96]

Music is the uncaught and the unwritten poetry of life. From hearing all these songs and sounds the poet finally realizes that each is a poem, that music indeed is the key which makes it possible for him to write in a new style, in a "new rhythmus."

One of the best uses of the germ motive is undoubtedly to be found in "Passage to India," where the original idea is expanded so that in its reappearance in "Passage to more than India," it leads into this most impassioned section:

> Passage to more than India!
> O secret of the earth and sky!
> Of you O waters of the sea! O winding creeks and rivers. . . .
> O morning red! O clouds! O rain and snows!
> O day and night, passage to you!

And then by way of climax to this Ulysses-like dedication:

> O my brave soul!
> O farther farther sail!
> O daring joy, but safe! are they not all the seas of God?
> O farther, farther, farther sail![97]

By way of prelude to "Whispers of Heavenly Death" Whitman wrote, "Darest thou now O soul Walk out with me toward the unknown region, where neither ground is for the feet nor any path to follow?" The prelude is to the twilight of life: "Labial gossip of night, sibilant chorals." In "That Music Always Round Me" the poet says in youth he did not always listen,

> But now the chorus I hear and am elated,
> A tenor, strong, ascending with power and health, with glad notes of daybreak I hear,
> A soprano at intervals sailing buoyantly over the tops of immense waves,
> A transparent base shuddering lusciously under and through the universe,
> The triumphant tutti, the funeral wailings with sweet flutes and violins, all these I fill myself with,
> I hear not the volumes of sound merely, I am moved by the exquisite meanings,
> I listen to the different voices winding in and out, striving, contending with fiery vehemence to excel each other in emotion;
> I do not think the performers know themselves—but now I think I begin to know them.[98]

Surely there can be no doubt that as Whitman drew nearer the close of his book and of his life he depended signally upon music

to make clear his meanings and he recognized clearly its influence
upon him. In the most spiritual of his poems, "The Mystic
Trumpeter," he used music solely for the illustration of his
spiritual awakening and change:

> Blow trumpeter free and clear, I follow thee,
> While at thy liquid prelude, glad, serene,
> The fretting world, the streets, the noisy hours of day withdraw,
> A holy calm descends like dew upon me,
> I walk in cool refreshing night the walks of Paradise,
> I scent the grass, the moist air and the roses;
> Thy song expands my numb'd imbonded spirit, thou freest,
>   launchest me,
> Floating and basking upon heaven's lake.

And in section seven the poet wrote:

> O trumpeter, methinks I am myself the instrument thou playest,
> Thou melt'st my heart, my brain—thou movest, drawest, changest
>   them at will;
> And now thy sullen notes send darkness through me,
> Thou takest away all cheering light, all hope,
> I see the enslaved, the overthrown, the hurt, the opprest of the
>   whole earth,
> I feel the measureless shame and humiliation of my race, it
>   becomes all mine,
> Mine too the revenges of humanity, the wrongs of ages. . . .[99]

And finally, in a chorus that sounds only too obviously like the
chorus of Beethoven's Ninth "Choral" Symphony—the last great
work from the pen of the old musician who had grown more
spiritual and mystical—the "Ode to Joy" set to music, Whitman
wrote:

> Now trumpeter for thy close,
> Vouchsafe a higher strain than any yet,
> Sing to my soul, renew its languishing faith and hope,
> Rouse up my slow belief, give me some vision of the future,
> Give me for once its prophecy and joy.
> O glad, exulting, culminating song!
> A vigor more than earth's is in thy notes,
> Marches of victory—man disenthral'd—the conqueror at last,
> Hymns to the universal God from universal man—all joy!
> A reborn race appears—a perfect world, all joy!
> Women and men in wisdom, innocence and health—all joy!
> Riotous laughing bacchanals fill'd with joy!

War, sorrow, suffering gone—the rank earth purged—nothing but
 joy left!
The ocean fill'd with joy—the atmosphere all joy! . . .
Joy! joy! all over joy![100]

Such is the final song in the great poetic structure of the *Leaves*.
It is true that other short poems followed, even the "Songs of
Parting," but "The Mystic Trumpeter" sounded the climax to
the poem. What follows is but coda which is as lengthy in Whitman's verse as it often is in music. But the matter is settled that
made up *Leaves of Grass*: the old man but takes his farewells.
These, even these, depend upon music, and he wrote in "Songs
of Parting":

O strain musical flowing through ages and continents, now
 reaching me and America!
I take your *strong chords, intersperse them,* and cheerfully pass
 them forward.[101]

In "Sands at Seventy" he writes:

After the dazzle of day is gone,
Only the dark, dark night shows to my eyes the stars;
After the clangor of organ majestic, or chorus, or perfect band,
Silent, athwart my soul, *moves the symphony true.*[102]

This is probably a perfect illustration of the power of music on
his senses. In the poem to "The Dead Tenor" he acknowledges
his indebtedness to the singer:

How much from thee! the revelation of the singing voice from
 thee!

 . . . .

The perfect singing voice—deepest of all to me the lesson-trial
 and test of all:
How through those strains distill'd—how the rapt ears, the soul
 of me, absorbing
Fernando's heart, *Manrico's* passionate call, *Ernani's,* sweet
 Gennaro's,
I fold thenceforth, or seek to fold, within my chants transmuting,
Freedom's and Love's and Faith's unloos'd cantabile. . . .[103]

Written in Whitman's seventieth year, this comes as final proof
of how much of what he heard in music he sought to translate into
his verse.[104] In "Goodbye My Fancy" Whitman writes:

... And now I *chant old age.* ...
As here in careless *trill,* I and my *recitatives,* with faith and love,
Wafting to other work, to *unknown songs,* conditions,
On, on, ye jocund twain! continue on the same![105]

In "Shakespeare—Bacon's Cipher" these words appear:

In each old song bequeath'd—in every noble page or text,
. . . .
A mystic cipher waits infolded.[106]

And so in the *Leaves,* the veins run with music.

It can hardly be claimed that Whitman's poetic devices are the direct result of musical influence, for he did make an occasional use of regular rhyme, as, for example, in "O Captain! My Captain!", and some concession to rhyme in the use of final participles. This device is freely illustrated in "Patroling Barnegat."

Waves, air, midnight, their savagest trinity *lashing,*
Out in the shadows their milk-white combs *careering,*
On beachy slush and sand spirits of snow fierce *slanting,*
Where through the murk the easterly death-wind *breasting,*
Through cutting swirl and spray watchful and firm *advancing,*
(That in the distance! is that a wreck? is the red signal *flaring?*)
Slush and sand of the beach tireless till daylight *wending,*
Steadily, slowly, through hoarse roar never *remitting,*
Along the midnight edge by those milk-white combs *careering,*
A group of dim, weird forms, struggling, the night *confronting,*
That savage trinity warily *watching.*[107]

The use of prepositional and participial phrases to give unity to a stanza was a more common device, as was the repetition of a single initial word. Some discussion of the resemblance of the Whitman verse line to the symphonic has already taken place. Poe was another poet besides Whitman who used initial repetition effectively, especially in "Ulalume," though Poe made constant use of end-rhyme as well. "Out of the Cradle Endlessly Rocking" illustrates how Whitman built up his stanzas.

Out of the cradle endlessly rocking,
Out of the mocking bird's throat, the musical shuttle,
Out of . . . .
Over . . . .
Down . . . . . .
Up . . . . . .
Out . . . . . .
From those beginning notes of yearning and love there in the mist,
From the thousand responses of my heart never to cease ...

I, chanter of pains and joys, uniter of here and hereafter,
Taking all hints . . .
A reminiscence sing.[108]

Critics have made much of this device of Whitman's for some time. Not so often mentioned are Whitman's experiments with near-rhymes or "discords," as Poe would have said, with a strikingly modern feeling for sound. That Whitman could write metrically regular rhymes is proved by his unimaginative early verse. But Whitman, the experimenter, wrote like this in "Song of the Broad-Axe":

Weapon shapely, naked, *wan,*
Head from the mother's bowels *drawn,*
Wooded flesh and metal bone, limb only one and lip only *one,*
Gray-blue leaf by red-heat *grown,* helve produced from a little
      seed *sown,*
Resting the grass amid and *upon,*
To be lean'd and to lean *on.*[109]

Far more commonly mentioned is the device of epanalepsis. This repetition of a word around which the phrases cluster is like a single repeated note with variations. The unity that the stanza achieves could hardly be improved upon. Poe, had he lived, would certainly have admired this repetitive technique, so like that of old English verse and the measure of *Hiawatha.* The parallelisms that had delighted the Beowulf poet also delighted Whitman. The lyrical quality is heightened by this device, as can be readily seen in this section from "Song of Myself":

I am he that walks with the tender and growing *night,*
I call to the earth and sea half-held by the *night.*

Press close bare-bosom'd *night*—press close magnetic nourishing
      night!
Night of south winds—*night* of the large few stars!
Still nodding *night*—mad naked summer *night.*

Smile O voluptuous cool-breath'd *earth!*
Earth of the slumbering and liquid trees!
Earth of departed sunset—*earth* of the mountains misty-topt!
Earth of the vitreous pour of the full moon just tinged with blue!
Earth of shine and dark mottling the tide of the river!
Earth of the limpid grey of clouds brighter and clearer for my sake!
Far-swooping elbow'd *earth*—rich apple-blossom'd *earth!*
Smile for your lover comes.

Prodigal, you have given me love—therefore I to you give love!
O unspeakable passionate love.[110]

But these matters, though indirectly related to music, are not
of as much moment here as is the difference that occurs in Whitman's style when he employs the long symphonic lines of the
larger portion of his book, lines like those just quoted, and when
he turns away from that poetic style to the highly vocal style of
the aria.

Whitman, like earlier poets, seems to have wavered between the
vocabularies of instrumental and vocal music. It should be obvious
that instrumental music had great influence upon the general style
of the poem, and though it is not possible to list here the myriad
references to music that Whitman made, the reader can quickly
satisfy his curiosity on this score. There were times, however, when
the Whitman line was purely vocal, and these times seem to have
occurred when the poet was most impassioned. Many of the lines
are invocations and directly address the reader. Others might well
have been those lines improvised at operas that Whitman heard.
How else account for the extremely personal, extremely pathetic
quality that the poet manages to infuse the verse with? The very
beats in the line suggest a musical parallel. Of *La Favorita,* one of
Whitman's favorite operas, the poet wrote:

The strains of death, too, come plaintively from his lips. Never
before did you hear such wonderful gushing sorrow, poured forth like
ebbing blood, from a murdered heart. Is it for peace he prays with that
appealing passion? Is it the story of his own sad wreck he utters?[111]

The rising line of excitement in a Whitman poem can be traced
as readily through the use of the "O!" in his best poems as if the
poet announced—"this is a song." In the same sense the prophetic
calm that came occasionally into his verse can be traced in the use
of the word "Lo!" in any given stanza. "Tears" might be the
poetic equivalent of the mournful aria Whitman referred to above
in which Fernando discovers that his love is lost to him.

O who is that ghost? that form in the dark, with tears?
What shapeless lump is that, bent, crouch'd there on the sand?
Streaming tears, sobbing tears, throes, choked with wild cries;
O storm, embodied, rising, careering with swift steps along the
    beach!
O wild and dismal night storm, with wind—O belching and
    desperate. . . .
O then the unloosen'd ocean,
Of tears! tears! tears![112]

Notice how the "O's" permit the release of strong emotion. Or the poet might have been listening to that same aria when he wrote the aria of the mocking bird in "Out of the Cradle Endlessly Rocking." The whole section is obviously a vocal one:

O night! do I not see my love, fluttering out among the breakers?
What is that little black thing I see there in the white?

And with greater excitement:

Loud! loud! loud!
Loud I call to you, my love!
High and clear I shoot my voice over the waves,
Surely you know who is here, is here,
You must know who I am, my love.[113]

Then the bird addresses the "low-hanging moon," accusing it of keeping his mate; then the land (with "carols of lonesome love") whereon he thinks that he sees her; and the rising stars, hoping that she will rise with them. After this come only the carols of loneliness, of night, of death, "O reckless despairing carols." But the bird suddenly hushes his song:

But soft! sink low!
Soft! let me just murmur,
And do you wait a moment you husky-nois'd sea,
For somewhere I believe I heard my mate responding to me. . . .

Hither my love!
Here I am! here! . . .
Do not be decoyed elsewhere. . . .

O darkness! O in vain!
O I am very sick and sorrowful. . . .

O past! O happy life! O songs of joy!
In the air, in the woods, over the fields,
Loved! loved! loved! loved! loved!

And the hush in the bird's song—"the aria sinking" and the boy understanding the "aria's meaning"—while all the other sounds of nature—the wind and the sea—continue, illustrates Whitman's attempt at many-voiced (polyphonic) verse. Finally complete despair, without a ray of hope, closes in and the bird song is a distillation of the memories of happier days—of that melody of bereavement so mixed with pain and sweetness that all poets have celebrated it. Here is Whitman's equivalent of "To a Skylark" and "To a Nightingale" but instead of talking about the bird, Whit-

man translates his song. The strong likeness of this poem to opera
appears in the line, "The aria sinking, all else continuing . . . ,"
following the italicized song of the bird. With stars, winds blowing,
sea incessantly moaning, even the echoes of the bird's song
sounding, the three voices speak to the boy:

> The colloquy there, the trio, each *uttering,*
> The undertone, the savage old mother incessantly *crying,*
> To the boy's soul's questions sullenly *timing,* some drown'd secret
>   *hissing*
> To the *outsetting* bard.[114]

The conclusion is symphonic, wherein the impassioned cries of
the bird certainly seem indebted to the "Italian dispensation."
There are several examples, which the reader will readily recall,
that further illustrate the principle that Whitman broke in frequently upon the symphonic line with an aria.

Another device, interesting to observe Whitman using, is that of
the question, which suggests the style of the early ballads:

> O how shall I warble myself for the dead one there I loved?
> And how shall I deck my song for the large sweet soul that has
>   gone?
> And what shall my perfume be for the grave of him I love? . . .
>
> O what shall I hang on the chamber walls?
> And what shall the pictures be that I hang on the walls,
> To adorn the burial-house of him I love? . . . [115]

Whitman had a fondness, too, in his more lyrical passages, for
the unit of three in a line. This can be observed in "Tears! tears!
tears!" Beat! beat! Drums!" "Shine! shine! shine!" "Loud! loud!
loud!" "Land! land! land!", etc. These hard-struck words, each
with its "caesura," precede lines which gradually lengthen into
what has been called "pyramid form." The length of the Whitman
line has infinite variation, a variation that is, in its way, an anticipation of the verse lines of Sidney Lanier. Whitman would have
agreed with Poe that it is quantity, and not regularity of syllables,
that makes verse and this is everywhere evident in his poetry. Two
stanzas like these from "When Lilacs Last in the Dooryard
Bloom'd" illustrate the extreme variety of metrical pattern—that
near speaking quality in this verse—which makes vocal what were
otherwise dumb emotions, in birds as well as humans. The contrast
between the passionate grief of the first stanza quoted and the
radiant calm of the second is a matter of metrics.

O powerful western fallen star!
O shades of night—O moody, tearful night!
O great star disappear'd—O the black murk that hides the star!
O cruel hands that hold me powerless—O helpless soul of me!
O harsh surrounding cloud that will not free my soul.

. . . .

Come lovely and soothing death,
Undulate round the world, serenely arriving, arriving,
In the day, in the night, to all, to each,
Sooner or later delicate death.

His verse line had no more precisely planned accentual system than has speaking or singing. In this sense Whitman's verse seems to have departed altogether from ordinary verse-rhymed patterns. Music, for instance, though it has equal units of time, flows uninterruptedly from measure to measure without undue attention to the fact that the first beat in every measure is thought of as the stressed beat. If the melodic line points up this fact, well and good; if not, the metrical or rhythmic pattern may pass almost unnoticed beneath the melodic pattern that has been established. So it is with Whitman's verse. It is actually difficult to define his metrics, and for identical reasons; it is the long symphonic lines that count, not the foot.

Any attempt at a detailed study of musical imagery in Whitman's verse would make a complete study in itself. Some clue to the nature of these images has appeared here in sections from "Proud Music of the Storm" and "The Mystic Trumpeter." However, these references are not the most common ones. More often music takes on some metaphysical significance in Whitman's vocabulary, and when he wants to make clear what he is doing in any verse, he seeks a parallel in music. "Thee for my recitative" he wrote. He spoke of the "clef of the universe." And he wrote a rather sentimental tribute to a great singer in "The Singer in the Prison." He used terms, like "embouchure," which reveal knowledge of instrumental music. He spoke of "romances," of hymns, of dance tunes, and he acknowledged in a score of ways, through the use of musical terms, that the poem depended structurally upon music. But it is not these overt uses of such terms that account for the music of the *Leaves.*

Perhaps the greatest single debt Whitman owes to music grew out of what he learned from it in the writing of finales or finishes or conclusions. What Whitman manages to do in a finale with words would be called a stretto by musicians. No other American poet, including Lanier, ever equaled Whitman's skill in writing a stretto. His conclusions to the great poems are artistically sure. The mighty waves that he manages to whip up, the pyramiding of emotion, the climactic struggle of all voices at once, the reader will himself recall. Equally skillful is the subsiding, the intimate conclusion that is characteristic of the great symphonies and of Whitman's verse. Only a poet who could write "big" poems could actually write symphonically.

Surely the place of music in Whitman's verse is of great importance. In "Specimen Days" he wrote:

Have not you . . . while listening to the well-played music of some band like Maretzek's, felt an overwhelming desire for measureless sound—a sublime orchestra of a myriad orchestras—a colossal volume of harmony, in which the thunder might roll in its proper place; and above it, the vast, pure Tenor—identity of the Creative Power itself—rising through the universe, until the boundless and unspeakable capacities of that mystery, the human soul, should be filled to the uttermost, and the problem of human cravingness be satisfied and destroyed?

Of this sort are the promptings of good music upon me. . . .[116]

But the effect of music upon the poet was not only metaphysical; he wrote of the cornet:

. . . it glides quickly in through my ears,
It shakes mad-sweet pangs through my belly and breast.

Speaking of the sound he loved best, that of the human voice, he said of the effect the orchestra had upon him:

The orchestra whirls me wider than Uranus flies,
It wrenches such ardors from me, I did not know I possess'd them,
It sails me, I dab with bare feet, they are lick'd by indolent waves,
I am cut by bitter and angry hail, I lose my breath,
Steep'd amid honey'd morphine, my windpipe throttled in fakes
    of death,
At length let up again to feel the puzzle of puzzles,
And that we call Being.[117]

And he wrote in "Democratic Vistas":

Then music, the combiner, nothing more spiritual, nothing more sensuous, a god, yet completely human, advances, *prevails, holds highest place; supplying in certain wants and quarters what nothing else could* supply. . . .[118]

To music then Whitman owes his diffuseness, his line, his form for verse, the inspiration for many of his poems, his rhythms, and some of the impassioned quality of his verse. Without making the slightest claim to completeness, this study has been made in the hope that future Whitman scholars will investigate along the lines of music as fully as they have explored other phases of his creative life.

Sidney Lanier

upon the poetry of Sidney Lanier—the last of the poets to be
dealt with specifically—is necessarily an ambitious project, for
each poem that he wrote was probably influenced in some way by
music. There is, however, a distinct difference in the quality and
kind of verse which preceded the Baltimore period, before he devoted much time to playing music professionally, and that which
followed when the possibilities of musical forms called forth that
series of experiments which constitute his best verse. It is indeed
unfortunate that the poet died only six years after his first mature
efforts in this direction saw publication. Though he lived nearly a
decade longer than Shelley, and had written half his total poetic
output by the Baltimore period, he was obviously but beginning to
hit his poetic stride when he succumbed to ill health. Less than a
quarter of his mature years was devoted to poetry; for the remainder he was businessman, lawyer, teacher, lecturer, musician,
and critic.

Lanier is the only professional musician in the annals of American poetry to achieve real fame as a poet. From 1873 on, a
substantial portion of his income depended upon his abilities as
an orchestral flutist and as a soloist. He was a kind of musical
phenomenon, for when he came to Baltimore, he lacked the professional training that most orchestral musicians had, and he could
scarcely sight-read orchestral material when he was hired to play
the first flute with the Peabody Orchestra.[1] But he had a flawless
technique and a beautiful tone, and in literally a matter of weeks

210

he was sight-reading material with the best of them.[2] He had the signal honor of being asked by Theodore Thomas to play with the New York Philharmonic, and he was fortunate to have Leopold Damrosch encourage him as a composer of flute music. Because we have no recordings of Lanier's playing, it is easy to forget that he achieved high rank as a musician in a matter of four years, having come virtually untrained among the virtuosi of the century. There can be no doubt of his talent for music, and it is hardly conjecture what his musical future might have been had he been born in the North or East where symphonic music was frequently heard.

He did extensive Shakespearean research, writing the first comprehensive essay on music of Shakespeare's day, tracing musical references in his works, and sounding out the current theories on rhyme as an indication of chronology in his verse and drama. In addition, he explored, as scientifically as he was able to, the physics and acoustics of music, a subject which had fascinated him since his college days when his ambition was to occupy a chair of the Physics and Metaphysics of Music at some college.

It was natural too that a poet interested in music should do a prosodic study based upon musical analogies, which would point up clearly the virtues of quantity in verse. Though Lanier's theories were challenged by Saintsbury, *The Science of English Verse* is still regarded as the best exposition of the quantity theory in English.[3]

This chapter is devoted chiefly to a study of the part that music played in influencing, improving, and changing the forms and the content of Lanier's verse. It is a study in poetic growth, for from the time that Lanier became fully aware of the possibilities of musical analogies in poetry, he began to take giant strides; and his century, fascinated by the two arts, hailed him as a great original poet. Though Lanier was endowed with a fine metrical sensitivity from the beginning, his was a search for a subject, a style, and a message. He was, at his death, no inconsiderable master of poetic technique.

By examining his musical life and musical theories, we may hope to account for a certain obscurity and experimentalism in his verse, and vitiate the charge that he wrote "sound" without sense.

Born in Macon, Ga., in 1842, Lanier, like the troubadours and the "flock of singing birds," had an early acquaintanceship with music. He said once in a letter to Paul Hamilton Hayne: "I could play passably well on several instruments before I could write legibly; and since then the deepest of my life has been filled with music, *which I have studied and cultivated far more than poetry.*"[4]

He began his musical education at five, and played, as a young child, piano, flute, guitar, violin, and organ.[5] His ability as a violinist was as marked as his flute virtuosity; his father forbade his continuing the study of the violin because of its effect upon him.[6] While still a school-boy, he organized an orchestra among his friends and directed it, as he was later to do when he was serving in the Confederate Army. His whole family was musical, and his sister learned music at boarding school, after the fashion of the day. Lanier commented upon the fact that in the South there were pianos, organs, flutes, and sundry other instruments in abundance in private homes.[7]

He early began making flute arrangements of music he liked, and adding flute parts to music already transcribed for some other instrument.[8] He tried his hand at writing music to Tennyson's "The Song of Love and Death" from *Lancelot and Elaine* and, from *The Miller's Daughter,* "Love that Hath Us in the Net," which was published three years after his death. While in prison at Point Lookout, Maryland, he entertained his fellow-sufferers by playing upon the flute as gladly as he had in his college days at Oglethorpe where he serenaded the ladies of evenings. (It was while he was in prison that he became the friend of Father Tabb, the famous poet-priest.) His only published piece of music from this period is a ballad dedicated to a child, Ella Montgomery, for locating him on the prison-ship and securing his release. The words and music to "Little Ella" were published by Offutt and Company in 1868.

While he was stationed with the Confederate troops at Norfolk, it was his habit to read German poetry, and he attempted a translation of Wagner's *Das Rheingold,* which has never been published. When he lost his German glossary to the enemy in 1863, he wrote his father for editions of Uhland, Lessing, Schelling, and Tieck. It may well be expected that the young poet absorbed from these readings many of his ideas for a literary life that would embrace music. He had tried his hand already at translations of Heine, Goethe, and Schiller. After Shakespeare, it is evident that the chief literary influence upon his life was that of German romantic poetry and prose. His first novel, *Tiger Lilies,* reveals the impress of his reading of the Germans and Carlyle, from whom he seems to have borrowed many ideas on trade. It should not be forgotten that though he read German at first laboriously, he had stood at the head of his graduating class at Oglethorpe, and that his literary gifts were so marked at this point and the desire for expression so strong his talent could have led him in purely literary directions.[9]

Tiger Lilies, published in 1867, was a young man's work and is filled with far too many ideas to achieve any harmonious arrangement as a novel. These ideas, by and large, center about the meaning that music had in the welfare of society, and reveal the musical knowledge which Lanier was early rather proud of in his continually interpolated musical passages, written just for this purpose of display. Most of Lanier's ideas on the art of music were formulated by the time he wrote this book, and he betrays his nineteenth century origin in his belief that music was The Art of that century.

Lanier was forced to try his hand at many kinds of work and writing, since he had many talents and was well endowed both as a teacher and lecturer. The fact that he did a little preaching on the side is revealing of his interest in man's "larger life"—a religious quality evident in his prose and verse. Certain large ideas seem to have been of such great importance to him that he expended his life demonstrating their truths. Like Whitman, whom he later frowned upon for his "formlessness," Lanier used as the leitmotifs in all his poetry and writing the ideas first expressed in *Tiger Lilies:* beauty, nature, love, music ("Music means harmony, harmony means love, and love means God"), and metaphysics. These ideas rush and sweep through this first novel, much as they do through *Leaves of Grass.* Garland Greever wrote of this tendency in Lanier's novel:

The German prose romance of the late eighteenth and early nineteenth century is a baffling genre. It is not primarily story. Though it rhapsodizes endlessly about art (especially music and poetry), it seeks rather than shuns incoherence and digression. . . . All of this was congenial to Lanier.[10]

Lanier's uncertainty as to his career was natural in one of strong and differing talents. For a while after his discharge from the Confederate Army he worked at being a clerk in his grandfather's hotel, at teaching, and finally, pressed by debt, at law, as his father wished. On a business trip to New York in 1869, however, he heard

all of the music that he could, including a performance of Halevy's
The Tempest. He wrote his wife ecstatically of this performance:

And my heart has been so full. . . . As the fair, tender notes came,
they opened . . . like flower-buds expanding into flowers under the
sweet rain of the accompaniment: kind Heaven! My head fell on the
seat in front, I was utterly weighed down with great loves and great
ideas and divine in-flowings and devout out-flowings, and as each note
grew and budded and opened, and became a bud again and died
into a fresh birth in the next bud-note, I also lived those flower-tone
lives, and grew and expanded and folded back and died and was born
again, and partook of the unfathomable mysteries of flowers and
tones.[11]

In 1870 Lanier was stricken with tuberculosis and for the rest
of his life he was constantly in search of a better climate. He went
at once to New York for treatment, and while there he heard
Christine Nilsson, who had just arrived in America, and Theodore
Thomas's orchestra. His excitement over the music he was hearing
is evident in the letters to his wife. Returning to New York for
further treatment in 1871, Lanier gave every evidence of a desire,
perhaps then unknown to himself, to be a part of the musical life
of America. He wrote of the orchestra:

. . . I went . . . and the *baton* tapped and waved, and I plunged into
the sea, and lay and floated. Ah! the dear flutes and oboes and horns
drifted me hither and thither, and the great violins and small violins
swayed me upon waves, and over-flowed me with strong lavations, and
sprinkled glistening foam in my face, and in among the clarinet as
among waving water-lilies, with flexible stems I splashed my easy way,
and so, ever lying in the music-waters, I floated and flowed, my soul
utterly bent and prostrate.[11a]

Certainly his was a soul hungry for music, and his descriptions
here of music in terms of nature are much like Whitman's, if more
"aesthetic."

Lanier made valiant efforts to recover his health and to engage
in the law practice which he apparently loathed with more than
ordinary hatred. His entire association with the business world
and law was one of protest, though occasionally he vowed to make
a good lawyer. But his health continued to fail, and by December
of 1872, Lanier had determined to forsake law and make what
efforts he could to restore his health.

From December 1872 to April 1873, Lanier pined in San Antonio, Texas, for the life on the Eastern coast, but his health was now so dangerously impaired that the Texas visit was thought necessary. Here he attended meetings of the Männerchor Society and began again to play the flute carefully, hoping to rebuild the power of his lungs. He played often for the musically interested in Texas. But 1873 was a decisive year. He determined to give up his profession entirely and came to Baltimore where the Peabody Orchestra was being formed. There he played for Asger Hamerik, pupil of von Bülow, protégé of Hector Berlioz, and conductor of the newly formed orchestra. Hamerik, who was impressed by Lanier's abilities, sent him down to New York with a letter to Theodore Thomas, and wrote of him later:

> To him as a child in his cradle music was given; the heavenly gift to feel and express himself in tones. His human nature was like an enchanted instrument, a magic flute, on the lyre of Apollo, needing but a breath or a touch to send its beauty out into the world. . . . His playing appealed to the musically learned and the unlearned, for he would magnetize the listener. . . . I will never forget the impression he made on me when he played the flute concerto of Emil Hartmann at a Peabody Symphony concert in 1878: his tall, handsome, manly presence, his flute breathing noble sorrows, noble joys, the orchestra softly responding. . . . He stood, the master, the genius. . . .[12]

Lanier played for Hamerik his own compositions for flute, among them "Field Larks and Blackbirds." Hamerik declared this to be the "composition of an artist."[13] Though he played also for Theodore Thomas, nothing seems to have come in the way of a professional engagement, and so in December of 1873 he was hired as first flutist by the Peabody Orchestra, formed under Hamerik's direction, and he moved to Baltimore for the season. His father and brother helped him financially at this point, since as a professional musician his earnings were exceedingly meagre. It may be assumed that Lanier felt, as his family probably did, that to delay longer in following his obviously "aesthetic" interests in music and poetry was unwise. His life span seemed definitely to be limited, and the move to Baltimore offered a rare opportunity to develop his two talents.

Lanier embarked almost immediately upon musical composition, for his midge dance or "Danse des Moucherons" was written for flute and orchestra during the first months in which he served with the orchestra. There seems to have been no happier period in Lanier's life than this first contact with the world of music.

Despite the fact that at first he did not even know how to follow the conductor's beats, he was soon proving himself in the world of professional music. His sight-reading ability improved virtually overnight, and his letters home describe the delight he took in playing chamber music. Though there were petty jealousies about his position, Lanier's relationship with the men who had given their whole lives to the study of music is remarkable for its sanity and calm. There can be no doubt of his really fine talent for music.

Lanier was also something of an inventor, experimenting with a long flute with which it would be possible to reach a low G. He used to enter one of the music shops to while away the time playing on the bass-flute; his playing called forth this comment from the proprietor, Badger:

Lanier is astonishing. . . . But you ought to hear him play the bass-flute. You would then say, "let me pass from the earth with the tones sounding in my ears." If he could travel with a concert troup and play solos on the bass-flute, I would get orders for fifty in a month. . . .[14]

In Baltimore he played with several Männerchor orchestras to supplement his income, as well as with the orchestra of the Concordia Theatre, in churches, and in private homes. He played as many out-of-town engagements as he could fill.[15]

His reactions to music were always dramatically emotional. He speaks repeatedly of the pain great music brought him, of the tears pouring from his eyes, and once after performing for a society in Texas he wrote his wife:

My heart which was hurt greatly when I went into the music-room, came forth from the holy bath of concords greatly refreshed, strengthened, and quieted. . . .[16]

The spiritual significance of music for Lanier was very great. He saw in music a great symbol of man's immortal yearnings, and some of the best writings in his letters are those concerned with music. In describing one of his concert performances he wrote to his wife:

. . . I had not played three seconds before a profound silence reigned . . . seeing which, and dreaming wildly of thee and feeling somehow, in an eerie and elfish and half-uncanny mood—I flew off into all manner of trills, and . . . cadenza monstrosities, for a long time, but finally floated down into *La Melancholie* (which, on the violin, ran everybody crazy some weeks ago here at a concert) which melted itself forth with such eloquent lamenting that it almost brought my tears:—and, to make a long story short, when I allowed the last note to die, a simultaneous cry of pleasure broke forth from men and women that almost amounted to a shout,—and I stood and received the congratulations that thereupon came in, so wrought up by my own playing with thoughts of thee I cd. but smile mechanically, and make stereotyped returns to the pleasant sayings, what time my heart worked falteringly, like a mouth that is about to cry. . . .[17]

The strongly "aesthetic" bent in Lanier, which revealed itself in his sentimental references to flowers and stars, coupled with the kind of emotional responsiveness to music apparent in these last quoted lines, seems almost effeminate, and repelled many of his readers. It was, however, this extreme sensitivity to sound and music which gave to his poetry its peculiar and original cast. But the fact that the poet could play as well as he did and stimulated the response from his audiences that he did, was, in many ways, a deterrent to his career as a poet, for here was also a kind of fame.

Lanier's best poetry dates from the year 1874 when he had finished his first season with the orchestra. Though the next seven years revealed a poetic growth almost unparalleled in American verse, the quantity of this poetry is not great. While Leopold Damrosch was encouraging the Georgia musician to further his musical studies, the Northern presses hailed his first major poem, "Corn," published in 1875. The success of "Corn" so stimulated Lanier's fancy that he set about immediately to write "The Symphony," wherein all of the instruments of the orchestra sing themes of various social significance in American life. This poem excited much curiosity in the art world, appearing as it did when synaesthesia had prompted tone poems, symphonic poems, and a variety of impressionistic musical studies. The possibilities of attempting musical form in verse stirred the creative imagination, and the poem passed for better than it was. Actually it was but an experiment.

However, the result was that Lanier achieved a kind of fame as a poet, while Charlotte Cushman and Bayard Taylor interested themselves in his behalf. It was Taylor who secured for Lanier the very envied opportunity to write the cantata ode for the first Centennial Celebration. The Centennial Cantata was performed May 10, 1876, with a chorus of 800 mixed voices and Thomas's orchestra of 150 musicians. The program opened with Richard Wagner's commissioned work, the *Centennial Inaugural March*, and it contained also a hymn by John Greenleaf Whittier, written for the occasion, and set to music by John Knowles Paine. The commission for the cantata came to Lanier as a special boon, since it gave him an opportunity to test his theories on the relationship of verse to music. Dudley Buck, the Connecticut musician whose compositions for the poetry of Poe are outstanding, shared honors with Lanier. The two worked well together and collaborated thereafter; particularly was Buck sympathetic to Lanier's theory that the poem for a cantata should be broad and general and that since it was to be primarily sung, with orchestral background, the words of the poem should be selected carefully "with reference to such quality as they will elicit when sung."

Lanier had been fully influenced by Wagner's writings on the relationship of music and poetry, and by the original poetry Wagner offered as libretti for his own operas. The growing emphasis on the orchestra in the nineteenth century, its perfect instrumental balance, and the ability of various choirs of instruments to express what had before been sung by the human voice, brought the orchestra to the fore, a fact which Lanier as a symphonic musician had recognized as well as had Wagner. Lanier was unfortunate in that his poem was published *before* the performance, without the music, and its vagueness unfavorably commented upon. It was felt that the poem alone had no meaning. Lanier was forced to defend it as a poem written *for* musical setting, in the newest sense. The performance justified his experiment. Poets like Francis Hopkinson in the eighteenth century, who were musicians as well and who were called upon to write cantatas, had adhered to the song-conception, but Lanier wrote with the symphony orchestra and the large chorus always in mind. Starke said of that occasion:

. . . neither Wagner's march nor the Whittier-Payne hymn was so acclaimed, as Lanier's and Buck's cantata. . . . The acclaim was not solely of Lanier's words nor of Buck's music, but of the music and words perfectly-wedded, and for this wedding Lanier was chiefly responsible.[18]

Daniel Coit Gilman, then president of Johns Hopkins University, said:

Lanier had triumphed. It was an opportunity of a life-time to test upon a grand scale his theory of verse. He had come out victorious.[19]

Gilman attempted at that point to arrange for Lanier a lectureship at Johns Hopkins on music and poetry, but was unsuccessful.

But other success did come from the cantata. Theodore Thomas engaged him for the following season (1877) to play with his orchestra. *Lippincott's Magazine* accepted for publication "Psalm of the West" as its centennial feature for the July issue, paying three hundred dollars for the ode. They also purchased the essay "From Bacon to Beethoven." *Scribner's* bought "The Orchestra of Today."

In 1877 Lanier was seriously ill and unable to fill either his position with the Thomas orchestra or the Peabody orchestra; but, settled in Tampa, Florida, he turned out some "nine or ten first-rate poems," among them two to Beethoven on the semi-centennial of his death. He also wrote "A Dream of the Age to Richard Wagner," wherein he pictured Wagner as the prophet of a new age when all work would be performed to strains of music. He returned to Baltimore "out of necessity" and played the following seasons, while his taste for literature and poetry increased. Though he wrote musical criticism for Baltimore papers and belonged to the music, not the literary society, he gave a course of "literary" lectures in a private home in the spring of 1878 to a group of ladies and gentlemen interested in Elizabethan literature. These were repeated successfully in successive years at Peabody Institute and eventually at Johns Hopkins where Gilman had finally (1879) succeeded in gaining him an appointment. Starke said that these lectures were based upon extensive research, during which time the poetic muse was all but silenced, except for the very fine "Sunrise" and "The Marshes of Glynn."[21]

But Lanier was burning himself out. He wrote, during this period, four books for boys,[22] numerous essays on Shakespeare, Chaucer, and the Middle English authors, as well as unpublished textbooks on Chaucer, Shakespeare, and the English sonneteers. Starke said these were not "produced merely as pot-boilers," but grew out of a deep and permeating interest in our older English literature.[23] In 1879 he wrote in eight weeks *The Science of English Verse,* a work in gestation for over two years. It was published the following year.

Lanier's death (1881) was exceedingly untimely, for his poetic ideas were in such a state of growth, and his final poems, "Sunrise" and "The Marshes of Glynn," in every way so new and excellent, that they seemed to prophesy a period of poetic fulfillment that Lanier never really lived to achieve. He left but one volume of verse, published in 1876 when many of his best poems were still

to be written. The growth in these last years, the steadily developing feeling for rhythm and sound, for treatment of idea, for scope
and breadth of form indicates that Lanier's poetic life should have
been longer. He did not leave any explanation for the type of
writing he finally came to, nor were these later efforts even widely
known. His fame has rested, unfortunately, upon such poetic curiosities as "The Symphony" and such lighter works as "Tampa
Robin."

At the time of his death Lanier was well regarded by his contemporaries as a talented poet, a capable musician, a successful
lecturer and teacher, and something of an essayist. He wrote frequently for the Baltimore papers and was in demand in civic
affairs concerned with the arts. Despite, however, his frantic efforts
in many directions to devote his life to the arts, he never earned
enough money even to support himself. His high moral earnest-
ness marks him as a Victorian and this "moral tone" weighted
down a great portion of poetry obviously lyrical. It was an anomaly
that Lanier felt poetry too to be a criticism of life, and a kind
of discordant quality marks these didactic poems because of his
naturally rich and sensuous imagery and his glittering poetic techniques. Some of the admiration he excited in his day grew out of
the battle he waged for art and morality under the most trying
of circumstances.

He left a considerable number of musical compositions and
pieces in preparation, the best of these being "Swamp Robins,"
"Sacred Memories," "Longing," and "Wind Song." His verses, in
turn, have inspired the effort of a host of composers, whom Anderson lists in the Centennial Edition.

It is often difficult to determine, when one looks at Lanier's life,
which was of greater importance to him personally—music or poetry. It should be noted that he wrote much of his verse early, and
apparently always hoped for a literary life, as the publication of
these early poems in lesser Southern journals would indicate. Also,
his study of German and the publication of *Tiger Lilies* may be
taken as some proof that the Baltimore musician was but earning
money to pursue his literary life more fully. On the other hand,
Lanier did write much of music from the beginning, and several
of his statements to friends indicate that he himself thought he was
more musician than poet. But he questioned early, in typical Victorian fashion, what service music might be in the social order.

I am more than all perplexed by this fact: that the prime inclination—that is, natural bent . . . of my nature is to music. . . . I have an extraordinary musical talent, and feel it within me plainly that I could rise as high as any composer. But I cannot bring myself to believe that I was intended for a musician, because it seems so small a business in comparison with other things, which, it seems to me, I might do. Question here: "What is the province of music in the economy of the world?"[24]

It has been seen to be a characteristic of poets who were musical or lyrical that they possessed some decided theories about the importance of music in the wider scheme of things. Lanier was no exception, and in some senses, his comments on music, which are surprisingly like those of his contemporaries and poetic peers, seem only to exaggerate the trend towards *synaesthesia* that was already in evidence. If Poe and Whitman worshipped music as superior poetry, Lanier, the musician, almost neglected to talk of poetry at all in his concern for the meaning of music. For him, music came to transcend religion itself in its spiritual power, and, like other nineteenth century figures, he felt the tremendous moral implication of music:

Greater and greater every year grow the multitudes of those who declare that no sermons, no words, no forms of any sort, avail to carry them on the way toward the desired sacred goal as do the tones of Palestrina, of Bach, of Beethoven . . . there comes but one testimony to the substantial efficacy of music in this matter of helping the emotion of man across the immensity of the known into the boundaries of the Unknown. Nay, there are those who go further than this: there are those who declare that music is to be the Church of the future, wherein all creeds will unite like the tones in a chord. . . .[25]

Despite the fact that most of the poets so far treated in this study were not practising musicians, Lanier's opinions and dicta on music are so fully in accord with their own views that almost more than anything else, he substantiates the sincerity of interest and the frequently intuitive knowledge of music that poets like Poe and Whitman had.

Like most nineteenth century lyrical poets, Lanier saw in music the panacea for a troubled world, and just as his musical gift exceeded that of other poets, so did his hope for music. He wrote:

. . . we are at the very threshold of those sweet applications we may hereafter make of that awful and mysterious power in music to take up our yearnings towards the infinite, at the point where words and all articulate utterance fail, and bear them onward to something like a satisfactory nearness to their divine object.[26]

In attempting, as a musician, to understand why there seemed to exist this close relationship between the infinite and music, Lanier said:

It must be that there exists some sort of relation between pure tones and the spirit of man by virtue of which the latter is stimulated and forced onward towards the great End of all love and aspiration. . . .[27]

Without answering *why,* Lanier asked why the "vibrations of the inner ear should endow man with so prodigious and heavenly an energy?" And this question led him to the formulation of his theory that music had a moral influence on man, a theory known to the Greeks and embodied in part by their doctrine of *ethos.*

I have so many fair dreams and hopes about music these days [1875]. It is a gospel whereof the people are in great need. I think the time will come when music, rightly developed to its now-little-foreseen grandeur, will be found to be a later revelation of all the gospels in one. . . .[28]

If Lanier had been alone in his feeling that music was endowed with supernal qualities, he might have been dismissed simply as an eccentric, but he was only one of the voices—many of them coming from Germany—at once the fountain-head of symphony and philosophy. His opinions are of unusual interest because music stimulated all his best verse.

In *Tiger Lilies,* his first book, Lanier took many an opportunity to philosophize and talk over musical matters.

For surely, the Art of today is music! . . . the art of painting has not struck its infinite roots into the domestic everyday-nesses of life, as the art of music has. There are not many homes in the land where one finds a painter's palette or a camera; but where is the cottage or hovel in which one will not find either a piano, a guitar, a flute, a violin, a banjo, a jews-harp, a whistling faculty, or a singing faculty?[29]

And, in writing of a concert of Lizst's, he turned again to the relationship of music and that "deeper life":

Lizst plays; we writhe under the music like the old priestess under the divine afflatus, so that our souls prophesy good things; and we shout in glory that the man there with his piano and his wondrous fingers has made conquest over the grim kingdom of the unutterable,— has spoken the otherwise unspeakable; and as we leave the concert room . . . our souls mount up to the very hem of the garment of God

. . . hearing, as we pass, the infinite music of the world's singing while they spin the thread of time. . . .[30]

Lanier even wrote of the omnipresence of music much as Whitman had:

The carpenter whistles to cheer his work, the loafer whistles to cheer his idleness. The church for life, and the bar-room for death; the theatre for tears and the circus for smiles; the parlor for wealth, and the street for poverty—each of these, now-a-days, has its inevitable peculiar orchestra . . . joy has gallops; sorrow has dirges; patriotism shouts its Marseillaise; and love lives on music. . . . From a christening to a funeral is seventy years; one choir sings at the christening, another choir sings at the funeral; all the life between, the dead man sang, in some sort, what times his heart could make. . . .[31]

And once, disappointed at a performance, he had written:

How well I now understand the foundation which music has, in the culture of the soul! A broad and liberal spirit wielding the baton tonight could have set the hearts of fifteen hundred people afire. As it was, they were (merely) greatly pleased. . . .[32]

He never abandoned the idea that music means more than people realize. He spoke of hearing two strains which were:

. . . full of majesty and simple sweetness. They bore to you soft breath from sunshiny woods, mingled with hum of purling waters of life and murmur of angel-talk; yet, in the midst of all, hinting by wild suggestions of a mystery that cannot be solved and a love that cannot be measured. The whole piece was like life and its end. It started with human yearnings and human failures; the second part brought religion and the third part spoke of heaven. . . .[33]

He went further than this. He believed that as music's power is felt among men, so the loveliness of morality is felt and so the race progresses. And he paid the typical romantic tribute to the greatness of Beethoven:

As for Beethoven . . . the educational value of his works upon the understanding soul . . . is unspeakable. . . . For in these works are many qualities which one could not expect to find cohering in any one human spirit. . . . I know not where one will go to find in any human product such tenderness, such variety of invention. . . . There is but one name to which one can refer in speaking of Beethoven: it is Shakespeare . . . so it is where Shakespeare ends that Beethoven begins.[34]

In one of the many philosophical discussions that take place in

Tiger Lilies, the young men, after revealing their familiarity with the ideas of Jean Paul, Emerson, and Carlyle on music, again turn to Beethoven:

What you say has occurred in poetry has also taken place, I think, in music. . . . Why do they talk of pre-Raphaelitism and not also of pre-Beethovenism and pre-Miltonism? These all mean surely nothing more than the close, loving, broad-minded study of Nature; and meaning this, they mean just what Raphael and Milton and Beethoven must have done. . . . Beethoven is to Chopin . . . as the sombre booming of the sea in a cave is to the heavenly murmur of a rivulet in a glen. So Milton to Tennyson and all the sweet house-hold poets of our day. . . . Those were grand, but these are beautiful; those were magnificent, these are tender; those were powerful, these are human![35]

Lanier was prone to generalize, and nothing ever seemed to give him as much pleasure as generalizing about the arts, and, more specifically, about music. It was music to which Lanier really seems to have devoted his thought. It was music which early inspired his soul, and poetry was only that "tangent" into which it sometimes shot. Though he came to a realization that his fame as a musician or composer would not be lasting, and though he was virtually self-taught as a musician, he never abandoned the effort to write music himself and to write about it. Its defiance of analysis sent the poet everseeking some new way of describing it:

The new-born child hears before he sees; the dying man hears after his eyes are forever dimmed: and so hearing is, as Richter says, "the first sense of the living" and the "last sense of the dying!" . . . Melody is as if one loved without reciprocation: harmony is the satisfaction of mutual love. Perhaps for this reason melody fascinates disappointed humanity and harmony pleases the satisfied angels.[36]

That music played an important role in Lanier's life is quite apparent; however, music was not the only force which distracted Lanier, the poet. One other reason why Lanier came so slowly to any obvious effort to fuse music and poetry was that he had a real interest in scholarship, and always sought the academic life. He probably would have done good work in musicology had the field then been open, for essays like "From Bacon to Beethoven," "The Orchestra of Today," "Mazzini on Music," and his Shakespeare essays, as well as "The Physics of Music," are genuine contributions to scholarship and criticism. Lanier was fascinated by science in his day, and did all he could to make of music an exact science. He had an analytical turn of mind; he was endowed with a certain perspicuity which made some of his theories read like newly discovered truths, and he had endless patience with the necessary detail work to prove a point.

Today his essays are almost unknown. Perhaps that is because many of them follow the line of "Music and Poetry" and the essay on "The English Novel": that is, they are syntheses of all knowledge current on these subjects at that time with an analysis of what the state of affairs actually was in the arts. Perhaps scholars today don't read Lanier's essays because they feel they have been superseded. Whatever the reason, the essays remain extremely provocative and worthy of much more attention than they have been accorded.

Kemp Malone wrote of Lanier's general scholarship and his Anglo-Saxon studies:

He had had no chance to get the professional training for research now available in most American universities; he taught himself. Moreover, his active interest in philology had come late in his career, and never won first place in his heart. In the circumstances, his scholarly achievement deserves generous recognition. This achievement was built up, of course, on a broad and solid foundation. Lanier entered academic scholarship a well-read man, at home in the world of literature, already a true philologist in the old sense of that word. And with his strong scientific interest it was natural for him to throw himself whole-heartedly into the new movement which everywhere was making the philologist a scientist in the field of letters. In his first Hopkins lecture, he sang the praises of exact scholarship, and put himself in the forefront of the fight for rigor and scientific precision in literary study. His lectures show him conscientious in taking account of the results achieved by contemporary investigators. They also show him deeply interested in the investigations themselves. . . . Given the health and strength to go on, he would surely have mastered the philological discipline and might well have become one of the leading Anglicists of his day. And though he had hardly begun his scholarly career when death brought it to an end, he left behind him a substantial body of learned writings.[37]

And of the large body of pioneering work Lanier did in testing his theories of rhyme as evidence of the chronology of Shakespeare's work, as well as capturing the *Zeitgeist* of Shakespeare's world in the essays on Shakespeare, Malone said:

The procedure and the conclusions are perfectly clear from the lectures themselves, to which the reader is referred with the assurance that he will find them learned, interesting, and characteristic both of Lanier and of his time.[38]

This scholarly turn of mind and the fund of information that Lanier drew upon by 1878 when he wrote *The Science of English Verse* led him often to use Shakespeare's poetry and drama, or Old English verse, to prove and explain his prosodic points.

Successful as both musician and lecturer, Lanier wrote in his final years, when the best of his poetry was being produced, a hurriedly prepared discussion of a subject that had long interested him. The debt owed to music in this prosodic study is that the poet thought music notation a far more accurate means for the transcription of the rhythms of verse than any prosodic notation so far devised. It is this debt which has confused some of his critics, who thought Lanier believed *all* poetry had been written with such musical values in mind. In addition, Lanier noted also, for the first time in prosodic history, the resemblance between speech tones and the singing voice. The success of this prosodic study can be gauged by noticing the indebtedness and approval of it by modern prosodists since 1880, among them E. C. Stedman, Julia P. Dabney, H. M. Alden, T. S. Omond, Egerton Smith, Henry Lanz, Gay Wilson Allen, and John Collins Pope.

Lanier's prosodic contribution lay in his recognition that standard verse rhythms, made up of like foot patterns, limited the flow of the line by such repetitions. His analysis of his own poems at this point, and the maturation of certain of his prosodic ideas, led him to believe that foot substitutions such as Poe sometimes made, and that all lyrical poets were prone to make, were nothing more than the efforts of poets to write in terms of the longer unit of the line rather than of the foot. He saw, and forecast in his own verse, the direction of modern verse toward lines made up of constantly shifting foot patterns which would eventually result in a defiance of standard prosodic scansions and would move in the direction of the freeness of music and prose. In this "modern" rhythmic pattern Lanier foresaw that only the musical measure would make clear the marking off of equal units of time. And he pointed out that from our earliest period poets of musical talent had felt this compulsion toward a freedom from exactly repeated foot forms— a fact which he demonstrated by applying musical scansion successfully to Old English verse as well as to the lyrical work of poets like Tennyson—simply another proof in the art world that the "modern" and primitive are much alike.

Lanier's work, long regarded as the best exposition of the quantity theory in prosodic history, met with the not inconsiderable weight of disapproval of George Saintsbury in his *History of English Prosody*, 1910-23. This cast such a pall over later prosodists that today prosodic theory lies, a virtual no-man's land, surrounded by a series of armed camps—those of the accentualists, those of the syllable-counters or advocates of foot forms, and those of the quantitists.

Since music had such an effect upon Lanier's prosodic theory and since it had much to do with the way in which he read and wrote verse, it is important to take notice of some of the valuable contributions he made and of the chief criticisms of his theory. Many criticisms of Lanier's quantity theory seem to grow out of a poor or careless reading of the work by critics or else out of their inability to cope with Lanier's surprisingly loose terminology. This latter fault Lanier, had he lived, would probably have been able to remedy. Also Lanier did not initially make his purposes clear, so that some critics did not fully understand why a musical staff was called into use, and others felt that his was no historical approach to the subject, as Saintsbury's was, for instance.

Saintsbury himself felt that *The Science of English Verse* was based upon a wholly wrong premise—a premise which directly interfered with his own staunch support of foot forms. His comments on Lanier's work are not helpful and are too slighting to clarify his own case. He seems to have felt, for one thing, that the only prosodic terms that were acceptable were those concerning foot forms, and anything else was "prosodically" wrong. He wrote:

The two main reasons why I have spoken disrespectfully (for I admit and maintain the disrespect) of musical *prosody* are as follows:— The first is that—without, I think, a single exception—the fruits of it are bad; and the scansions, as far as they allow themselves to be comprehended in prosodic terms at all, prosodically wrong. The second is the hopeless disagreement of the exponents.[39]

Harriet Monroe called Saintsbury's refusal to attempt to understand Lanier's theories tantamount to "a refusal to determine whether the sun goes around the earth or the earth around the sun in a treatise on astronomy."[40] But it should be remembered that Saintsbury did not deny the importance of quantity in prosody.[41]

He fully admitted that equal units of time were the rhythmic bases of poetry, but he wanted exactly preserved foot forms within these units. His quarrel lay with musical scansion which he felt did not so much interfere with accent as it interfered with foot forms. Poets, he felt, had to compose *in terms of feet*. They could not work with musical staffs, thinking of abstract note values and intricate rhythmic patterns, for words themselves, he felt, argued against this system. He must have felt that the musical analogy would destroy foot forms eventually so that rhythmic flow rather than strongly marked and repeated rhythms would characterize such verse (as it did.) And he would have, in part, agreed with Johannes Andersen, who wrote in *The Laws of Verse* a critique on musical scansions:

. . . supposed absolute equality misled Sidney Lanier in his musical scansion. He made the temporal units, the "feet," actual bars, restoring definite quantity to iambs and trochees. Poetry, however, by no means has the regularity of music; and whilst an iamb may be, and often is, short-long in actual quantity, it as often is not; and the trochee may be, but more often is not, long-short in quantity. While the musical element certainly enters largely into poetry, musical scansion leads to erroneous results. . . .[42]

Poe did not use musical notation; he demanded for a proper reading of his verse exactly measured values for the syllables that he had written. As a matter of fact, Poe more often than not deplored lapses from a one to one-half system.[43] Yet it is hardly in line with critiques on Poe as a poet to think of his exceptionally fine rhythms as "erroneous results," irrespective of the opinion one may hold of Lanier's abilities. This quantity system is not the classical quantity system where all syllables had certain assigned long or short values. Under this new system, the poet deliberately chooses to make his syllables of a certain length in accord with the rhythmic pattern he is developing. The poet, in this way, is much freer than he was under the old classical quantity system, and he is also free from adhering only and exactly to the same foot forms as poets had in the eighteenth century. This freedom was anathema to Saintsbury, who said: "Only by recognizing the independent personality of different feet can the true nature of English verse be understood; and, when once you leave that citadel of strength, you enter upon a labyrinth. . . ."[44] How right Saintsbury was about the labyrinth is illustrated by modern poetry and the musical verse of writers like Lanier and Whitman. Whether one approves of the quantity system or not, there is certainly much in Saintsbury's point that under the older foot forms, matters prosodic were much more stable, even if one had to occasionally slay the reputations of poets who did not see fit to follow foot forms. Saintsbury was no poet and did not analyze the creative principles at work in constructing verse. But he did know how he wanted to read and scan it.

Though, on the whole, Saintsbury's method of commenting on Lanier is reprehensible,[45] and though he makes errors like saying Lanier would do away altogether with accent (while reminding the reader that he himself is not primarily an accentualist),[46] he does make one point that has nothing to do with rhythm: he attacks the question of *timbre* as Lanier explained it in "speech-tunes," pointing out, quite rightly, that the analogy he drew to music was faulty.[47]

Ever since the Saintsbury period, and it is significant that no other critic of authority has attacked Lanier, some scholars have left the prosodic *onus probandi* with Lanier. Even Paull F. Baum, who edited the Centennial Edition of *The Science of English Verse,* and therefore should have known better, does an interesting job of legerdemain in keeping his own opinions in the air, aside from so innocuous a statement as this about the work: "He had nevertheless a fresh theory with a new and fundamentally sound idea in it, and even though he misapplied the idea, and almost wilfully obscured it with irrelevancies and false detail, he commands our respect and admiration."[48]

Baum does little to clarify the position this prosody holds today. One might even readily and justifiably question whether there was anything so "new" about the quantity system—a fact even Saintsbury paused long enough to mention—for the Renaissance poets were among the first to attempt the return to classical quantities and in this way stumbled upon the newer quantity theory, largely because Renaissance verse in Italy was all sung verse. The singing of words to music naturally establishes quantity in the verse line.

Though Baum did outline the prosodic works which preceded and followed Lanier's,[49] he did not treat carefully the chief differences in these works and Lanier's. It is not the concern of this study to "place" *The Science of English Verse,* except insofar as such a "placing" contributes to an understanding of Lanier's verse and influences those *poets* who became practitioners of the quantity theory. The subject here is, after all, poetry, not *just* prosody: but since Lanier's work comes closer to a study of all phases of poetry than any other up to this time, the writer must be forgiven for straying a little in these pastures. For the longer one looks at Lanier's prosodic work, the more impressive grows the contribution he made.

The Science of English Verse is surely worthy of defense against strictures like William Thomson's, which Baum felt were "difficult to refute."[50] Thomson had written that Lanier believed (1) that "quantity is the sole and sufficient basis of rhythm," and (2) that "the office of accent cannot begin until rhythm is established." He also wrote that Lanier was (3) "heavily weighted down by two preoccupations, the one that of music, the other that of the classical iambus and anapest"; he felt that Lanier had (4) "blundered about the bar" because he wrote the iambus ⏑ ⏑ while he felt it should be written ⏑ ⏑ ⏑ ,[51]—whatever that means. These may not have been the most severe criticisms of Lanier's work, but the chances are that they are or Baum would hardly have quoted them and been so impressed by them. It is worth noting that Thomson had once been quick to agree with Lanier when he wrote his *The Basis of English Rhythms* in 1904;[52] but after being singled out for attack by Saintsbury in 1910, he published *The Rhythm of Speech* (1923), with the changes of opinion indicated, in part, above.

It is well at this time to turn to *The Science of English Verse* to let Lanier defend himself in his own words. Of criticism number one Lanier wrote:

A clock which ticks seconds may be said to set up a primary rhythm for the ear which hears each recurrent tick. Those ticks are exactly alike: they fulfill the definition of primary rhythm, which describes it as a conception resulting from a similar event recurring at equal (or simply proportionate) periods of time.[53]

. . . .

But this primary rhythm may be considered a sort of primordial material, which the rhythmic sense of man always tends to mould into a more definite, more strongly-marked, and more complex form that may well be called secondary rhythm. . . . The tendency to arrange any primary units of rhythm into groups, or secondary units of rhythm, is so strong in ordinary persons, that the imagination will even effect such a grouping when the sounds themselves do not present means for it. . . .[54]

It will be of use to mention here, by way of anticipation, that it is secondary rhythm which is usually meant by the term "rhythm" in ordinary discourse, and that the variations in pitch and in intensity by which we saw it effected among the clock-ticks are what is called "accent" in English treatises.[55]

This, from Lanier, does not warrant Thomson's statement that he considered "quantity" the "sole and sufficient basis of rhythm." Lanier never indicated that it was either "sole" or "sufficient." He did say:

Time is the essential basis of rhythm. "Accent" can effect nothing, except in arranging materials already rhythmical through temporal recurrence. Possessing a series of sounds temporally equal or temporally proportionate, we can group them into various orders of larger and larger groups . . . by means of accent; but the primordial temporalness is always necessary.[56]

That Thomson fell into the error he did in his second stricture is Lanier's fault, for he used the term "rhythm" too loosely, wavering always between time and accent, and often forgetting to call one *primordial* rhythm and the other secondary or the truly rhythmic.

Thomson erred on his own account when he accused Lanier again of preoccupation with the classical iambus, for he could easily have read:

In point of fact, quantity is inseparable from all English words; though it is shifting, exactly as in music (that is, the same sound may be used either for a "short" or a "long," according to its varying relations with its neighboring sounds); and it is not limited to the single proportion, 1 to 2, but exists clearly in the further proportions of 1 to 3, 1 to 4, 1 to 5 and so on. . . .[57]

This "shifting" value of the English syllable and word is exactly what differentiated it for the poet's use from the classical quantitative values and gave such freeness to English verse.

Thomson's last point is by no means clear to me from his annotation, but certainly his idea that Lanier "blundered" about the bar is a strange one, for Lanier knew where the accents fell in music. Again it is Lanier's terminology that must have misled Thomson.

Many criticisms that are still leveled at Lanier's work are

concerned with his readings of lines,[58] and it has already been observed how Saintsbury deplored them. It should be pointed out, however, in defense of musical scansions and the quantity theory, that in all schools of prosodic thought there are differences—and extreme ones, within a given school—in the reading of lines. Baum said of this tendency:

> But nothing is duller than disputes about another man's scansions. Not only is agreement almost impossible and persuasion hopeless, what with our individual prepossessions and the frailty of our ear and taste . . . but often in fact a particular scansion is no true test of the theory at all, because the theory will sometimes lead a man to violate even his own conscience.[59]

A large portion of Lanier's contributions to our understanding of the rhythms of poets and poetry has been substantiated by the passage of time; though some of his insights still have not been scientifically proved and wait upon our further experiments in the physics of sound, it can be claimed that Lanier was the first prosodist to make completely clear the fact that poetry is not a written art, but always a sound art.[60] This realization Poe was conscious of when he wrote: "As yet written verse does not exist."[61] But Lanier was the first to make indubitably clear what that fact meant for poetry. Calvin S. Brown, the most recent critic and writer in the allied fields, drew heavily upon Lanier here.[62]

In some ways recognition of the fact that poetry is a sound art makes the quantity theory more understandable, for reading verse aloud slows down the tempo and exaggerates the values of the syllables to such an extent that even the "pure" accentualist must realize that syllables are being forced to occupy the time relationships that the poet had in mind. The mind's voice in reading poetry, as in reading music, is rapid and does not supply the proper values of either form of notation. It was for this reason that Poe always insisted upon an exaggeration of the time values in reading "The Raven," or any of his verse, and this quality marks verse like Vachel Lindsay's "Congo," where a correct reading demands that the strictly defined rhythms be made obvious.[63]

Lanier's understanding of music led him to differentiate between prosodical length (duration) and accent (stress or emphasis). In verse, until Lanier's time, length and accent or stress had been treated as though they were one and the same thing. Lanier's belief that they are different poses a new prosodic problem. If he is right—and it was for this failure to differentiate between the two that Lanier criticized Poe's prosodic markings—prosodists are faced with a need for another method of marking scansions. This new means for such markings Lanier found in the musical notation. He said Poe's essay was "permeated by a fundamental mistake—Namely, that the accent makes every syllable *long*. . . ."[64] However, what is true of music may not be as true of verse. Even Lanier admits that the average ear is badly trained to detect any subtle differences in intensity (or, in verse, heavy and light stress) except those at the far ends of each scale.[65] Is the stressed syllable in verse necessarily the long syllable, and if so, is that lengthening a matter of habit or is the more intense sound actually a lengthened sound? Questions such as these still abide in prosody and wait upon acoustical experiment. If the long syllable can be something other than the stressed syllable, and if the stressed syllable can be actually a short syllable in point of time, perhaps Lanier's rhythms would appear less varied than they do now. It may also be that an answer to this question would obviate many of the existent difficulties in prosodic terminology. It would account for lines in modern verse where the so-called "hovering accent" appears, quite apart from the length of the syllables. This is what Coleridge was groping toward when he eschewed foot forms and wrote on a principle of accent groupings, quite apart from long and short syllables. In music the repeated stress occurs on the first of every measure, though stress can be shifted anywhere in the unit of time (measure) at the will of the composer. It is the repetition of this stress at expected places that makes syncopation such a delight in music when a kind of counter rhythm is suddenly interpolated, occurring on the half or unstressed beat. In poetry this syncopation results from the sudden shift of foot form or pattern of stress after such a long period of regularity has occurred that the rhythms seem to have an established pattern. The best syncopation of verse results from a flow of, perhaps, iambs suddenly interrupted by a cross current of dactyls which move "three" against "two."

Lanier also pointed out, long before others, that the chief distinction between music and verse lay in "the difference between the scale of tones used in music and the scale of tones used by the human speaking voice."[66] And he wrote at some length on the fact that whereas the musical scale is tempered and made up of arbitrarily selected tones, the speaking voice is limited in scale only by sounds the ear can clearly distinguish; and while the voice has a more limited range, it has also many tones of less than a half step.[67]

The question of primary and secondary rhythms, as Lanier understands them, has already been touched upon. He made a further contribution in pointing out that any two speech sounds bear some time relationship to each other such as 1 to 3, 1 to 4, etc. In prose this relationship may be so close as not to be apparent, but it is the chief characteristic of poetry that this ratio should be quite obvious, the rhythms thus forced into this relationship. Foot forms limit the ratio between sounds somewhat; modern verse is inclined to the view that subtlety of rhythmic pattern, such as occurs in music and prose, is more interesting. Thus the ratios are usually less apparent in modern verse than the older 1 to 2 form; and modern verse lines, for this reason, have a kind of unhampered flow down the page like prose, because of this more subtle rhythm. Eighteenth century forms, and even, for that matter, Poe's rhythms, point up the exact ratios more clearly than later verse.

Lanier's work with logical as well as rhythmic accent is provocative. His statement that rhythmical accent establishes the rhythm while logical accent "disestablishes" it is perspicuous. He was conscious of the "rest" in verse, which Poe termed, ambiguously, the "caesura," and he too pointed out that it was this quality in verse which made the quantity theory so necessary. He was not, however, enlightening about the stanza, though his own verses came to fall into freer forms than most poets approved. However, he must have felt that his stanzas were "organic" because he deplored lack of form; and yet he failed to realize how closely he was paralleling Whitman, whom he had criticized for "formlessness."

Many of Lanier's insights are worth repeating, though it is impossible to do so in any detail. He said, for instance, that written English words "constitute a system of notation for rhythm, precise as to the larger orders but susceptible of varying interpretations as to the primary rhythms to the extent of minute differences of utterance. . . ."[68] Few poets, outside of Poe, ever made better use of the English language as a notational system, distributing syllables like notes.

He said that "the liberty of arranging at pleasure the individual time-relations (or primary rhythms) . . . is availed of by poets to make their rhythms melodious, varied, and characteristic."[69] Like Poe he illustrated his quantity thesis best by reference to the silences in poetry which are intrinsic to a line, not part of either a foot or accentual system and wholly dependent upon *time*. He illustrates this through Tennyson's "Break, break, break. . . ."[70] He pointed out how often poets like to use the triplet in verse, just as the musician does, to stretch (elongate) a time unit to its utmost.[71] He also pointed out that the good poet immediately makes known to his reader his metrical system by the first lines of verse and the syllabic distribution of the words. He warned poets particularly against the use of a single word as a rhythmic unit since the lines constructed from such units are thus open to several possible interpretations. It should be noted that Lanier did actually very little with logical accent, a field in which Bayard Q. Morgan has done much recent exploration. Lanier, however, at least recognized the power of logical accent, as he did of pronunciation accent.

Lanier's work with "three rhythm," by which he means the iamb and the trochee, is based largely upon excerpts and readings from Old English verse, for which he established a strong temporal rhythm in a day when some scholars were still denying that Old English verse even had a distinguishable rhythm. His contribution here lay largely in the work with the unaccented syllables which too many nineteenth century scholars considered a matter of indifference. Since the quantity system is quite as much concerned with the values of unaccented as with accented rhythmic units, Lanier's work pioneered in Leonard's direction. One of the most surprising developments in this chapter is the obvious ease with which Old English falls into musical scansion.[72] That much of Old English verse was a kind of chant or recitative is known, and its inherent musical properties make musical scansions most satisfactory. Anglo-Saxon rhythmic patterns are usually readily apparent from the opening words, and the parallels Lanier drew between this verse and that of Swinburne and Whitman are happy ones. Music like "Sumer is icumen in/Lhude sing Cucu" naturally adapts to musical scansion. One might take issue with scansions of *Piers Plowman,* wondering why the bar was not so arranged that the accented beat formed trochees rather than iambs, but so might one wonder at the Prologue to the *Canterbury Tales* and the "Knightes Tale," as well as Hamlet's soliloquy; but musical scansion is perfect for Longfellow's verse, the "Fight at Finnesburg," Tennyson, and, of course, Poe. Ballad rhythms, as in "Agincourt" and Coleridge's "Christabel," take on a crystalline quality under notational scansions. And surely one of his finest contributions lay in the section on Shakespeare's use of the rhythmic accent when, in discussing his blank verse, Lanier wrote:

> We can see him [Shakespeare] learning to think in verse . . . he finally made his whole technic a constitutional grace, so that his passion flowed with a hereditary pre-adaptation to rhythm.
> . . . This method of working with a constant inward reference to the great average and sum of men, and with an absolute reliance upon their final perception, is the secret of that infinitely varied rhythm which we find plashing through all the later blank verse of Shakespeare. . . .
> Perhaps every one has observed that particularly in Shakespeare's later plays he seems absolutely careless as to what kind of word the rhythmic accent may fall on. Sometimes it is on the article *the,* sometimes the preposition *of,* sometimes the conjunction *and.* . . .
> This apparent carelessness is really perfect art. It is the consummate management of dramatic dialogue in blank verse, by which the wilder rhythmic patterns of ordinary current discourse are woven along through the regular strands of the orderly typic lines.[73]

At this point Lanier illustrates one of his most brilliant insights into Shakespearean blank verse, writing it first with musical notation for its underlying (*typic,* he calls it) rhythms, which the reader is at once in absolute disagreement with, and then noting rhythmically the *actual* reading of the lines according to meaning. By a comparison of the two he illustrates, with amazing clarity, that the typic form *does underlie* the actual, and that the variations from the typic are what most please us because the typic rhythms sound through the actual unconsciously.[74]

In this most prescient chapter, Lanier, unfortunately, since this is the fullest exposition of his ideas through application of notational values to familiar verse, fails to make clear that his musical scansions often are basic rhythmic scansions rather than reading patterns or secondary rhythms themselves. He does not sufficiently stress this fact, and it is not until one has reached nearly the end of that chapter and has waded through his re-appraisal of metrical tests to determine the chronology of Shakespeare's plays that the key or clue is dropped that makes his musical scansions, when they seem at fault, only the raw material from which the poet worked and possibly departed. And when the readings are happy it is because that poet was consciously adhering to or forcing a "typic" rhythm. Lanier, the musician, is often suggestive rather than explanatory, and though much of his material in these early chapters is done in too much detail, most of his ideas suffer from lack of development. That he must have realized this, after reading the first review, can be gathered from the fact that he set about instantly to revise the work—a revision hindered by his early death.

The succeeding chapters in section I, following the climax reached in chapter three on rhythm in English verse, are a vast emptiness in which Lanier does nothing whatsoever with the line, the stanza, and logical accent. Here his poor organization is most apparent, for he had already said originally in the first chapter much of what he had to say, and he did not wish to repeat himself, even by way of illustration. Then he had placed alliterative groupings with logical accent when they undeniably belonged to the section on "The Tunes of English Verse." His final chapter in this section on rhythm is exceedingly weak; and it is difficult to see why a separate chapter had to be made of three or four pages for four rhythms in English, which are but dactyls and anapests and could have been illustrated along with three rhythms in a chapter on basic rhythmic patterns in English. It is obvious that the writer, in sketching the whole thing out hastily in eight weeks, did himself a terrible injustice.

By the time Lanier reached section II of his work he was exhausted, and it is true that this section was slighted by the poet.[75] But haste is not the only reason that section II is not well written. Actually the whole field of speech tunes is just now being explored, and Lanier's genuine prophetic recognition that rhyme belongs in a discussion of speech tunes and not only in a discussion of rhythm is typical of the thought that did go into the book. He began with a most prescient discussion of speech tunes, pointing out "what delicate variations in meaning were effected by uttering the same words to a different tune,"[76] and illustrating how much of the meaning of a given sentence or question is altered by the tones in which it is spoken, which have a pre-arranged and understood meaning. He reiterated that the range of the speaking voice was limited and employed variations of less than half steps; he even suggested a possible scale constructed on the basis of these smaller intervals for the average two octave voice. Further than this the poet does not go, though men like Bayard Q. Morgan are continuing research along these lines.[77]

The colors of speech, beginning with the section on rhyme, had a short and unhappy development, for Lanier threw out the pregnant suggestion that harmony and melody differed in verse, and then, rather than force himself into thinking through what he had begun, he did a kind of history of rhyme which is of little value to students today. He revealed a partiality for internal rhyme while cautioning the poet against too many rhymes too near each other in "tone color." In his brief discussion of vowel-colors he applauded the careful and fairly wide distribution of vowel sounds in a line. He was wholly conscious of the effect of alliteration upon the rhyme scheme, and spoke of its purpose as that of varying the pattern. He was favorable to mild and hidden alliterative patterns rather than those which were "loud." Again his conclusion is weak, and he seems to have ended the book at the point where hopes were highest that an ear trained as his was and an imaginative faculty fertile as his was, coupled with a rather astonishing breadth of knowledge, would lead far into the exploration of those mysteries of verse which, until his few chapters, had remained almost untouched.

It is easy to fall into the habit of saying that "the trouble with Lanier was. . . ." The trouble does not lie so much with Lanier as it does with the fact that art is long, and two arts twice as long. Had he lived much longer, he might have given us the final word prosodically, and then again he might not have. His book as we have it has many inaccuracies in it, and fails at many points. It is not always clear; it is poorly organized, and, at the most inauspicious moments, Lanier begins to wave the blue flower, which in his case is the rose, and quite confounds his logic with transcendental theories about the nature of rhythm in the universe, all of which date his work and his thinking. However, no one else in the English language on either side of the ocean had written anything nearly so comprehensive, so thoughtful and thought-provoking about verse in the year 1880, and even Saintsbury's work can not be compared, for it is an historical approach like that of the Renaissance prosodists and not a probing of what constitutes poetry.

This book was not a handbook for beginners nor was it actually by a beginner in the fullest sense of that term, for Lanier had written his "Physics of Music" for publication and almost had it in the press when he decided to amplify the material and make a book of it. It does not purport to teach how to write poetry, nor does it lay down rules for the writing of verse. What it actually is is an *analysis* of verse, laying bare those constituents that had so far defied analysis or treatment, such as the quantity element in modern English, the question of the relationship of typic and reading rhythms in verse, the matter of rhyme as both a rhythmic and "color" function in verse, and alliteration and syzygy.

Whole schools of prosodic theory were spurred by Lanier's little book. J. C. Pope, after years of working with Old English verse, came to the conclusion that a line was best scanned by musical notation. He concluded that if verse was rhythmic one should be able to beat time to it, and he spoke highly of his debt to Lanier.[78] Baum lists the many contemporary critical opinions on the book, concluding that the prosodic consensus today is favorable to *The Science of English Verse*.[79] Gay W. Allen wrote favorably of it[80] and Bayard Q. Morgan is continuing research along lines suggested in Lanier's work on speech tunes. Evelyn H. Scholl, writing in *PMLA*, in 1948, on the conflicting theories of prosody, bore out the quantity theory in her study of Renaissance verse.[81] Wilbur Schramm's recent experiments in rhyme indicate that Lanier was moving in the right direction,[82] and the heavy dependence on Lanier of Calvin S. Brown's fine work proves how prophetic the book actually was.[83] Compounded of naively stated truths and of startling bits of erudition, the book remains today the only outstanding prosodic work of a poet writing in his own field of an art he knew intimately. He had a finer background for writing than we can expect to find again.

In any discussion relating Lanier's verse to music, the element of paradox must at once be recognized. For though Lanier was a professional musician as well as poet, and thus might be expected to represent the ultimate virtues of musical-poetic productions, he must not be thought of as the successor to the symphonic conceptions of Whitman. For Whitman had so early an exposure to symphonic music of the best sort that the accounts Lanier leaves of hearing the symphony in New York in 1871-72 seem, by comparison, pathetic. And though Lanier was brought up in a musical family, so much of his early youth was given to war and so many of the following years were spent in the South during Reconstruction when the arts began a serious lag, that he may be said to have spent the formative years of a poet's life in a kind of musical drought.[84] His early verses, for this reason, exhibit only those musical tendencies natural to a lyrical poet interested in music, and his was initially a song conception for verse, not a symphonic one. His interests in the beginning were in the poetic conceits and musical sounds of the syllables, this though he was nearly a quarter century younger than Whitman.

It is also significant that Lanier's location virtually segregated him from the mainstream of nineteenth century verse in America. Most of his poetic readings were in German and French literatures, and aside from a friendship with Paul Hamilton Hayne, who was similarly situated, and imitations of Poe, Coleridge, and Byron, the young poet could not be said to be widely read in modern verse. He did not even read Whitman's verse until 1878, when his own was largely written. Thus Lanier's growing awareness of musical forms for verse runs parallel, in many respects, to Whitman's own recognition of the symphony and its form. That Lanier moved into another later musical conception for verse, impressionism, comes almost too late in his life to be anything but provocative. It does indicate, however, how rapidly the poet transformed musical ideas and art concepts into poetry.

Lanier served a long apprenticeship to poetry, however, and from his earliest youth was writing his father for criticisms on his more serious poetic efforts. His father seems to have been quick to recognize the extravagances of the young poet, and Lanier realized early that his was to be, among other things, a pruning job. Before he even began the study of law in 1868, he had written over seventy poems, nearly half of all the poems he was ever to write. It is impossible here, and unnecessary, to treat in any detail any large portion of Lanier's verse, but in order to show the linguistic and poetic growth which the poet made away from his earliest completely aesthetic terminology to a kind of love for Anglo-Saxon phrasings, it will be necessary to look at some of these early poems. The influence of Chaucer upon the poet in 1872 was salutary, for he came to love the diction of our native tongue. And he wrote in 1873 to Peacock, when the influence of the symphony began its hold upon him: ". . . but *one cannot forget Beethoven,* and somehow all my inspirations came in these large and artless forms, in simple Saxon words, in unpretentious and purely intellectual conceptions. . . ."[85]

Lanier's poetic growth is one of the most exciting and promising in our language. From imitations of Poe and Coleridge, and later efforts imitative of Swinburne, Tennyson, Morris, and Browning, Lanier gradually evolved, by a series of experiments, and in distinct stages, his own style peculiarly related to his interest in music and his growing recognition of the relationship of the two arts. In 1864 the young Lanier was writing of his determination to see if he had the talent to make a poet of himself; ten years later, in

1875 with the publication of "Corn," he received the answer, after a long period devoted to teaching, law, and music.[86]

The lyrical elements in Lanier's verse are strongly evident from the very beginning, and his first verse appears in Poe-like stanzas with already marked attention to rhythmic variation and subtle combinations of sound:

> A lone wolf by a castle-ruin howled,
> A moon between black drift-clouds scowled
>   With baleful leer—
>
> Wind through age-eaten port holes moaned
> And weirdly shrieked wild wailings, toned
>   Like cries of fear—[87]

The Gothic quality in this sixteen-year-old's verse is more imitative than the instinctive artistry with which his ear directed him into a smooth pattern where "wolf," "with," "wind," "weirdly" and "wild wailings" bind the two stanzas together. Then the shift of *o* sounds from the initial position in the first stanza to the final position in the first lines of stanza two gives sound unity to the grouping. He apparently knew intuitively how to space sounds in a line, for the melody leans heavily upon *o, e, i,* and the alliterative *l* sounds. His fine innate rhythmic sense led him to write the fore-shortened third lines.

Three years later, however, the writer was trying his hand at his "three-fold" metaphors which result often in unpleasant conceits. Here the alliterations are exaggerated and the poem is deficient in taste.

> Thou rippleless, dim lake, enspelled
>   By the basilisk eyes of stars, at night:
> With thy lilies calm as sweet thoughts, upheld
>   On thy bosom's waveless chrysolite. . . .
> Float the Unloved to the lilies, O Lake,
> And cover the Loveless with lilies, Good Lake;
> No flowers on land (in life!) had she:
> Let her have flowers (in death!), in thee.[88]

This tendency toward a style that is an elaborate weaving of sounds began to characterize a good portion of Lanier's writing from this time on. Here the poet is exaggerating the *l* sounds without too much regard for the total effect upon the reader. The poem, in many ways, is in poorer taste than the first because of words like "rippleless" and "enspelled" which appear in one line, and phrases like "waveless chrysolite" which offer a plethora of "l" sounds. It is a mistake, however, to think the poet here is only carried away with the musical sounds of the liquids, or with questions of balance like "in life" and "in death," etc. Actually, this poem is also heavily weighted by the poet's sentimental message, so like Thomas Hood's, which stultifies the flow of the lines, while his meaning, because of the welter of sounds, evades the reader as completely as possible. Poe's attempt at indefiniteness was a quite different matter. Lanier's is no attempt to imitate music, but rather an effort to be ultra profound, to "impact" into every word and phrase meaning that is in no wise clarified by the extreme music of the sounds he writes in. This "impacted" quality is in every way foreign, as an element in verse, to the truly lyrical, but it was Lanier's misfortune that he had both sound and sense in some of his verse beyond the limit of enjoyment.

Since Lanier was always conscious of music, almost any of his early poems have some connection with music. One of his first poems to receive recognition outside the South was "Life and Song." Written in 1868, it was reprinted in Baltimore and New York periodicals, and it represents the second style in which Lanier wrote his verse: the clearer of the two, the less impacted, and the less concerned with melody within the line. It uses the clarinet as the symbol of Song:

> If life were caught by a clarionet,
>   And a wild heart, throbbing in the reed,
> Should thrill its joy and trill its fret
>   And utter its heart in every deed,
>
> Then would this breathing clarionet
>   Type what the poet fain would be;
> For none o' the singers ever yet
>   Has wholly lived his minstrelsy,
>
> Or clearly sung his true, true thought,
>   Or utterly bodied forth his life,
> Or out of Life and Song has wrought
>   The perfect one of man and wife;
>
> Or lived and sung, that Life and Song
>   Might each express the other's all,
> Careless if life or art were long
>   Since both were one, to stand or fall:
>
> So that the wonder struck the crowd,
>   Who shouted it about the land:

> *His song was only living aloud,*
> *His work a singing with his hand!*[89]

The poem is chiefly characterized by a more judicious separation of alliterative sounds so that *l, b, d, f,* and *s* are scarcely prominent sounds, while *t* and *th* are rather apparent. It was natural that this poem should achieve some wider popularity since it was simple in form and rhythmic concept and maintained a unity of tone that he was not, at this time, always successful in maintaining.

More typical of the "aesthetic" poems from this period is "Betrayal," which embodies much that was best in this style of writing, and much that was bad. A far more lyric poem than "Life and Song," and one that in its colors and references immediately suggests Villon, the poem adds to its imitative qualities a certain artistic surety that is promising.

> The sun has kissed the violet sea,
>   And burned the violet to a rose.
> O Sea, O Sea, mightst thou but be
>   Mere violets still? Who knows? who knows?
>   Well hides the violet in the wood:
>   The dead leaf wrinkles her a hood,
>   And winter's ill is violet's good;
>   But the bold glory of the rose,
>   It quickly comes and quickly goes—
>   Red petals whirling in white snows,
>   Ah me!
>
> The sun has burnt the rose-red sea:
>   The rose is turned to ashes gray.
> O Sea, O Sea, mightst thou but be
>   The violet thou hast been to-day!
>   The sun is brave, the sun is bright,
>   The sun is lord and love and light;
>   But after him it cometh night.
>   Dim anguish of the lonesome dark!—
>   Once a girl's body, stiff and stark,
>   Was laid in a tomb without a mark,
>   Ah me![90]

Here the rhymes have an interesting pattern, with a quatrain at the beginning and two sets of lines rhyming in threes. The lines themselves are rhythmically pleasing with occasional foot substitutions, and the imagery, while vivid, does not carry any intellectual burden. The only lines over which the reader really hesitates are the fourth lines in each stanza—those which change the color violet of the sea to the flower, violet, so that the whole first sequence seems a badly mixed metaphor. The sentimental touch at the close, the ever-recurrent death of young ladies, pleased Lanier as it had Poe and later many a Victorian. But young Lanier never seems to know quite what the significance of the death is, so that his poems are not made more effective by the reference. It has been pointed out that Lanier, who believed in a message for verse, really had very little to say in his early poetry.[91]

The two rhyme schemes most characteristic of Lanier are the alternate rhyming lines of the quatrain, usually employed in his simpler lyrics, and the three-line rhyming stanza, which seems to have been a favorite pattern of Whitman's too. This particular pattern was effective in that it made possible a repetition or a balanced phrasing with the third line usually directed toward the next unit of three lines, or else gave a kind of finish to the first two. In "Nirvana," for instance, he employed this technique, usually with the third line acting in the nature of a revelation, while its patterning was already established as a familiar one:

> Through seas of Dreams and seas of Phantasies,
> Through seas of Solitudes and Vacancies,
> And through myself, the deepest of the seas,
>   I strive to thee, Nirvana, etc.[92]

Another noticeable characteristic of Lanier's work, which he found troublesome at first but which toward the end of his life was becoming one of his most pleasing stylistic devices, was the conversational line. By this I mean that the poet sometimes departed from any ordinary poetic pattern and began to write a blank verse of marked sincerity and heightened expression. At first the employment of this non-poetic personal approach was stilted and spotty, since the poet employed the personal style in the most personal of matters and the poem reflected a kind of self-pity. Later, as his understanding grew of what was to be, for him, the most fortunate choice of subject matter—nature—the personal element took on the color of a prophetic voice, separated from the material, and yet perfectly conscious of judging it. The earliest employment of the personal blank verse line in Lanier can be seen in "June Dreams, in January." Written as the direct outgrowth of the poet's sadness at his inability to earn his livelihood by writing, and immediately preceding the period devoted to the study of law—a profession taken up in dire necessity—Lanier exhibits his sentimental style in the introductory little poem which deals with June, flowers, night, winds, and night sounds. It is better in its actual imagery than it at first appears to be—like most of Lanier's work—and it is followed by almost perfect blank verse rhythms. The final section, not quoted here, completes the story, in which a friend, "Dick Painter," comes in and carries off the poem to a critic who happily approves it; and so the final scene deals with the happiness of the poet. It is interesting that the little domestic scenes ensue as they do, because it indicates that Lanier, even though he failed at dialect writing, certainly had some talent for the narrative poems so popular in the gift annuals of the time. The poem opens with regular enough quatrains:

> O tender darkness, when June-day hath ceased,
>   —Faint odor, of the crushed day-flower born,
> —Dim, visible sigh out of the mournful East
>   That cannot see her lord again till morn:
>
> And many leaves, broad-palmed towards the sky
>   To catch the sacred raining of star-light:
> And pallid petals, fain, all fain to die,
>   Soul-stung by too keen passion of the night:
>
> And short-breath'd winds, under yon gracious moon
>   Doing mild errands for mild violets,
> Or carrying sighs from the red lips of June
>   What aimless way the odor-current sets:
>
> And stars, ring'd glittering in whorls and bells,
>   Or bent along the sky in looped star-sprays,
> Or vine-wound, with bright grapes in panicles,
>   Or bramble-tangled in a sweetest maze,
>
> Or lying like young lilies in a lake
>   About the great white Lotus of the moon,
> Or blown and drifted, as if winds should shake
>   Star-blossoms down from silver stems too soon, . . .
>
> And long June night-sounds crooned among the leaves,
>   And whispered confidence of dark and green,
> And murmurs in old moss about old eaves,
>   And tinklings floating over water-sheen!

However, in fairness to Lanier it should be pointed out that even this little poem, compounded of sights, scents, and sounds, is superior in many respects to the ordinary verse of less talented writers. Quatrain one with its image of "tender darkness" as an "odor" "crushed" from the "day-flower" is a better than average sensuous image. That it lies next to another idea—that dark is the "visible sigh" of "mournful East" separated from the sun—does not, of course, help either image. The delineation of the light upon leaves in the next stanza is sure promise of the fine, almost superfine, nature detail that was to characterize the last and best of Lanier's verse. Here is the repetition of compound words like "star-light" and "soul-stung." Two images again surfeit the line: the "sacred raining" of star-light upon broad palms, and the color of the leaves lying pallid under the "too keen passion of the night." The third quatrain misses rather badly, but the next, with its imagery surely depending upon the sight of decorations of a Christmas tree, is quite successful, as is the re-shaped lilies-on-lakes material with the happy phrasing of the "great white lotus of the moon." In these verses it should be noted that the poet introduces considerable variation within the line and that the words are many syllabled so that the rhythm is unmistakable; it should also be obvious that the poet has set up a springing, bounding line, caught at each end—at one by the rhymes, at the other by the introductory "ands" and "ors," while the fullness of the line billows out between. The poet is obviously skillful, for he has no difficulty with either rhyme or rhythm. Like most of Lanier's early verse, and this belongs to his early period, it errs in having a too-muchness—always the sign of a youthful but important talent. The same ease is observable in the fine blank verse lines—fine that is, rhythmically, though the telling of the story here is also quite successful:

> Then he that wrote, laid down his pen and sighed;
> And straightway came old Scorn and Bitterness . . .
> "I'll date this dream," he said: "So: Given, these,
> On this, the coldest night in all the year,
> From this, the meanest garret in the world,
> In this, the greatest city in the land,
> To you, the richest folk this side of death,
> By one, the hungriest poet under heaven,
> —Writ while his candle sputtered in the gust,
> And while his last, last ember died of cold,
> And while the mortal ice i' the air made free
> Of all his bones and bit and shrunk his heart . . .
> —Read me," he cried, and rose, and stamped his foot
> Impatiently at Heaven, "read me this"

(Putting th' inquiry full in the face of God)
"Why can we poets dream us beauty, so,
But cannot dream us bread? Why, now, can I
Make, aye, create this fervid throbbing June
Out of the chill, chill matter of my soul,
Yet cannot make a poorest penny-loaf . . ."
And, late, just when his heart leaned o'er
The very edge of breaking, fain to fall,
God sent him sleep. . . .[94]

The remarkable thing about this essentially unpoetic matter is that because of a certain well-placed repetitiveness and a wonderful ear for alliterative spacing, it remains poetry.

Lanier was one of the masters of the single line refrain, which he usually modified in successive strophes of the poem. "On Huntingdon's 'Miranda' " is a good example of this sort of thing. However, aside from a keener awareness of rhythmic possibilities in verse and a noticeable ease in grouping rhythms in a line, Lanier does not exhibit until 1874 more of a tendency than other lyric poets to fuse music and verse.

By 1874 Lanier had had access to the superior cultural life of Baltimore with its newly founded conservatory of music and its new university, Johns Hopkins. He had been a professional symphonic musician for a season, and was already experimenting in the physics of sound with the apparatus available at Peabody. He had written more music in that year than he had written before, and there was a marked growth in the technical quality of the poems published in this period. "Corn," written in 1874, is the most maturely conceived of any of Lanier's poems and exhibits all of the virtues and the vices that were to characterize his best verse.

"Corn" was inspired by a return to his native Georgia, whose war-scarred and deserted cotton lands seemed to him a symbol of all that had become wasted in the South. In the hope of restoring the productivity of the South by arousing interest in the planting of corn he wrote this poem, the most complex he had yet conceived. Its success grew directly out of its fine nature descriptions, the subtlety of the rhythms, and the message which the poet intended to convey. Again there is the surfeit of detail which may be likened to that of certain tapestries, each corner of which is elaborated, and whose intricacies are such that the eye at close range is wearied by an attempt to discern the fuller meaning in the weaving. Yet the curious and interested find in the poem a kind of finical perfection, a latter-day baroque quality which seems hardly indigenous either to the English tongue or to the period in which Lanier wrote. This quality in Lanier's verse, which differentiates it wholly from anything written before or after, so that he seemed to have struck off in the direction of an originality almost divorced from standard conceptions of verse, was fed upon springs too hidden for imitation and repels some readers while it fascinates others.

To talk of ordinary poetic considerations in the poems from 1874 on is to offer only a partial appraisal of Lanier's work, for though his rhymes had given patterns, though he used recognizable rhythms, and though all that can be said of the work of any lyrical poet can be said of Lanier, these are not the distinctive features of his work. One must initially recognize that here is an exercise of the intellect, an exercise of the fancy, of the understanding, of the ear, and of the memory. Here are threads from many different skeins; and in attempting to trace their rightful source, one is likely to become lost in a blur of color. There is almost a disfigurement of the original conception of the poem in the bloating which takes place in every portion. There is a probing of particulars that often reveals too much, so that some details stand starkly forth which seem to need muting. And the complexity of key ideas and their treatment take on a character—since they are worked out in such detail—like baroque music; the lines fairly spring from the page in a whirling concatenation of sound and sense.

This element in Lanier's work is so far removed from the poetic tradition—though when Lanier read Whitman late in life he was fascinated and instantly recognized the musical quality of his verse—it can only be said to have originated from a musical mind, a mind trained in subtleties beyond ordinary comprehension, a mind given to indefinitely defined general impressions with detailed treatment of portions of ideas, a mind full of the endless varieties which make up the sudden shifts of emotion we experience in music and of the repetitions which give pleasure. Lanier's ideas dip and merge after the fashion of music; the stanzas form and change. With "Corn" a certain complexity in his verse becomes a settled style which runs parallel to the simplicity and beauty of his song style. "Corn" is by no means the best example of this tendency toward the complex structure in Lanier: it is simply the first of the important poems in this *genre*.

The poem opens with a detailed comparison of the green woods and human characteristics like sight, touch, breath, and sound, a comparison that is inverted before the strophe ends, so that the human is described in terms of nature. This device of inversion is common musical treatment of an idea. It should be noted immediately that this is a kind of descriptive verse, depending upon light and shadow and the human senses for the totality of the impression.

> To-day the woods are trembling through and through
> With shimmering forms, that flash before my view,
> Then melt in green as dawn-stars melt in blue.
> The leaves that wave against my cheek caress
> Like women's hands; the embracing boughs express
> A subtlety of mighty tenderness;
> The copse-depths into little noises start,
> That sound anon like beatings of a heart,
> Anon like talk 'twixt lips not far apart.
> The beech dreams balm, as a dreamer hums a song;
> Through that vague wafture, expirations strong
> Throb from young hickories breathing deep and long
> With stress and urgence bold of prisoned spring
> And ecstasy of burgeoning.
> Now since the dew-plashed road of morn is dry,
> Forth venture odors of more quality
> And heavenlier giving. Like Jove's locks awry,
> Long muscadines
> Rich-wreathe the spacious foreheads of great pines,
> And breathe ambrosial passion from their vines.
> I pray with mosses, ferns and flowers shy
> That hide like gentle nuns from human eye
> To lift adoring perfumes to the sky.
> I hear faint bridal-sighs of brown and green
> Dying to silent hints of kisses keen
> As far lights fringe into a pleasant sheen.
> I start at fragmentary whispers, blown
> From under-talks of leafy souls unknown,
> Vague purports sweet, of inarticulate tone.[95]

The three-line rhyme pattern here, with its interpolated duple rhymes, the pacing of the rhythms as they move toward a rhyme ending, the balance in the lines themselves and between lines, depending upon compound words or participial or prepositional phrases, carry along the vivid and richly descriptive imagery. Lines such as appear in "Corn" will probably never achieve any widespread popularity because every part of them contains pockets of

sustained interest and demands more attention from the reader
than he is likely to give to lyrical verse. This strange hybrid creation of Lanier's, compounded of sound and sense, is at times so
minutely realistic as to defy the term poetry, yet is always couched
in the most musical sounds. The colors, hues, and scents that
mingle in the verse are obviously aesthetic. The message is an
anomaly. Yet the poem succeeds, despite a surfeit of rich imagery
that calls up a comparison to young Keats. Here are "dew-plashed
roads" and "muscadines" whose vines "rich-wreathe" the "fore-
heads" of great pines. Here is almost a naturalist's interest in
nature that bespeaks not only his Southern origin but an original,
personal viewpoint of nature. The next, more prosaic strophe,
comes as a relief in its simplicity:

> I wander to the zigzag cornered fence
> Where sassafras, intrenched in brambles dense,
> Contests with stolid vehemence
>   The march of culture, setting limb and thorn
>   As pikes against the army of the corn.
>
> There, while I pause, my fieldward-faring eyes
> Take harvest, where the stately corn-ranks rise,
>   Of inward dignities
> And large benignities and insights wise,
>   Graces and modest majesties.
> Thus, without theft, I reap another's field;
> Thus, without tilth, I house a wondrous yield,
> And heap my heart with quintuple crops concealed.[96]

There is nothing in these lines to repel the reader; as a matter
of fact syzygy is subtle, the rhymes obvious, and the images
sharpened and clear. The "zigzag fence" and "sassafras" present
an interesting tonal combination, while the poet elevates with
ease the thought from the ranks of corn to the soul's harvesting.
The simplicity of these lines suggests the work that Frost has done
in our own time with the same kinds of subjects.

Lanier begins to draw his moral from the tallest stalk of corn
and compares the creative soul with the corn:

> Soul calm, like thee, yet fain, like thee, to grow
> By double increment, above, below;
>   Soul homely, as thou art, yet rich in grace like thee,
>   Teaching the yeoman selfless chivalry
>   That moves in gentle curves of courtesy;
> Soul filled like thy long veins with sweetness tense,

> By every godlike sense
> Transmuted from the four wild elements. . . .
>
> As poets should,
> Thou hast built up thy hardihood
> With universal food,
>   Drawn in select proportion fair
>   From honest mould and vagabond air;
> From darkness of the dreadful night,
>   And joyful light;
>   From antique ashes, whose departed flame
>   In thee has finer life and longer fame;
> From wounds and balms,
> From storms and calms,
> From pots-herds and dry bones
>   And ruin-stones.
> Into thy vigorous substance thou hast wrought
> Whate'er the hand of Circumstance hath brought;
>   Yea, into cool solacing green hast spun
>   White radiance hot from out the sun.
> So thou dost mutually leaven
> Strength of earth with grace of heaven;
>   So thou dost marry new and old
>   Into a one of higher mould;
> So thou dost reconcile the hot and cold,
>   The dark and bright
> And many a heart-perplexing opposite,
>   And so,
>   Akin by blood to high and low,
> Fitly thou playest out thy poet's part,
> Richly expending thy much-bruiséd heart
>   In equal care to nourish lord in hall
>   Or beast in stall:
>   Thou took'st from all that thou might'st give to all.[97]

The constant creation of metaphor came only too often to the poet, who was immersing himself in Shakespeare studies, together with some occasional affectations of the Elizabethans, their vivid colors, and their multi-voiced music. The last strophe of "Corn" contains these initial lines addressed to the over-worked land, which lead to a powerful conclusion.

> Old hill! old hill! thou gashed and hairy Lear
> Whom the divine Cordelia of the year,
> E'en pitying Spring, will vainly strive to cheer. . . .[98]

"Corn" was certainly one of the best poems of 1875 (the year it was published). Not only did the poet handle his themes with greater ease than before, but he began to find a style which, though ornate, carried important ideas and many memorable images.

The change in stanza form which dates from "Corn" must be ascribed to Lanier's interest in music, for before this poem, his stanzas have recognizable metrical groupings. With "Corn," however, the poet's stanzas become markedly "organic." Actually here they represent different views of the subject: first the descriptive, then the personal ones, and finally those which deal with various phases of the comparison of the "Corn-captain" with the poet. Though Lanier continued also to write quatrains and other verse forms, after this point his stanzas achieve greater length and no longer are metrical in grouping, for, as often as not, any one stanza may have any number of metrical shifts in it.

The musician's knowledge, which Lanier wisely did not push too fully in poetry, can be seen in poems like "In Absence." Here the nearness of the poet again to his Renaissance models exhibits itself in his preoccupation with love, the physical presence of love, and with God, who now plays a very important role in the life of Lanier, who knows that his time is measured. And though Lanier's excessive love for this life in all its forms of nature, humanity, and art remains unchanged, there appears persistently in the poetry from 1874 on an awareness of God as something quite apart from music—which he once felt was a quite adequate substitute. Here the poet writes of his wife:

I

>The storm that snapped our fate's one ship in twain
> Hath blown my half o' the wreck from thine apart.
>O Love! O Love! across the gray-waved main
> To thee-ward strain my eyes, my arms, my heart.
>I ask my God if e'en in His sweet place,
> Where, by one waving of a wistful wing,
>My soul could straightway tremble face to face
> With thee, with thee, across the stellar ring—
>Yea, where thine absence I could ne'er bewail
> Longer than lasts the little blank of bliss
>When lips draw back, with recent pressure pale,
> To round and redden for another kiss—
>   Would not my lonesome heart still sigh for thee
>   What time the drear kiss-intervals must be?

II

>So do the mottled formulas of Sense
> Glide snakewise through our dreams of Aftertime;

> So errors breed in reeds and grasses dense
>   That bank our singing rivulets of rhyme.
> By Sense rule Space and Time; but in God's Land
>   Their intervals are not, save such as lie
> Betwixt successive tones in concords bland
>   Whose loving distance makes the harmony.
> Ah, there shall never come 'twixt me and thee
>   Gross dissonances of the mile, the year;
> But in the multichords of ecstasy
>   Our souls shall mingle, yet be featured clear,
>   And absence, wrought to intervals divine,
>   Shall part, yet link, thy nature's tone and mine.[99]

This second strophe is the first actual sustained use Lanier made of musical metaphor. Here music serves as an illustration of his belief that in Heaven there is no separation from the loved one. The figure begins with a reference to the musical staff where "by Sense" we rule the time and the distance or space between notes. Lanier points out that no such staff appears in Heaven where intervals are not measured unless they be in "harmony" and where no dissonances of any kind separate note from note and love from love. In this divine land souls will exist like notes in harmony, each a part of a common chord and yet remain separate "featured clear" and individual elements in the perfect melody. And absence —or separation—will link the chords as a result of the just intervals which make for greater harmony.

Comparisons like these in Lanier's verse are well conceived and carried through. It is rarely, indeed, in his mature verse, that Lanier ever fails to sustain a figure, and yet it is, in some senses, to his disadvantage that as a poet he possessed either more erudition or, in some cases, simply more scientific and aesthetic interest in the subjects upon which his figures are based than readers generally care about. Lanier suffers from what so great a poet as Shakespeare once suffered: charges of irregularity, obscurity, and complexity. Each gradually began to find his audience limited, and in our time, unless some further evaluation of Lanier's work is attempted, his reputation will probably suffer a complete eclipse, for Lanier seems apart from the main stream of contemporary writing, despite the modernity of his rhythmic patterns. Like Bach, to draw another eminent comparison, Lanier composed with something of an academician's quality in his early work, and with an appeal to the intellect and the abstract which immediately limits his audience. However, he also treated contemporary questions with seriousness in his verse—a treatment rendered almost anomalous by his obviously lyrical bent.

Lanier's best verse moves toward two large stylistic groupings: the complex, impressionistic treatment of nature, and the simpler, beautiful song structures. The first came to have all the heightened emotional quality of the baroque; the second the simple dignity of the classical song.

It was, of course, inevitable that a man who was playing symphonic music every day, and attempting the composition of flute music, should eventually come to grips with the idea of writing a symphony in verse. It should be noted, however, that despite Lanier's recent acquaintance with the symphony, this was never a familiar poetic medium for him, and that he excelled at verse "pieces" rather than the lengthy profound symphony. He does not even mention such a relationship of forms in *The Science of English Verse,* and though, had he lived, he might have returned to and mastered the style of the symphony, he had abandoned the attempt in his last efforts.

It is evident though, for a while, that the symphony seemed to Lanier to open up new possibilities for verse. He was a-tremble at these possibilities and wrote to Peacock that writing "The Symphony" had seized him like a "James river ague,"

And I have been in a mortal shake with the same, day and night, ever since. I call it "The Symphony": I personify each instrument in the orchestra and make them discuss various deep social questions of the times, in the progress of the music. It is now nearly finished: and I shall be rejoiced thereat, for it verily racks all the bones of my spirit.[100]

The success of "The Symphony" rests on its rhythmic superiority and on its originality and experimental nature.[101] In his letters to his wife, written during the frequent separations made necessary by the travels for his health and his trips as a musician, Lanier had written for her virtually programme notes of the music that he played; in short, he readily transcribed the feeling of the music into words. "The Symphony," however, is less successful as a poem than it might have been had he developed his ideas here much as he had in the letters, as, for instance, we see Whitman doing where an aria or a symphony is only the structure on which that poet improvised. Lanier was eminently suited to do the same thing. Instead, he turned, in "The Symphony," to the mechanical and less successful, if more obvious, experimental device of announcing each instrument in the orchestra and letting it sing a certain definite theme. Now this simply cannot be done successfully, for the announcement of the instrument automatically cuts in upon the introspection of the symphony with something that is no part of it; and Lanier's experiment must always be regarded as something far beneath what he was capable of. However, he was the first American poet to move consciously into these pastures, and it is as an experiment that his poem must be considered. It is unfortunate that far too many critics, intrigued by the possibilities of new poetic form and the freshness of this approach, have taken "The Symphony" as an example of Lanier's best work. They have written well of it, better probably than it deserves, for Lanier moved a long distance from this effort in two years. One critic said:

The most concise definition of art is unity in variety. Surely "The Symphony" admirably fulfils that definition. There is a great variety in the subject matter: a severe condemnation of trade with a plea for the poor, by the violin; the beauties of nature, sung by the flute; a searching denunciation of man's inhumanity to woman, by the clarionet; an offer of knightly service to women by the horn; a plea for innocence in life by the hautboys; a final paean of victory for love by the bassoons. All this variety of subject is given with the varying effects of the different instruments, now fast in short, snappy lines, now slow, stately, sonorous in long full lines, now in the depths of despair and misery, now on the heights of faith and love. The thread of unity in it all is the common attack on Trade and the plea for heart and love in life. It is by no means perfect in execution, and fails in many points in diction and in rhythm, but as a whole it is a wonderful poem in the greatness of its idea and the adequacy and fitness with which it is carried out, and the wonderful harmony that it contains, to say nothing of individual lines of striking beauty in thought and melody. It is furthermore very significant in its suggestion as to the possibilities of poetry in the future.[102]

The last line of this critique is the most significant, for Lanier's verse has made possible the finer work of Conrad Aiken with the symphony, and surely those efforts of John Gould Fletcher in the same direction.

"The Symphony" is extremely uneven in quality and cannot in any way be compared with the larger design by which Whitman shaped his *Leaves of Grass*.[103] Lanier's effort is a minor poem, not approximating the symphony in either length or style, except for some rather obvious overtures in that direction. However, his was a pioneering work, and he had the vision of a symphonic poem, if not the fulfillment of it. His attempts to create, in verse, themes for each instrument are—aside from the flute theme—such mechanical efforts that they are almost laughable. The creaking of the machinery is evident throughout the poem, and Lanier realized how bad the effort was almost immediately. However, he did succeed in illustrating in verse "bridge" passages in music, and the flute's "song" is memorable. Of the passage which illustrates the tone of the flute in the orchestra what criticism can be offered? Nature, of which the flute sings, is beautifully described:

> But presently
> A velvet flute-note fell down pleasantly
> Upon the bosom of that harmony,
> And sailed and sailed incessantly,
> As if a petal from a wild-rose blown
> Had fluttered down upon that pool of tone . . .
> From the warm concave of that fluted note
> Somewhat, half song, half odor, forth did float,
> As if a rose might somehow be a throat:
> "When Nature from her far-off glen
> Flutes her soft messages to men,
> The flute can say them o'er again;
> Yea, Nature, singing sweet and lone,
> Breathes through life's strident polyphone
> The flute-voice in the world of tone.
>   Sweet friends,
>   Man's love ascends
> To finer and diviner ends
> Than man's mere thought e'er comprehends.
>   For I, e'en I,
>   As here I lie,
> A petal on a harmony,
> Demand of Science whence and why
> Man's tender pain, man's inward cry,
> When he doth gaze on earth and sky?
> I am not overbold:
>   I hold
> Full powers from Nature manifold.
> I speak for each no-tongued tree
> That, spring by spring, doth nobler be,
> And dumbly and most wistfully
> His mighty, prayerful arms outspreads
> Above men's oft unheeding heads,
> And his big blessing downward sheds.
> I speak for all-shaped blooms and leaves . . .

Grasses and grains in ranks and sheaves;
Broad-fronted ferns and keen-leaved canes,
And briery mazes bounding lanes,
And marsh-plants, thirsty-cupped for rains,
And milky stems and sugary veins . . .
All shynesses of film-winged things
That fly from tree-trunks and bark-rings; . . .
All limpid honeys that do lie
At stamen bases, nor deny
The humming-birds' fine roguery,
Bee-thighs, nor any butterfly;
All gracious curves of slender wings,
Bark-mottlings, fibre-spiralings,
Fern-wavings and leaf-flickerings;
Each dial-marked leaf and flower-bell
Wherewith in every lonesome dell
Time to himself his hours doth tell;
All tree-sounds, rustlings of pine cones,
Wind-sighings, doves' melodious moans . . .
Yea, all fair forms, and sounds, and lights,
And warmths, and mysteries, and mights,
Of Nature's utmost depths and heights,
—These doth my timid tongue present,
Their mouthpiece and leal instrument. . . .[104]

The interludes, or the "bridge" passages that occur in the music as Lanier has conceived it, are fortunate. He wrote passages like these (the first marks the throbbing undertone the orchestra sets up for the flute melody):

And then, as when from words that seem but rude
We pass to silent pain that sits abroad
Back in our heart's great dark and solitude,
So sank the strings to gentle throbbing
Of long chords change-marked with sobbing—
Motherly sobbing, not distinctlier heard
Than half-wing openings of the sleeping bird,
Some dream of danger to her young hath stirred.[105]

and the different pacing to introduce the clarinet:

Thereto a thrilling calm succeeds,
Till presently the silence breeds
A little breeze among the reeds
That seems to blow by sea-marsh weeds. . . .[106]

But the poorness of the concept that has each instrument sing

of social problems can best be seen if the reader thinks of the
nature of the symphony, what its appeal is, and how, like the long
passage quoted, the mind may dream of elements in nature. But
it is difficult to imagine the human mind busying itself with such
sentiment as makes up a portion of "The Symphony." Passages
which illustrate the voices beside the flute are dialogues, which
Lanier probably hoped would take care of the difficulty he en-
countered in attempting to make many voices sound together as
they actually do in a symphony. But these are not the introspective
dialogues, the conversations between instruments that one might
expect. They lack the sweep and meaning found in Whitman's
work. Here, instead, the instruments sing exactly worded and
limited themes, such as trade, the protection of womanhood, etc.,
themes which are noble enough but far too exact for musical
parallels. Note here how the "Lady Clarionet" begins her song, and
her song doesn't improve later:

> "O Trade! O Trade!" the Lady said,
> "I too will wish thee utterly dead
> If all thy heart is in thy head. . . ."[107]
> . . . .
> There thrust the bold straight forward horn
> To battle for that lady lorn,
> With heartsome voice of mellow scorn,
> Like any knight in knighthood's morn.
>   "Now comfort thee," said he,
>   "Fair Lady.
> For God shall right thy grievous wrong. . . .[108]

The poem is replete with such "pathetic fallacies," and it is
Lanier's misfortune that, because this early experiment in musico-
poetic structure piqued the curiosities of many people, it has been
more often found in anthologies and thus has had wider fame
than it deserves. Unfortunately, the poem is often regarded as
Lanier's best work since it fits in with what is known of the dual
interests of his life. That he never regarded it as such is evident
from his early abandonment of the purely symphonic structure as
unsuited to his style. But later poems give evidence that he realized
how fully he had failed here, for never again does he write like
this in terms of music:

> And ever Love hears the poor-folks' crying,
> And ever Love hears the women's sighing,
> And ever sweet knighthood's death-defying,

And ever wise childhood's deep implying,
But never a trader's glozing and lying.
"And yet shall love himself be heard
Though long deferred, though long deferred:
O'er the modern waste a dove hath whirred:
Music is Love in search of a word."[109]

This sentimental approach which makes "The Symphony" so
uneven a poem, and which obviously would repel many who might
otherwise have admired his experiment, is offset in the poem by
occasional successful figures of speech, one of which, near the close
of "The Symphony," is based upon music:

Life! Life! thou sea-fugue, writ from east to west,
    Love, Love alone can pore
    On thy dissolving score
Of harsh half-phrasings,
    Blotted ere writ,
And double erasings
    Of chords most fit.
Yea, Love, sole music-master blest,
May read thy weltering palimpsest.
To follow Time's dying melodies through,
And never to lose the old in the new,
    And ever to solve the discords true—
    Love alone can do.[110]

Here we have a successful reference to life, as a sea-fugue, written
horizontally on music paper, which only Love can make melody of
since the flux, "the dissolving score" of life, makes it a record of
errors, blottings, and welter.

The real contribution of "The Symphony" lies in Lanier's
effort to follow the form of the symphony with its bridge passages.
The title, "The Symphony," appearing widely as it did in 1875,
undoubtedly led other poets to make the more recent efforts in
the direction of this form. Since music has rarely been divorced
from poetry, it was natural that in the nineteenth century the
form of the symphony should inspire imitation. Certainly composers were already doing *tone poems*. Lanier was the first poet to
title his poem a symphony, though he actually did little work with
the symphony as a form, and borrowed eventually only its breadth
and sweep. From 1875 on, his poems take on considerably greater
length, unless they are song poems. "The Symphony," however,
brought Lanier considerable notice and the friendships of Char-

lotte Cushman and Bayard Taylor, the latter then a major literary
figure. Taylor was impressed by Lanier's combinations of talents,
and exerted his influence to see that the offer to write the Centennial cantata for the Centennial celebration came to the one
American skilled in both arts. And on the merits of "Corn" and
"The Symphony" the offer was made to him.

Lanier's "The Centennial Meditation of Columbia" marks the
high tide of his obvious musico-poetic interest, and all of the experimentation that went into it moved in the direction of freer
forms for poetry.[111]

"The Centennial Meditation of Columbia" made Lanier's
name famous. It also acquainted him fully, for the first time, with
the musico-dramatic principles of Richard Wagner and the free
forms he evolved as libretti for his operas, for Lanier was writing
his first "libretto." The influence of Wagner is apparent in the
poem.[112] It is a short poem for the amount of thought, care, and
heartbreak that went into it. It wasn't written to be published
separately, and is not a good "occasional" poem. Its concept was
musical from start to finish. Invited to write the verses for the
music of Dudley Buck, New York composer, to be performed by
Theodore Thomas's chorus and orchestra for the Fourth of July
Centennial Celebration, and included among such already famous
names as Whittier, Taylor, Lowell, and Wagner (who was commissioned to write an overture for the occasion), Lanier was selected to do the cantata because of his familiarity with both music
and poetry.[113] There was much excitement among the newspaper
critics over the first Centennial celebration and the forthcoming
poem, and it was published in advance of its performance with
near-disastrous results. As a poem, it was too diffuse. As a poem
for music, it was overwhelmingly successful. Lanier wrote Peacock
about the first draft of it:

I've written the enclosed. Necessarily I had to think out the musical
conceptions as well as the poem, and I have briefly indicated these
along the margin of each movement. I have tried to make the
whole as simple, and as candid as a melody of Beethoven's. At the
same time expressing them in such a way as could not be offensive
to any modern soul. I particularly hope you'll like the Angel's Song,
where I have endeavored to convey, in one line each, the philosophies
of Art, of Science, of Power, of Government, of Faith, and of Social
Life. Of course I shall not expect that this will instantly appeal to
tastes peppered and salted by Swinburne and that ilk; but one cannot

forget Beethoven. . . . I adopted the trochees of the first movement because they *compel* a measured, sober, and meditative movement of the mind; and because too they are not the genius of our language. When the trochees cease and the land emerges as a distinct unity, then I fall into our native iambics. . . .[114]

Lanier continued, pointing out that "the words of the poem ought to be selected carefully with reference to such quality of tone as they will elicit when sung." He was not interested in writing a poem to be read, but writing one that would fit the orchestra of one hundred and fifty and the chorus of eight hundred singers. Lanier felt, quite rightly, that "only general conceptions" were "capable of being rendered by orchestral music," and that "the subordinate related ideas must be sketched in gigantic figures" contrasting with each other in "broad outlines of tone color."

Knowing this, he composed in terms of sound rather than idea, in movements rather than in words or even lines; and he wrote his text not with the reader but the musical composer in mind.[115]

Dudley Buck was pleased with the poem he had to set to music, and he cautioned Lanier against undue anger at critics who understood none of the complex ideas that had led to the creation of the poem. He asked for many more Lanier poems to set to music. That Lanier never republished the poem does not mean he felt it was a failure; only that it would not be understood if merely read.

During the writing of the poem Lanier maintained constant correspondence with Bayard Taylor, who originally was to write the "Hymn" for that occasion. One of Lanier's first letters about his other intentions in the poem stated that it "afforded room to give the musical composer an opportunity to employ the prodigious tone contrasts of sober reflection, the sea, lamentation, a battle, warning, and magnificent yet sober and manly triumph and welcome. . . , that it [the poem] ought to be, not rhymed philosophy, but a genuine song, and lyric outburst. . . .[116]

Bayard Taylor, perhaps because he understood the pioneering effort of Lanier, liked the idea from the beginning and praised the poem for its "originality and lyric fire." Lanier was delighted and replied:

. . . I'm particularly charmed to find that you don't think the poem *too* original. I tried hard to think—in a kind of average and miscellaneousness. . . .

You see, I had to compose for the musician as well as the country;

and had to cast the poem into such a form as would at once show well in music (where contrast of movement between each adjacent part, in *broad bands of color,* was, from the nature of the art, a controlling consideration). . . . I wished, indeed, to make it as large and as simple as a Symphony of Beethoven's. If it does not come up to this, I've failed. . . .[117]

But Taylor was not pleased with the first version in its complete form; so on January 15, 1876, Lanier wrote Taylor again:

. . . hoping that you will let me know if it seems to you entirely large, simple and melodious. . . . I have had constantly in mind those immortal melodies of Beethoven, in which, with little more than the chords of tonic and dominant, he has presented such firm, majestic ideas. . . . Of course, with the general world . . . I do not expect to obtain the least recognition of the combination of child-like candors and colossal philosophies which I have endeavored here to put in words: but I do wish to know whether to *you* the poem, as you now see it, comes near this ideal. I desire the poem to be perfect.[118]

Some indication of the care that went into this short poem of sixty lines is illustrated by Lanier's careful *adaptation* of metre to various meanings of the poem:

I put the *Farewell, dear England,* into the Mayflower strophe, be-cause Mather relates that the people on the vessel actually stood up and cried out these words as they were departing. I also rewrote the stanza you did not like: and then inserted a whisper chorus, (of the Huguenot and Puritan, in dactyllic measure) to prepare by its straining pianissimo, for the outburst of jubilation. . . .[119]

Taylor responded to this by saying it was "in every way better than the first draft" and was what it "purports to be,—a cantata, not an ode—with the musical character inherent in its structure."

The cantata ode tells really very little about the history of America, aside from the original colonists' arrival and the hard-ships endured. This is somewhat unexpected since the poem might have dealt with the formation of the Union or the Revolutionary War or any other phase of American life. However, the poet chose those subjects most powerfully suited to musical accompaniment, and when it is recalled that the cantata was to last about twenty minutes, and in its final form had about eight divisions in it for the composer to illustrate, it can be immediately seen that it is excellent for musical setting. The introduction is written in large generalities suited to music of the graver sort; the first chorus has behind it the weltering sound that the symphony so well achieves.

The next division is more specifically choral, depending upon the quality of the human voice, weeping, wailing, and prophesying a kind of disaster. Then all of the voices sound from the forces that attempt to thwart the great dream, coming in a minor key, followed by full symphony and chorus to represent the various trials, war, terror, and evils in various shapes. All these sweep to a mighty climax: "No, Thou shalt not be!" This commands silence, and then "Hark," the forces form to fight for survival and swell finally to a "jubilant chorus" which flowers into the Angel's song warning America that only so long as Art is used for a good end, in the name of love; that only so long as Science is so dedicated; that only so long as the power of America "harms no Dove"; that only so long as law is respected among men will America maintain her greatness and her leadership. This was Lanier's message to America, and he was to say much of the same thing in his "Psalm of the West." One look at the poem titled "The Centennial Meditation of Columbia" will convince the reader that it should not have been published without the music. It is more a libretto than a poem.

A Cantata

From this hundred-terraced height,
Sight more large with nobler light
Ranges down yon towering years:
Humbler smiles and lordlier tears
Shine and fall, shine and fall,
While old voices rise and call
Yonder where the to-and-fro
Weltering of my Long-Ago[120]
Moves about the moveless base
Far below my resting-place.

Musical Annotations, Full Chorus: sober, majestic progression of chords.

Mayflower, Mayflower, slowly hither flying,
Trembling westward o'er yon balking sea,
Hearts within *Farewell dear England* sighing,
Winds without *But Dear in vain* replying,
Gray-lipp'd waves about thee shouted, crying
    No! It *shall not be!*

Chorus: the sea and the winds mingling their voices with human signs.

Jamestown, out of thee—
Plymouth, thee—thee, Albany—
Winter cries, *Ye freeze:* away!
Fever cries, *Ye Burn;* away!
Hunger cries, *Ye starve:* away!

Quartette: a meagre and despairing minor.

Full chorus: return of Vengeance cries, *Your graves shall stay!*
the MOTIVE *of the*   Then old Shapes and Masks of Things,
second movement,   Framed like Faiths or clothed like Kings—
but worked up with   Ghosts of Goods once fleshed and fair,
greater fury, to the   Grown foul Bads in alien air—
climax of the shout   War, and his most noisy lords,
at the last line.   Tongued with lithe and poisoned swords—
                Error, Terror, Rage, and Crime,
                All in a windy night of time
                Cried to me from land and sea,
                  No! *Thou shalt not be!*

                    Hark!

A rapid and intense   Huguenots whispering *yea* in the dark,
whisper—chorus.   Puritans answering *yea* in the dark!
                Yea, like an arrow shot true to his mark
                Darts through the tyrannous heart of Denial.
                Patience and Labor and solemn-souled Trial,
                  Foiled, still beginning,
                  Soiled, but not sinning,
                Toil through the stertorous death of the Night,
                Toil when wild brother-wars now-dark the
                    Light,
                Toil, and forgive, and kiss o'er, and replight.

Chorus of jubilation,   Now Praise to God's oft-granted grace,
until the appeal of   Now Praise to Man's undaunted face,
the last two lines in-   Despite the land, despite the sea,
troduces a tone of   I was: I am: and I shall be—
doubt; it then sinks   How long, Good Angel, O how long?
to pianissimo.   Sing me from Heaven a man's own song!

Basso Solo: the good   "Long as thine Art shall love true love,
Angel replies: Long as thy Science truth shall know,
                Long as thine Eagle harms no Dove,
                Long as thy Law by law shall grow,
                Long as thy God is God above,
                Thy brother every man below,
                So long, dear Land of all my love,
                Thy name shall shine, thy fame shall glow!"

Full chorus: jubila-   O Music, from this height of time my Word
tion and welcome.   unfold,
                In thy large signals all men's hearts Man's
                    Heart behold:

> Mid-heaven unroll thy chords as friendly flags
> unfurled,
> And wave the world's best lover's welcome to
> the world.[121]

The printing of this poem six weeks before it was performed as a cantata subjected Lanier to much unjust criticism. He thought of replying to one of the *Tribune* critics, saying that many people would otherwise come to its final perusal with the "prepossession that the author of it was stupidly ignorant of the first principles which should guide a writer of text for music. This prepossession is a wrong on the public."[122] It was reasonable that he should be offended by such comments as "Walt Whitman with the jim-jams," "Jabberwocky in its sententious Gravity," and a "communication from the spirit of Nat Lee, rendered through a Bedlamite medium."[123] He wanted to print his defense. Writing Taylor, he defended the poem as only sixty lines long, containing the broad outlines of the past, present, and future of the country. He said further that rhythms were chosen for their descriptive characters:

. . . the four trochaic feet of the opening strophe measure off reflection, the next (Mayflower) strophe swings and yaws like a ship, the next I made *outré* and bizarre and bony simply by the device of interposing the line of two and a half trochees amongst the four trochee lines; the swift action of the Huguenot strophe of course required dactyls: and having thus kept the first part of the poem (which describes the time before we were a real nation) in metres which are as it were exotic to our tongue, I now fall into the iambic metre—which is the genius of English words—as soon as the Nation becomes secure and firm.[124]

Lanier also mentioned attempting to produce in the Jamestown stanza the ghostly effects of the bassoon "by the use of the syllable *ee* sung by a chorus." He hoped in the future that whenever the papers carried the complete poem without printing at least the "piano score," his explanation of the poem might appear with it.[125] Dudley Buck attempted to assuage Lanier's despair. He asked Lanier if there were "any little bits" lying around which he could set to music, and pointed out to Lanier that the more intelligent the reader of the poem was, the more he appreciated it. Shortly after the performance Theodore Thomas made his offer to Lanier to join the New York Philharmonic Society as additional flutist. Daniel Coit Gilman, president of Johns Hopkins University, wrote most favorably of the poem after passing through a period of some doubt as to its meaning:

At length came the cantata. From the overture to the closing cadences it held the attention of the vast throng of listeners, and when it was concluded loud applause rung through the air. A noble conception had been nobly rendered. Words and music, voices and instruments, produced an impression as remarkable as the rendering of the Hallelujah Chorus in the nave of Westminster Abbey. Lanier had triumphed.[126]

The actual performance of the cantata marked Lanier for success. It meant a lectureship at Johns Hopkins and wide-spread fame as a poet with a new and practical theory. Buck's music was fully equal in quality to the verse and seemed admirably suited. The recording that was made of this cantata in 1936 reveals that Lanier understood the technique that today is so freely employed on the radio by cantata writers for special occasions. As a matter of fact, its dramatic and musical appeal is such that it is the natural progenitor of "Ballad for Americans" and in no way is less effective.

It may be said that it was the Centennial ode which gave greatest impetus to Lanier's musical conceptions for verse, for in writing it he became conscious for the first time of the possibilities of suiting rhythms exactly to the sense of the verse—and this stood him in good stead in all his later writings. He excelled as a matter of fact, thereafter, in rhythmic descriptions in lines of verse, altering the rhythms with the sense.

The other contribution to his creative thought came in the impression that he was able to give in words of some mood or large idea. This writing in general terms, this suitable "impressionism" was an intimate part of the style which he finally realized in his last poems.

After "The Centennial Meditation of Columbia," Lanier's ideas on the possibilities for music-poetic verse were formed. This is the period when he wrote freely a number of fine lyrics, and poems like "The Bee," "Clover," and "Psalm of the West."

"Psalm of the West" was consciously intended as a symphony in verse. Its length, his determination that it should "carry or create its own musical accompaniment," and his intention of writing additional music to go along with this "Choral Symphony,"[127] prove how deeply preoccupied he was with verse of a musical nature. If many of his late poems are ballad-like, perfect song-structures, "Psalm of the West" is his best effort at symphonic structure, and far superior technically to the poem titled "The Symphony," if we remember that it was to be also a "choral idiom."

For "Psalm of the West" was written to fulfill a commission for a Centennial Ode in *Scribner's Magazine*. It was an even more ambitious work than the earlier ode and is several steps further along in artistic concept than was the original Symphony.[128] Here the movements between choral elements are bridge passages inherent to the poem. The length of "Psalm of the West" prohibits detailed discussion.[129] It is actually a choral medium, for many of the lines are italicized for the actual singing of them. It concerns the growth of America, from its birth as an idea in nature to its discovery and population. It is the longest poem Lanier ever wrote, and in this respect more nearly approximates the scope and breadth of the symphony, but like his other ode, it does not and cannot read too well, because of his theories of a proper "libretto" for music. The stanzas and the rhythmic patterns follow the shifts in idea in the poem, much like movements in a symphony. It was Lanier's effort to sum America in song, using the scope and breadth of the symphony as a *pierre de touche*.

These poems, the two choral odes and "The Symphony," inspired Lanier and it is natural that he wrote most of his best lyrics in 1876-77. He said:

As for me, life has resolved simply into a time during which I want to get upon paper as many as possible of the poems with which my heart is stuffed like a schoolboy's pocket.[130]

During the Southern period when the poet was making a final fight for health in Georgia and Florida he wrote those few poems which were to give him any lasting fame: "The Bee," "The Stirrup Cup," "To Beethoven," "To Richard Wagner," "Song of the Chattahoochee," "The Mocking Bird," "Tampa Robins," and "Evening Song." The simple forms of these poems, with the opportunity for nature descriptions or praise of music, seem to be the best Lanier had so far conceived. "Evening Song" has had some remarkably beautiful song settings, and it was written for such a purpose. Its song-like simplicity is noticeable as well as the ease with which the nature metaphor is handled:

> Look off, dear Love, across the sallow sands,
>   And mark yon meeting of the sun and sea;
> How long they kiss, in sight of all the lands!
>   Ah, longer, longer, we.
> Now in the sea's red vintage melts the sun,
>   As Egypt's pearl dissolved in rosy wine,

And Cleopatra Night drinks all. 'Tis done!
  Love, lay thine hand in mine.
Come forth, sweet star, and comfort Heaven's heart;
  Glimmer, ye waves, round else unlighted sands;
O Night, divorce our sun and sky apart—
  Never our lips, our hands.[131]

Lanier listened to Schubert's songs and defined the perfect poetic song as "expressing but a single idea . . . in the simplest, noblest, most beautiful, and most musical words. . . ."[132] Always a good song poet, Lanier's poems for music improved with his connection with Dudley Buck and through the collaboration they so happily achieved. Buck regarded "Evening Song" as nearly a perfect lyric: "simply lovely." The imagery here is exceedingly simple, yet rich in color. The mood is quiet, reflective, and ideally suited to the treatment of music, which deals best in large simplicities and introspective ideas. Each stanza of this lyric—and it took Lanier years of practice to learn to write so simply—is capable of being treated as a "tone mood" since one technique which Lanier surely learned from his study of Schubert was that the mood of love and descriptions of nature are ideally suited to musical settings. In 1876 he wrote his poem "To Beethoven" and in 1877 "To Richard Wagner." A part of his tribute to Beethoven is quoted here.

O Psalmist of the weak, the strong,
  O Troubadour of love and strife,
Co-Litanist of right and wrong,
  Sole Hymner of the whole of life,

I know not how, I care not why,—
  Thy music sets my world at ease,
And melts my passion's mortal cry
  In satisfying symphonies. . . .

      . . . .

Yea, it forgives me all my sins,
  Pits life to love like rhyme to rhyme,
And tunes the task each day begins
  By the last trumpet-note of Time.[133]

This poem is quite lengthy, as is the tribute "To Richard Wagner." Wagner, who shared with Lanier advanced ideas on the composition of poetry for music and who wrote many essays on the subject of the interaction of the arts, also interested Lanier because of his strong opinions on the subjects of economics and politics. Lanier wrote:

> O Wagner, westward bring thy heavenly art.
>   No trifler thou: Siegfried and Wotan be
> Names for big ballads of the modern heart.
>   Thine ears hear deeper than thine eyes can see.
> Voice of the monstrous mill, the shouting mart,
>   Not less of airy cloud and wave and tree,
> Thou, thou, if even to thyself unknown,
> Hast power to say the Time in terms of tone.[134]

"Song of the Chattahoochee" has been universally accepted as one of the most unusual poems in American poetry. Most of the inherent musicality does not stem from repetitive consonants or rhyme or alliteration; it is not, in short, melodious—but it has a structure that is repetitive, impetuous, and ideally suited to the subject. Half of the wonder in Lanier's verse surely grows from the unmusical subjects of which he makes a kind of pure music. His similarity to Whitman can be noticed in the construction of prepositional phrases in "Song of the Chattahoochee," written in 1877 after his ideas on music and poetry had crystallized:

> Out of the hills of Habersham,
> Down the valleys of Hall. . . .
>
> In the clefts of the hills . . .
> In the beds of the valleys. . . .

This parallelism of pattern is borne out in the rest of the structure, where even many of the lines attain a singular balance.

The most important thing about "Song of the Chattahoochee," and the quality which differentiates it from all previous nature writing, is the poet's approach to the river itself, which approach is extremely personal, and yet altogether lacking in any ordinary descriptiveness on the poet's part. Here the verse lines become the river's voice, just as Debussy's music became the wind's voice. This is an "impression" of the river told in the flow and ebb of rhythm. The poem excels in its rhythmic freedom. While the larger foot patterns may be thought of as running dactyls, there is a constant releasing of sounds through these, followed by a springing return to the shorter leaps of trochees, interrupted at points by sluggish spondees, etc., so that the poet is obviously more interested in the movement to the two repetitious lines at the end of each stanza than he is concerned with foot patterns. He is writing in musical or (rather here) in poetic phrases—prepositional and verbal—and balanced clauses.

Both his alliterative patterns and the use he made of equal time units rather than foot patterns are everywhere noticeable. The important concern of the poet was with the rush and flow of the river, and his effort was expended to keep the stanza in a fluid shape, with occasional little springing phrases to push the metrical pattern down the page. His use of parallel structure, alliteration, and logical syllabic groupings can be seen in this stanza as well as any other:

> I *hurry amain* to *reach the plain,*
> *Run the rapid* and *leap the fall,*
> *Split at the rock* and *together again,*
> *Accept my bed,* or narrow or wide,
> And flee from folly on every side
> *With a lover's pain* to *attend the plain*
>   Far from the hills of Habersham,
>   Far down the valleys of Hall.[135]

The series of verb phrases culminating in "and flee," move the poem downward to the completion of that stanza. The alliterative devices in "run the rapid and leap the fall," and "flee from folly" are only the apparent links in the stanza; not quite so obviously alliterative is "hurry amain" and "reach the plain," and "lover's pain," "narrow or wide," etc. The rhyming device, suspending a return to "fall" until the last word in the stanza, moves through a pattern inverted from -am, -all, -ain, to -ain, -am, -all. This pattern of rhyme inversion works in every stanza. Lanier was fond of varying rhythms from iambs:

> The rushes cried *Abide, abide,*
> The willful waterweeds held me thrall

to dactyls. Note also his consciousness of a choral element in nature.

Another device used here is that of making the first stanza the voice of the Chattahoochee, and the second and third the voices, successively, of the rushes and reeds, and the various "overleaning" trees. The fourth strophe introduces not only colors and gemlike minerals, but spondaic rhythms which lengthen the line and widely space the emphases; these really slow down the flow of the movement and impede, just as the sense of the poem signifies:

> The white quartz shone, and the smooth brook-stone
> Did bar me of passage with friendly brawl,
> And many a luminous jewel lone
> —Crystals clear or a-cloud with mist,
> Ruby, garnet and amethyst—
> Made lures with lights of streaming stone
>   In the clefts of the hills of Habersham,
>   In the beds of the valleys of Hall.[136]

The imagery here is sharply cut, clear, sparkling. Then the final strophe occurs with the voice of the Chattahoochee saying that all depends upon the call of the lordly "main." Here all of the lines point in the direction of the verb "calls" and fall from "downward" and "and":

> But oh, not the hills of Habersham,
>   And oh, not the valleys of Hall
> Avail: I am fain for to water the plain.
> Downward the voices of Duty call—
> Downward, to toil and be mixed with the main,
> The dry fields burn, and the mills are to turn,
> And a myriad flowers mortally yearn,
> And the lordly main from beyond the plain
>   Calls o'er the hills of Habersham,
>   Calls through the valleys of Hall.[137]

All the rhythms are alternately bound and released, caught, and sprung free. Parallelisms, short internal rhymes, and a certain ebbing and flowing from the initial line repetitions are caught in successive and alternate rhyme endings. The poem is, of course, a slight one, lacking many of the graver overtones so often found in Lanier's work. But it is a little art-work, not simple, delighted in for its tiny and perfectly wrought mosaic rhyme scheme.

Music is the subject of "To Nannette Falk-Auerbach," one of the great nineteenth century Beethoven interpreters, as it is in the humorous but rather fine little verses "To Our Mocking Bird Died of a Cat" with its original figure of speech:

> Trillets of human,—shrewdest whistle-wit,—
>   Contralto cadences of grave desire . . .
> Bright drops of tune, from oceans infinite
> Of melody, sipped off the thin-edged wave
> And trickling down the beak. . . .
> Ah me, though never an ear for song, thou hast
>   A tireless tooth for songsters: thus of late
>   Thou camest, Death, thou Cat! and leapst my gate,

And . . . snatched away, how fast, how fast,
My bird—wit, songs, and all—thy richest freight
Since that fell time when in some wink of fate
Thy yellow claws unsheathed and stretched, and cast
Sharp hold on Keats, and dragged him slow away,
And harried him with hope and horrid play—
Ay, him, the world's best wood-bird, wise with song—
Till thou hadst wrought thine own last mortal wrong. . . .

Nay, Bird; my grief gainsays the Lord's best right.
The Lord was fain, at some late festal time,
That Keats should set all Heaven's woods in rhyme,
And thou in bird-notes. Lo, this tearful night,
Methinks I see thee, fresh from death's despite . . .
Methinks I hear thy silver whistlings bright
Mix with the mighty discourse of the wise,
Till broad Beethoven, deaf no more, and Keats,
Midst of much talk, uplift their smiling eyes,
And mark the music of thy wood-conceits,
And halfway pause on some large courteous word,
And call thee "Brother," O thou heavenly Bird![138]

Though his 1876 volume of verse was published while the poet lay seriously ill, he was writing from Tampa in 1877, "I 'bubble song' continually these days, and it is as hard to keep me from the pen as a toper from his tipple,"[139] (which has a sound to it surprisingly like Emily Dickinson). And all of 1878 he was writing poems like the above, and reading for the first time Walt Whitman and Emerson.

Lanier's relationship to Whitman already has been the subject of much discussion. Most critics have recognized the strong interest of both poets in moving toward something new in the way of poetic forms, and though Lanier wrote Whitman that he disagreed with him on all matters referring to form and "taste" in poetry, he recognized the "modern song at once so large and so naive . . . propounded in such strong and beautiful rhythms."[140] Anderson commented astutely on this relationship between the two men: "Perhaps the greatest likeness is between Whitman's practice and Lanier's theory."[141] Though *The Science of English Verse* made no direct reference to *Leaves of Grass*, Anderson called attention to the fact that Lanier must have had it sometimes in mind.[142]

"The Marshes of Glynn" is undoubtedly one of the best poems Lanier ever wrote. It is full of his complex rhythmic patterns, overlaid with alliteration, and a muted syzygy. It was never widely published because it was not finished until July, 1878, long after the collected poems had been published. All of the qualities that represent the inwoven style which is peculiarly Lanier's own can be found in this poem. Here are all the devices for moving the line and concluding the stanza that have been observed in incipient stages. Here is all the minutely wrought detail that blurs the larger outline with its vividness. Every corner, every facet of one man's impression of the marsh is explored, and the large symbol of the marsh sweeps into the poet's heart so that he no longer fears the unending, unknown, and water-flooded areas. Here Lanier has made of the marsh a wonderful mystic symbol:

> Oh, what is abroad in the marsh and the terminal sea?
>> Somehow my soul seems suddenly free
>> From the weighing of fate and the sad discussion of sin
>> By the length and the breadth and the sweep of the marshes of
>> Glynn. . . .

The sense of light and shadow that plays initially on the leaves of the live oaks plays fitfully throughout the poem, now blazing here in clarity, now shadowing and suggesting. It is noticeably true that these marsh poems have a rhythmic perfection—dactyls tying line to line—with innumerable substitutions of feet and subtleties of phrases, of melodic interplay, but they also have a freeness in the stanza that may have been in part inspired by the evolution of cantata odes and poems like "Psalm of the West." Perhaps the chief influence upon this great poem of Lanier's—and it is considered his best poem by many critics—was the Maryland Musical Festival of 1878 which Lanier undoubtedly took part in, and which he reviewed. One of the most striking phases of the review is his interest in Beethoven's worship of nature, as revealed in the Seventh Symphony, Mendelssohn's "Calm of the Sea," and the beauties of Wagner's "Siegfried Idyl," of which he wrote:

> This is the explanation of much of the difficulty which most persons feel in perceiving the drift of Wagner's pieces. Probably it will be long before the ears of average audiences will be practised to such keenness that they can detect the multitudinous melodies which arise, sing together, vanish, and re-appear, all through the *Idyl*. . . . To follow these through their sinuous windings and interweavings is possible only to a practised ear and concentrated attention. . . .[143]

Certainly there was much in the Festival that excited the poet, and "The Marshes of Glynn" came from his pen only two months later. It differs in many respects from any previous poem; Lanier's consciousness of God is everywhere apparent in it; and the longer lines sweep with artistic surety. The poet's personal impression of nature is bound up with religion. Stanza two begins with a reference to the lights and darks of the woods while the sun is still high:

> Beautiful glooms, soft dusks in the noon-day fire,—
> Wildwood privacies, closets of lone desire,
> Chamber from chamber parted with wavering arras of leaves,—
> Cells for the passionate pleasure of prayer to the soul that grieves,
> Pure with a sense of passing of saints through the wood,
> Cool for the dutiful weighing of ill with good. . . .[144]

Here the flickering light, reference to the cathedral-like woods and arches, and the "wavering arras of leaves" parting hermit chambers constitute only a part of the stanza's beauty: the careful handling of time within the phrases, with their varied rhythms, is another. Rich imagery and verbal music combine here, while foot forms give way to a flowing, changing accentual pattern.

Another influence that acted upon this poem was Lanier's discovery for the first time of Whitman (1878) and his profound appreciation of *Leaves of Grass*. Whitman's feeling for nature could hardly have escaped Lanier. The lengthened lines that stretch across the Whitman page suggest the wide "Marshes of Glynn." Lanier, for the first time, seems to have found here a sufficiently broad and powerful subject with which to deal.

Part of the beauty of "The Marshes of Glynn" comes not only from the treatment of the woods, the marshes, and the sea as facets of nature the poet no longer fears, but also from the reverence felt for nature which the poet seems to be exhibiting fully for the first time. Here are scarcely any lines of even length. How Lanier's varied rhythmic patterns run across the page, urged on by "and" and the development of the idea of a cessation of works as evening sets in and the sun sinks, can be seen in this stanza:

> But now when the moon is no more, and riot is rest,
> And the sun is a-wait at the ponderous gate of the West,
> And the slant yellow beam down the wood-aisle doth seem
> Like a lane into heaven that leads from a dream,—
> Ay, now, when my soul all day hath drunken the soul of the oak,
> And my heart is at ease from men, and the wearisome sound of the
> stroke
> Of the scythe of time and the trowel of trade is low,
> And belief overmasters doubt, and I know that I know,

And my spirit is grown to a lordly great compass within,
That the length and the breadth and the sweep of the marshes
   of Glynn
Will work me no fear like the fear they have wrought me of
    yore. . . .
  Oh, now, unafraid, I am fain to face
   The vast sweet visage of space.
  To the edge of the wood I am drawn, I am drawn,
Where the gray beach glimmering runs, as a belt of the dawn,
  For a mete and a mark
  To the forest-dark:—
   So:
Affable live-oak, leaning low,—
Thus—with your favor—soft, with a reverent hand,
(Not lightly touching your person, Lord of the land!)
Bending your beauty aside, with a step I stand
  On the firm-packed sand,
    Free
By a world of marsh that borders a world of sea. . . .[145]

The final impression the poet leaves in this tone poem of nature is that of the sea spilling over into the marsh, flooding it in silver veins which reflect the last rosy glow of the sun. And then the whirring wings of some homeward bound bird sound in the looming dark and silence. And it is night. Finally the quite wonderful lines which query the shapes that appear in dreams, and those other final dreams:

And the sea lends large, as the marsh: lo, out of his plenty the sea
  Pours fast: full soon the time of the flood-tide must be:
    Look how the grace of the sea doth go
  About and about through the intricate channels that flow
    Here and there,
    Everywhere,
Till his waters have flooded the uttermost creeks and the low-lying
    lanes,
   And the marsh is meshed with a million veins,
  That like as with rosy and silvery essences flow
   In the rose-and-silver evening glow.
    Farewell, my lord Sun!
The creeks overflow: a thousand rivulets run
'Twixt the roots of the sod; the blades of the marsh-grass stir;
Passeth a hurrying sound of wings that westward whirr;
Passeth, and all is still; and the currents cease to run;
   And the sea and the marsh are one.

How still the plains of the waters be!
The tide is in his ecstasy.
The tide is at his highest height:
   And it is night.

And now from the Vast of the Lord will the waters of sleep
   Roll in on the souls of men,
  But who will reveal to our waking ken
  The forms that swim and the shapes that creep
    Under the waters of sleep?
And I would I could know what swimmeth below when the tide
    comes in
On the length and the breadth of the marvelous marshes of Glynn.

The rhythmic principle again is quantitative, for nearly every line represents quick and fairly subtle rhythmic changes from dactyls, and yet the logic of the inner voice speaking is not at all disturbed by the underlying rhythms and the sense is not obscured. The old question—what dreams may come when we have shuffled off this mortal coil—was perplexing the poet. The superiority of "The Marshes of Glynn" lies not alone in its rhythmic fecundity, nor in its memorable imagery, but also in the suiting of the rhythms and the tonal colors of the words to the mood of the poem. Despite the deceptive quietness of the wood, there is a passionate quality in the lines in which the first person "I" appears, in the "oh's," and in the final questioning. On the whole, the poem is a quiet, almost reflective piece of writing, lacking the pacing of many of Lanier's verses. But the lines which deal with the movement of water—the sea—move quickly. Note how the poet smoothly calls attention to the sea; then how the "intricate" channels hold it back; then how it quickly flows "here and there—everywhere" till it again spreads out smoothly and has flooded the lands. And when the poet turns to a philosophical idea, how the dignified lines roll across the page, not only in length, but also in sound pattern: "And now from the Vast of the Lord will the waters of sleep. . . ." Then note the careful spacing of vowel sounds as an alternate "Roll in on the souls of men" and the final line—"On the length and the breadth of the marvelous marshes of Glynn."

In 1878 when this poem was written, Lanier had learned to handle completely the music of his lines, the complexity of his ideas, the alliteration of his syllables, and the organic shaping of a poem through some great mystical or spiritual experience. In short, he had found his subject matter, and his moral sense enlarged itself into a powerful faith in God, and his love for nature served as a wonderful symbol of that faith.

One of his last poems, "A Ballad of Trees and the Master," written for music in the simple lyrical song style he also mastered, has been set to music and recorded. It is one of the most beautiful songs he wrote:

> Into the woods my Master went,
> Clean forspent, forspent.
> Into the woods my Master came,
> Forspent with love and shame.
> But the olives they were not blind to Him,
> The little gray leaves were kind to Him,
> The thorn-tree had a mind to Him
> When into the woods He came.
>
> Out of the woods my Master went,
> And he was well content.
> Out of the woods my Master came
> Content with death and shame.
> When Death and Shame would woo Him last,
> From under the trees they drew Him last;
> 'Twas on a tree they slew Him—last
> When out of the woods He came.[147]

Lanier's preoccupation with trees and the days in the wilderness resulted in this significant religious poem. He suggested harp-accompaniment for this late poem. The simplicity and dignity of this song mark it for posterity.

"Sunrise," the last expression of the consumptive poet who loved life with such passion that its delineation led to charges of obscurity, is in reality another marsh hymn, with the same spiritual significance, but lacking in the philosophic quiet that the first is built upon. "Sunrise" seems almost imbued with the poet's life blood. It exhibits in the fullest degree his passion for nature and all of his poetic devices at once. It approaches a climax amid a luxuriant flowering of image and sound, and a strain and upward reaching that come from the very depths of his fevered soul. His worship of the sun in terms of nearly pagan joy, in Christian symbols, in terms of its meaning for man and for one particular dying man, almost overwhelms the music of the verse by the heavy freight of ornate and elaborate imagery that frets it. There is nothing easy or simple in Lanier's "Sunrise" and those who come to it lightly feel some despair that anything which sounds so melodious should

appear at first too obscure for perception. Reading Lanier's late
poetry is not easy, and even a good reader must repeat and repeat
the pattern of the lines to realize how profoundly thought out the
rhythms and many of Lanier's thoughts are. "Sunrise," for instance, demands a creative effort from the reader fully proportionate to the poem itself. In the creation of a word picture attempting
to capture the actual feeling of dawn itself rising out of the sea,
the various steps leading up to that sunrise all have their different
rhythmic modes and patterns like movements in music. The poem
itself is written in a series of hushed stanzas, while the ear strains
for the sounds of dawn with the whispering leaves, and the old
"alchemist" marsh "distilling silence." Occasionally the poet's easy
circling and bounding rhythms dissuade the reader that anything
of moment is being said, and yet here the poet is describing a state
of tension which music alone had never achieved by a climbing,
straining, piling up of sound that waits and waits for a single tone
to dash the whole structure. In the verse, the poet has reached that
quiet, breathless moment in nature which heralds the dawn. Here
the stars gleam in the dome of night while beauty and silence
strain forward:

> Oh, what if a sound should be made!
> Oh, what if a bound should be laid
> To this bow-and-string tension of beauty and silence a-spring,—
> To the bend of beauty the bow, or the hold of silence the string!
> I fear me, I fear me yon dome of diaphanous gleam
> Will break as a bubble o'er-blown in a dream,—
> Yon dome of too-tenuous tissues of space and of night,
> Over-weighted with stars, over-freighted with light,
> Over-sated with beauty and silence, will seem
> But a bubble that broke in a dream,
> If a bound of degree to this grace be laid,
> Or a sound or a motion made.[148]

Then the wonderful description of that first movement, so vibrant in feeling that it suggests only the parallel of Whitman's
"Out of the Cradle Endlessly Rocking" where the same speaking
quality of the verse, the same address to nature occurs. Lanier's
capture here of the immediacy of the action is musical, and reads
like an improvisation of Grieg's "Morning." The images, however,
are very clearly conceived, like the movement of expectation in
the marsh-grass; the duck, sailing silently around the river bend.
It may seriously be doubted whether any better description of

dawn with so carefully sustained a crescendo has been achieved in the English language. How it fits the descriptive quality of music in describing our alive senses in listening for sound:

> But no: it is made: list! somewhere,—mystery, where?
>   In the leaves? in the air?
>   In my heart? is a motion made:
> 'Tis a motion of dawn, like a flicker of shade on shade.
> In the leaves, 'tis palpable: low multitudinous stirring
> Upwinds through the woods; the little ones, softly conferring,
> Have settled, my lord's to be looked for; so; they are still;
>   But the air and my heart and the earth are a-thrill,—
> And look where the wild duck sails round the bend of the river,—
>   And look where a passionate shiver
>   Expectant is bending the blades
>   Of the marsh-grass in serial shimmers and shades,—
> And invisible wings, fast fleeting, fast fleeting,
>   Are beating
> The dark overhead as my heart beats,—and steady and free
>   Is the ebb-tide flowing from marsh to sea . . .
>   And a sailor unseen is hoisting a-peak,
>   For list, down the inshore curve of the creek
>   How merrily flutters the sail,—
>   And lo, in the east! Will the East unveil?
>   The East is unveiled, the East hath confessed
> A flush: 'tis dead; 'tis alive: 'tis dead, ere the West
> Was aware of it; nay, 'tis abiding, 'tis unwithdrawn:
>   Have a care, sweet Heaven! 'Tis Dawn. . . .[149]

Unfortunately for Lanier, too many times the first strophe of this poem has been quoted to illustrate his metrical practice, and readers have found it, out of context, quite devoid of sense. The impressionistic descriptions of the rising sun itself are twofold: first the golden rays of the sun are described with Dionysiac jubilation and then a different, slower pacing as the great orb itself rises from the sea:

> Now a dream of a flame through that dream of a flush is uprolled:
> To the zenith ascending, a dome of undazzling gold
> Is builded, in shape as a bee-hive, from out of the sea:
> The hive is of gold undazzling, but oh, the Bee,
>   The star-fed Bee, the build-fire Bee,
>   —Of dazzling gold is the great Sun-Bee
>   That shall flash from the hive-hole over the sea. . . .[150]

The dactyls of which Lanier was so fond quickly change, when the sun itself is hailed, to the spondees so native to a rather primitive rhythmic beat:

> The star-fed Bee, the build-fire Bee
> . . . is the great sun Bee. . . .

Punctuated rhythm like this can appear any place in a stanza in the last verses of Lanier, indicating the greatest freedom within a line. Then again the slow paced dactylic line:

> Not slower than Majesty moves, for a mean and a measure
> Of motion,—not faster than dateless Olympian leisure
> Might pace with unblown ample garments from pleasure to
>   pleasure,—
> The wave-serrate sea-rim sinks, unjarring, unreeling,
>   Forever revealing, revealing, revealing,
> Edgewise, bladewise, halfwise, wholewise,—'tis done!
>   Good-morrow, lord Sun!

The sun is finally greeted as a symbol of power, of strength, first as a creative force, and then as a symbol of security for the dying man:

> O Artisan born in the purple,—Workman Heat,—
> Parter of passionate atoms that travail to meet
> And be mixed in the death-cold oneness,—innermost Guest
> At the marriage of elements . . .
> Thou, in the fine forge-thunder, thou, in the beat
> Of the heart of a man, thou Motive,—Laborer Heat: . . .
> Yet ever the artist, ever more large and bright
> Than the eye of a man may avail of:—manifold One,
> I must pass from thy face, I must pass from the face of the Sun:
> Old Want is awake and agog, every wrinkle a-frown;
> The worker must pass to his work in the terrible town:
> But I fear not, nay, and I fear not the thing to be done;
>   I am strong with the strength of my lord the Sun:
> How dark, how dark soever the race that must needs be run,
>   I am lit with the Sun.
>
>   Oh, never the mast-high run of the seas
>   Of traffic shall hide thee,
> Never the hell-colored smoke of the factories
>   Hide thee,
> Never the reek of the time's fen-politics
>   Hide thee,
> And ever my heart through the night shall with knowledge abide
>   thee,

And ever by day shall my spirit, as one that hath tried thee,
Labor, at leisure, in art,—till yonder beside thee
  My soul shall float, friend Sun,
    The day being done.[151]

Lanier revised "Sunrise" extensively and it has been highly praised by a variety of critics, many of whom saw relatively little in his earlier verse. It was called exceptionally original and his poems were called "so entirely unlike the poems of the day, that one has no standard to judge them by."[152] The English journals in particular hailed Lanier's verse, and, said the *Spectator,*

There is more of genius in this volume than in all Poe's poems, or all Longfellow's, or all Lowell's. . . . Lanier is an original poet,—more original, we think, than the United States has ever yet produced, more original than any poet whom England has produced during the last thirty years.[153]

And the London *Times* called him "the greatest master of melody of any of the American poets."[154] After arriving in Samoa, Stevenson was asked what he would do for intellectual companionship, and pulling the poems of Lanier from his pocket, he replied: "I am always well-companioned so long as I have this."[155] And Hamlin Garland, strangely enough, was fascinated by Lanier's verse. He wrote:

His verse puzzled me at first by its complexity, but it grew in music with each rereading.

Eager for more knowledge of this singer, I read every accessible article by him or about him, . . . every obtainable comment, until at last I felt it my duty to let the world know (so far as I was able) the message this poet, this thinker, had given me. . . .

. . . In opening his volume of verse, I chanced upon "Sunrise" and was instantly and profoundly stirred by its freedom of form, its wealth of thought, its intricacy of metaphor and its glorious music, and yet the subtleties of the metaphors, the changes in the rhythm, like the infinite shimmering lights of a near-seen landscape, distracted me. To this day "Sunrise" lives with me more closely than any other nature poem.

This striving after something dimly seen and dimly felt I soon discovered arose from an overwhelming musical tendency, which made of Lanier first of all a singer, establishing the lyric quality of his writing as absolutely as it did that of Blake or Shelley. . . . He was too intellectual, too masterful, too original, too sane to be affected by Poe. . . . He was lyric not as Poe was lyric; rather he was symphonic. . . .

"Whatever else his poetry may not be, it is perfect song," I said to my pupils. "It has a flexible, variant, vibrant quality which is well-nigh unapproached by any American poet."

Curious as it may seem to other lovers of Lanier, I found much in common between "The Marshes of Glynn" and Whitman's "Out of the Cradle Endlessly Rocking."

Whitman is wilder, sterner and more iconoclastic than Lanier, yet both were poets of cosmic sympathy. With singularly individual outlook on nature, each believed in uttering himself in characteristic fashion, each instinctively avoided conventional forms. I found no difficulty in loving and admiring them, both.[156]

Coulson and Webb made a considerable study of Lanier's contemporary status as a poet and found a surprising difference in the reactions of critics and poets, as well as general readers, to Lanier's verse.[157] A partial explanation for this phenomenon must lie in the fact that not all of Lanier's work appears in anthologies, and that what does appear is often something he surpassed quickly. His early experiments, taken singly, while interesting in proving how rapidly he mastered a medium, are too slight to gain for him lasting fame as a great poet. If Lanier's reputation is to be succored in any way, a genuine effort must be made to see that his later poems have wide currency. In the Centennial Edition of Lanier's works Anderson wrote:

. . . [his poems] achieve the impression of freedom by carefully chosen and consciously controlled devices, sparingly employed but of considerable variety: occasional extremes of line-length, the frequent use of run-on lines, skillful foot-substitutions, and the reproduction in words of all the sound effects known to the ear of the professional musician. Others had made such experiments before him, of course; Lanier's contribution lies in the elaborateness with which he tried to combine music and poetry, and this is the explanation of why his poems are both liked and disliked. . . .[158]

Thus, it can be seen that the influence of music upon the poetry of Sidney Lanier can scarcely be overestimated. It is responsible for the kinds of poetry that he wrote; it had much to do with his concept of the line and the pacing of that line. Sometimes he threw off a spate of syllables like a group of notes in music with swiftness and excitement; at other times the accents are widely separated and the line lengthened by sonorous consonants so that it quietly eddies across the page. His stanzas after 1874 were elongated by the greater musical force which coursed through them, and the shifts between these strophes became subtler so that the poems gained in unity. He came to feel late in life less dependence upon end rhyme, and more dependence upon epanaphora, and all of the lines in a poem were directed toward a climax achieved not so much in the meaning as in the verbal coloring and rhythmic resolution. His rhythms, which were often very regular, in general, and in the best verse, came to have a complete freedom from repeated foot forms so that scarcely a line of "Sunrise" had the same feet in it. This freedom from foot forms makes for music in verse because, like music, when the only criteria are equal temporal values, melody is freed. But Lanier used foot forms with conscious success, interpolating exact patterns at sudden intervals to bring a kind of order to an idea and differentiate or emphasize a point. Sometimes dactyls or anapests appear, with their repetitious rhythms, and are swung faster and faster through a line as he handles his syllables like notes in music, until finally the tension breaks and the rhythms flood out from the feet in widely undulant waves. His stanzas seem to have little relationship with rhymes, but they do have some primitive relationship to the phrasal units with which Lanier preferred working. The speaking quality of many of his lines he learned from handling the choral medium.

But Lanier's was also a symphonic conception, though all of the voices were subservient to the melody or subject that he had chosen. This homophonic, or "symphonic," quality can be seen at work in "The Marshes of Glynn" and "Sunrise," both superior to "The Symphony." Here are three voices sounding in "Sunrise" all of which await the sun's arrival: the marsh, the sea, and the wood:

> The little green leaves would not let me alone in my sleep;
> Up-breathed from the marshes, a message of range and of sweep,
> Interwoven with wafture or wild sea-liberties, drifting,
> Came through the lapped leaves sifting, sifting,
> Came to the gates of sleep.

Not only are three voices announced but the pattern of this verse follows the sense of the lines, so that the thought of sleep impels "drifting, sifting, sifting" as repetitive soft sounds of leaves in nature and leads to dreams—the next section. The poet finally awakens:

> I have come ere the dawn, O beloved, my *live-oaks,* to hide
>   In your gospelling glooms,—to be
> As a lover in heaven, the *marsh my marsh* and the *sea my sea.*

The poet then addresses himself first to the leaves of the live-oak which he treats as symbols of conscience and passions:

> And there, oh there
> As ye hang with your myriad palms upturned in the air,
>   Pray me a myriad prayer.

Then he turns to the marsh which is an

> Old chemist, rapt in alchemy,
>   Distilling silence. . . .

And finally the sea, which sweeps into the marsh, glimmering beneath the stars:

> The tide's at full: the marsh with flooded streams
> Glimmers, a limpid labyrinth of dreams.
> Each winding creek in grave entrancement lies
> A rhapsody of morning-stars. . . .

Then the period of strain and quiet listening sets in which is so rarely described in the present in poetry:

> Oh, what if a sound should be made!
> Oh, what if a bound should be laid. . . .

And suddenly the slightest movement among leaves, and then the soft movement of winds up through the woods, the air, "my heart," and the earth—the marsh grass bends in the breeze, and a sail catches the wind, while dawn comes. And then the sun rises slowly above the horizon:

> Now a dream of a flame through that dream of a flush is uprolled. . . .

And the sea and the marsh and the woods and "my soul" are the various voices that greet their "lord Sun." The poet closes with a tribute to the might and power of the sun.

Lanier's last two poems are in the nature of "tone" poems, showing many of the qualities that must cause him to be placed among that group of artists appearing at the end of the century who came to be called impressionists. One of these qualities is love for color and, specifically, for the play of light and shadow. Another is the extremely subjective and personal reading of the poet's experience into nature, which gives to his descriptions something of an air of obscurity; in fact, so personal is the reaction that the wealth of finical detail—like pointillism in painting—obscures the general outline and meaning of the poem until one steps back and observes the larger sweep of the poet's canvas that gives an over-all "impression" of nature divorced from "real" nature.

Impressionism, in its reaction against the realism that followed the romantic movement, was more individual in its expression than almost any other "movement." In poetry it found its expression in the symboliste work of the French: Baudelaire, Rimbaud, Verlaine, Valery, etc., whose theories had been profoundly influenced, initially, by Edgar Allan Poe. In music, so disparate a group as Wagner, an early musical "symboliste," Resphighi, Franck, Berlioz, Debussy, Grieg and a host of minor "nationalistic" composers have all been called "impressionists." Closely related to descriptive or programme music, impressionism excels in the capture of the fleeting moment in nature. Grieg was dealing in impressionism in "Morning" from *Peer Gynt*. Debussy's personal impression of "Clouds" is one of the more famous musical impressions. In some ways the impressionism of painters such as Monet, Cezanne, Renoir, to name only a few, was a higher kind of realism than had before existed in painting. It is true that the outline itself was frequently blurred by the painter's intellectual judgment of nature, but nature had never before been so conceived and painted. For this reason those paintings, intellectually, possess great popularity and significance. In all of the arts, impressionism was the effort to suggest a thing by its human appeal, by relating it to some human faculty to a far greater extent than had ever before been attempted.

Since impressionism received fullest development in painting, some comment on that movement might help here; Lang said of impressionism:

. . . it is rather the sum total of man's experiences and observations, his artistic temperament . . . the painters fled into the open . . . declaring color the carrier of life; and since they endeavored to apprehend life in its minute momentary aspects, they reduced color to its finest particles. The final aim was an art bent on seizing the impressions of volatile, scurrying moments. . . .

Contour and silhouette have lost most of their qualities, the forms are dissolved into color patches. If we still want to find rhythm in these pictures we must seek it in the *innumerable color particles,* in the most subjective oscillation of the subtle color patterns. This rhythm, flickering restlessly, can no longer be abstracted from content and form; it rests on the relationship of theme, form, and color, receiving its validity exclusively from the creator.[159]

How much of this can be applied to Lanier's verse must rest

with the eye of the beholder, but certainly there is much to be said
for his impressionistic style in the last works, for the elaborate
daubs of color and detail (pointillism). Since impressionism has
never adequately been explored in American poetry, it is understandable that Lanier's attempts should exist now in a sort of demi-
monde. For the "art for art's sake" school has hardly yet received
adequate treatment either on the continent or in England. This
parallel to impressionism explains Lanier's surprising success with
such apparently unlyrical subjects as "Corn" and "The Marshes
of Glynn." Lang said of this faculty: "The sensuous, corporeal,
and actual stimuli of color and light become the main subjects,
while the importance of the concrete subjects is minimized."[160]

It is important to remember that impressionism existed inde-
pendently in verse, as it did in music and painting, before it became a movement. All of the impressionistic poets "struggle
against rhyme, verse, and strophe," and demand "free rhythm,"
according to Lang. In music, the only binding quality is that of
mood and the treatment of the "fleeting" moment. Impressionistic music is colorful, blurred, mystic, dreamy. Debussy typifies
musical impressionism. Certainly there is this personal subjective
approach to nature in Lanier, and the initial difficulty the reader
feels when first he hears (sees) trees so described as in the "Marshes
of Glynn" can be rightly understood as impressionism:

> Glooms of the live-oak, beautiful-braided and woven
> With intricate shades of the vines that myriad-cloven
>   Clamber the forks of the multiform boughs—
>   Emerald twilights,—
>   Virginal shy lights,
> Wrought of the leaves to allure to the whisper of vows,
> When lovers pace timidly down through the green colonnades
>   Of the dim sweet woods, of the dear dark woods,
>   Of the heavenly woods and glades,
> That run to the radiant marginal sand-beach within
>   The wide sea-marshes of Glynn;—

Agreed that this is a kind of nature realism, it is only such realism as stems from the personal impression of a sensitive musician
or poet, just as the impression of dawn and the rising sun move
along, in point of time, with the actual rising of some sun. In this
strange temporal quality Lanier seems again to be doing in poetry
what music can do—recreating and sustaining the interest in the
poem in that very moment, as a musician would in music. This is

a difficult task and an almost original one that Lanier has attempted, for while music can depend upon a lulling of tone, a crescendo of interest by rhythm, melody, and intensity—and intensity was a quality that Lanier borrowed freely from music—poetry is faced with either using repetitive patterns or else with striking off new ideas which will sustain the flow of music to the climax. The richness of Lanier's poetic fancies made possible poetry such as he wrote, where every movement forward is impelled along that same line by the addition of some fancy in the same vein.

It is the immediacy and vibrancy more than anything else in this last verse of Lanier's that suggest a musical analogy, for only music, not art, shared with poetry the ability to be created and enjoyed in the moment. Music is wonderfully suited to sound the hush and the first stirrings of nature; it is something new when a poem achieves that same sort of effect. These little "tone poems" of Lanier's seem to owe to music their conception and their form. The lines in themselves, unlike the Whitman line, lack the symphonic quality; they are melodious. Lanier's verses would make good programs or program notes for a symphony on such a theme. There is the provision for the same sort of intensity and climax music handles so well. Descriptive poetry and descriptive music were the best products of Lanier's imagination. Lanier belongs to the lesser, finer workers in tone and colors that made up a certain coterie in the arts as the century waned.

It must therefore be admitted in any study of Lanier's verse that the influence of music was most profound. It shaped his stanzas; it was responsible for the forms and kinds of verse he wrote; it resulted in attempts at musical parallels: of symphonies in verse, of choral elements in verse, and of a kind of musical impressionism transferred to verbal terms. Though he wrote sonnets, the development of his musical gift led him into always greater structural irregularities, until in his "programme music," "The Marshes of Glynn" and "Sunrise," he seems to have followed only the forms of music. Add to these his numerous songs and the excellence of his musical images, and one can say of Lanier's verse, quite apart from the metrical dexterity and melodic beauty it often revealed, that if music had not been known to him his verses as we know them simply would not exist. He was a natural song poet, like Poe; he became fascinated by the symphonic forms of his day, like Whitman; but it is quite apparent now that the best poems he wrote were musical "impressions." It is probably true that Sidney Lanier will someday be recognized as America's first great impressionistic poet and only a very musical poet would attempt to write in terms of such sounds and colors.

LOOKING FORWARD

After 1880, in what has been called the "twilight interval" in American poetry, a number of minor poets wrote a series of lyrical and impressionistic poems conservatively indebted to music in title, in content, in imagery, in sound pattern, and in rhythms. E. C. Stedman, R. H. Stoddard, Lizette Woodworth Reese, Edward Rowland Sill, Father Tabb, and Richard Watson Gilder, to name a few, wrote verses indicative of an interest in music, if not a very thorough-going recognition of its possibilities in alliance with verse. The poems of Emily Dickinson, late published as they were, reveal, by contrast, the same general kind of transcendental interest in music that Emerson had had and a marked feeling for "dissonance" in rhyme and rhythmic irregularities.

The twentieth century interest in prosody and its relationship to music, generated by *The Science of English Verse,* was given impetus in 1901 by Julia P. Dabney's *The Musical Basis of Verse,* T. S. Omond's *A Study of Metre* and *English Metrists* in 1907, and Johannes Carl Andersen's *The Laws of Verse* in 1928. In England, Gerard Manley Hopkins and Coventry Patmore *(Amelia,* 1878) had already experimented with new rhythms, and Hopkins' "sprung-rhythms" were greeted as something new, though they are as old as Greek music and verse. Robert Bridges' attempts to define the types of prosodic patterns in *Milton's Prosody* and his own experiments with quantitative values had their effect upon American verse. Karl Shapiro's annotated study, *A Bibliography of Modern Prosody,* 1948, indicates how important the position of music is in recent prosody.

The importance of music in American poetry increased perceptibly in the second and third decades of the twentieth century with that experiment in verse, so indebted to Poe and the French symboliste poets, known as Imagism. One of the basic tenets of the imagist group, a tenet which has not been sufficiently explored, was that the imagist line must be identified with the musical phrase. Much of the interest in *vers libre* and polyphonic prose during this poetic "renaissance" thus had its source in music. The concern of the poets to write in terms of cadence rather than of line and the attempts to write orchestral verse grew out of the preoccupation of the imagists with music.

Ezra Pound, for instance, whose writings have received praise for their precision and delicacy, made a considerable study of the poets of the Middle Ages, of the minnesingers and meistersingers, and of the troubadours and their musical forms. His interests in Provençal poetry led him into discussions of music. His essays in *Make It New* reveal his interest in the relationship of speech and music, and his concern with the staccato and legato effects of the "hanging together of words" has been constant. He was responsible for the editing of several Vivaldi manuscripts and wrote an opera on François Villon which was presented in Paris and broadcast in London. Many of his poems were written to tunes and snatches of songs he knew. He still writes often in Provençal musical forms.

Harriet Monroe, editor of *Poetry Magazine* during its greatest period, from 1912 to 1920, was an ardent champion of quantity and the *vers libre* movement as well as the "new poetry." Most of the innovations that appeared in metrics were discussed in her magazine, and the "new" poets themselves found their work welcome.

Amy Lowell, the chief champion of polyphonic prose in *Can Grande's Castle* (1918) and of orchestral verse, was herself a writer of *vers libre* and acknowledged her debt to Debussy in *Men, Women and Ghosts* (1916). William Carlos Williams has been concerned for a number of years with the problem of the verse line and the cadence and their relationship to music.

The troubadour poets, Vachel Lindsay and Carl Sandburg, are both vibrant examples of the influence of music upon modern verse. Lindsay's famous jazz rhythms, said to owe their origin to the Moody hymnal and to the Negro spiritual, depend upon the recitative, a declamatory style allied to music. Lindsay's deliberate attempt to write verse for music, to indicate the exact metrical performance of his verse with its dextrous, syncopated, rhythmic patterns owes much to his knowledge of music. And Sandburg's return to the role of strolling troubadour is almost as genuine an appreciation of sung verse as Lindsay's was. Publication of the *American Song Bag* was the result of his interest in balladry. Alfred Kreymborg, musician, whose editorship of *Others* had so much to do with the *vers libre* movement, was an experimentalist with new rhythms and "new forms" in *Mushrooms* (1916) and wrote much on the effect music had upon his verse in his autobiography, *Troubadour* (1925). Arthur Guiterman is another poet whose work was indebted to music.

Though it is hardly feasible simply to list here all of the poets who have made use of music in their verse during the first half of this century, certainly three men who have experimented most widely with the form of the symphony, though their styles diverge at many points, deserve some further recognition. These men are John Gould Fletcher, T. S. Eliot, and Conrad Aiken—each of whom, after his fashion, has done much to explore the possibilities of instrumental music—largely the symphony—in verse.

John Gould Fletcher, one of the original imagists, made no secret of his musical obsession, and, in many ways, was responsible for calling the possibilities in the form of the symphony to the attention of both Aiken and Eliot. Fletcher, however, did not fully explore that form himself, but turned instead to the writing of "impressionistic" sketches and "symphonies in color" which make up the bulk of his musical verse in *Preludes and Symphonies* (1922). These "color" symphonies were anticipated by Sidney Lanier's own work in impressionism, though Fletcher's impressions differ in length and in their preoccupation with color. His longest attempt to follow the symphonic form was *Sand and Spray,* a "Sea Symphony" published in 1915 together with his theories on the use of music in the writing of verse—*Irradiations*. In his autobiography, *Life Is My Song* (1937), he made further allusion to his musical preoccupation. He made important attempts at what has come to be called "verbal orchestration" and polyphonic prose, but the limits of his work can best be seen when compared to and contrasted with that of Conrad Aiken.

Aiken has, so far, most fully developed in American verse the possibilities of musical parallels. The nebulous quality of his imagery, which critics have sometimes deplored, owes its origin, as we have seen in the works of Poe, Whitman, and Lanier, to the fact that he is working always with the musical parallel in mind. Aiken is one of the most successful of American poets in his use of the cadence and his concern with the musical phrase in verse, largely because of the sensitivity of his ear. He has attempted, and is attempting, to re-create, in his psychological studies, the mind's voice itself with its tossing and merging images, and to do this he has chosen the parallel of the symphony. Much as Whitman began to do, he introduces and merges his themes. He exhibits his knowledge of music in his careful development of themes, but he works always with an eye for the pitfalls into which Lanier had fallen in his early attempts to approximate symphonic form. Aiken releases the verse from its musical parallel whenever the form of the latter would impinge fatally upon the poem. He says himself that the sounds of music are approximated in his mind by the sounds and rhythms of verse.

Often Aiken abandons the method of the symphony altogether for a kind of musical "impression" which differs patently from that of Fletcher. Actually Aiken seems closer to that later movement in art known as "expressionism" in which the artist views every subject subjectively, in the light of his personal experiences. In this sense Aiken appears to be an "expressionist," if terminology alone is an aid to the understanding of a man's style. Aiken's symphonies are carefully planned, on the whole, and his use of thematic material often recalls the leitmotif. The most symphonic of his poems, such as "The Charnel Rose" (1915), "Jig of Forslin" (1915-16), "The House of Dust" (1916), and "Senlin" (1918)—the latter written as a tone poem—have been collected and recently republished in a volume called *The Divine Pilgrim* (1948). Calvin S. Brown, who also sees in Aiken's work the fullest development of music in verse, has written a special chapter on Aiken in *Music and Literature* and promises to do much more work in this direction in the near future.

Despite the obviously cerebral appeal of T. S. Eliot, it cannot be denied, and is not denied in the recent critical accounts of his metrics and his poetry, that he is one of the two living American poets most concerned with drawing upon music in his verse. Eliot's dependence upon music is intellectual and formalistic, but it is also the source of the strange and portentous emotionalism that moves the reader. His use of the symphonic parallel in *The Waste Land* has received critical recognition, as has his use of the simpler, if more tightly conceived patterns of chamber music in *Four Quartets*. Eliot's use of symbols is often a musical one, and since he is, in many ways, the foremost of the practicing symbolists, his kinship to Richard Wagner is close. Eliot wrote out, in *The Music of Poetry* (1942), many of his ideas on music and attempted to explain the line and phrase as both musical and poetic. Recent studies reveal that he handles syllables much as Lanier did, that is, quantitatively. Music, in the case of both Aiken and Eliot, is a most suitable source of inspiration, for while Aiken attempts to represent the emotional response of a sensitive individual to the world (expressionism), Eliot attempts the creation of the special world of the intellectual who has largely rejected his environment (abstractionism); and both of these attempts are likened in style and feeling to music. Certainly further studies are needed to reveal the exact purposes and working media of each of these three modern poets.

Notes

1. See John Murray Gibbon, *Melody and the Lyric* (London: J. M. Dent, 1930), 25. The Venetian Ambassador to the Court of Henry VIII said of the singers at the Chapel Royal: "Their voices are really divine, and as for the deep bass I do not believe they are equalled in the world."
2. See Merwin M. Kastendiek, *England's Musical Poet: Thomas Campion* (New York: Oxford University Press, 1938), 38; and Bruce Pattison, *Music and Poetry of the English Renaissance* (London: Methuen & Company, Ltd., 1948), 96-98. Cf. also Gibbon, 86f.
3. For a fuller discussion of metrical psalmody see Hamilton Macdougall, *Early New England Psalmody* (Brattleboro: Stephen Daye Press, 1940), chapters I-VIII; Henry W. Foote, *Three Centuries of American Hymnody* (Cambridge: Harvard University Press, 1940), chapters I-VI; and Edward S. Ninde, *Nineteen Centuries of Christian Song* (New York: Fleming H. Revell Company, 1938), 81-92.
4. Luther borrowed melodies from the *Ludi Spiritualis* of the Franciscan brothers; from the melodies of the Bohemian brethren, followers of John Hus; from Gregorian chant and from the Minnesingers. He also borrowed the ballads and popular tunes of the day. He saw no reason why "the devil" should have "all the good tunes."
5. Calvin's psalter also contains many of the popular French hunting songs of the day familiar to Marot, and many a tune of like secular nature.
6. O. G. Sonneck, *Early Concert Life in America* (Leipzig: Breitkopf & Hartel, 1907), 7.
7. Evert and George Duyckinck, *Cyclopedia of American Literature* (Philadelphia: Wm. Rutter & Company, 1875), I, 201.
8. See Percy Scholes, *The Puritans and Music* (London: Oxford University Press, 1934), 2.
9. Quoted in *Chronicles of the Pilgrim Fathers*, ed. Ernest Rhys (London: J. M. Dent & Sons, 1910), 362.
10. See Thomas Goddard Wright, *Literary Culture in Early New England*, (New Haven: Yale University Press, 1920), 16; 70.
11. See the *Complete Poetry and Selected Prose of John Milton* (New York: Modern Library, 1948), 13-14.
12. See Scholes, 56f.

13. Quoted in Samuel Eliot Morison, *Harvard College in the Seventeenth Century* (Cambridge: Harvard University Press, 1936), I, 116.
14. *Ibid.,* p. 116.
15. See Reverend N. H. Chamberlain, *Samuel Sewall and The World He Lived in* (Boston: DeWolfe, Fiske & Company, 1897), 148.
16. Quoted in Foote, 78.
17. Quoted in Foote, 93, from *The Reasonableness of Regular Singing* (1720).
18. Quoted in Scholes, 54.
19. *The Boston News-Letter,* December, 1731.
20. See Foote, 136. Also *Church Music and Musical Life in Pennsylvania* (Philadelphia: Publications of the Pennsylvania Committee on Historical Research of America, 1927), II, 163, for a discussion of the performances of his symphonies.
21. Quoted in John Tasker Howard, *Our American Music* (New York: Thomas Y. Crowell Company, 1946), 22.
22. These French public concerts began in 1725 in Paris.
23. Quoted in William Arms Fisher, *Notes on Music in Old Boston* (Boston: Oliver Ditson Company, 1918), 15.
24. See Sonneck, 10.
25. See Howard, 23.
26. See *The Diary of Samuel Sewall* (Boston: the Massachusetts Historical Society, 1878-1882), III, 285. Nahum Tate and Nicholas Brady wrote a version of the psalms of Anglican service that was accepted in 1696 and was referred to as the "new version" of the Psalter.
27. See Howard, 49.
28. See Foote, 117.
29. See Howard, 56f.
30. *Ibid.,* 28.
31. See *A Benjamin Franklin Reader,* ed. N. G. Goodman (New York: Thomas Y. Crowell Company, 1945), 102.
32. Quoted in O. G. Sonneck, *Francis Hopkinson and James Lyon* (Washington, D. C.: H. L. McQueen, 1905), 113.
33. See Howard, 31.
34. Sonneck, *Francis Hopkinson and James Lyon,* 163.
35. *Ibid.,* 117.
36. *Ibid.,* 183.
37. See Edward J. Smith, "Benjamin Franklin as a Musician," *Musical Digest,* XXIX (November, 1947), 12.
38. *The Writings of Benjamin Franklin,* ed. Albert Henry Smyth (New York: The Macmillan Company, 1906), IV, 380f.
39. *Ibid.,* V, 530-533 *passim.*
40. Henry Edward Krehbiel, *The Philharmonic Society of New York* (New York and London: Novello, Ewer & Company, 1892), 23.
41. Krehbiel said that excellent orchestras existed in America fifty years before the founding of the Philharmonic. See *ibid.,* 23ff. See the Bibliography for a listing of the numerous sources upon which this section is based.
42. This first serious American orchestra played together until 1824.
43. See the *Salem Gazette,* December 16, 1818.
44. *Dwight's Journal* was preceded by the *Enterpeiad; or Musical Intelligencer—* devoted to the Diffusion of Musical Information and Belles Lettres in 1820; the *Boston Musical Gazette* in 1838; the *Musical Magazine* in 1839 in Boston, and by eight other music magazines in New York. His was of greatest importance, however, since it was published in 1852 and ran continuously until 1881. From 1820 to 1898 there were, altogether, thirty-three music magazines and journals founded in America. See Howard, 741-2.

CHAPTER II

1. George Sandys, living in the Virginia colony in 1636, had written a "Paraphrase of a Psalm of David."
2. Foote seems to feel that most of the ministers were too lazy to help in the translations and that the bulk of the work fell upon Welde, Mather, and Eliot. See Henry W. Foote, *Three Centuries of American Hymnody* (Cambridge: Harvard University Press, 1940), 140.
3. *Bay Psalm Book* (New York: Prepared for the New England Society, in the City of New York, 1903), preface.
4. *Ibid.*
5. *Ibid.*
6. *Ibid.*
7. Ainsworth's melodies were based upon a collection of psalm-tunes by Este published in 1592, as well as upon the melodies of Sternhold and Hopkins and the French and Dutch lines of the day with their greater variety of metres. Este gave place-names to his tunes, a practice which Ravenscroft later copied. There were fifty-eight tunes in the Este Psalter. See Foote, 31.
8. See Hamilton C. Macdougall, *Early New England Psalmody* (Brattleboro: Stephen Daye Press, 1940), 12. Macdougall has a detailed study of the psalm tunes in the *Scottish Psalter,* classifying them modally.
9. *Ibid.*, 16.
10. "The music used for a long time before the year 1690 was mostly written in their *Psalm Books* . . . the number of tunes thus written rarely exceeded five or six. . . ." George Hood, *A History of Music in New England* (Boston: Wilkins, Carter and Co., 1846), 52.
11. Macdougall, 35.
12. Quoted in Foote, 94.
13. See *ibid.*, 95-111.
14. Quoted in Macdougall, 27.
15. *Bay Psalm Book*, introduction, vii; see also Foote, 35.
16. See Foote, 42-43.
17. *Bay Psalm Book*, introduction, viii-ix.
18. There is difference of opinion over the extent of Milton's influence in seventeenth century American verse. Certainly Mather knew *Paradise Lost* before 1698 in writing *Magnalia*. Thomas Goddard Wright, *Literary Culture in Early New England* (New Haven: Yale University Press, 1920), 143-45. See also Charles Francis Adams, "Milton's Impress on the Provincial Literature of New England," *Proceedings Massachusetts Historical Society,* XLII (1909), 154-170.
19. Harold S. Jantz, *First Century of New England Verse* (n.p.: Antiquarian Society of Massachusetts, 1944).
20. *Ibid.*, 30-32, *passim.*
21. See Ola Winslow, *American Broadside Verse* (New Haven: Yale University Press, 1930).
22. For a fuller discussion of elegiac verse in America, see Wright, 82-95.
23. Quoted by Jantz, 77. The italics are mine.
24. *The Works of Anne Bradstreet,* ed. John Howard Ellis (New York: P. Smith, 1932), 340f.
25. *Ibid.*, 154f.
26. *Ibid.*, 130.
27. *Ibid.*, 345-349 *passim.*
28. *Ibid.*, 355.
29. *Ibid.*, 153.
30. *Ibid.*, 166.

31. *Ibid.,* 373. The italics are mine.
32. *Ibid.,* 100f.
33. *Ibid.,* 379. The italics are mine.
34. *Ibid.,* 17.
35. *Poetical Works of Edward Taylor,* ed. Thomas H. Johnson (New York: Rockland Editions, 1939), 11.
36. *Ibid.,* 67.
37. *Ibid.* 100-101. The italics are mine.
38. *Ibid.,* 107-108.
39. The gamut, or scale, originated as a term by a tenth century musician, Guido of Arezzo, who introduced the syllable system for the scale, taking the names for his syllables from the first words in a Sapphic "Hymn to St. John the Baptist." *Ut* in place of *do* gives rise to the expression *gam-ut* for running the scale from bottom to top.
40. *Ibid.,* 109.
41. *Ibid.,* 124.
42. *Ibid.,* 175.
43. *Ibid.,* 135.
44. *Ibid.*
45. *Ibid.,* 141.
46. *Ibid.,* 150.
47. *Ibid.,* 176-177.

CHAPTER III

1. See Burton A. Milligan, "An Early American Imitator of Milton," *American Literature,* XI (1939), 200-206.
2. See Mather Byles, *Poems on Several Occasions* (New York: The Facsimile Text Society by Columbia University Press, 1940) for some of his verse.
3. Quoted in Arthur W. H. Eaton, *The Famous Mather Byles* (Boston: W. A. Butterfield, 1914), 109.
4. *Ibid.,* 111.
5. Byles could never have heard Bach nor his music, though the style of the fugue was in great popularity in America until 1750.
6. See Eaton, 108.
7. See John W. Davenport, "The Ode in American Literature" (Chapel Hill: University of North Carolina, Ph.D. dissertation, 1934), 142.
8. See O. G. Sonneck, *Francis Hopkinson and James Lyon* (Washington, D. C.: H. L. McQueen, 1905), 110-113.
9. *Miscellaneous Essays and Occasional Writings of Francis Hopkinson* (Philadelphia: Reprinted by T. Dobson, 1792), III, 6. Subsequent references will be to the *Writings of Francis Hopkinson* unless otherwise indicated.
10. See Sonneck, 63-76.
11. *The Writings of Francis Hopkinson,* III, 54.
12. This is, of course, another traditional association of music with love. Shakespeare and Plato would both have recognized it.
13. *Writings of Francis Hopkinson,* III, 21-30 *passim.*
14. *Ibid.,* 11-12.
15. *Ibid.,* 167.
16. *Ibid.,* 190.
17. *Ibid.,* 74.
18. One of his best is certainly the simple "A Morning Hymn."
19. See Davenport, 80. Dryden's "Song for St. Cecilia's Day" is the first work of a

major poet in cantata form. Gray's "Ode for Music" was performed in 1759 with music by Dr. Randall. Gray's other pindaric ode, "The Bard," is filled with references to music.

20. *Writings of Francis Hopkinson,* 80-82 passim.
21. Actually England during the Restoration did much to further the cantata ode as a literary form, as well as musical. The chief figure in England was John Blow. See Henry Leland Clarke, "John Blow: A Tercentenary Survey," *Musical Quarterly,* XXXV (July, 1949), 415.
22. *Writings of Francis Hopkinson,* 86-88 *passim.*
23. *Ibid.,* 184.
24. *Ibid.,* 59-60.
25. See *Juvenile Poems on Various Subjects by Thomas Godfrey* (Philadelphia: Henry Miller, 1765), iv.
26. *Ibid.,* 58.
27. The expression of these ideas alone—of "love, fear, terror, and compassion"—mark Evans as a romanticist.
28. Nathaniel Evans, *Poems on Several Occasions* (Philadelphia: John Dunlap, 1772), preface, vii-ix.
29. *Ibid.,* 35.
30. *Ibid.,* B-2.
31. *Ibid.,* 5. The italics are mine.
32. *Ibid.,* 33.
33. *Ibid.,* 41ff. Italics are mine.
34. *Ibid.,* 135.
35. *Ibid.,* 82f.
36. *Ibid.,* 74-78 *passim.* Italics are mine.
37. *Ibid.,* 108-109.
38. *Ibid.,* 110-111.
39. Paine's life-long excesses left him impoverished. He was extremely popular as a poet in his own day and could sell almost any verse he wrote.
40. See *The Cambridge History of American Literature,* eds. Trent, Erskine, *et al.* (New York: The Macmillan Co., 1946), I, 179.
41. *The Works in Verse and Prose of the Late Robert Treat Paine* (Boston: J. Belcher, 1812), xiv.
42. "Practically every one of Paine's odes was intended to be sung for some public festival." Davenport, 129.
43. *The Works in Verse and Prose of the Late Robert Treat Paine,* 111.
44. Paine wrote his first "Fire Ode" in 1794 and his last in 1809, and was well paid for all of them.
45. *The Works in Verse and Prose of the Late Robert Treat Paine,* 248-249.
46. He was, for a while, even a theatre critic during the 1793-4 season.
47. *The Works in Verse and Prose of the Late Robert Treat Paine,* 256-7.
48. The reader would be interested to note how carefully Paine suited words to melody in this case. See *ibid.,* 213.
49. Coleridge, in commenting on the sweetness of Spencer's verse, said it arose from his *alternate alliteration,* which formed a melodic pattern. See *The Best of Coleridge,* ed. Earl L. Griggs (New York: Ronald Press Company, 1934), 373.

CHAPTER IV

1. James Huneker, *Bedouins* (New York: Charles Scribner's Sons, 1920), 82.
2. See Johann J. Winckelmann, *History of the Art of Antiquity* (1764), trans. G. Henry Lodge (London: J. Chapman, 1850).

3. See Schopenhauer's essays on "Early Greek Philosophy," "Thoughts Out of Season," the "Case of Wagner," and "Human—All Too Human" for his comments on music.

4. Quoted in Alfred Einstein, *Music in the Romantic Era* (New York: W. W. Norton & Company, 1947), 24.

5. "On the Metaphysics of Music," *The World as Will and Idea* (London: Paul, Trench, Trübner and Company, 1891), III, 233. Schopenhauer wrote further: "Music, far from being a mere accessory of poetry, is an independent art, nay, the most powerful of all the arts. . . ." See *ibid.*, 232. For a more complete discussion of the dominance of music in the century see Einstein, who has collected much philosophical comment on music in the century.

6. See Frederick W. Sternfeld, "The Musical Springs of Goethe's Poetry," *Musical Quarterly*, XXXV (October, 1949), 514.

7. See Paul Henry Lang, *Music and Western Civilization* (New York: W. W. Norton & Company, 1941), 736.

8. Coleridge wrote in 1833: "I could write as good verses now as ever I did if I were perfectly free from vexations, and were in the *ad libitum* hearing of fine music which has a sensible effect in harmonizing my thoughts, and in animating and as it were, lubricating my inventive fancy." Quoted in *The Best of Coleridge,* ed. Earl L. Griggs (Boston: Ronald Press Company, 1934), 543.

9. See Esme J. H. Howard, *Music in the Poets* (London: Duckworth Press, 1921), 43ff.

10. See "To Charles Cowden Clarke," "Isabella," and "The Eve of St. Agnes," for musical references.

11. See Calvin S. Brown, *Music and Literature*. Athens, Georgia: University of Georgia Press, 1948.

12. Schoenberg attempted, in his *Pierrot Lunaire* and the "Ode to Napoleon," to indicate the pitch line to be followed in the reading by a notation. See Calvin S. Brown, "The Poetic Use of Musical Forms," *Musical Quarterly,* XXX (January, 1944), 88, 8. Schoenberg hoped in this fashion to establish the exact performance of sounds in the reading of his verse.

13. See Edward Lockspeiser, *Debussy* (London: J. M. Dent & Sons, 1936), 35-37 *passim.*

15. Philip Freneau, though he wrote nature verse, treated nature quite differently. Dana's nature poems are simple and lyrical. Freneau's are more freighted with learning and sensuous imagery.

16. Richard Henry Dana, Sr., *Poems and Prose Writings* (Boston: Russell, Odiorne, and Company, 1833), 136f.

17. Quoted in Parke Godwin, *A Biography of William Cullen Bryant* (New York: D. Appleton and Company, 1883), I, 276f.

18. He ranged Milton and Shakespeare against Pope and Dryden.

19. See William Ellery Leonard, "Bryant and the Minor Poets," *Cambridge History of American Literature* (Now York: The Macmillan Company, 1917), I, 266.

20. See Van Wyck Brooks, *The World of Washington Irving* (The World Publishing Company, 1944), 253.

21. Bryant read Greek readily and made experiments in Latin prosody. See Godwin, 34f; 227n.

22. See the *Literary History of the United States,* eds. Spiller, Thorp, et al. (New York: The Macmillan Company, 1948), I, 303.

23. *Cambridge History of American Literature,* I, 275.

24. See Tremaine McDowell, *William Cullen Bryant* (New York: American Book Company, 1935), lvi.

25. Other hymns included the "Hymn of the City" and "Hymn of the Sea." His better songs include the "Song of the Sower" and "Love's Seasons: A Song."
26. Quoted in Godwin, 20. This is a tribute to the old "fuguing" tunes of William Billings.
27. Quoted in *ibid.*, 277f.
28. See *Prose of William Cullen Bryant,* ed. Parke Godwin (New York: D. Appleton and Company, 1884), I, 6.
29. James Grant Wilson, *The Life and Letters of Fitz-Greene Halleck* (New York: D. Appleton and Company, 1869), 406.
30. See William Cullen Bryant, *Some Notices of the Life and Writings of Fitz-Greene Halleck* (New York: Printed by New York Evening Post, 1869), 15.
31. *Ibid.*, 27.
32. "He has a taste for music, and plays the flute admirably. As I owe to his acquaintance many a pleasant hour, he has become endeared to me. . . ." So Halleck wrote his sister. Quoted in Frank L. Pleadwell *The Life and Works of Joseph Rodman Drake* (Boston: The Merrymount Press, 1935), 115.
33. See *ibid.*, 63.
34. See *ibid.*, 142.
35. See *ibid.*, 143.
36. *The Culprit Fay and Other Poems* (New York: George Dearborn Company, 1835), 39.
37. See Pleadwell, 286. Drake was a lover of opera.
38. See Homer F. Barnes, *Charles Fenno Hoffman* (New York: Columbia University Press, 1930), 144.
39. See *Poems by George Pope Morris* (New York: Charles Scribner's, 1883), 225.
40. *Poems by the Late Dr. John Shaw* (Philadelphia: Edward Earle and J. Coale, 1810), 230.
41. *Ibid.*, 233.
42. Thomas Olive Mabbott and Frank L. Pleadwell, *The Life and Works of Edward Coote Pinkney* (New York: The Macmillan Company, 1926), 119.
43. *Ibid.*, 124.
44. *Ibid.*, 32.
45. *Ibid.*, 104.
46. *Ibid.*, 120.
47. *Ibid.*, 128.
48. *Ibid.*, 113.
49. *Ibid.*, 190.
50. *Areytos, or Songs and Ballads of the South* by William Gilmore Simms (Charleston: Russell & Jones, 1860), 282.
51. *Poems by William Gilmore Simms* (New York: Redfield, 1853), II, 79.
52. *Ibid.*
53. *Lyrical and Other Poems* by William Gilmore Simms (Charleston: Ellis & Neufville, 1820), 76.
54. *Areytos,* p. v.
55. *Ibid.*, 6-7.
56. *Ibid.*, 16.
57. *Virginalia—Songs of My Summer Nights* by T. H. Chivers (1853), iv.
58. *Ibid.*, v.
59. *Ibid.*
60. *Ibid.*
61. *Ibid.*, 21.
62. *Ibid.*, 22.
63. *Ibid.*, 25.
64. *Poems of Henry Timrod* (Boston: Houghton Mifflin Company, 1899), 116.

65. *Ibid.*, 141. This is South Carolina's State Song. The music for it was composed by Anne Burgess.

66. *Ibid.*, 26.

67. *Ibid.*, 31.

68. *Complete Poems of Paul Hamilton Hayne* (Boston: D. Lothrop and Company, 1882), 229.

69. *Ibid.*, 376.

70. Quoted from the *Early Letters of George William Curtis to John Sullivan Dwight,* ed. George Willis Cooke (New York: Harper and Brothers, 1898), 58.

71. See Honor McCusker, *Fifty Years of Music in Boston* (Boston: Trustees of the Public Library, 1938), 8.

72. See Lindsay Swift, *Brook Farm* (New York: The Macmillan Company, 1900), 63.

73. "Music as a Means of Culture," *Atlantic Monthly,* XXVI (September, 1870), 322-323.

74. See *The Writings of Margaret Fuller,* ed. Mason Wade (New York: The Viking Press, 1941), 6, 29, 40, 46, 66, 366 et passim.

75. The *Dial,* I (July, 1840), 124.

76. The *Dial,* III (July, 1842), 53.

77. See *Poems by Jones Very,* ed. William P. Andrews (Boston: Houghton, Mifflin and Company, 1883), 11. See also William Bartlett, *Emerson's Brave Saint* (Durham: Duke University Press, 1942).

78. See *Ralph Waldo Emerson,* ed. Frederic I. Carpenter (New York: American Book Company, 1934), xli.

79. *Ibid.*, xl.

80. See *The Journals of Ralph Waldo Emerson* (Boston: Houghton Mifflin Company, 1909-1914), II, 48.

81. *Ibid.*, III, 85f.

82. *Ibid.*, V, 269.

83. *Ibid.*, IX, 358-9.

84. *Ibid.*, III, 19-20.

85. *Ibid.*, V, 121.

86. *Ibid.*, 138.

87. *Ibid.*, 145.

88. *Ibid.*, 492.

89. *Ibid.*, III, 464.

90. *Ibid.*, 457. It is interesting to think he had actually heard this instrument.

91. *Ibid,* V, 255.

92. *Ibid.*, 269.

93. *The Works of Ralph Waldo Emerson* (New York: Tudor Publishing Company, n.d.), IV, 93.

94. *Ibid.*, 26.

95. *Ibid.*, 116.

96. *Ibid.*, 243.

97. *Ibid.*, 242.

98. *Ibid.*, 73f.

99. *The Complete Works of Ralph Waldo Emerson: Poems,* ed. Edward Waldo Emerson (Cambridge: Riverside Press, 1904), IV, 85. Subsequent references to poetry are to this edition.

100. "To Ellen," 93.

101. "Merlin," 120.

102. Thoreau, it is true, also wrote irregular stanzas, yet Emerson's could have been regular enough. This section quoted from "Merlin" reveals when his irregularities occur: as the content becomes forceful the metrical pattern is broken.

103. "Bacchus," 126.

104. "The House," 129. Emily Dickinson wrote quatrains very much like this, and used music in an almost identical fashion in her verse.

105. "The Harp," 237-239 passim.

106. See Leonora Cranch Scott, *The Life and Letters of Christopher Pearse Cranch* (Boston: Houghton Mifflin Company, 1917), 129-280 passim.

107. He said that he visited some ladies there who were, in point of fact, musical, poetical. "I go there every day, sing, play the flute, chat. . . ." See *ibid.*, 26-27.

108. *Ibid.*

109. *Ibid.*, 48.

110. *Ibid.*, 78.

111. *Ibid.*, 90.

112. *Ibid.*

113. *Ibid.*, 190.

114. *Ibid.* William Henry Fry, music critic for the *Tribune*, operatic composer and writer, championed American compositions and opera in English at a time when America had fallen under the sway of Italian operatic influence. He was the strongest nineteenth century proponent of American composition. However, neither Richard Storrs Willis nor Dwight could be persuaded to admire his "Santa Claus Symphony." George Bristow wrote the second American opera for public performance and joined Fry in a defense of American compositions.

115. From *Satan: A Libretto* (Boston: Roberts Brothers, 1874), 2.

116. Quoted in McCusker, 19.

117. *The Complete Poetical Works of Henry Wadsworth Longfellow*, ed. Horace E. Scudder (Boston: Houghton Mifflin Company, 1893), 1.

118. *Ibid.*, 56.

119. *Ibid.*, 207.

120. *Ibid.*, 218.

121. *Ibid.*, 26.

122. *Ibid.*, 27.

123. *Ibid.*, 104.

124. *Ibid.*, 169.

125. *Henry Wadsworth Longfellow*, ed. Odell Shepard (New York: American Book Company, 1934), xlii-xliii.

126. James Lightwood, *Music and Literature* (London: Epworth Press, 1931).

127. Holmes spoke learnedly of the Amati and Stradivarius, of the fifty-eight pieces of the violin, of its centuries of aging. See *ibid.*, 146.

128. *Ibid.*, 152.

129. Quoted in *ibid.*, 151.

130. *Ibid.*, 153.

131. MS. Letter from Sidney Lanier (August 3, 1880), Holmes Collection: 2, H. O. Library of Congress.

132. See *ibid.*

133. See H. T. Henry, "Music in Lowell's Prose and Verse," *Musical Quarterly*, X (October, 1924), 570-572.

134. *Ibid.*, 550.

135. *Ibid.*

136. *Ibid.*, 559.

137. *Ibid.*, 557.

138. *Ibid.*, 572.

CHAPTER V

1. See N. Bryllion Fagin, *The Histrionic Mr. Poe* (Baltimore: Johns Hopkins Press, 1949), 135ff for a discussion of verbal melody in Poe's verse.

2. See Mary E. Phillips, *Edgar Allan Poe: The Man* (Chicago: John G. Winston Company, 1926), I, 38.

3. See *ibid.*, pp. 31-39. Arnold was organist at Chapel Royal and an opera and oratorio writer.

4. Quoted in *ibid.*, 44.

5. For accounts of Elizabeth Poe see Arthur H. Quinn, *Edgar Allan Poe* (New York: D. Appleton Company, 1942), 4-6; Mary E. Phillips, 51-60; and George E. Woodberry, *Edgar Allan Poe* (Boston: Houghton Mifflin Company, 1913), 3-11.

6. Quoted by Phillips, I, 69.

7. "In speaking of my mother you have touched a string to which my heart fully responds. To have known her is to be an object of great interest in my eyes." Quoted in Quinn, 237.

8. See *ibid.*, 4f.

9. See the *Complete Poems of Edgar Allan Poe,* ed. J. H. Whitty (Boston: Houghton Mifflin Company, 1917), 198. Poe copied many of these old songs out into notebooks.

10. Poe was in and around the Burns country at Irvine while abroad.

11. See Woodberry, 24.

12. See Fagin, 38.

13. See *Edgar Allan Poe,* eds., Margaret Alterton and Hardin Craig (New York: American Book Company, 1935), introduction, xxi, n. 19.

14. "I have made prosody, in all languages which I have studied, a particular subject of inquiry." See Poe's letter to Nathaniel Beverly Tucker (Professor of Law, William and Mary College), December 1, 1838, in Quinn, 236.

15. Gessner Harrison, who became an Oxford language professor, ranked only three places above Poe at the University of Virginia. See Alterton and Craig, xxiii, and Quinn, 100. Poe stood easily in the top five per cent of his class.

16. See Fagin, 47-49. Whitty said that his voice was "musical and cultivated." See 188.

17. Several biographers mention this fact. The instrument was widely used by young men of the day. See Killis Campbell, *The Mind of Poe* (Cambridge: Harvard University Press, 1933), 11.

18. See Quinn, 198.

19. *Ibid.*

20. See Fagin, 47.

21. See "Light and Sound," *Marginalia. The Works of Edgar Allan Poe* (New York: Charles Scribner's Sons, 1927), VII, 341. Subsequent references to this edition are titled *Works.*

22. See Woodberry, 24.

23. He knew Bellini's "La Sonnambula" and "Norma," which were then popular in America. He also apparently knew Verdi's "Hernani" first heard in America at the Astor Place Theatre in 1846. Opera was a medium Poe was particularly well equipped to enjoy.

24. See "A Singular Association," *Marginalia, Works,* VII, 329, 311.

25. See *ibid.*, 319, 335.

26. See *ibid.*, 266, 319, 335; and Fagin, 127.

27. Quoted in *The Letters of Edgar Allan Poe,* ed., J. W. Ostrom (Cambridge, Massachusetts: Harvard University Press, 1948), I, 257f. Italics are mine.

28. See *Works,* VI, 256-259 for his comments on Thomas Moore, Byron and Coleridge.

29. *Ibid.,* 12.

30. See *The Complete Tales and Poems of Edgar Allan Poe* (New York: Modern Library, 1938), 998, n. 1.

31. From "A Chapter of Suggestions," *Works*, VIII, 331.
32. *The Complete Tales and Poems of Edgar Allan Poe*, 236.
33. *Ibid.*, 237. At this point Poe introduced the poem "The Haunted Palace."
34. See *ibid*, 271. Note the references to the opera "Hernani," and how the use of music sets the general tone of the story.
35. *Ibid.*, 285.
36. *Ibid.*, 297.
37. Bellini (1801-1835) was, perhaps, the best loved Italian composer in America.
38. *Complete Tales and Poems of Edgar Allan Poe*, 458.
39. *Ibid.*, 606-607.
40. *Ibid.*, 252.
41. *Ibid.*, 699f.
42. *Works*, VIII, 272f. See also his criticisms of H. F. Chorley and C. P. Cranch.
43. *Ibid.*
44. See *ibid.*, VII, 319.
45. See *ibid.*, VIII, 274.
46. *Ibid.*
47. *Ibid.*, 275. Italics are mine.
48. *Ibid.*, VI, 10f. This is another tribute to the greater power of music.
49. *Ibid.*, 28. This association of music with the soul is typical of the nineteenth century.
50. *Ibid.*, 11f.
51. *Ibid.*, 12.
52. *Ibid.*
53. See May Garretson Evans, *Music and Edgar Allan Poe: A Bibliography* (Baltimore: The Johns Hopkins Press, 1939), for a complete bibliography of musical settings of his verse. It is interesting to note that most settings of Poe's verse were written more than fifty years after his death.
54. Letter to Professor Tucker, quoted to Quinn, 236. The italics are mine.
55. "It may be said, indeed, that we are without a treatise on our own verse." *Complete Tales and Poems of Edgar Allan Poe*, 909.
56. *Ibid.*, 910.
57. *Ibid.*, 913. Italics are mine.
58. *Ibid.*, 915.
59. "If the relation does not exist of itself, we force it by emphasis, which can, of course, make any syllable as long as desired." *Ibid.*
60. "Lines being introduced, the necessity of distinctly defining these lines *to the ear* . . . would lead to a scrutiny of their capabilities *at their terminations*." *Ibid.*, 916. It should be noted here that Poe says that poetry appeals to the ear—"as yet written verse does not exist." *Ibid.*
61. Poe is following Bryant's lead here. The attack on "blending" heralded the arrival of the Romantic movement in American verse. Poe had always the utmost respect for Bryant and his work. See Spiller, I, 303 for a discussion of Bryant by Poe.
62. "The point of *time* is that point which, being the rudimental one, must never be tampered with at all." See *Complete Tales and Poems of Edgar Allan Poe*, 921. This is certainly an anticipation of Lanier's *time* as primary rhythm. Italics are mine.
63. *Ibid.*
64. *Ibid.*, 924.
65. *Ibid.*, 909.
66. See Fagin, 145-146.
67. Quoted in *ibid.*, 157.

68. Poe's desire to make of verse a verbal music led him to the most careful analysis of the poet's working material yet known in English or American verse.

69. See Richard C. Pettigrew, "Poe's Rime," *American Literature,* IV (May, 1933), 151-159.

70. See Wilbur L. Schramm, "A Note About Rime," PMLA in Bayard Q. Morgan's "Review of *Music and Literature,*" *Comparative Literature,* II (Fall, 1950), 372.

71. Half the effect of "Ulalume" is secured by the pitch, melodic, and rhythmic variations on the main (repeated) themes. The reader is fascinated by the slightest slips in the line, as a listener is excited by an anticipated variable in the melodic pattern of Ravel's "Bolero" or Debussy's "Afternoon of a Faun."

72. This *rime riche* Pettigrew particularly approved of. Personally I find it often cheaply effective.

73. Bayard Q. Morgan, writing of rhythms and pitch in West German verse, said that "the double alliteration" of the first half line is commonly accompanied by *equality of pitch.* We have largely lost the power of hearing the pitch relationship of speech . . . but the relationships exist and some day perhaps they will be rediscovered." See Morgan, *loc. cit.*

74. Syncopation seems always to draw out the "linked sweetness."

75. He insisted strongly upon an even metrical flow in versification. Recently the modernity of "The Bells" has been remarked upon because it must be read in "sounds and tempos." See Fagin, 149.

76. Fagin commented that hearing Vachel Lindsay read "The Bells" was a greater experience than hearing a Rachmaninoff setting of it. See *ibid.,* 147.

77. Poe was interested in a limited, repetitive pitch pattern; after all, bells sound in only about four pitches, and toll repeatedly in his poem.

78. I suspect that Poe's verse will live long for this reason, and that he knew it; there will always be G. B. Shaws not wearied by verbal music. Great meditative verse will probably always attract readers. But Poe deliberately chose to sing the Sirens' songs which intoxicate and lure.

79. See a discussion of verse techniques in T. S. Eliot, *The Music of Poetry* (Glasgow: Jackson & Company, 1942), 28.

80. See W. L. Werner, "Poe's Theories and Practice in Poetic Technique," *American Literature,* II (May, 1930), 163ff.

81. *Ibid.*

82. *Works,* VIII, 273.

83. Note Poe's effect upon the French. See Spiller, I, 341, for a brief discussion of his influence on the Symboliste poets who tried to emulate his suggestive, musical qualities.

84. Poe said the ending of "Ulalume" was scarcely clear to himself. See *ibid.,* 339.

85. Quoted in Fagin, 155.

86. Poe's imagery is unusually associative, just as Keats's imagery was. See Richard Harter Fogle, *The Imagery of Keats and Shelley* (Chapel Hill: University of North Carolina Press, 1949) for a discussion of *synaesthesia* in these young romantics.

87. See Joe J. Jones, "Poe's 'Nicean Barks'," *American Literature,* II (January, 1931), 433-437. Jones traces the term to Poe's reading of Catullus who fled to the ancient and Asiatic city of Nicea by boat to forget his love for the faithless Clodin. He also prefaces his comments with a survey of earlier theories.

88. Proust's suggestive powers often depend upon a remembered scent which opens for the reader a world of associations. See the opening chapters of *Remembrance of Things Past.* It is not unreasonable to assume that Poe's larger pattern for "Helen" was the Ulysses story, with certain notable changes.

89. Quoted in Fagin, 147.

90. See *The Writings of Margaret Fuller,* ed., Mason Wade (New York: Viking Press, 1941), 401f, for her comments on the phrase "Universal Valley."
91. Politian says the voice fell, "into my heart of hearts." See "Scenes from 'Politian'," *Complete Tales and Poems of Edgar Allan Poe,* 984ff.
92. *Ibid.,* 992. Italics are mine.
93. *Ibid.,* 998. Italics are mine.
94. *Ibid.,* 996.
95. This "sound of silence on the startled ear" reminds one of Keats's "heard melodies are sweet, but those unheard are sweeter."
96. *Complete Tales and Poems of Edgar Allan Poe,* 999. The sound that "sprang" from the spirit which bears the "burthen" to the charm the maiden sang is bearing a *bass* or accompaniment to her own song—not a refrain. That Poe knew enough about music to interject such a line with insouciance argues for his early knowledge of music.
97. *Ibid.,* 1000. Italics are mine.
98. *Ibid.,* 1006. Italics are mine.
99. *Ibid.,* 1010. Italics are mine.
100. *Ibid.,* 1013. Italics are mine.
101. *Ibid.,* 1012. Italics are mine.
102. *Ibid.,* 1015.
103. *Ibid.,* 1022.
104. *Ibid.,* 1024. Italics are mine.
105. *Ibid.,* 1025. Italics are mine.
106. By this I mean that it is more limited in its suggestiveness, and therefore more popular, just as program music which says "here is what you are to think of at this point" is more popular.
107. See Gay Wilson Allen, *American Prosody* (New York: American Book Company, 1935), 83.
108. See Werner, *loc. cit.,* 158.
109. The use of the *leit-motif,* or symbol, by Poe is well illustrated here. The "kingdom by the sea" is the most obviously recurring idea in the poem, and appears in some form in each stanza. Wagner developed a similar technique in music.

CHAPTER VI

1. In "A Backward Glance O'er Travel'd Roads" Whitman wrote in resume: "For grounds for *Leaves of Grass,* as a poem, I abandoned the conventional themes . . . none of the stock ornamentation, or choice plots of love or war, or high, exceptional personages of Old-World song . . . no legend, or myth, or romance, nor euphemism, nor rhyme. . . ." *The Complete Poetry and Prose of Walt Whitman,* ed. Malcolm Cowley (New York: Pellegrini & Cudahy, 1948), I, 471.
2. Quoted by Hamilton W. Mabie in "American Life in Whitman's Poetry," *The Outlook,* LXXV (September 5, 1903), 72.
3. Louise Pound concluded that operatic music formed the basis for the verse of Whitman, and she traced many of the references to opera in his verse. She commented that while Whitman was in New Orleans he could have heard opera four times a week. She felt Whitman's frequent use of musical terms like recitative, clef, etc., was always poetic and knowledged. See Louise Pound, "Walt Whitman and Italian Music," *American Mercury,* VI (September, 1925), 58-62.
4. See Calvin S. Brown, *Music and Literature* (Athens, Georgia: The University of Georgia Press, 1948), 178-194.

5. Faner's dissertation, in fully revised form, appeared as *Walt Whitman & Opera* in 1951.

6. See Frederik Schyberg, *Walt Whitman,* trans., E. A. Allen (New York: Columbia University Press, 1951), 62ff.

7. See Sculley Bradley, "The Fundamental Metrical Principle in Whitman's Poetry," *American Literature,* X (January, 1939) 437-459, and Autrey N. Wiley, "Reiterative Devices in *Leaves of Grass,*" *American Literature,* I (May, 1929), 170, among others.

8. Most of this material came from the manuscript collections of the Library of Congress and at Duke University. The Trent Collection Notebooks at Duke University have since been published as *Faint Clues & Indirections,* eds. Clarence Gohdes and Rollo Silver (Durham, North Carolina: Duke University Press, 1949). Hereafter Trent Collection material will appear abbreviated as T. C. since my references are to these manuscripts.

9. Though most biographers since Holloway mention this point, there is no evidence that Jeff had any unusual talent.

10. See "A Backward Glance O'er Travel'd Roads," *The Complete Poetry and Prose of Walt Whitman,* I, 477.

11. This prose work remained, rather fortunately, unpublished.

12. *The Uncollected Poetry and Prose of Walt Whitman,* ed., Emory Holloway (New York: P. Smith, 1932), II, 99.

13. See James Huneker, "A Visit to Walt Whitman," *Ivory Apes and Peacocks* (New York: Charles Scribner's and Sons, 1917), 27.

14. Bettini appeared at Castle Garden in 1851; Alboni in 1853. Both especially thrilled him.

15. See Hamilton W. Mabie, 72.

16. *Ibid.*

17. See Emory Holloway, *Whitman* (New York: Alfred A. Knopf, 1926), 91.

18. *Ibid.,* 90.

19. See *The Complete Poetry and Prose of Walt Whitman,* II, 14f.

20. *Ibid.,* 526. Italics are mine.

21. *Ibid.,* 158. Italics are mine.

22. *Ibid.*

23. *Ibid.,* 35.

24. *Ibid.,* 38.

25. *Ibid.,* 63.

26. *Ibid.,* 510.

27. He was something of a singer and often sang plantation songs and ballads. He was fond of reading aloud and used to read Dante to the waves and spout Homer on Fifth Avenue busses. In youth he even had a fling on the stage, and he heard during his lifetime the oratory of Channing, Fanny Kemble, and Father Taylor, among others.

28. *The Complete Poetry and Prose of Walt Whitman,* II, 84.

29. *Ibid.,* 85ff.

30. Quoted by Huneker, 24.

31. *The Complete Poetry and Prose of Walt Whitman,* II, 80f. Italics are mine.

32. *Ibid.,* 82.

33. *Ibid.,* 91.

34. See note 37 *infra.*

35. "The greatest poet is not he who has done the best; it is he who suggests the most . . . and who leaves you much . . . to complete in your turn." *The Complete Poetry and Prose of Walt Whitman,* II, 301-302 *passim.*

36. James A. Rooney, "Whitman and Alboni," *Poughkeepsie Daily News,* from Trent Collection, catalogue 62-22, no. 16.

37. *The Uncollected Poetry and Prose of Walt Whitman*, I, 258f.

38. Trent Collection: Catalogue 33, no. 40, 17.

39. *Ibid.*, no. 22.

40. *Ibid.*

41. T.C.: catalogue 20, no. 36, 14.

42. T.C.: catalogue 30, no. 37, 15.

43. *Ibid.* Whitman crossed out the word *poem,* indicated by parentheses.

44. T.C.: catalogue 34, no. 31, 25.

45. T.C.: catalogue 101, no. 26, 35

46. T.C.: catalogue 31, no. 38, 15.

47. T.C.: catalogue 126, no. 25, 46.

48. *Ibid.*

49. *Ibid.*

50. See *ibid.*

51. Faner, 207.

52. Quoted by Robert Haven Schauffler, *Beethoven: The Man Who Freed Music* (New York: Doubleday, Doran & Company, 1929), 531.

53. *Ibid.*, 497.

54. E. T. A. Hoffmann, "Beethoven's Instrumental Music," trans. Oliver Strunk, *Source Readings in Music History* (New York: W. W. Norton and Co., 1950), 778.

55. T.C.: catalogue 31, no. 38, 15.

56. *The Complete Poetry and Prose of Walt Whitman,* I, 473.

57. "A Song for Occupations," *op. cit.,* I, 213.

58. See Gay Wilson Allen, *Walt Whitman Handbook* (Chicago: Packard and Co., 1941), 210 for a discussion of this change.

59. "From Paumanok Starting," *Complete Poetry and Prose of Walt Whitman,* I, 51-52.

60. *Ibid.*, 56. Italics are mine.

61. *Ibid.*, 58. Italics are mine.

62. "Song of Myself," *op. cit.,* I, 77. Italics are mine. Embouchure is not a term used commonly. Its use assumes quite an understanding of music. Whitman misuses here the term a little, I believe, despite the correctness of his general application of it.

63. The reader will find it interesting to watch the various themes the poet treats impinging upon each other and piling up after the fashion of music.

64. "Song of Myself," *op. cit.,* I, 102-103. This is a revealing passage. The poet is conscious of the reiterated final chords in music which sound the close of a musical number. Future poetic references are to this same edition and volume.

65. *Ibid.*, 105.

66. *Ibid.*, 113.

67. *Ibid.*, 113f. This remarkable close at once points up the poet's mortality and his immortality, and in this fashion manages to embody in verse much of the pathos and inspiration of great music.

68. "Children of Adam," 115. Italics are mine. All subsequent poetic references are to Volume I of this text.

69. *Ibid.*, 137.

70. "Salut au Monde," 149.

71. *Ibid.*, 174f.

72. "Song of the Redwood Tree," 206. Italics are mine.

73. *Ibid.*, 219f. Italics are mine.

74. "France," 229f. Italics are mine.

75. "As I Ebb'd with the Ocean of Life," 244.

76. *Ibid.*

77. *Ibid.*, 245.
78. Bradley believes "Tears" is the best example of pyramid verse Whitman wrote. He said it was like a "large wave or breaker with three crests." He thought the rhythmic principle was quantity. See Bradley, 443ff.
79. "First Songs for a Prelude," 261ff. Italics are mine.
80. *Ibid.*, 264. Italics are mine.
81. *Ibid.*, 265.
82. *Ibid.*
83. *Ibid.*, 284.
84. *Ibid.*, 288f. Italics are mine.
85. *Ibid.*, 296.
86. Whitman's association of death with pulsing, laving water is often apparent in the poetry of Bryant whom he admired.
87. These forms come first to mind because implied in each is the return of a given theme. True sonata form handles only two themes (A and B), not three.
88. See Schauffler, 530.
89. "When Lilacs Last in the Dooryard Bloom'd," 302.
90. "By Blue Ontario's Shore," 307.
91. *Ibid.*, 322. Italics are mine.
92. "Proud Music of the Storm," 356ff. Italics are mine.
93. The horn, like the lyre, is a romantic musical reference, here signifying that revenge will triumph and honor force Ernani to suicide. In this poem Whitman celebrates Italia's peerless compositions above all others.
94. A reference to *"La Favorita"* of Donizetti.
95. "Proud Music of the Storm," 360. Italics are mine. Whitman's eclecticism in music is apparent in this poem.
96. *Ibid.*, 360f. Italics are mine.
98. This drawing together of the universe through music was a common reference throughout Whitman's verse. "That Music Always Round Me," 391.
99. "The Mystic Trumpeter," 405.
100. This poem is the last of the great Whitman poems in power.
101. "Songs of Parting," 425. Italics are mine.
102. "After the Dazzle of Day," 435. Italics are mine.
103. "The Dead Tenor," 443. Italics are mine.
104. There can be hardly any doubt that the "Italian dispensation" under which he was bred had had its influence—a strong one—upon him.
105. "On, on the Same, ye Jocund Twain," 456. Italics are mine.
106. This poem appears in the last of the faint clews Whitman left. It precedes the little poem which says only in a "long long course" will his poems reach fruition. He felt they, like the Shakespeare cipher, had never been ferreted out.
107. The total effect of identical "rhymes" in participial endings is not melodious, but it keeps the lines moving like waves that break themselves on each final syllable.
108. This is a fine example of the series of phrases that move irresistibly toward the subject, thus unifying a stanza.
109. The inner rhythmic pattern here is remarkable. It is based strongly upon the quantity system, and in its syncopations is a direct anticipation of Vachel Lindsay's "The Congo."
110. The cluster of phrases around *earth* takes us back to the verses of "Hiawatha" and to the unifying devices of Old English Verse. Since the repeated word comes initially, the lines eddy outward freely—constantly repeating the process of sound and with all the fascination attendant upon the eddy. See Wiley, 161-170.

111. *The Uncollected Poetry and Prose of Walt Whitman*, I, 258. This is certainly a reference to Fernando who grieves for his own lost state of peace and his lost love. Compare this to the song of the bereaved thrush.
112. The passionate sorrow reminds the reader of the sobbing bells and moaning, groaning bells of Poe. See "Tears," 246.
113. The yearning in the voice of the bird, here first made vocal, Whitman says, was "wonderful causing tears."
114. The young bard here first learns the secret. Italics are mine.
115. "When Lilacs Last in the Dooryard Bloom'd," 301.
116. *The Uncollected Poetry and Prose of Walt Whitman*, I, 256.
117. "Song of Myself," 86.
118. *The Complete Poetry and Prose of Walt Whitman*, II, 211.

CHAPTER VII

1. See Lanier's letter to Clifford Lanier, January 4, 1874 in the *Sidney Lanier Letters*, eds. Charles R. Anderson and Aubrey Starke, Centennial Edition, (Baltimore: The Johns Hopkins Press, 1945), VIII, 425f.; IX, 8. Subsequent references to this edition will appear only with the volume title and number.
2. *Ibid.*, 28ff.
3. Gay Wilson Allen wrote: "It is doubtful whether any other prosodist has presented the quantity argument with such clarity and force as we find in *The Science of English Verse*." See Gay W. Allen, *American Prosody* (New York: American Book Company, 1935), 277-306, for his comments. Cf. also *The Science of English Verse*, II, xxx-xxxviii.
4. Quoted in Dorothy Blount Lamar, *Sidney Lanier, Musician, Poet, Soldier* (Macon, Georgia: J. W. Burke & Company, 1927; [1940], 12.
5. See Aubrey Starke, "Sidney Lanier as a Musician," *Musical Quarterly*, XX (October, 1934), 384.
6. See William R. Thayer, "Letters of Sidney Lanier to Mr. Gibson Peacock," *Atlantic Monthly*, LXXIV (July, 1894), 16.
7. See "From Bacon to Beethoven," *Essays on Music"*, II, 289.
8. See Starke, *loc. cit.*, 386.
9. He said of himself at this time: "The difficulty with me is not to write poetry," but, conversely, "Whatever turn I have for Art is purely musical; poetry being with me, a mere tangent into which I sometimes shoot." See *Letters*, VIII, 347.
10. See *Tiger Lilies and Southern Prose*, V, xxf.
11. "A Poet's Musical Impressions," The Letters of Sidney Lanier, ed. Henry W. Lanier, *Scribner's Magazine*, XXV (May, 1899), 623.
11a. *Ibid.*, 624.
12. Quoted by Norman C. Schlichter, "Sidney Lanier—Musician and Poet," *Quarterly Review,* (October, 1899), 327-328.
13. See Starke, 389.
14. See "A Poet's Musical Impressions," 626.
15. He traveled to Wheeling, West Virginia, and Macon, Georgia, to give concerts. See Starke, 390.
16. "A Poet's Musical Impressions," 625.
17. See *Letters*, VIII, 329f.
18. See Starke, 394.
19. *Ibid.*
20. *Ibid.*, 395.
21. *Ibid.*, 396.

22. He wrote redactions of Percy, Froissart, the Mabinogian, and Malory.
23. Starke, 395.
24. Quoted in Edwin Mims, *Sidney Lanier* (Boston: Houghton Mifflin Company, 1905), 38-39.
25. "From Bacon to Beethoven," II, 287.
26. "The English Novel," IV, 131.
27. "From Bacon to Beethoven," II, 287.
28. "A Poet's Musical Impressions," 625.
29. *Tiger Lilies*, V, 173f.
30. *Ibid.*, 173.
31. *Ibid.*, 30.
32. "A Poet's Musical Impressions," 630.
33. *Tiger Lilies*, V, 92.
34. "From Bacon to Beethoven," II, 290. "I look to see America the home of the orchestra, and to hear everywhere the profound messages of Beethoven and Bach to man." *Ibid.*
35. *Tiger Lilies*, V, 90.
36. "Retrospects and Prospects," V, 291.
37. *Shakespeare and his Forerunners*, III, xvi-xvii.
38. *Ibid.*, xxiv.
39. See Richard Webb and Edwin R. Coulson, *Sidney Lanier, Poet and Prosodist*, (Athens, Georgia: The University of Georgia Press, 1941), 87.
40. Harriet Monroe, *Poets and Their Art* (New York: The Macmillan Company, 1932), 290. Miss Monroe advocated a complete discard of foot forms and a classification of all rhythms into "3 times and 4 times."
41. "Every one who ever used the words 'long' and 'short,' and who did not go a-wandering after accentualism, had always known the temporal character of our rhythms." George Saintsbury, *A History of English Prosody* (London: The Macmillan Company, 1923), III, 494.
42. Johannes Andersen, *The Laws of Verse* (Cambridge: The University Press, 1928), 12.
43. See Edgar Allan Poe, *Complete Tales and Poems* (New York: Modern Library, 1938), 915.
44. Saintsbury, 497.
45. Baum wrote of Saintsbury's criticisms: "Much of his condemnation of Lanier is more brisk than logical, and what it comes to is that prosodically they dwell on different stars." *The Science of English Verse*, II, xxxiii.
46. See note 41 above.
47. See Saintsbury, 496.
48. *The Science of English Verse*, xxxviii.
49. See *ibid.*, xxx-xxxvii.
50. See *ibid.*, xxxvi.
51. See *ibid.*, xxxv-xxxvi.
52. *Ibid.*, xxxiii.
53. *Ibid.*, 51f.
54. *Ibid.*, 51-52 *passim.*
55. *Ibid.*, 53.
56. *Ibid.*
57. *Ibid.*, 56.
58. See note 49 above.
59. *Ibid.*, xxxix.
60. *Ibid.*, 22.
61. Poe, *Complete Tales and Poems*, 916.

62. Calvin S. Brown, *Music and Literature* (Athens, Georgia: The University of Georgia Press, 1948), 8-12.

63. It is the exaggerations of ordinary quantitative properties in poems like the "Congo" which make them seem so rhythmical.

64. *The Science of English Verse,* 11, n. 2.

65. *Ibid.,* 33.

66. *Ibid.,* 31.

67. *Ibid.,* 47f.

68. *Ibid.,* 60ff.

69. *Ibid.,* 77.

70. *Ibid.,* 108.

71. This results in a kind of syncopation. Thus he indicated that "typic" rhythms could only be decided by looking at the "sum of appearances" in the verse. See *ibid.*

72. See *ibid.,* 113-122.

73. *Ibid.,* 166.

74. *Ibid.,* 168-174. The relative nearness of the two patterns is illustrated more freely than I have ever seen before.

75. Lanier said initially here that his work was but an "outline," an "elementary work" written in the hope of promoting research in these fields. See *ibid.,* 196.

76. *Ibid.,* 211.

77. Bayard Q. Morgan has an interesting study in his unpublished manuscript: "Question Melodies in English."

78. Pope said his own theory of the rhythm of Anglo-Saxon verse "sprang from a study of Sidney Lanier's pioneering work." See J. C. Pope, *The Rhythm of Beowulf* (New Haven: Yale University Press, 1942), Preface.

79. ". . . the *consensus* appears to be that Lanier was in general nearer right than wrong . . ." *The Science of English Verse,* xxxvii.

80. Allen wrote further: " . . . a great part of his treatise is scientifically correct, and all of it is challenging and suggestive." See Allen, 271-285 *passim.*

81. See Evelyn H. Scholl, "English Metre Once More," *PMLA,* LXIII (March, 1948), 293-326.

82. Schramm's experiments proved Lanier's theories about rhyme to be valid. Rhyme is a phase of speech tunes, for experiments prove that the voice will leap as much as a full octave to return to a rhyme pitch. See Wilbur S. Schramm, "A Characteristic of Rime," *PMLA,* L (December, 1935), 1223-1227.

83. See Calvin S. Brown, Chapters II-IV, 7-31.

84. Lanier wrote Bayard Taylor in 1875: "I could never describe to you what a mere drought and famine my life has been, as regards that multitude of matters which I fancy one absorbs when one is in an atmosphere of art, or when one is in conversational relation . . . with persons who have . . . done large things." See *Sidney Lanier Letters,* IX, 230.

85. Thayer, "Letters of Sidney Lanier to Gibson Peacock," 25.

86. "Corn" was received by a small but very appreciative audience. As a result of this poem and "The Symphony," Lanier became friends with Peacock, Bayard Taylor, and Charlotte Cushman.

87. *Poems,* I, 224.

88. *Ibid.,* 5.

89. *Ibid.,* 16.

90. *Ibid.,* 19.

91. See Anderson's comment in *ibid.,* xxviii.

92. *Ibid.,* 19.

93. *Ibid.,* 29.

94. *Ibid.,* 30f.

95. *Ibid.*, 34f.

96. *Ibid.*

97. *Ibid.*, 36f.

98. *Ibid.*, 39.

99. *Ibid.*, 42f.

100. *Letters*, IX, 182.

101. Lanier said of "The Symphony": "I have dared *almost* to write quite, at my ease in the matters of rhythm, rhyme, and substance, in this poem. You will be glad to know that it has had a grand success." *Ibid.*, 203.

102. Webb and Coulson, 66f.

103. Anderson said that there was "no attempt made to parallel the structural design of a symphonic composition. Instead, this is a sort of counterpart to programme music . . ." *Poems*, I, xliii.

104. *Ibid.*, 48-50 *passim.*

105. *Ibid.*, 48.

106. *Ibid.*, 52.

107. *Ibid.*

108. *Ibid.*, 53.

109. *Ibid.*, 56.

110. *Ibid.*, 55f.

111. Actually his experiments here and with his later "Centennial Ode" matured his conception of musical verse and made possible his later attempts at impressionism.

112. Lanier wrote: ". . . the gigantic illustrations of Richard Wagner . . . have . . . widened the province of orchestral effects to such a magnificent horizon that every modern musical composer, whether consciously Wagnerite or not, is necessarily surrounded with a new atmosphere which compels him to write for the whole orchestra, and not for the human voice as a solo instrument . . ." "The Centennial Cantata," II, 263.

113. It was Bayard Taylor's recommendation that the commission for the cantata ode go to Lanier, whom he knew, at that time, only as a "promising" writer.

114. Thayer, *loc. cit.*, 25.

115. See *Poems*, I, xlvii.

116. *Letters*, IX, 295.

117. *Ibid.*, 296f.

118. *Ibid.*, 297f.

119. *Ibid.*, 298f.

120. This line, which seems more ambiguous than most, Lanier explained to the composer, Dudley Buck, as indicating the "weltering flow" of the remote past breaking like a sea against the firm existence of our Republic. See *Letters*, IX, 301.

121. *Poems*, I, 60-62.

122. *Letters*, IX, 349.

123. *Poems*, I, xlvi.

124. *Letters*, IX, 353.

125. *Ibid.*, 354.

126. Quoted by Lincoln Lorenz, *The Life of Sidney Lanier* (New York: Coward-McCann, Inc., 1935), 162.

127. The music Lanier wrote to "Psalm of the West" was entitled "Choral Symphony" after the pattern of Beethoven and Wagner. Unfortunately the music manuscript has never been found.

128. Lanier wrote: "By the grace of God my Centennial Ode is finished. I now only know how divine has been the agony of the last three weeks during which I have been rapt away to heights where all my own purposes as to a revisal of

artistic forms lay clear before me, and where the soul travail was of choice out of multitude." *Letters*, IX, 350.

129. It runs forty-one pages, and it is important to remember that the writing of this poem taught Lanier more about the choral idiom and the symphonic orchestra than any writing to date.

130. See *Poems*, I, xlix.

131. *Ibid.*, 88.

132. *Ibid.*, 1.

133. *Ibid.*, 88-90 *passim.*

134. *Ibid.*, 103.

135. *Ibid.*

136. *Ibid.*, 104.

137. *Ibid.*

138. *Ibid.*, 117-118 *passim.*

139. *Letters*, IX, 428.

140. See Aubrey Starke, "Lanier's Appreciation of Whitman," *American Scholar*, II (October, 1933), 399.

141. *Poems*, I, lxi.

142. *Ibid.* Anderson felt that the recognition on Lanier's part of "rhythmic but un-metric" verse to be written without line divisions was due to Whitman's influence.

143. "The Maryland Musical Festival," II, 326f.

144. *Poems*, I, 119.

145. *Ibid.*, 119ff.

146. *Ibid.*, 121.

147. *Ibid.*, 144.

148. *Ibid.*, 147.

149. *Ibid.*

150. *Ibid.*, 148.

151. *Ibid.*, 148f.

152. *The London Quarterly,* quoted in *Ibid.*, lxxxvii.

153. *Ibid.*

154. *Ibid.*

155. Quoted in Oliver Huckel, "The Genius of the Modern in Lanier," *Johns Hopkins Alumni Magazine*, XIV (June, 1926), 164.

156. Hamlin Garland, "Roadside Meetings of a Literary Nomad," *Bookman*, III (December, 1929), 404.

157. Coulson wrote: "Lanier's acceptance today by poets and students of poetry and versification has enabled the poet's fame to beat down the barriers which persisted after a long period of civil strife . . . Lanier's position as one of America's first ranking poets is secure." See Webb and Coulson, 102f.

158. *Poems*, I, lxxixf.

159. Paul Henry Lang, *Music in Western Civilization* (New York: W. W. Norton & Company, 1941), 1014f.

160. *Ibid.*, 1016.

Bibliography

Adams, Charles Francis, "Milton's Impress on the Provincial Literature of New England," *Proceedings Massachusetts Historical Society,* LXII (May, 1909), 154-170.

Aiken, Conrad, *The Divine Pilgrim.* Athens: University of Georgia Press, 1948.

Allen, Gay Wilson, *American Prosody.* New York: American Book Company, 1935.

————, *Walt Whitman Handbook.* Chicago: Packard and Company, 1946.

Allen, Hervey, and Mabbott, Thomas Olive, *Poe's Brother.* New York: George H. Doran Company, 1926.

————, *Israfel.* New York: George H. Doran Company, 1926.

Alterton, Margaret, and Craig, Hardin, *Edgar Allan Poe,* New York: American Book Company, 1935.

Andersen, Johannes, *The Laws of Verse.* New York: Macmillan Company, 1928.

Anderson, Charles, ed., *Sidney Lanier Centennial Edition,* 10 vols. Baltimore: Johns Hopkins Press, 1945.

Andrews, Wm. P., ed., *Poems by Jones Very.* Boston: Houghton Mifflin Company, 1883.

Apel, Willi, *Harvard Dictionary of Music.* Cambridge: Harvard University Press, 1944.

Arvin, Newton, *Whitman.* New York: Macmillan Company, 1938.

Bailey, Marcia Edgerton, *A Lesser Hartford Wit, Dr. Elihu Hubbard Smith.* Orono: University of Maine, 1928.

Baldwin, Lillian, *A Listener's Anthology.* New York: Silver Burdette Company, 1948.

Barnes, Homer F., *Charles Fenno Hoffman.* New York: Columbia University Press, 1930.

Bartlett, William Irving, *Jones Very, Emerson's "Brave Saint."* Durham: Duke University Press, 1942.

Bay Psalm Book. New York: Prepared for the New England Society, 1903.

Beeson, Mrs. Leola Selman, *Sidney Lanier at Oglethorpe University.* Macon, Ga.: J. W. Burke & Company, 1936.

Bennett, E. K., *A History of the German Novelle.* Cambridge, England: The University Press, 1938.

Biermann, Berthold, *Goethe's World.* New York: New Directions, 1949.

Bradley, Sculley, "The Fundamental Metrical Principle in Whitman's Poetry," *American Literature,* X (January, 1939), 437-459.

Bradley, William A., *William Cullen Bryant.* New York: Macmillan Company, 1905.

Brawley, Benjamin, *History of the English Hymn.* Nashville: Abingdon-Cokesbury Press, 1932.

Bridges, Robert, ed., *Poems of Gerard Manley Hopkins.* London: Oxford University Press, 1940.

Brooks, Cleanth, *Understanding Poetry.* New York: Henry Holt & Company, 1938.

————, *The Well Wrought Urn.* New York: Reynal & Hitchcock, 1947.

Brooks, Van Wyck, *The Times of Melville and Whitman.* New York: E. P. Dutton & Company, 1947.

————, *The World of Washington Irving.* New York: E. P. Dutton & Company, 1944.

Brown, Calvin S., *Music and Literature.* Athens: University of Georgia Press, 1948.

————, "The Poetic Use of Musical Forms," *Musical Quarterly,* XXX (January, 1944), 87-101.

————, *Tones into Words.* Athens: University of Georgia Press, 1953.

Bryant, William C., *Some Notices of Fitz-Greene Halleck.* New York: New York *Evening Post,* 1869.

Bukofzer, Manfred F., *Music in the Baroque Era.* New York: W. W. Norton & Company, 1947.

Byles, Mather, *Poems on Several Occasions.* New York: The Facsimile Text Society by Columbia University Press, 1940.

Caldwell, Luther, ed., *An Account of Anne Bradstreet, the Puritan Poetess.* Boston: Damrell & Upham, 1898.

Cambridge History of American Literature, eds. W. P. Trent, John Erskine, *et al.* New York: Macmillan Company, 1946.

Campbell, Killis, *The Mind of Poe.* Cambridge: Harvard University Press, 1933.

Canby, Henry Seidel, *Walt Whitman, An American.* Boston: Houghton Mifflin Company, 1943.

Carpenter, Frederic I., *Ralph Waldo Emerson*. New York: American Book Company, 1934.

Chamberlain, Reverend N. H., *Samuel Sewall and the World He Lived In*. Boston: DeWolfe, Fiske & Company, 1897.

Chase, Lewis, *Poe and His Poetry*. London: George G. Harrap & Company, 1913.

Chronicles of the Pilgrim Fathers, ed. Ernest Rhys. London: J. M. Dent & Sons, 1910.

Church Music and Musical Life in Pennsylvania in the Eighteenth Century, 3 vols. Philadelphia: Printed for the Committee on Historical Research, 1926-47.

Clark, Harry H., ed., *Poems of Freneau*. New York: Harcourt, Brace and Company, 1929.

Clarke, Henry Leland, "John Blow: A Tercentenary Survey," *Musical Quarterly,* XXXV (July, 1949), 412-420.

Cohen, Helen Louise, *Lyric Forms from France*. New York: Harcourt, Brace and Company, 1922.

Collins, Fletcher, "Chaucer's Understanding of Music." Yale: Unpublished Ph.D. Dissertation, 1934.

The Complete Poems of Paul Hamilton Hayne. Boston: D. Lothrop, 1882.

The Complete Tales and Poems of Edgar Allan Poe. New York: Modern Library, 1938.

Cooke, George Willis, *John Sullivan Dwight*. Boston: Small, Maynard & Company, 1898.

————, *Early Letters of George William Curtis to John Sullivan Dwight*. New York: Harper and Brothers, 1898.

Cowie, Alexander, *John Trumbull, Connecticut Wit*. Chapel Hill: University of North Carolina Press, 1936.

Cowley, Malcolm, ed., *The Complete Poetry and Prose of Walt Whitman,* 2 vols. New York: Pellegrini & Cudahy, 1948.

Cozzens, Frederic S., *Fitz-Greene Halleck*. New York: Frederic Cozzens, 1868.

Cranch, Christopher P., *Ariel and Caliban*. Boston: Houghton Mifflin Company, 1887.

————, *Satan: A Libretto*. Boston: Roberts Brothers, 1874.

Crossley-Holland, Peter, *Music in Wales*. London: Henrichson Editors, Ltd., 1948.

Dabney, Julia P., *The Musical Basis of Verse*. New York: Longmans, Green & Company, 1901.

Daiches, David, *Robert Burns*. New York: Rinehart & Company, 1950.

Dana, Richard Henry, Sr., *Poems and Prose Writings*. Boston: Russell, Odiorne and Company, 1833.

Davenport, John Stewart, "The Ode in American Literature." University of North Carolina: Unpublished Ph.D. Dissertation, 1934.

Dent, Edward J., *Opera*. New York: Penguin Books, 1940.

Deutsch, Babette, *Honey Out of the Rock*. New York: D. Appleton-Century Company, 1925.

The Dial. 4 vols. Boston: Weeks, Jordon, 1840-1844.

Dickinson, Helen and Clarence, *Excursions in Musical History*. New York: H. W. Gray Company, 1917.

Dorian, Frederick, *The History of Music in Performance*. New York: W. W. Norton & Company, 1942.

Drake, Joseph Rodman, *The Culprit Fay and Other Poems*. New York: George Dearborn, 1835.

Dreiser, Theodore, *Moods, Philosophic and Emotional*. New York: Simon and Schuster, 1936.

Drew, Elizabeth, *T. S. Eliot, The Design of His Poetry*. New York: Charles Scribner's Sons, 1949.

Duyckinck, Evert A. and George, *Cyclopedia of American Literature*. Philadelphia: Rutter & Company, 1875.

Dwight, John Sullivan, "Music As a Means of Culture," *Atlantic Monthly*, XXVI (September, 1870), 322-323.

Eaton, Arthur W. H., *The Famous Mather Byles*. Boston: W. A. Butterfield, 1914.

Eidson, John Olin, *Tennyson in America*. Athens: University of Georgia Press, 1943.

Eliot, T. S., *Collected Poems*. New York: Harcourt, Brace and Company, 1930.

————, *The Music of Poetry*. Glasgow: Jackson & Company, 1942.

Einstein, Alfred, *Music in the Romantic Era*. New York: W. W. Norton & Company, 1947.

Ellis, John H., ed., *The Works of Anne Bradstreet*. New York: P. Smith, 1932.

Emerson, Edward Waldo, ed., *The Complete Works of Ralph Waldo Emerson*. Cambridge: Riverside Press, 1904.

Engle, Paul, *American Song*. New York: Doubleday, Doran & Company, 1934.

Evans, May Garretson, *Music and Edgar Allan Poe; A Bibliography*. Baltimore: Johns Hopkins Press, 1939.

Evans, Nathaniel, *Poems on Several Occasions*. Philadelphia: John Dunlap, 1772.

Fagin, N. Bryllion, *The Histrionic Mr. Poe*. Baltimore: Johns Hopkins Press, 1949.

Faner, Robert D., "Operatic Music and the Poetry of Walt Whitman." University of Pennsylvania. Unpublished Ph.D. Dissertation, 1947.

————, *Walt Whitman & Opera*. Philadelphia: University of Pennsylvania Press, 1951.

Fausset, Hugh I., *Walt Whitman*. New Haven: Yale University Press, 1942.

Fisher, William A., *Notes on Music in Old Boston*. Boston: Oliver Ditson Company, 1918.

Fletcher, John Gould, *Irradiations, Sand and Spray*. New York: Houghton Mifflin Company, 1915.

————, *Selected Poems*. New York: Farrar & Rinehart, 1938.

Fogle, Richard H., *The Imagery of Keats and Shelley*. Chapel Hill: University of North Carolina Press, 1949.

Foote, Henry W., *Three Centuries of American Hymnody*. Cambridge: Harvard University Press, 1940.

Ford, Ford Madox, *The March of Literature*. New York: Dial Press, 1938.

French, J. Milton, *The Life Records of John Milton*. New Brunswick: Rutgers University Press, 1949.

Freneau, Philip (introduction by Harry H. Clark), *Letters on Various Interesting and Important Subjects*. New York: Scholars' Facsimiles and Reprints, 1943.

————, *Poems Relating to The American Revolution*. New York: W. J. Middleton, 1865.

Gardner, W. H., *Gerard Manley Hopkins*. New Haven: Yale University Press, 1948.

Garland, Hamlin, "Roadside Meetings of a Literary Nomad," *Bookman*, III (December, 1929), 392-406.

Gaye, Phoebe F., *John Gay*. London: Collins Publisher, 1938.

Geiringer, Karl, *Haydn, A Creative Life in Music*. New York: W. W. Norton & Company, 1946.

Gerson, Robert A., *Music in Philadelphia*. Philadelphia: Theodore Presser Company, 1940.

Gibbon, John M., *Melody and the Lyric from Chaucer to the Cavaliers*. London and Toronto: J. M. Dent & Sons, 1930.

Godfrey, Thomas, *Juvenile Poems*. Philadelphia: Henry Miller, 1765.

Godwin, Parke, *A Biography of William Cullen Bryant*. New York: D. Appleton and Company, 1883.

Gohdes, Clarence, and Silver, Rollo, eds., *Faint Clues & Indirections*. Durham: Duke University Press, 1949.

Graf, Max, *Composer and Critic*. New York: W. W. Norton & Company, 1946.

Greenslet, Ferris, *James Russell Lowell*. Boston: Houghton Mifflin Company, 1905.

Grierson, H. J. C., *Metaphysical Lyrics and Poems of the Seventeenth Century*. Oxford: The Clarendon Press, 1936.

Grout, Donald Jay, *A Short History of Opera*. New York: Columbia University Press, 1947.

Hale, Edward E., *James Russell Lowell and His Friends*. Boston: Houghton Mifflin Company, 1899.

Halleck, Fitz-Greene, *Alnwick Castle with Other Poems*. New York: George Dearborn, 1836.

Hanford, James Holly, *John Milton, Englishman*. New York: Crown Publishers, 1949.

Harrison, Gabriel, *John Howard Payne*. Albany, N. Y.: Joel, 1875.

Hatfield, J. T., *New Light on Longfellow*. Boston: Houghton Mifflin Company, 1933.

Heller, Otto, *Studies in Modern German Literature*. Boston: Ginn & Company, 1905.

Henry, H. T., "Music in Lowell's Prose and Verse," *Musical Quarterly*, X (October, 1924), 546-573.

Hewett-Thayer, Harvey W., *An Anthology of German Literature in the Nineteenth Century (1795-1910)*. Princeton: Princeton University Press, 1932.

Hieble, Jacob, *An Outline of German Literature*. Ithaca, N. Y.: Thrift Press, 1935.

Hilbert, Werner, *Die Musikaesthetik der Fruhromantik*. Jena: G. Schmidt, 1911.

Hillyer, Robert S., *First Principles of Verse*. Boston: The Writer Inc., 1938.

Holloway, Emory, ed., *The Uncollected Poetry and Prose of Walt Whitman*, 2 vols. New York: P. Smith.

————, *Whitman*. New York: A. A. Knopf, 1926.

Home, Suzanne, *Wilhelm Meister and His English Kinsmen*. New York: Columbia University Press, 1930.

Hood, George, *A History of Music in New England*. Boston: Wilkins, Carter & Company, 1846.

Hovey, Richard, *To the End of the Trail*. New York: Duffield & Company, 1908.

Howard, Esme J. H., *Music in the Poets*. London: Duckworth Press, 1921.

Howard, John T., *Our American Music*. New York: Thomas Y. Crowell Company, 1946.

Howard, Leon, "The Influence of Milton on Colonial American Poetry," *Huntington Library Bulletin*, IX (April, 1936), 63-69.

Huneker, James Gibbon, *Bedouins*. New York: Charles Scribner's Sons, 1920.

————, *Ivory Apes and Peacocks*. New York: Charles Scribner's Sons, 1915.

An Introduction to Literature and the Fine Arts. Lansing: Michigan State College Press, 1950.

Jantz, Harold S., *The First Century of New England Verse*. Worcester: Published by The American Antiquarian Society, 1944.

Johnson, Thomas H., ed., *The Poetical Works of Edward Taylor*. New York: Rockland Editions, 1939.

Jones, Joe J., "Poe's Nicean Bark," *American Literature,* II (January, 1931), 433-437.

Journals of Ralph Waldo Emerson. Boston: Houghton Mifflin Company, 1909-1914.

Kastendiek, M. M., *England's Musical Poet: Thomas Campion.* New York: Oxford University Press, 1938.

King, A. H., *Chamber Music.* New York: Chanticleer Press, 1948.

Klemm, Gustave, "Poet, Man and Musician," *Etude Music Magazine,* LIX (May, 1941), 300-342.

Kobbé, Gustave, *The Complete Opera Book.* New York: G. P. Putnam's Sons, 1935.

Krehbiel, Edward H., *The Philharmonic Society of New York.* New York: Novello, Ewer & Company, 1892.

Kreymborg, Alfred, *Troubadour.* New York: Liveright Inc., 1925.

Lang, Paul H., *Music in Western Civilization.* New York: W. W. Norton & Company, 1941.

Lamar, Dorothy Blount, *Sidney Lanier, Musician, Poet, Soldier.* Macon, Georgia: J. W. Burke & Company, 1927 [1940].

Lanier, Henry W., ed., "A Poet's Musical Impressions," The Letters of Sidney Lanier, *Scribner's Magazine,* XXV (May, 1899), 622-633; 745-752.

Lessing, G. E., *Selected Prose Works.* London: G. Bell and Sons, 1879.

Letters of Edgar Allan Poe, ed. J. W. Ostrom. Cambridge: Harvard University Press, 1948.

Lightwood, James T., *Music and Literature.* London: The Epworth Press, 1931.

Lindsay, Vachel, *Going to the Stars.* New York: D. Appleton and Company, 1926.

Lockspeiser, Edward, *Debussy.* London: J. M. Dent & Sons, 1936.

Lorenz, Lincoln, *The Life of Sidney Lanier.* New York: Coward-McCann, 1935.

Lowell, Amy, *Ballads for Sale.* Boston: Houghton Mifflin Company, 1927.

————, *Tendencies in Modern American Poetry.* New York: Macmillan Company, 1917.

————, *What's O'Clock.* Boston: Houghton Mifflin Company, 1925.

Mabbott, Thomas, and F. L. Pleadwell, eds., *The Life and Works of Edward Coote Pinkney.* New York: Macmillan Company, 1926.

Mabie, Hamilton W., "American Life in Whitman's Poetry," *Outlook,* LXXV (September 5, 1903), 66-78.

Macdougall, H. C., *Early New England Psalmody.* Brattleboro, Vermont: Stephen Daye Press, 1940.

MacLeish, Archibald, *Poetry and Opinion.* Urbana: University of Illinois Press, 1950.

Masters, Edgar Lee, *Whitman*. New York: Charles Scribner's Sons, 1937.

————, *Vachel Lindsay*. New York: Charles Scribner's Sons, 1935.

Matthews, Brander, *A Study of Versification*. Boston: Houghton Mifflin Company, 1911.

Matthiessen, F. O., *The Achievement of T. S. Eliot*. Boston: Houghton Mifflin Company, 1935.

McCusker, Honor, *Fifty Years of Music in Boston*. Boston: Trustees of the Public Library, 1938.

McGlinchi, Claire, "American Literature in American Music," *Musical Quarterly*, XXXI (January, 1945), 101-119.

McGreevy, Thomas, *Thomas Stearns Eliot*. London: Chatto & Windus, 1931.

Mertins, Louis and Esther, *The Intervals of Robert Frost*. Berkeley: University of California Press, 1947.

Meyer, Ernest, *English Chamber Music*. London: Lawrence & Wishart, 1946.

Miller, Joaquin, *Songs of the Sierras and Sunlands*. Chicago: Morrill, Higgins & Company, 1892.

Milligan, Burton A., "An Early American Imitator of Milton," *American Literature* XI (May, 1939), 200-206.

Mims, Edwin, *Sidney Lanier*. Boston: Houghton Mifflin Company, 1905.

Monro, Daniel B., *Modes of Ancient Greek Music*. Oxford: Clarendon Press, 1894.

Monroe, Harriet, *Poets and Their Art*. New York: Macmillan Company, 1932.

Moore, Douglas, *From Madrigal to Modern Music*. New York: W. W. Norton & Company, 1942.

Morgan, Bayard Q., "Review of *Music and Literature*," *Comparative Literature*, II (Fall, 1950), 370.

Morison, Samuel B., *Harvard in the Seventeenth Century*, 2 vols. Cambridge: Harvard University Press, 1936.

Naylor, R. W., *The Poets and Music*. London: J. M. Dent & Sons, 1928.

————, *Shakespeare and Music*. London: J. M. Dent & Sons, 1931.

Nef, Karl, *Outline of the History of Music*. New York: Columbia University Press, 1935.

Nettl, Paul, *The Book of Musical Documents*. New York: Philosophical Library, 1948.

Newman, Ernest, *Wagner As Man and Artist*. New York: Garden Publishing Company, 1941.

Ninde, E. S., *Nineteen Centuries of Christian Song*. New York: Fleming H. Revell Company, 1938.

Nitze, William A., *Arthurian Romance and Modern Poetry and Music*. Chicago: University of Chicago Press, 1940.

Nitze, William and Dargan, B. Preston, *A History of French Literature.*
New York: Henry Holt & Company, 1927.

Oberholtzer, Ellis P., *The Literary History of Philadelphia.* Philadelphia: George W. Jacobs & Company, 1906.

Oliver, Alfred Richard, *The Encyclopedists as Critics of Music.* New York: Columbia University Press, 1947.

Omond, T. S., *A Study of Metre.* London: A. Noring, Ltd., 1907.

Oxford History of Music. London: Oxford University Press, 1929.

Paine, Robert Treate, *The Works in Verse and Prose.* Boston: J. Belcher, 1812.

Palmer, G. H., *The Life and Works of George Herbert.* Boston: Houghton Mifflin Company, 1926.

Parrott, T. M., and Thorp, W., eds., *Poetry of the Transition* (1850-1914). New York: Oxford University Press, 1936.

Parrington, Vernon L., *The Connecticut Wits.* New York: Harcourt, Brace and Company, 1926.

Pattison, Bruce, *Music and Poetry of the English Renaissance.* London: Methuen & Company, Ltd., 1948.

Pellisier, Georges, *Le Mouvement Litteraire au XIX Siecle.* Paris: Libraire Hachette, 1905.

Pettigrew, Richard C., "Poe's Rime," *American Literature*, IV (May, 1932), 151-159.

Phillips, Mary E., *Edgar Allan Poe: The Man.* Chicago: John C. Winston Company, 1926.

Pleadwell, F. L., ed., *The Life and Works of Joseph Rodman Drake.* Boston: Merrymount Press, 1935.

Poe, E. A., *Al Aaraaf.* New York: Printed for Facsimile Text Society, Columbia University Press, 1933.

Poems by George Pope Morris. New York: Charles Scribner's, 1883.

Poems by the Late Doctor John Shaw. Philadelphia: Edward Earle, 1810.

Poems of Henry Timrod. Boston: Houghton Mifflin Company, 1899.

Poetical Works of William Cullen Bryant. New York: D. Appleton and Company, 1909.

Pope, John Collins, *The Rhythm of Beowulf.* New Haven: Yale University Press, 1942.

Pound, Ezra, *Personae.* New York: Liveright Publishing Company, 1926.

————, *The Cantos of Ezra Pound.* New York: New Directions, 1948.

————, *Pavannes and Divisions.* New York: A. A. Knopf, 1918.

Pound, Louise, "Walt Whitman and Italian Music," *American Mercury*, VI (September, 1925), 58-63.

Pratt, Waldo S., *Music of the Pilgrims.* Boston: Oliver Ditson Company, 1921.

Quinn, Arthur H. and Hart, Richard H., eds., *Edgar Allan Poe Letters and Documents*. New York: Scholars' Facsimile and Reprints, 1941.

Quinn, Arthur H., *Edgar Allan Poe*. New York: D. Appleton-Century Company, 1942.

————, *The Literature of the American People*. New York: D. Appleton-Century-Crofts, 1951.

Reese, Gustav, *Music in the Middle Ages*. New York: W. W. Norton & Company, 1940.

Reese, Lizette W., *A Wayside Lute*. Portland: Thomas B. Mosher, 1909.

Robertson, John W., *Edgar A. Poe: A Psychopathic Study*. New York: G. P. Putnam, 1923.

Rollins, Hyder Edward, *Keats' Reputation in America to 1848*. Cambridge: Harvard University Press, 1946.

Rusk, Ralph L., *The Life of Ralph Waldo Emerson*. New York: Charles Scribner's Sons, 1949.

Sachs, Curt, *Our Musical Heritage*. New York: Prentice Hall, 1948.

Saintsbury, George, *A History of English Prosody*, 3 vols. London: Macmillan Company, 1923.

Schauffler, Robert H., *Beethoven: The Man Who Freed Music*. New York: Doubleday, Doran & Company, 1929.

Schlichter, Norman C., "Sidney Lanier, Musician and Poet, *Quarterly Review*, X (October, 1899), 622-759.

Schramm, Wilbur L., "A Characteristic of Rime," *PMLA*, L (December, 1935), 1223-1227.

Scholes, Percy A., *The Puritans and Music*, London: Oxford University Press, 1934.

Scholl, Evelyn H., "English Metre Once More," *PMLA*, LXIII (March, 1948), 293-326.

Schopenhauer, Arthur, *The World as Will and Idea*. London: Paul, Trench, Trubner and Company, 1891.

Schutte, A. P., "Facts About Poe," *University of Virginia Record*, Extension Studies, X (April, 1926), 7-25.

Schyberg, Frederik, *Walt Whitman*, trans. E. A. Allen. New York: Columbia University Press, 1951.

Scott, Leonora Cranch, *The Life and Letters of Christopher Pearse Cranch*. Boston: Houghton Mifflin Company, 1917.

Scudder, Horace E., ed., *The Complete Poetical Works of Henry Wadsworth Longfellow*. Boston: Houghton Mifflin Company, 1893.

Shapiro, Karl, *A Bibliography of Modern Prosody*. Baltimore: Johns Hopkins Press, 1948.

————, *English Prosody and Modern Poetry*. Baltimore: Johns Hopkins Press, 1947.

Shepard, Odell, *Henry Wadsworth Longfellow*. New York: American Book Company, 1934.

Shuster, G. N., *The English Ode from Milton to Keats*. New York: Columbia University Press, 1940.

Simms, William Gilmore, *Areytos or Songs and Ballads of the South*. Charleston: Russell & Sons, 1860.

————, *Lyrical and Other Poems*. Charleston: Ellis & Neufville, 1820.

————, *Poems*. New York: Redfield, 1853.

Smith, Edward J., "Benjamin Franklin as a Musician," *Musical Digest,* XXIX (November, 1947), 10-12.

Smyth, Albert Henry, *The Writings of Benjamin Franklin*. New York: Macmillan Company, 1906.

Sonneck, Oscar G., *Early Concert Life in America*. Leipzig: Breitkopf & Hartel, 1907.

————, *Francis Hopkinson and James Lyon*. Washington: H. L. McQueen, 1905.

Spiller, Robert E., Willard Thorp, *et al.*, eds., *Literary History of the United States,* 3 vols. New York: Macmillan Company, 1948.

Starke, Aubrey H., *Sidney Lanier*. Chapel Hill: University of North Carolina Press, 1933.

————, "Lanier's Appreciation of Whitman," *American Scholar,* II (October, 1933), 398-408.

————, "Sidney Lanier as a Musician," *Musical Quarterly,* XX (October, 1934), 384-400.

————, "Sidney Lanier, Man of Science in the Field of Letters," *American Scholar,* II (October, 1933), 388-397.

Stedman, E. C., *Alice of Monmouth*. New York: Charleton Publishers, 1864.

————, *Blameless Price and Other Poems*. Boston: Fields, Osgood & Company, 1869.

————, *Songs and Ballads*. New York: Printed for Book Fellows' Club, 1884.

Sternfeld, Frederick W., "The Musical Springs of Goethe's Poetry," *Musical Quarterly,* XXXV (October, 1949), 514.

Stoddard, R. H., *Recollections, Personal and Literary*. New York: A. S. Barnes and Company, 1903.

Stringham, Edwin J., *Listening to Music Creatively*. New York: Prentice-Hall, 1943.

Strunk, Oliver, *Source Readings in Music History*. New York: W. W. Norton & Company, 1950.

Swift, Lindsay, *Brook Farm*. New York: Macmillan Company, 1900.

Taggard, Genevieve, *Life and Mind of Emily Dickinson*. New York: A. A. Knopf, 1930.

Taylor, Bayard, *The Poet's Journal*. Boston: Ticknor and Fields, 1863.

————, *Studies in German Literature*. New York: G. P. Putnam's Sons, 1891.

Thayer, W. R., "Letters of Sidney Lanier," *Atlantic Monthly,* LXXIV (July, 1894), 14-28.

Thomas, John W., *James Freeman Clarke, Apostle of German Culture to America.* Boston: H. W. Luce Company, 1949.

Thompson, Benjamin, *His Poems,* ed. H. J. Hall. New York: Houghton Mifflin Company, 1924.

Todd, Mabel Loomis and Bingham, Millicent T., eds., *Bolts of Melody: New Poems of Emily Dickinson.* New York: Harper & Brothers, 1945.

U.N.E.S.C.O., *Goethe Homage.* Printed in Zurich, Switzerland: UNESCO, Paris, 1949.

Van Doren, Mark, ed., *Samuel Sewall's Diary.* New York: Macy-Masius Publishers, 1927.

Verniyer, Grace O., *Famous American Composers.* New York: Thomas Y. Crowell Company, 1944.

Wade, Mason, ed., *The Writings of Margaret Fuller.* New York: Viking Press, 1941.

Wakefield, A. M., *Ruskin on Music.* London: George Allen, 1894.

Ward, Reverend Nathaniel, *The Simple Cobbler of Aggawam in America.* Boston: James Munroe and Company, 1843.

Warren, Austin, *Richard Crashaw.* Baton Rouge: Louisiana State University Press, 1939.

Webb, Richard and Coulson, Edwin R., *Sidney Lanier, Poet and Prosodist.* Athens: University of Georgia Press, 1941.

Wegelin, Oscar, *Early American Poetry.* New York: P. Smith, 1930.

Werner, W. L., "Poe's Theories and Practice in Poetic Techniques," *American Literature,* II (May, 1930), 157-165.

Whitty, J. H., ed., *Complete Poems of Edgar Allan Poe.* Boston: Houghton Mifflin Company, 1917.

Wiley, Autrey N., "Reiterative Devices in *Leaves of Grass,*" *American Literature,* V (May, 1929), 161-170.

Willis, N. P., *Poems.* New York: Clark & Austin, 1846.

Winckelmann, Johann J., *History of the Art of Antiquity,* trans. G. Henry Lodge. London: J. Chapman, 1850.

Winslow, Ola, *American Broadside Verse.* New Haven: Yale University Press, 1930.

Winters, Yvor, *Primitivism and Decadence.* New York: Arrow Editions, 1937.

Woodberry, George E., *Edgar Allan Poe.* Boston: Houghton Mifflin Company, 1913.

The Works of Edgar Allan Poe, 8 vols. New York: Charles Scribner's, 1927.

Wright, C. H. C., *French Classicism.* Cambridge: Harvard University Press, 1920.

Wright, Thomas G., *Literary Culture in Early New England.* New Haven: Yale University Press, 1920.

MANUSCRIPTS

Lanier MS Collection, Sidney Lanier Room at Johns Hopkins University, Baltimore, Maryland.

Poe MS Collection, Valentine Museum, Richmond, Virginia.

Whitman MS Collection, Trent Library at Duke University, Durham, North Carolina.

Whitman MS Collection, Library of Congress, Manuscript Division, Washington, D. C.

Index